Baltic Sea

E. POMERANIA

Dan[zig]

[BRAN]DENBURG

R. Warthe

[...]burg

POLAND

R. Vistula

Warsaw

SILESIA

Peitsch

R. Oder

Breslau

[Dr]esden

[T]eplitz

Prague

BOHEMIA

[Wi]en

Cracow

MORAVIA

IMPERIAL HUNGARY

Munkacz

Brünn

Oesterlitz

HUNGARY

Guntersdorf

Ernstbrünn

Tyrnan

Schemnitz

[Bish]opric Passau

AUSTRIA

Vienna

Nitra

Miscolz

Linz

Pressburg

Eger

Amstetten

Neuhäusel

Weiner Neustadt

Raab

Gran

[S]alzburg

Makazell

Oldenbourg

Budapest

STYRIA

TRANSYLVANIA

GEORGE STEPNEY
1663-1707
DIPLOMAT AND POET

*Portrait of George Stepney (1705), by Sir Godfrey Kneller. Courtesy,
National Portrait Gallery.*

George Stepney

1663-1707
Diplomat and Poet

Susan Spens

James Clarke & Co
Cambridge

In Grateful Memory of
Dr Albert Hollaender
Late Keeper of the Manuscripts at
The Guildhall Library
and Editor in the Public Record Office

He gave unfailing help and advice
to the author

James Clarke & Co.
P.O. Box 60
Cambridge
CB1 2NT

British Library Cataloguing in Publication Data:
A catalogue record is available from the British Library.

ISBN 0 2276 7940 7

Printed in Great Britain by Redwood Books, Trowbridge

Contents

Illustrations

Author's Note

Quotations: These are given as they appear in the original documents; hence the lack of accents appearing in the French quotes: for all writers of the period were delightfully idiosyncratic. Words or names in squared brackets have been added, for clarification.

Dating: Until 1700 the difference between the English calendar and that used on the Continent was 10 days, after 1701 it was 11 days. Hence 'Old Style' (o.s.- English) and 'New Style' (n.s. - Continental). Many writers indicated both, e.g. 10/20 January. Confusingly, the year ended on 25 March in England, but on 31 December on the Continent. In this volume the year is taken to end on 31 December, so the date above would be indicated 10/20 January 1698/99.

Acknowledgments: The author and publishers gratefully acknowledge a grant towards the costs of publication kindly made by The Scouloudi Foundation in association with the Institute of Historical Research. The author owes gratitude to the staff of the British Library (Department of Manuscripts). Mr Peter Barber (Deputy Map Librarian, BL) and Dr Frances Harris most kindly advised her. At the Public Record Office the archivists, past and present, at Chancery Lane and at Kew have always been helpful. Relevant manuscripts held by the Bodleian Library, Oxford, were ready for perusal when the author visited the Library in November 1988. Within the United Kingdom the following people are remembered with appreciation for their help with research, 1986-1993: Ms Sonia Anderson, Historical Manuscripts Commission, London. Dr R G Asch, German Historical Institute, London. Mr David J Brown, Scottish Record Office, Edinburgh. Mr Gareth Fitzpatrick, Administrator, Boughton House, Northamptonshire. Mr John Forster, Education Officer, Blenheim Palace, Oxfordshire. Mr Victor Gray, County Archivist, Essex. Dr Dorothy B Johnston, Keeper of the Manuscripts, University of Nottingham Library. Mr Alan Kucia Archivist, Trinity College Library, Cambridge. Mr John Owen, County Archivist, Dyfed. Mr Alwyn J Roberts, Department of Manuscripts and Records, National Library of Wales. Mr Malcolm Taylor, Librarian, English Folk Dance and Song Society. Ms Rachel Watson, County Archivist, Northamptonshire.

The late Mrs Winifred Gil of Lewes and Miss Audrey Fellowes of Norwich patiently supplied Latin translations. Miss Joan Chreseson and Miss Shelagh Freeman helped with the technicalities of English prosody. It would not have been possible for the author to have worked in London without the kind hospitality of Miss Heather Coltman. In Hove, Mr Brian Port of Express Letterheads Ltd and his assistants have always given cheerful assistance. In Vienna Frau Dr Christiane Thomas of the *Haus- Hof u. Staatsarchiv* took great trouble to check transcriptions from the archives. Her colleagues, in particular Dr Leopold Auer (a specialist of the seventeenth and eighteenth centuries), were always helpful. Frau Dr Brigitte Reiffenstein (Department of English, University of Vienna) provided references to Stepney's poetry. Dr Roland and Frau Dr Eugenia Stöckelle guided the author around the archives and libraries in that city. In Germany thanks are especially due to Dr Gieschen *Niedersächsisches Hauptstaatsarchiv,* Hanover. Dr Leukert *Staatsarchiv,* Dresden (1988). Herr Bernhard Reichel *Stadtarchiv,* Frankfurt/Main. Dr Sielemann *Staatsarchiv,* Hamburg. Herr Georg Strobel *Heimatmuseum,* Höchstädt a.d.Donau. Dr Siegfried Wenisch *Staatsarchiv,* Würzburg; in France, to M. Bernard Weigel *Archives municipales,* Wissembourg

For acknowledgments regarding copyright, see **Notes and References**.

Abbreviations

ADB	*Allgemeine Deutsche Biographie*
Add.MS	Additional manuscript
Bodl.	Bodleian Library Oxford
BL	British Library
Cal.Tr. B	Calendar of Treasury Books
Coxe	William Coxe, *Memoires of the Duke of Marlborough* (London, 1820)
CSPD	Calendar of State Papers (Domestic)
DNB	Dictionary of National Biography
f.	folio
Gachard	L.P. Gachard *Receuil des anciennes ordonnances de la Belgique. III Serié, Tome 2 1706-1715* (Brussels, 1867)
Hengelmüller	Ladislas, Baron Hengelmüller, *Hungary's Fight for National Existence* (London, 1913)
HHStA	*Haus- Hof- u. Staatsarchiv*
HMC	Historical Manuscripts Commission
t'Hoff	B. van t'Hoff, *The Correspondence 1701-11 of John Churchill. First Duke of Marlborough. and Anthonie Heinsius. Grand Pensionary of Holland* (The Hague, 1951)
IGI	International Genealogical Index
Luttrell	Narcissus Luttrell, *A Brief Historical Relation of State Affairs from September1678 to April 1714* (Oxford, 1857)
Michaud	J.Fr.Michaud, *Biographie Universelle ancienne et moderne* (Paris, 1854)
misc.	miscellaneous
MS	manuscript
Murray	Sir George Murray, *Letters & Dispatches of John Churchill, Duke of Marlborough* (London, 1854)
n.s.	new style
o.s.	old style
PRO	Public Record Office
Röder	Philipp Röder, ed. *Kriegs- u. Staats-schriften des Markgrafen Ludwig Wilhelm v. Baden über den spansichen Erbfolge-krieg* (Karlsruhe, 1850)
Snyder	Henry L. Snyder, ed. *The Marlborough-Godolphin Correspondence* (Oxford, 1975)
VCH	Victoria County History
Zedler	Johann Heinrich Zedler, ed, *Universal Lexicon* (Leipzig & Halle, 1740)

Introduction

George Stepney's name has achieved only a passing mention in the writings of eminent historians, from Bishop Burnet to Sir Winston Churchill. The compilers of the *Dictionary of National Biography* accorded him a page, and his portrait hangs, with those of other members of the Kit-Cat Club, in the National Portrait Gallery. His correspondence, however, comprises sixty one volumes divided between the Public Record Office and the British Library. A few papers are to be found in the Bodleian Library, Oxford, the National Library of Wales and the Record Offices of Westminster, Dorset and Carmarthenshire. References to his career occur in the archives of Berlin, Vienna, Frankfurt/Main and Brussels.

The purpose of this book is to use the rich legacy of these sources to amplify the known outline of his life, allowing him to tell his own story. Although he left instructions in his will that his private papers were to be destroyed – and this injunction was obeyed – his official correspondence and the surviving series of his Letter Books reveal enough about his circumstances to permit this task to be carried out.

Stepney grew up during the last quarter of the seventeenth century, in England a time of reconstruction after the turmoil of the Civil War, and equally a period of developing autocracy in government. King Charles II had resumed his throne in 1660. With great skill he so handled his successive parliaments that for the last four years of his reign he was able to do without that assembly altogether, thanks largely to hidden subsidies received from his cousin, Louis XIV of France. That monarch had experienced in childhood the smell of revolution at the time of the *Fronde*. When in 1661 he took responsibility for his country he was determined to achieve absolute monarchy. He succeeded. Most of the sovereign princes of Europe tried to emulate him.

Yet Louis made a grave error. Partly to enhance his own glory, and partly to occupy the time and talents of his possibly dangerous nobility, he embarked on the series of offensive summer-time wars, the *Réunions*, in an attempt to extend the borders of France to the Rhine and beyond. Thus Louis incurred the enmity of certain German princes and of the Dutch Republic.

The Thirty Years War, which had engulfed parts of Germany, had ended in 1648 (apart from some raiding by the various *condottieri* who wished it to continue). But there had been no decisive victory either by catholic or protestant contenders. Owing to the long-standing practice of partible inheritance - that is, the division of land and property between all the sons of a family - the country had become a conglomeration of small states. True, some had achieved greater strength than others. The seven most important princes comprised the Electoral College who voted for the Holy Roman Emperor of the German Nation. Usually, but not automatically, the Emperor was a member of the Habsburg dynasty which, in the seventeenth century, also supplied the King of Spain. In 1658 the Habsburg candidate, Leopold I, then eighteen years old, was duly elected. *Augustissime Caesar* were the words used to address him. Yet his actual power was very limited and the apparatus of government was unwieldy. The Archbishop/Elector of Mainz (Catholic) was the Chancellor of the Empire, but appointed a deputy to run the affairs of state. This man resided in Vienna, as did the Emperor. The *Diet* (Parliament) usually met at Ratisbon (*Regensburg)* at infrequent intervals. The imperial court, at Vienna, consisted of officials whose loyalty lay either towards the Empire itself (the *Reich*) or to the Habsburg family as landowners (the *Hof*). The princes, nobility and cities of the Empire were supposed to contribute to the Emperor's support. But he lacked ready cash and had to rely on receiving money from his subjects in return for promised favours of land or office. In times of crisis he turned to Jewish moneylenders.

The other Catholic Electors were the Archbishops of Trèves (*Trier)* and Cologne *(Köln)*, together with the Elector of Bavaria. The Elector Palatine (whose jumbled territories lay along the Rhine) was at the beginning of the century a protestant prince. However by mid-century the inheritance had become catholic. This fact did not prevent the Palatinate suffering the ravages of Louis XIV's armies.

In northern Germany the reformed religion continued under the Electors of Brandenburg and Saxony. The rulers of Hanover, who aspired to an electorate, were also protestant. It would be wrong, however, to believe that the dynastic disputes of the late seventeenth century were caused by religion. Acquisition of land was for most rulers the reason for war. Religious fervour was more often evinced by the middle classes - the Huguenot trades-people who abandoned France after the revocation of the Edict of Nantes in 1685; or the catholic monks and nuns who advanced the counter-reformation in Austria and Hungary.

The principal opponent of Louis XIV's aggression turned out to be William Henry, Prince of Orange, together with his dour and capable countrymen, the Dutch. These people had always been obliged to contend with their main enemy, the sea. In 1648 the seven provinces which comprised their Republic finally confirmed their independence from Spain. The Prince was not their ruler, but merely *Stadhouder,* or defender of the land. Being seamen the Dutch, as well as the English, had built up a trading network overseas which extended both east and west. It was not for nothing that both countries came to be known as the Maritime Powers. Trade by sea was always cheaper and easier to arrange than the carriage of goods overland. The two nations fought trade wars during the 1660s. The Dutch gained a victory in the Thames, but New Amsterdam became New York. In 1672, when the French invaded Holland, the Prince of Orange (then aged 22) commanded the dykes to be breached so that the flooded land would save the city of Amsterdam. For the next 30 years he continued his implacable opposition to France.

In 1688 France again declared war on Holland and the German Empire. By the following year the Prince of Orange was established as King of England, replacing the pro-French James II. George Stepney, who was serving in Hamburg at the time of the Glorious Revolution, had to decide what to do. Like most of his contemporaries he opted to continue his career under the new monarch. In following his progress the reader is given an insight into the complexities of the struggle against the French, both during King William's Nine Years' War and later in the first years of the War of the Spanish Succession when the Duke of Marlborough was in command of the English forces. By that time Stepney was the most experienced of the English Envoys in the German-speaking world.

The diplomat personified the well-educated professional man who was becoming indispensable to government in early-modern Europe. The system of education was universally based on the classical languages, the history and myths of Greece and Rome. Latin was still used for the drafting of treaties, but increasingly the spoken language of diplomacy was French.

In England positions in government service could be bought,

and were often treated as an heirlooms, being passed from father to son. Pay was minimal, but a clerkship was valuable owing to the fees which could be extracted from petitioners for the king's bounty. It was usually necessary for a young man to seek a patron who might provide an opening. The nobleman would be willing to help, because by so doing he would demonstrate his 'interest' at court, and hence the regard in which he would be held by his sovereign. George Stepney's correspondence reveals his continuing anxiety about patronage, up to and including the last year of his life.

In all countries the ties of kinship were strong. Stepney was sometimes to turn to quite distant relatives for financial help. In the later part of his career he was to further the prospects of two of his cousins. His letters to his sisters shew the gradually improving status of spinsters at the turn of the seventeenth/eighteenth centuries. Neither of these girls married, but seemed to lead comfortable and independent lives.

Across Europe, the situation of *les misérables* was dire. In some respects suffering transcended class. In the pre-anaesthetic age a war wound was as agonizing to the officer as to the private soldier. Smallpox killed in the palace as it did in the slums. But plague hit the poor the worst, if only because the rich could afford to flee. Famine could anywhere result from a bad harvest, but was more prevalent in Europe than in post-civil-war England because of the ravages of advancing armies during summer campaigns. Stepney was to remark on the comparative affluence of the English labourer as compared with his European counterpart. Continental landowners took trouble to protect their lands from the incidence of war, the Habsburg family being particularly diligent and successful in this aim.

During Stepney's years abroad the arts of peace flourished. Palaces, churches and houses were being built or improved. Although the greatest age of European painting had passed, gentlemen considered themselves connoisseurs and eagerly sought works of art to adorn their properties. Scientific enquiry was pursued, and in England membership of the Royal Society was considered an honour. Drama, literature and poetry were appreciated and practised. Stepney was acclaimed in his own day as a poet, although admiration for his verses did not continue beyond the first half of the eighteenth century. A new appraisal of his work, together with a list of his poems, is included in these pages.

During his diplomatic career of 21 years Stepney spent only one complete year (1700) in England. His papers throw light on the ideas and the customs of his day across the panorama of northern Europe, from London to Hamburg, Berlin and Warsaw, via the Hague through the valleys of the Rhine and the Danube to Vienna, and thence eastwards into Hungary. 'His life was busy, and not long,' commented Samuel Johnson. As these pages will shew, Stepney made good use of the span of life allotted to him.

I *Antecedents*

My grandfather was an extravagant man, and never made provision for 3
sons, whereof Bernard (the eldest) is now living (a Batchelour) as a
Gentleman on his means. My father, George, (ye 2d Brother) was Groom
of ye Privy Chamber only, & dyed when I was only 3 years old wch has
exposed me to seek my Fortune wch however by my Mother's care my
education (who is a Moseley of ye Ancoats in Lancashire) & by yr
friendship in ye College & Patronage since has ever been plentifull &
honourable & I hope by my diligence may be more so.[1]

Thus did George Stepney, diplomat, writing to his friend and patron
Charles Montagu, describe his family background. But properly to
understand his inheritance – or lack of it – it is necessary to go
back three generations and consider not only his father, but his
grandfather and great-grandfather, because all three were younger
sons and hence had to make their own way in the world.

The founder of the Pembrokeshire branch of the Stepney family
was a lawyer named Alban (d. l611), who in 1559 left the family
home at Aldenham in Hertfordshire, and came to Wales in the train
of Bishop Richard Davies, then carrying out a visitation. In 1561
Alban was appointed Receiver-General of the diocese of St.
Davids.[2] He made two successful marriages, which brought
him estates (including that of Prendergast, now a suburb of
Haverfordwest) in what was then known as 'little England'. He
also fathered five children. The eldest son, John, later became the
first baronet Stepney of Prendergast, whose descendants continued
prominent in South Wales for two centuries. Thomas (grandfather
of George the diplomat) was Alban's third boy. He was born in
1591, studied at Cambridge and then joined the royal court, where
he seems to have been something of a favourite of James I, who
knighted him. At least Thomas had the good luck to be present
when, in 1622, that monarch fell off his horse into a bog in
Theobalds Park. Thomas came to the rescue and was promised
£3,500 upon his marriage. But few Stuart promises were actually
carried out, and Thomas vainly petitioned Charles I, a few years
later, to make good James's generous words.[3] For a younger son,
marriage in the seventeenth century was a serious affair, and could

advance or retard the career of a budding courtier. Thomas Stepney made two attempts: first to a Hampshire widow, which failed. The wife died, and there is no trace of any estate accruing to the bridegroom. His second marriage was made in 1624 to Mary, granddaughter and heiress of Sir Bernard Whetstone of Woodford Hall, Essex. Whatever were Thomas's expectations of this second marriage, no property came his way; and indeed after 1630 he disappears from history into the general social chaos of the English Civil War.

But three of Thomas's four children had some influence on the life of his grandson, George Stepney the diplomat. The eldest was 'Uncle Bernard', who never married, but is referred to from time to time in George Stepney's correspondence. As the latter advanced in dignity, so did Bernard make application to his nephew for favours or loans, the last of which was forgiven him in George's will in 1707. The second of Thomas's sons was George Stepney senior; but before considering him, mention should be made of Rowland, the third boy (who died as a young man), and of the one girl born into the family. Her name was Margaret, and she was later to marry George Lewis, Minister at Abergwili (near Carmarthen) and become the mother of the wily Erasmus Lewis (1671-1754) who in the early eighteenth century became secretary to Robert Harley, Earl of Oxford, and who was also the heir and disposer of all George Stepney's papers.[4]

George Stepney senior was apprenticed to the Grocer's Company of the City of London. This fact was carefully concealed by his son (the diplomat); and it is indeed possible that the relevant page in the List of Apprentices of the Grocer's Company covering the years 1629-1666 has been tampered with. Between 1656 and 1663 the senior George's name appears with depressing regularity in the Minute Book of the Company as borrowing £100 and being admonished to find securities for repayment. Nevertheless this second son of Sir Thomas must have traded as a grocer, for he took his own younger brother, Rowland, as apprentice in the year 1662. Their father was listed as deceased.[5]

It can be assumed that George Stepney senior was born about 1626 or 1627. Before 1657 he had married Jane Moseley, and was living in the parish of St Swithun's, London Stone, where the first two children of the marriage, Frances and Dorothy, were christened in 1657 and 1659 respectively. By the time the diplomat was born on 30 July 1663 the family had moved to the parish of St Martin-in-the-Fields, Westminster, where they lived on the 'water-side' of

the high street (near Charing Cross). The house was known as
Wilmot House. George and Jane Stepney leased it from the Countess
of Rochester at a rack-rent of £120 per annum. The house was
large, three-storied, with a kitchen on the ground floor and a cellar
beneath; the reception rooms above measured 94 feet by 34. From
a survey made in 1650 its worth per annum was said to be £65. In
1664 the rate books record 'a great losse by fyre.' No details survive
of this event, but at the time of George Stepney senior's death in
1669, he was known to have owed Lady Rochester £70.[6]

In October 1664 the diplomat's father was appointed Groom of
the Privy Chamber (supernumerary), having purchased the place
for £300. The board wages were 3s. 4d. per day. George was granted
an immediate livery of £40 0s. 6d., and this amount should have
been repeated year after year. But the board wages were never paid,
nor was the £40 per annum. In February 1669 George petitioned
the King to be allowed to dispose of his place, the amount of the
sale remaining unknown. George was ill, and heavily in debt. His
successor as Groom of the Privy Chamber (William Cooke) was
probably the same individual who bought his goods when these
were seized, appraised and sold by the Bailiff of Westminster as
part settlement of the debts. The value of the goods was £40 10s.[7]

These dramatic events took place in 1670, when George Stepney
the diplomat was 7 years old, and his elder sisters 13 and 11 years
respectively. The goods seized comprised all the kitchen equipment,
including the childrens' three porringers. Beds, blankets and bed
linen; chairs, tables, carpets and rugs; curtains and hangings; small
odd things and lumber; all were dragged away. The Stepney papers
contain no reference to this event, so the children may not have
been present. But as an adult George Stepney frequently expressed
his utter horror of getting into debt, and he was punctual in paying
any sums which he owed. One cannot but think that his father's
hand-to-mouth existence made a deep impression on him.

The individual who bore the brunt of George Stepney senior's
indebtedness, illness and death was his wife Jane. She was a lady
of determined personality, who guided and shaped her son's early
life. Documentary evidence of her own upbringing does not exist,
but some points can be gleaned from county records, wills, and
from her son's correspondence.

Jane's story begins in Manchester; she was christened in what
later became the cathedral on 11 September 1627. The Moseleys
of Ancoats in Lancashire made their living by the cloth trade. One
of their most distinguished members was Sir Nicholas (1564-1617)

who moved south and eventually became Lord Mayor of London. Jane's grandfather, Anthony, was the younger brother of the Lord Mayor. He stayed in Manchester and became the father of a numerous family, of whom the youngest son, Rowland (b. 1603) made a very early marriage – he was only 15 – to a lady named Isabel Dodge. There were at least four children of the marriage, of whom Jane was the third. The Moseleys were a large clan, many of whom were caught in the turmoil of the Civil War. During the interregnum the parliamentary Committee for the Advancement of Money was active in Lancashire, assessing the values of royalist estates. They caught up with cousins of Jane's, Nicholas and Francis Moseley of Colleyhurst, and from the documents it is evident that Jane's father Rowland was dead before August 1651 (the date of the assessment), and also that Jane and her younger sister Frances had each been left £100 by an uncle.[8]

A bride with a known dowry was quite enough to tempt George Stepney senior. But there is no record of his courtship or marriage with Jane. Possibly she may have travelled south to take up a position in the household of one of the London Moseleys, but there is no evidence. Similarly, nothing is known of her husband's activities before he became a grocer. There is a record of a George Stepney who, in 1651 and 1652 was actively assisting Daniel Searle (merchant of London and later Governor of Barbados) in 'discovering' the debts of royalists for the benefit of the parliamentary government. This man unsuccessfully petitioned for one fifth of the money concerned. There is no certain identification with the diplomat's father, although such an activity seems to have been in keeping with his character. Moreover this George Stepney was described as being 'of Westminster.'[9]

The last illness of the diplomat's father is described in detail in papers surviving from a court case of the year 1684, when Jane Stepney (widow) and her 'brother', James Partridge, were sued in the court of Chancery by one John Sawyer, who complained at length that moneys owing to him by the late George Stepney had been withheld by the two defendants, and that they had satisfied other creditors before himself. The equally lengthy defence provides the inventory of the Stepney house, and the financial status of Jane's husband at the time of his death in 1669. Jane had been paid £9 10s. by her husband's debtors; his wearing apparel was valued at only £1 10s.; he was owed about £300 by the King; and the contents of the house were valued at £40 10s.

But the chief interest in these documents lies in the relationship of widow Jane with James Partridge. He could hardly be her brother, unless he had changed his name. There is no record that he was a brother-in-law. Yet George the diplomat in his will in 1707 left £50 to 'my honoured Uncle Captain James Partridge.' It is also surprising to learn that in 1670, when Jane had taken out letters of administration for her husband's estate, James Partridge promptly sued her in the court of King's Bench at Westminster for payment of bonds into which he had entered as surety for the deceased George. The sum involved was about £200; hence the seizure of the goods from the house near Charing Cross. It is possible that this was a collusive action, in order to save Jane from the attentions of other more rapacious creditors. It is also possible – although there is no proof – that James Partridge was the protector of the widow Jane. A man of the same name was a noted bookseller and publisher, and from 1682 to 1694 lived in Spring Gardens, Whitehall.[10]

In her defence of the 1684 court case, Jane Stepney was emphatic that she had repaid her husband's debt to the Countess of Rochester as well as other smaller debts 'out of the... money which she hath gotten by her owne industry since his death.' So what was Jane's industry which enabled her, the provider for three children, to clear her husband's debts, equip her son for his school-days at Westminster and later on to support him from time to time when the delays in Treasury payments grew unbearable? In 1669, when George Stepney senior died, Jane stood possessed of very little. Any dowry which she had brought with her into the marriage would legally have belonged to her husband, and all her property was his.

Jane made her will in 1688 (she died in November 1694). Among other small bequests she left her son George £10 per annum to be paid 'out of the rents issues and profitts of my house or houses situated and being neare Scotland Yard in the parish of St. Martin.' It seems most likely that Jane's property was used as a lodging house by officials of the court, and that Jane earned a living as a landlady. In 1695 George Stepney the diplomat congratulated his sisters that John Ellis (Assistant Secretary of State) was about to become their lodger. In writing home, the diplomat often sent greetings to friends (sometimes unnamed) at the 'Black Boy.' In the small world of the Whitehall officials, everybody knew everybody else. During Jane's lifetime, and after her death, George her son was from time to time involved in protecting the 'door': that is, an entrance from the house into the Court, to save residents the trouble of going round to the official gate. Such an entry would enhance the rents which a landlady could charge.[11]

George Stepney held his mother in high regard. 'Honour'd Mother' was the salutation which he used in his letters. He always acknowledged his debt to her in providing for his education. In his own will, he echoed his mother's phrase in proudly asserting that all his possessions, apart from Jane's gifts to him, had been acquired 'by my owne Labour and Industry.' Jane did what she could for her children, who remained friends to each other and – perhaps because none of them ever married – continued to cultivate the bonds of mutual respect and support.

II *Education*
(1676-1686)

> I heartily lament my good old Master: He deserves a good Poem
> and ought to have a Book in tribute to his memory from both
> Universities: If all his Scholars who are ab[ou]t Town attend his
> Funerall (as I hear they will) the followers may be as numerous as
> those to the Queen; and if they are not Mourners at his death I am
> certain there is not one but has shedd Tears upon his account in
> his Life-time. . . . I hope a weighty Stone may be lay'd on him, to
> keep him from walking: For it would be a double horror to any of
> his Scholars to see a Ghost [of] such a Master.[1]

George Stepney was writing in 1695 on learning of the death of the
renowned Headmaster of Westminster School, Dr Richard Busby,
who came to the school in 1638 and taught there until his death.
The regime was fearful, to twentieth-century eyes; but Busby
appreciated the clever boys, of whom Stepney undoubtedly was
one.

The qualifications for entry into Westminster were strict: a boy
was expected to be acquainted with the rudiments of grammar, the
eight parts of speech, and to be able to write moderately well. After
one or more years at the school, boys were examined for places
among the 40 King's Scholars, where Stepney found himself in
1676, at the age of 13. There is no record of his primary schooling
up to that date: Jane Stepney took care of her son's early education
(as he often admitted), but it is not known whether she taught him
herself or sent him to the local school at St Martin-in-the-Fields,
which had been in existence since 1614.[2]

It cannot have been easy for Jane to provide for her son. Apart
from his clothes, an annual Christmas gift of one guinea was
expected from parents to the Headmaster, and half a guinea to the
second master. At the annual election of the scholars, those already
there feasted at the expense of the newcomers. Once elected,
Stepney would have received about £3 a year for his food, and two
marks (13s. 4d. or about 66p) for a gown.

The scholars lived in the school, in a building which formerly had been a granary. The day began with the morning call '*Surgite!*' at 5.00 a.m., prayers in the dormitory in English and in Latin, followed by washing of hands and faces at the open-air pump in the cloisters. Study began soon after 6.00 a.m. and continued until dinner at 12.00 noon. It is not known whether in the seventeenth century the boys were given any breakfast. They were always hungry: senior boys who could compose clever (Latin) epigrams – and were encouraged to do so – were rewarded with food from the Headmaster's table. Work on Latin or Greek continued all day, until supper at 6.00 p.m., after which scholars were allowed 'small beer.' Although for junior forms bedtime was set at 8.00 p.m., the studious older boys were expected to go on working for another two hours or more.

There was some relief: a Saint's Day (falling on a week-day) was treated as a 'play' or holiday, and other free half-days might be granted by the Dean. There were no long holidays, but for about four weeks during the summer the Scholars moved to College House in Chiswick (then in the depths of the country) where discipline was more relaxed and (it is hoped) they could enjoy the fresh air and some exercise. At Westminster, a classical play was performed each year; Shrove Tuesday was celebrated by the cook tossing a pancake (for grabs by the boys) over the bar which divided Upper from Under School. At Christmas, there was a Saturnalia.[3]

In the last quarter of the seventeenth century, the city of Westminster backed on to open country. It was possible to walk through fields from St James' Park to Hampstead or Highgate. But the marshes of Tuttle Fields lay immediately to the south and south-west. The area was damp. George Stepney grew up (as he himself remarked) to be 'of low stature.'[4] To the modern mind, he suffered from malnutrition.

However, though Stepney may have suffered physically from his days under the care of Dr Busby, mentally he was extraordinarily well equipped for his future career. He achieved a first-class command of Latin, and only slightly to a lesser extent of Greek. Both languages had been instilled by constant repetition of grammatical rules and of passages learned by heart. Therefore Stepney's aural memory was trained from his boyhood years. He remembered, accurately, what people said to him: he could contradict statements with which he did not agree, using logic as his weapon. During his whole career Latin was used as the language in which treaties between states were formulated. Stepney, as did some of his friends, collected the texts of various treaties which could be used as examples of nicely worded clauses conveying a precise meaning. In later years the excellence of Stepney's Latin was praised by his contemporaries, as was his mastery of modern languages. These last were not taught at Westminster, so Stepney's ability must have been derived from his good memory and agile mental processes. Another omission – it could be said – to the Westminster curriculum was any study of the works of Shakespeare. There is no reflection of the greatest of poets in Stepney's writing, although references to classical Latin authors, and to Dryden, are often to be found. However, the greatest (unconscious) influence on Stepney's English prose was undoubtedly the Authorised Version of the Bible, and the *Book of Common Prayer*. This is not surprising, considering the long periods of time spent by all the boys in Westminster Abbey, every Sunday, attending morning and evening prayer. All boys were expected to summarise the sermon after service, either in Latin or English. While Stepney was not particularly devout, and never wished to take holy orders, the phrasing of his letters often mirrors passages in the Bible or Prayer Book which had caught his attention, or which he knew by heart.

Daily life at Westminster in the last quarter of the seventeenth century was anything but dull. The Popish Plot of 1678-9 and the exclusion crisis of a few years later would have been as hotly debated within the school as outside. Boys could sometimes attend debates in the House of Commons; the Law Courts when in session were held in Westminster Hall. The bustling life of the Court and the City was taking place only yards away from the school. There is no record of George Stepney's reactions to political life while he was a schoolboy. But he did establish a most important friendship, with Charles Montagu (1661-1715), the later promotor of the Bank of England, who became Earl of Halifax. Charles entered Westminster School in 1675, a year earlier than Stepney, and he too was clever with the Latin language, composed epigrams and poetry and was a favourite of the Headmaster. A grandson of the Earl of Manchester of Civil War fame, Charles moved in a higher social circle than did Stepney. Nevertheless Manchester House in 'Chanel Row' [later Cannon Row] was close to the Stepney home in Scotland Yard, and Charles called on Jane Stepney from time to time. As he developed in social prominence so were the Stepney sisters careful to wait on him in Whitehall if they wished any favour for their brother. Charles did indeed protect and promote his friend. Stepney was well aware of this fact and throughout his life returned thanks for Charles' goodwill.

In June 1682 George Stepney was 'sped away' from Westminster School to Trinity College Cambridge as head of the election i.e. in first place. His tutor was James Smallwood, a man not much older than himself, who had been a King's Scholar at Westminster in 1671 and was elected head to Trinity College in 1674. He later took holy orders and became an army chaplain. Stepney himself was admitted as a Pensioner, duly matriculated, and the following year, on 9 May, became a Scholar. He took his B A on 17 February 1686 (Ash Wednesday), being fourth *in ordo senioritatis*. Eventually he took up a Fellowship on 6 July 1689, which he held for the usual period of ten years.[5]

Sadly, no letters have survived from Stepney during his college years, but he enjoyed his time at Cambridge to the full.

> From fellow of Trin.Coll to become Master is sincerely all the vanity I have. . . . But I must not flatter myself by thinking those employments are bestowed so lightly. [6]

So wrote Stepney to a friend in 1693. But in Cambridge he considered himself a poet. His first claim to fame was a Latin poem written in honour of the marriage of Princess Anne to Prince George of Denmark in 1683. Two years later, in common with many undergraduates, he celebrated the accession of King James II with a poem which later caused him to be suspected of being a Jacobite. But the 20 lines contain no greater flattery than the similar compositions of his contemporaries, including Charles Montagu. The students were merely contributing to the University's book of condolence and congratulation to the new monarch, at a time when the Stuarts were at the height of their power. Stepney's poem to King James was followed, some months later, by a satirical piece, *On the University of Cambridge burning Monmouth's picture, 1685, who was formerly their Chancellor.* This begins:

> Yes, fickle Cambridge, Perkins found this true
> Both from your rabble and your doctors too,
> With what applause you once receiv'd his Grace,
> And begg'd a copy of his God-like face;
> But when the sage Vice-Chancellor was sure
> Th'original in limbo lay secure,
> As greasie as himself he sends a Lictor
> To vent his loyal malice on the picture.

The poems published on the accession of King James II drew both Charles Montagu and Stepney to the attention of Charles Sackville, Earl of Dorset (1643-1706). This man, astute and lazy, was a patron of many literary figures of his day. He had already greatly assisted

Matthew Prior (1664-1721) by educating him at Westminster School and St John's College Cambridge. Prior came to Westminster in 1681, a year before George Stepney left, and during his Cambridge days collaborated with Charles Montagu in composing a cruel and witty parody of John Dryden's poem *The Hind and the Panther.* The boys called their version *The City Mouse and the Country Mouse.* The biographers of the eighteenth century (Samuel Johnson, Ned Ward) noted that the careers of the three young men, Montagu, Prior and Stepney, were all furthered by Lord Dorset. By 1724, when memoirs of the Kit-Cat Club began to appear, all three were grouped together as 'My Lord Dorset's Boys' and it was assumed that the Earl spirited them away to be greeted with admiring attention by the wits of London Town. The reality is more prosaic. Charles Montagu was undoubtedly introduced to London society by Lord Dorset, but Stepney certainly and Prior probably remained in Cambridge. Montagu, in a long poem, described Stepney as

Gentle George . . . [who] . . . must still, must still write on.

The anonymous author of the preface to *The Works and Life of Lord Halifax* (London, 1715) states that although Montagu accepted Lord Dorset's invitation, Stepney

desir'd to be excus'd, out of his love to a retir'd life.

The reason for Stepney's reticence was probably his mother's lawsuit, described in Chapter I. And George was likely to fear the expense of social life in London. In 1684 he had written a poem dedicated *To the Earl of Carlisle upon the Death of his Son before Luxembourg,* lamenting the death of Frederick Christian Howard, killed at the siege of Luxemburg that summer:

He's gone! and was it then by your Decree)
Ye envious Pow'rs, that we should only see)
This Copy of your own Divinity)
Or thought ye it surpassing Human State
To have a Blessing lasting as 'twas great?
Your cruel Skill you better ne'er had shown
Since you so soon design'd him all your own.[7]

But this long effusion, over several pages, seems not to have brought to the author any patronage. So, as soon as he had completed his BA degree in 1686 Stepney began, of necessity, to seek employment in the world of 'business.'

III *Apprenticeship*
(Hamburg 1686-1689)

> All I know of Sr G Etherage (with whom I should have gone, but
> that ye gentle Knight bilk'd me, as he used to do his Creditors) is
> that he was allowed 300ᴵᴵ [£300] for his Equipage, wch all ye
> Town knew, for (by ye same Token) he lost his money at Play the
> day after he had receiv'd it.[1]

At the turn of the year 1685-6 George Stepney, while preparing at
Cambridge for his Bachelor of Arts examination, was also seeking
employment in the diplomatic service. King James II had selected
Sir George Etherege (?1635-1691) to represent him in Ratisbon
(now better known as Regensburg in Germany) where the Diets of
the Holy Roman Empire usually took place. Etherege was a leading
figure in English Restoration society: he was witty, a good French
speaker, and the author of three highly successful comedies which
included *The Comical Revenge:* or *Love in a Tub.* It is not known
who introduced Stepney to Etherege, but the appointment appeared
to be firm:

> if I had not been supplanted 4 days before Sir George was to
> embarque after as many months attendance by the Interest of Dr.
> Wynne, who put his Brother-in-law over my Head.[2]

Thus early in his career did Stepney learn of the pitfalls which beset
a young graduate of the seventeenth century, if he could not rely on
influential relatives or friends to help him.

It was usual for a young man who wished a diplomatic
appointment to apply for the post of secretary to one of the King's
representatives abroad. These individuals enjoyed differing degrees
of importance, and salary. At the top were the Ambassadors, who
often had the additional role of Plenipotentiary – that is, the power
to negotiate a treaty. Then came the more usual rank of Envoy.
Finally, the King might appoint a Resident – someone to deal with
routine business in a post where diplomatic activity was not
expected to be great.

A secretary would accompany his chief abroad, or join him at
his post, and would become part of the 'family' – a group which

was not restricted to blood relations, but which included the whole household, chaplains, servants and even horses, who were maintained and fed by the head of the mission. Pay was minimal. Stepney in his first post earned £20 a year. His duty as secretary was mainly to write, copy and dispatch letters; but also to deal with administrative and consular matters.

George Stepney always feared that he would fall into debt, so it is doubtful whether he would have been happy with Etherege. After his disappointment he took up another introduction, to Sir William Trumbull (1639-1716), who in 1685 was preparing to go as Envoy Extraordinary to the King of France. Ten years later, when Trumbull had been promoted by King William III to be Secretary of State, Stepney wrote to him:

> I know not, Sir, if you remember that it is now nine years ago that
> I offred you my Service when you was going for France (so early
> was my ambition to be known to you) my dear Lord Falkland
> gave me a letter for you, wch I deliver'd at Drs commons, but you
> was already provided with Mr. Tempest.[3]

So, from Cambridge George did sometimes travel to London. 'Doctors Commons' was a college in London for doctors of civil law. Jane Stepney once suggested to her son that he should take up residence there. George did not agree. It appears that in his student days (or earlier) he had made the acquaintance of Anthony Cary, fifth Viscount Falkland, to whom he used to refer as 'my first patron.' The Cary family (which included the famous Lucius, killed at the battle of Edgehill during the Civil War) had property at Aldenham, Hertfordshire, where the elder branch of the Stepney family also lived. In May 1694 Falkland was appointed Envoy and Plenipotentiary to the United Provinces of Holland, but sadly he died of smallpox before he could take up his duties. He does not appear to have helped Stepney in any way except by providing the introduction to Trumbull: nevertheless George always wrote of him with great affection.[4]

It is not known how George Stepney came to consider the post which he subsequently accepted, that of secretary to Sir Peter Wyche (1629-?1699), who in 1686 was the English Resident in Hamburg. The most obvious link between the two men is that Wyche's son John was a contemporary of Stepney's both at Westminster and at Trinity College, where he studied under the same tutor, James Smallwood. Early in 1686 Sir Peter Wyche in Hamburg wrote to Sir William Trumbull, then ambassador in Paris, recommending his son John as secretary. As far as is known, John never went to

Paris; but George Stepney did get a job in Hamburg.[5]

Sir Peter Wyche was the son, brother and father of diplomats. His father (also Sir Peter – d. 1643) had been Ambassador at Constantinople. His younger brother Cyril had a distinguished career in public service, and was at one time appointed Ambassador to the Turks. Sir Peter's eldest son, John, although he failed on his first attempt at employment as secretary in Paris, nevertheless eventually followed his father as Resident at Hamburg. John's three younger brothers were all traders. Wyche himself had had a varied career. He was a Fellow of the Royal Society; a Portuguese linguist, who had been Resident at Lisbon; he had served briefly in Russia, at Vienna and also Modena. In 1678 he was appointed to the Hanse Towns (of which Hamburg was the chief), and served there until 1681. He was a known Roman Catholic, and so in 1685 King James II reappointed him to his former post in Hamburg where, as soon as he had presented his credentials in May of that year, he wrote to the Senate to remind them not to permit their port to be used to further any rebellion against King James.[6]

Wyche worked hard. He rarely let slip an opportunity for reporting home, which meant that he wrote letters at least twice a week. He always used the services of a secretary: only the subscript and signature on his letters are in his own hand. From evidence of the handwriting, George Stepney began work in Hamburg on 7 May 1686. It is not known when he left Cambridge, but in doing so he abandoned his first chance of a Fellowship at Trinity College, which his friends had been predicting for him.

At the end of the seventeenth century the Imperial Free City of Hamburg was surrounded by predatory powers. To the north lay the Dukedom of Holstein-Gottorp, whose ruler was a client of Sweden, but who had recently been dislodged from his patrimony by the Danish king. This latter was the City's most dangerous enemy.

To the east lay the Dukedom of Mecklenburg, itself flanked by the growing power of Brandenburg under its Great Elector. To the south, the Dukedom of Brunswick-Lüneburg was divided between the Dukes of Brunswick-Zell (Celle) and Brunswick-Calemberg, or Hanover. The City, governed by an elected *Bürgermeister*, Senate and Council, existed for and because of its trade. Its main trade route with the German hinterland was the River Elbe. This waterway was by no means free. Each state along its route could and did impose tolls on the merchandise carried. The City could do little but acquiesce, cherish its commerce and do its best to keep its boundaries intact.

The King of England maintained a diplomatic representative in the City owing to the long-standing existence there of the English Company of Merchant Adventurers. Over the years the Company had gained substantial privileges and property. Its trade was in cloth – the woollen cloth that continued to be England's chief export. Its ships returned to England laden with the supplies of the Baltic: timber and iron, ropes and tar.

The English Company (as it was known) considered itself to be largely independent both of the City authorities and of its own government in London. It owned the 'English House' in the Gröningerstrasse, Hamburg, abutting on to the churchyard of St Katherine. Meetings of the Court (the governing body of the Company in Hamburg) took place in the English House, as did the church services, conducted according to the Anglican ritual. The Company's headquarters were in London, and its officials travelled between the two cities. According to the Company, the business of the King's Resident in Hamburg was to lend support to its affairs in all matters, but to refrain from interfering with the normal course of trade. During his first term of office as Resident, between 1678 and 1681, Sir Peter Wyche had got on well with the Company, who had praised his ability and industry.[7]

A leading member of the English Company was Francis (Franc) Stratford. This man later became George Stepney's banker, and the two corresponded over a number of years. Stratford was accused of Jacobite leanings. This was quite true; as was also his subsequent support for King William III. In other words, Stratford's aim in life was to make money. He would support any government in power at a given moment, and would lend to it – as he did to individuals – against interest. Stepney knew this perfectly well. The knowledge did not prevent him from treating Stratford as a confidant.

In 1686 the internal situation of the City of Hamburg was not to the liking of the English Resident. Two years previously the conservative and moderate *Bürgermeister*, Mürne, had been forcibly displaced by a radical party, known as 'the 30', who were widely regarded as a traitorous group supporting the pretensions of King Christian V of Denmark to rule the City.

The situation was complicated because the 30 had fallen out with the neighbouring Duke of Zell, who normally protected Hamburg from any Danish incursion. The Hamburg Senate had caused to be burned a paper which related the City's disfavour in the eyes of the Holy Roman Emperor in Vienna. The Duke of Zell took umbrage at the Senate's action, and his representative in Vienna assaulted a Senator from Hamburg who was attending the imperial court. The Duke's forces also devastated some land which belonged to the City, although his soldiers withdrew because the Envoys of the Emperor and the King of Denmark joined in vigorous diplomatic protests at Zell. Then the Elector of Brandenburg intervened, and to demonstrate his displeasure at the outrage committed against the City's Senator 'revenged himself' on the estates of the Duke of Zell's Envoy in Vienna. This was the state of affairs when George Stepney, aged nearly 23, took up his pen to write, at the dictation of the English Resident in Hamburg, a four-page relation [i.e. dispatch] addressed to the Earl of Middleton, Secretary of State in Whitehall:

> Hamburg May yᶜ 7 1686
> My Lord,
> The D of Zell hath returnd an answer to yᶜ letter this Senate wrote to him, in wch he plays with them, tells yᵐ he took well the Civility of it and their desires of a fair accomodation, but at yᶜ same time yᶜ Burgeosy taking a resolution so contrary to the tenor of it, & so much in defyance of him, he must have an explanation of it, knowe where lyes yᶜ power of this Magistracy, & wᵗʰ whom he is to treat.

Meanwhile an Aulic [Imperial] Counsellor had arrived in Hamburg in order to mediate between the City and Zell, and had received a deputation from the Senate. Sir Peter Wyche commented that he would like the City to be quiet, for the sake of trade. But the forces of Zell and those of Hamburg were on either side of the river. Zell had taken prisoners, and warships were being armed at Harburg. The Landgrave of Hesse and his lady were at Berlin; and the Elector [of Brandenburg] was going to Cleves on 17 May. Wyche reported a possible alliance between the King of France and the Elector of Cologne, Bishop of Münster. Then

> The Force of France & Savoy hath totally destroyed yᶜ people of yᶜ vallies, who broke yᶜ treaty they had once agreed to, because That at the Counsell of Constance . . .'twas concluded That noe promise to Hereticks was binding, & they would not venture unarm'd to leave their Country.

The dispatch continued with news from Upper Germany: on the first Monday in June there would be an assembly at Augsburg, to which were invited the Circles of Franconia, Bavaria, Suabia and the Upper Rhine, to discuss a projected military alliance between the Emperor and these states of the Empire.

The King of Sweden was assembling 16,000 men, thereby provoking the 'jealousy' of Denmark. Conferences had taken place at the Hague between the ministers of these two crowns about provision of men for the Emperor's use in Hungary. The Danes said they had none: the Swedes that only exercise was intended. If the Holstein question could be settled, observed Wyche, peace would reign.

Letters from Vienna reported the victory of Generals Heusler and Mercy against Serasquier and 4,000 Turks, and against Teckely [Thököly] plus 1,000 rebels and tartars, near Segedin. An account of the battle would follow.[8]

This first letter of George Stepney's diplomatic career has been set out in some detail because it illustrates the tangled European situation into which he had suddenly been thrust. Wyche received against payment newsletters from all over Europe as well as collecting information from his own contacts. Stepney, who liked and admired Wyche, followed his first master's example.

The modern reader of this dispatch will pick out, as of particular interest, the projected journey of the Great Elector of Brandenburg to his estates in Cleves. There, the Elector would meet the Prince of Orange, who wished to engage him among the anti-French powers in Europe. The persecution of the Protestants of the Swiss valleys is the theme of the third paragraph. The Edict of Nantes had been revoked in France the previous year, and already the flood of Huguenot refugees into Protestant Europe was under way.

Wyche then reported the state of the League of Augsburg, set up in March 1686 and comprising the Emperor, the Dutch, Spain, Savoy, Sweden, and the German electorates of the Palatinate, Saxony and Bavaria. All were ranged against the territorial ambitions of Louis XIV of France. The importance of the invitation to 'the Circles' of the Empire to join was that these middle-class citizens would be required to find the money for their own defence.

The Resident next related the perpetual discord between Denmark and Sweden; and the Emperor's need for troops to take part in his equally perpetual struggle against the Turks in eastern Europe. Accounts of battles were always studied with great interest by the statesmen and military commanders of the day. Stepney later on would send many such documents to Whitehall.

On 18 May 1686 Wyche received an important visitor, in the person of Baron 'Frytag'. This was Franz Heinrich, Baron von Fridagh zu Gödens, the imperial Envoy to Brandenburg, who had also arrived in Hamburg in order to mediate in the quarrel between the Senate and the Duke of Zell. Three days later, Wyche reported somewhat breathlessly that the Danish Minister (Mons. Paul(e)), who was *en poste* in Hamburg, had been recalled into Denmark for hurried consultations overnight, and had returned as swiftly:

> and . . . thereupon he was advised to give ye Senate notice to take care of ymselves, & ye City (wch Zeale of his ye 30 misconstrued, & took to reflect on ym, who own their being often with Monsr Paule & ye Danes) made soe great a noise here, yt by ye entreaty of some of this Company I made noe Scruple to send yesterday my Secretary to ye reigning Burgermaster to desire him to lett me knowe if they apprehended any danger imminent over ym, yt I might be able truly to informe ye K. my Master (who had convinct this Governemt of his inclinations to ym) & yt his subjects who had soe great an Interest here might have as much warning as could be to save their Estates.[9]

This was George Stepney's first diplomatic mission. The Senate returned a soft answer: no danger was anticipated. But, as Wyche observed in his dispatch, the Danes were disguising their preparations and ten French men-of-war were under way to the Sound.

At the same time Sir Peter embarked on a request which was made with unfailing regularity by most English envoys during their service overseas: the plea was for money. Wyche had been a year in his post and had not had a penny out of the Exchequer. He begged Lord Middleton to intercede with the Treasury on his behalf. Stepney, alas, would find himself writing many similar letters in years to come. It was of course usual for all correspondents of the late seventeenth century, both English and foreign, to begin and end their letters with the utmost ceremony. Wyche was no exception. The following is an example (taken at random) of the way in which he would conclude a letter to the Earl of Middleton:

> Never being without a becoming sence of my great obligations to yr Lp, & of my need of yr continued good Patronage, I strive by these to square ye esteeme, zeale & fervancy wch are to make me second to none in being
> My Lord,
> Yr Ls: most obedient and
> most humble servant
> PETER WYCHE

Wyche continued to report regularly on the imperial assembly at Augsburg. He obtained his information from newsletters, and by July 1686 it is likely that he was leaving this routine reporting to his secretary. On 8 July a letter was dispatched to London which contained much detail on the assembly, with Latin quotations. A separate sheet was included, listing 'The Army & Officers projected to be rais'd by ye Allyance treated on at Augsburg.' This gives a count, in thousands of men, of the troops expected to be raised by the Emperor, the Kings of Sweden and Spain, and including those of the Circles of the Upper Rhine, Franconia and Suabia. The total expected was 60,000. The names of the commanders were listed, under the Commander-in-Chief, the Prince Waldeck.[10]

It is true that this information was probably of academic interest to King James II. But similar lists, provided by Stepney in later years, were anything but academic to King William III. Unwittingly, Wyche was providing excellent training to a man who would become one of King William's most assiduous servants.

Meanwhile Danish pressure on the City of Hamburg was increasing. By 20 August, the Danes were on the march, 'the 30' were eclipsed, the ancient government was resettled and a tax was being raised. By this time Hamburg was being supported both by Brandenburg and by the Duke of Zell, despite the latter's recent dispute with the Senate. The King of Denmark now announced that all he wanted was a formal acknowledgement of homage by the City: otherwise he would destroy the place. Here George Stepney takes up the story:

> Upon this news, I was dispatched expresse with letters to him in behalfe of ye English Colony here . . . and were to expect noe favourable distinction if His Bombs executed wt he threatened, but must have their share in ye publique Calamity. With these instructions I traveled all night in quest of ye Court, & next morning (Sunday ye 22 of August) found ym at their Devotions.
> . . . I could get nothing but a denouncing of Anguish, Desolation and Woe; and might reasonably expect noe lesse than Hamburgh in flames on my returne.

The siege lasted from 21 August to 10 September. The City's troops defended its sconce [the outworks] with spirit, and inflicted 1,000 casualties on the attackers. Their sallies were less successful, and at one time it was feared that the sconce had been betrayed by Danish sympathisers. But the King of Denmark too had his difficulties: he feared his army would starve; the City always managed to keep two gates open for provisions. And as Stepney remembered in later years, the King's artillery did not arrive as planned. Wishing an honourable reason for retreat, the King employed the foreign ministers to advise the Senate to submit. The envoys in question included Sir Peter Wyche and his colleague Sir Gabriel Sylvius, who was accredited to and accompanied the King of Denmark. During the negotiations Sylvius interfered constantly with Wyche's function and tried to deal directly with the City. Wyche was furious: Stepney was sent to and fro; but eventually Wyche earned a rebuke from Whitehall and had to respond by disclaiming to London any idea of enmity between himself and Sylvius.

The King of Denmark at last agreed to desist, and removed his troops. He demanded 300,000 Crowns and an island, and that the forces in support of Hamburg should also withdraw. The City refused these terms, and demanded the release of their ships, and free commerce on the Elbe. On 16 September, the defending horse from Brandenburg and Lüneburg marched out, the City's battery on the island was demolished, the ships were released by Denmark (but lost two thirds of their cargo) and the Elbe was promised to be opened. The King of Denmark returned to Copenhagen, leaving his partizans to suffer. Stepney watched the execution of two of the men, the bodies being buried under the gallows 'and their heads exalted on ye Gates.' He added, in his account of this grisly incident, that confiscation of the traitors' estates would not do the public much good, 'they having been (as always are projectors of new Government) men of desperate fortune'.[11]

After the siege, life in the City of Hamburg returned to normal. Early in November a cold snap caused the river Elbe to be blocked by ice, so that the commercial traffic which had been released by the King of Denmark was again at a standstill. About this time George Stepney received a letter from Dr Owen Wynne, Under-Secretary of State:

> Your mother is concern'd at your absence, there being as she says severall fellowships like to be shortly Vacant in your College: you may gett Sr Peter to engage Mr. Cook to be your friend in procuring the King's letter.[12]

Since the spring of 1686 both Jane Stepney and Charles Montagu had been anxious that George should not lose his chance of a fellowship at Trinity College by reason of his absence overseas. George himself had already been in touch with his friend Timothy Bedford – a Fellow of the college – to ask his help in persuading the Master and seniors that his absence in Hamburg should be no impediment to his election as a Fellow. Bedford had been successful in this task, and wrote to George accordingly on 16/26 April 1686. Charles had called on Jane Stepney in London and recommended her to apply for a royal mandate, now that the regulations for applicants were being changed. As Charles now explained to George:

> There is no body that knows either you or the College that can be ignorant how certain you were to come in by the Election of all the Fellows if they had votes, and tho' 'tis no wonder you should affect that honourable way of proceedings in which you might be

sure to succeed, yet the sails must shift with the winds; least [sic] while you ly in expectation of a Direct Gale the market be overstockt and your voyage lost.[13]

Trinity College was doing its best to defer admitting Fellows on mandates: nevertheless both Charles and Jane agreed that this was now the safest way to proceed, and accordingly George's humble petition was sent to Whitehall [see Appendix I]. The surviving copy is undated, but was no doubt composed by George on receipt of Montagu's letter quoted above. Curiously, George confused his father with his grandfather, and therefore some eighteenth-century historians referred to him as the son, and not the grandson of Sir Thomas Stepney, Knight. The royal mandate duly followed [Appendix II], dated 17/27 July 1687, from Windsor.

Sir Peter Wyche had added his influence with Lord Middleton in favour of his secretary's fellowship at Trinity College, and was quick to acknowledge Middleton's help in the matter, explaining that Stepney was too modest to express his thanks himself to the Secretary of State. This was true: but gentle George may well have had a motive other than shyness for his reticence towards Middleton. Catholic influence in England was increasing. Although the letters to Stepney which survive from the year 1686 – those from Montagu and from Bedford – read as though written to a man of known Whig persuasion, yet Stepney worked for a Catholic diplomat and by April 1687 Wyche was openly attending Mass at the French Resident's chapel in Hamburg. It could not be denied that Stepney had obtained his Fellowship by the mandate of the Catholic King of England. These are the reasons why nineteenth-century historians have tended, at least obliquely, to charge Stepney with turning his coat from Jacobitism to a blatant Protestantism during the course of his early career. Such charges are made with hindsight. During 1686-7 Catholicism was riding high all over Europe, and for all Stepney knew he might have to accommodate himself to the ancient faith for his entire lifetime. His desire for the fellowship at Trinity College was natural. He enjoyed the collegiate life; he wanted to continue his poetry; and above all he wanted a little financial independence. His Fellowship would bring him in about £35 a year, and he would live free in College. But he did not need to emphasise his thanks to Middleton on this occasion.[14]

Timothy Bedford wrote to Stepney to congratulate him on the mandate. Another similar letter came from David Egert, a diplomatic clerk then serving in Stockholm, to whom Stepney had been obligingly kind when Egert passed through Hamburg on his way to his post. Egert would later apply unsuccessfully to Stepney to join him in Dresden as clerk. He now passed on greetings to others he had met in Hamburg, and from his letter is derived a rare glimpse of George Stepney's companions during his first post. These included a Mr Wotkuir, a housekeeper (unnamed but masculine) and 'Mr Storar.' The name of this last recurs in the Stepney correspondence. John Storer was a minor administrative official – one of those who make the world comfortable for the more senior ranks. Stepney later would ask him to send books, a coffee pot and even red potatoes. Another friend from Hamburg days was Mat(thew) Grey (or Gray), probably a member of the English Company. George Stepney refers to him as a musician, an acquaintance of Storer's, and already in 1693 laid up with gout. In later years Stepney was credited with having many friends ('cronys') in Hamburg and he always expressed willingness to return there as Resident, although this post never came his way.[15]

During the summer of 1687 a social event occurred: the arrival of Prince George of Denmark (husband of the English Princess Anne) at Glückstadt. Wyche hastened thither to make his compliment and took his secretary with him. The first encounter was not however with Prince George, but with Sir Gabriel Sylvius, Wyche's old rival. The Prince was missing, and the possibility was discussed that he might have been attacked by pirates. But eventually he turned up, carriages having to be pressed to transport his baggage. A little later in the year Isabella Lady Wyche arrived in Hamburg. She had been lady-in-waiting to Queen Catherine (Charles II's widow), for whom she had great affection. Stepney helped Lady Wyche with her correspondence, sometimes addressing the outer cover of her letters. He seems to have been attracted to her maid, Millison, to whom he refers some seven years later.

Sir Peter had other more pressing affairs on his mind. The Duchess of Modena, mother of James II's wife, Queen Mary Beatrice, had died, and Wyche was ordered into mourning by the Earl of Sunderland. This was an expensive business for any diplomat. Not only must he appear in black, but servants, carriages and horses had to be similarly attired. Wyche twice asked for his expenses to be paid.[16]

Christmas 1687 came and went. Wyche wrote home, emphasising the 'quiet & devotion of ye Holydays.' On 24 January 1688

> I was this morning awakened by very ill news wch was brought
> me off [sic] an Englishman who late last night was by a Frenchman

> . . . kild on these streets; as I heard the Malefactor was in hold, I
> sent my Secretary this morning to ye Judge to be by at his
> examination, who confest ye fact, & on whom I shall press justice
> may be done.

The dead man was not one of the Company, but had led 'noe good
life' for six months and was going under an assumed name. He had
lost his life as a result of a drunken quarrel. Wyche decided to seek
a 'prosecution of blood' for murder. Meanwhile the funeral of the
victim had to be arranged. This incident is typical of the consular
duties which in the seventeenth century were expected of all
diplomats.[17]

Despite the exigencies of post-days, and the copying and re-
copying of letters for the twice-weekly mail, George Stepney was
not neglecting his artistic career as a poet. In February 1688 his
friend Charles Montagu somewhat surprisingly married Anne,
Countess of Manchester, the widow of the third Earl of Manchester
who was Charles' uncle. Stepney sent a poem in congratulation
(regrettably lost) and received a letter from Anne in
acknowledgement.

In March a very distinguished visitor came to Hamburg in the
person of John George III, Elector of Saxony and senior member
of the house of Wettin which was to play such an important part in
Stepney's later career. Wyche naturally wished to compliment (as
the custom was) the Elector, and sent Stepney to beg an audience
from the Captain of the Elector's Guard. But the Elector was
travelling incognito, and would see nobody. Wyche reported
disapprovingly that the Elector and the Duke of Holstein

> eat & drink a l'Almand every day together, & goe as often to our
> Operas, wch are permitted in Lent to entertain them.[18]

At the beginning of June 1688 Wyche reported a snippet of news.
At the time of writing he could never have realised its significance.
This was that 'Benting' – i.e. Hans-Willem Bentinck (1649-1709),
the later Earl of Portland – had been sent by his master the Prince
of Orange to condole and compliment the new Elector of
Brandenburg on the death of the latter's father, the Great Elector.
Bentinck went on to visit Cassel, and Wyche was near the mark
when he stated that

> a strong & firm allyance [is] being aimed at between Saxony,
> Brandenburg, Lunenburg, Hessen and the States.

But what Bentinck was in fact arranging was German support for
the Prince's projected invasion of England.[19]

Also in June arrived in Hamburg the happy news – as far as

Wyche was concerned – of the Queen of England's safe delivery of a son. Wyche rejoiced, and wrote excitedly that he was seeking an audience of the Duke of Holstein; he would give a collation 'tonight' for the whole English Company, then for the 'Publique Ministers' in Hamburg, and after them the Senate. Fortunately the celebrations were to be allowed in the Extraordinaries [i.e. in Wyche's expense account] and the Resident had at last received some cash from the Treasury. Years later, Stepney recalled the insistence of the Duke of Holstein upon his correct styles and titles. He was entitled to be addressed as 'Serenissimo.' Stepney himself carried the letter from King James II to the Duke, notifying the birth of the Prince of Wales.

> Chanc[ll] Ahlfeldt enquired if ye Title were upon ye letter, and if it had chanced to have been omitted, I am perswaded he would neither have received the letter, nor have given audience to Sir Peter Wyche who sent me.[20]

Wyche was duly received by the Duke, who honoured the English Resident with his presence at dinner in early July, in celebration of the royal birth.

However, storm-clouds were gathering for the Resident. A Deputy of the Company had died, and Wyche passionately desired to be elected in his place. He applied for a royal letter, but was refused, and by mid-August he had been turned down (with contumely) by the Company, who elected a man from their own ranks. Wyche's religion had been held against him.[21]

And now, in August, events in Europe were taking a sinister turn for the Catholic Resident in Hamburg. 'Benting' had arranged the march of about 23,000 Brandenburg and Lüneburg troops southward towards Cleves. Anti-Stuart rumours were rife in Holland. By 4 September, it was rumoured that the Dutch fleet would sail for England. The Resident's secretary, however, was engaged in quite another matter: Wyche was informed that the Duke of Zell had decided to send 100 stags to King James II, and he (Wyche) was to organise transport. The fate of the unfortunate beasts is not known.[22]

At the end of October, George Stepney was writing, at Wyche's dictation:

> Wee had this day from Holland ye certaine news with wt Parade and confidence all was embarqued on ye fleet, & that the Pr [of Orange] was to goe on board on Wednesday. The Judge of all the World is to doe the Right, by wch ye Crown is long yet to flourish on His Mat[ies] head, & his enemy in ye fatall year off [sic] 88 again to be cover'd with shame – Blessings on His Maty, & those who

venture with him.[23]

News of the actual invasion of England reached Wyche from Holland. He was aware that intelligence from this source had to be in part regarded as propaganda. Information from England was slow to arrive: 'the Pacquet Boats goe noe more.' However, by 13 November Wyche had received mail from Flanders and Holland and he knew that the Prince of Orange had landed in England, but he did not know where. Meanwhile, the city of Mannheim had been taken by the French, and Coblenz had been reduced to a heap of stones.

Wyche was now corresponding with Edmund Poley, then Envoy in Stockholm. Stepney continued to write down his chief's increasingly despairing comments on the situation in England:

21 December 1688

The inclosed (received this morning) is to tell you Such amazing News off ye Queen & Pr of Wales one day, & ye King ye next leaving ye K[dome], that I believe 'twill put yr fortitude to it, if you can compose yrselfe to business within ye same time 'tis yet since I receiv'd ye blow . . . all my thoughts are contriving to Subsist in my old age, wch will be an hard matter to doe, Soe totally ruin'd is

Sir

Yr most obedient &
most humble Servant
Pet Wyche [24]

However, Isabella Wyche in England wrote to her husband in January 1689 that she was 'not too much cast down in affliction.' The Prince of Orange had taken on the government of England by popular request. But the new government ignored the Resident in Hamburg completely. Wyche had received no letters. He did hear from King James in France, who told him to correspond with Lord Melfort, now his Secretary of State. [25]

The coronation of the new King and Queen, which took place in London on 11 April 1689, was celebrated by the English Company in Hamburg with feasting at the house in the Gröningerstrasse, and with music, dancing and games. Salutes were fired by the English ships in the port; fireworks were provided in the evening.[26]

George Stepney's opinion on these events has never been revealed. He was still at his post in Hamburg when, at the end of May 1689, he received a letter marked 'For Mr. George Stepney at Hamburg to be delivered to his own hands privately.' It was written from London on 12/24 May and ran as follows:

Sr

Being shortly designed from hence in qualitie of Resident to the Government of Hamburg, some of your friends, & relations have beene with me, desiring me to receive you for my Secretary in that employment, to wch I have the more readily agreed, upon the recommendations of Mr. Mountague, & Dr. Wynne, who gave me a very good character of you, but howsoever wth condition, that it may be with the good liking, & consent of my old school-fellow & acquaintance Sir Peter Wych, unto whom I have wrote by this post.[27]

Sir Paul Rycaut continued his letter by requesting a quick answer, to reach him before he set off. He also asked if Wyche would leave him his house, otherwise he would need another, possibly a Company house. He implied that Stepney would arrange these matters for him. The letter ends, 'Your affectionate humble servant', which might imply that he and Stepney were already acquainted, although there is no other evidence for this. Wyche had heard of the possibility of Rycaut's arrival, but had had no word of any further payments due to himself, a matter which caused him great anxiety. One day after Rycaut's letter (and before it could possibly have arrived in Hamburg), Wyche wrote in his own hand to an unknown addressee:

My Secretary Mr. Stepney who hath served mee so long with dexterity fidelity & ability hath for some months been prest by his Mother to return into England wch desire (tho coming from her) hee hath deferred yesterday hee shewed mee two lines from her wch peremptorily commanded him to come away immediately and to take his passage on to a vessel wch probably may sail toomorrow. . . . I oppos'd to his Mother's commands the great inconvenience I should receive by his so suddaine departure and no more able to performe my correspondence. . . . but that beeing convinc'd (as I am) that tis his interest to goe into England I desir'd him to stay with mee [one] month more wch after arguing with himself hee [hath] consented to doe, wch I must take very well.[28]

And take ship the young man did, some time during the month of June. Sir Peter Wyche left Hamburg on 2 June (according to the City archives) for a ten-year exile in Lisbon. In August 1689 Sir Paul Rycaut duly arrived to take up his duties to the Hanse towns. He corresponded with Stepney in a friendly way for many years, but was not to enjoy his services as secretary. Stepney's apprenticeship was over.[29]

IV *Tutelage*
(Brandenburg, 1690-1691)

> Many eminent men . . . who had no estates of their own, sought
> possession of others: but the king did not readily grant their
> requests; and that [he] could not gratify them all, he sent many of
> those, who boasted of their merits, out of the way: . . . Mr James
> Johnston, still well known, both on account of his father's death,
> and his own good services, to the elector of Brandenburgh, on
> the recommendation of Dr. Burnet.[1]

On 6 July 1689 George Stepney was admitted as a Fellow of Trinity
College, Cambridge, at a ceremony held in the College chapel. His
presence at the Fellowship ceremony was obligatory, as he had
been warned by his friend Timothy Bedford. It can be assumed
that for the rest of the year Stepney lived in College. His stipend
was probably his only income: perhaps his mother also made him a
small allowance. In her will (drawn up in December 1688) Jane
left her son £10 a year for as long as he held his Fellowship at the
University of Cambridge, and no longer. Jane added, that if George
should at any time settle himself either in Oxford or Cambridge, he
was to have a lump sum of £50 to help him. She died at the end of
October 1694. The second provision of her will concerning George
was never required. In order to augment his income Stepney may
have hoped for fees or presents as honoraria for his poetry; but
there is no certain record that any of his verses were written during
1689. During the last days of the year, at Cambridge, he received a
letter from his friend Charles Montagu:

> Sr   Dec 24, 1689
> I have a small proposal to offer you, wch is more considerable
> [for] the manner of its being offer'd, than any other ways: for Mr
> Vernon came very frankly & kindly to tell me, that [if] you would
> go Secretary to Mr Johnson who is sent with the character of
> Envoyé to Brandenburgh he would recommend you, this I was
> extremely pleased at since it convinc'd me that Mr Vernon did
> remember the Promises he had made Me. This is the case, and if
> this be worth your acceptance 'tis at your service: and Mr Johnson
> is so far civil, that he has promised Me, if you will come up to
> Town, and speak with Him, if you should not agree matters, he

will defray the expence of your journeys, so that 'tis my opinion
that you would do best to come up to Town, tho you should not
be fond of going into the same climate again (for I have no other
exception to [it]) that you may discourse with Mr. Johnson, and
thank Mr. Vernon for his kindnesse, and then wee will discourse
this matter further.

I am

Your most Humble servt

Cha: Montague

My service to all
our friends particularly
to the Coll, and
John Laughlin.[2]

It is noticeable that Montagu was now addressing Stepney with
formality. Gone are the casual forms of 'dear George' or 'gentle
George.' Charles was already a Member of [the Convention]
Parliament; he had purchased a post as Clerk to the Privy Council
for £1,500, and he had been introduced to King William III. His
patronage was the greatest lever in Stepney's advancement, and
would continue to be so over the years. He had (probably) brought
Stepney to the attention of Lord Dorset; now he was to introduce
him to James Vernon senior (1646-1727), later Secretary of State,
who had toiled long in government service and who was known as
'Father Vernon' to several of William III's younger diplomats.
Vernon did indeed treat Stepney paternally and encouraged his
protegé when the latter met with disappointments.

James Johnston (1655-1737), the newly-appointed Envoy to
the Elector of Brandenburg, was a younger son of the Earl of
Warristoun who lost his head for treason at the Restoration. James
was evacuated to Holland, for safety, and studied civil law at Utrecht
University, where it may be presumed he made the acquaintance of
the young Prince of Orange, who had been a student at the same
University. Johnston was said to have been employed by Henry
Sidney, Lord Romney, on a secret mission during the year 1688 in
favour of the Glorious Revolution. According to one eighteenth-
century report:

He is very honest & yet something too credulous & suspicious;
endued with a great deal of Learning & Virtue; is above little
Tricks, free from Ceremony; & would not tell a Lye for the world.[3]

Johnston was not ungenerous in offering to pay Stepney's expenses
for the journey to London in the event of his refusing the post
offered. It seems to have been his last generous act towards his
secretary: Stepney accepted the offer, but the relationship between

the two men was not happy and Stepney frequently complained of the Scot's meanness and of his reluctance to treat his new employee as anything other than a servant.

Before the new Envoy left England he was paid £500 for his equipage (i.e. his coach, horses and servants), plus one quarter's advance on his 'ordinary' salary of £5 a day. The 'ordinary' was reckoned to commence from the date of departure 'out of the presence.' For Johnston this meant 24 January 1690, when he 'kissed hands and departed on that employ.' He went, accompanied by his servants, coach and goods to Gravesend, to take ship for the Continent.[4]

For the next four months the movements of the Envoy and his secretary are obscure. Johnston was in duty bound to take up his post with the Elector of Brandenburg without undue delay. Frederick III (1657-1713), who had succeeded the Great Elector in the spring of 1688, was not the man his father had been, but he was at pains to emphasise the greatness of his inheritance by the use of ceremony and display. He disliked the business of state, and avoided it where he could be making frequent and sudden journeys from one part of his patrimony to another, and the domains of the house of Hohenzollern included not only Brandenburg/Prussia but also territory in south-western Germany, the Duchies of Cleves, Jülich and Berg. On 1 March 1690 (n.s.) the Elector was reported to be in Königsberg in east Prussia: it is unlikely that Johnston was in attendance.[5]

Storms during January 1690 held up the voyage of the Earl of Portland (Hans-Willem Bentinck) to Holland, and no doubt delayed Johnston's departure too. Portland's task was to establish in the Hague the congress of the Grand Alliance of all the powers which were opposed to France. The League of Augsburg (set up by the Emperor to try to combat French incursions into Germany) was already in being, but King William had no intention of committing himself to an assembly which was based so far away from the United Provinces and from his new kingdom of England. From 1690 for the next 12 years the Hague was the centre of the anti-French coalition and doubtless Johnston made his way there. The first firm news of his arrival was given by the gifted and industrious secretary of the English Embassy at the Hague, William Aglionby (d. 1706), who reported on 4/14 April that Johnston had arrived, but was indisposed and was expected to stay for some days. By the beginning of May the Envoy had recovered, at least sufficiently to start his journey to Berlin, travelling by way of Hanover and Zell, and, it may be inferred, accompanied by his secretary. The call at Hanover was of importance to Stepney, although at the time he could not have realised its significance. The Duchess (later Electress) of Hanover was Sophia (1630-1714), the twelfth child of Frederick, Elector Palatine and Elizabeth, ('the Winter Queen'), daughter of James I of England. By 1690 Sophia had been married to the Duke of Brunswick-Calemberg (Hanover) for 32 years. She had succeeded in creating at Hanover a cultivated and educated court which was illuminated by the presence of Gottfried Wilhelm Leibniz (1646-1716), the great mathematician and philosopher. Stepney was soon to become one of Leibniz's 1,028 correspondents. In 1690 Sophia was not yet regarded as the heiress-presumptive to the throne of England. Nevertheless she was always proud of the fact that she was James I's granddaughter, and was invariably kind to travellers who arrived from England.[6]

The next stop for Johnston and his party was at Zell. The ruler of this Dukedom (part of the Brunswick inheritance) was George William (1624-1705), brother-in-law to Sophia. One of King William III's early acts had been to dispatch an Envoy to the Brunswick courts and in 1690 this peripatetic post was held by Sir William Dutton Colt (d. 1693). Johnston immediately addressed himself to Colt, partly to pick up mail (sent on from the Hague) and to discuss Germanic affairs with him, having particular regard to the task which was the first duty of all King William's Envoys: to make arrangements for as many German troops as possible to be available for the continuing war against the French. Colt was a kindly man, and wrote of his contentment at having made Johnston's acquaintance. He was kind, too, to Stepney, and asked the latter to write often – meaning that Stepney should supply the routine reports which were the duty of most secretaries. Johnston changed horses at Zell, leaving some of his own with Colt, under the care of a groom. With fresh horses, Johnston and Stepney set out for Berlin.[7]

The date of the Envoy's arrival at his post is not known. However, he was there in time to organise the investiture of the Elector of Brandenburg with the Order of the Garter. In this he was assisted by Gregory King (1648-1712), Lancaster Herald, who had arrived from England by way of Hamburg. The ceremony took place on 6/16 June 1690. George Stepney played a minor role and kept a careful record of all that happened, including Johnston's speech in 'ffrench, Latin and High Dutch' [i.e. German], which he (Stepney) later sent to Colt when the latter was charged with a similar mission to the Elector of Saxony. Johnston himself later sent to London an expense account to cover '6 coachmen, 30 footmen, 24 trumpeters, 2 drummers etc.' This entourage had been hired for the occasion. The lavish display was intended to demonstrate the power and the glory of the new King of England. William III needed to gain recognition of his kingly title, particularly because his deposed father-in-law, James II, was the guest of the King of France.[8]

No sooner was the Garter ceremony performed than the Elector (and perforce the foreign Envoys) immediately made plans for a hurried journey to his Rhenish dominions. There was need for haste. The successful commander of the imperial forces, Charles, Duke of Lorraine, had died in April. His successor, Prince Waldeck, was facing a massive French army. Johnston, writing in Berlin on 17/ 27 June, told his correspondent:

The Elector is to be at Wesel on the 29th: I go all this night.

The court duly got to Wesel – that cross roads, on the Rhine, where north-south and east-west European traffic met – but it was too late. Without the support of the Brandenburg army Prince Waldeck was defeated by the French at the battle of Fleurus, on 1 July (n.s.) 1690. A month later, Johnston was writing to Colt from Grez:

I wrote to you from Wesel. I must now use Mr. Stepney's hand as I hope you will do the like for ye heat & dust in travelling do so disorder my eyes that I cannot write myself.

Johnston continued by complaining of the quarters which had been allocated to him; and he then described the various components of the allied army, calculating that about 50,000 men might still take the field:

The Elector's troops are very good. The Victory in Ireland [the battle of the Boyne] gives us courage; & the News of it came so seasonably, that otherwise wee should have done nothing . . . . It is glorious for ye King, but a dear-bought glory, that nothing goes right but where He is.

Johnston's apology to Colt for not writing with his own hand was to excuse himself for a lack of courtesy. Stepney later wrote the bulk of his huge correspondence himself, and only allowed copies of his letters to be made by secretaries. The use of the plural, in the second excerpt quoted above, relates to the Elector of Brandenburg in this instance:

that otherwise wee should have done nothing.

This was a common device used between diplomats (often with irony) to indicate the court to which they were accredited. Stepney followed Johnston in this practice.[9]

Two weeks later, from Brussels, Stepney himself wrote to Colt. This is the first letter under Stepney's own signature which has survived:

> Hon^d Sir   Brussels 7/17 August 1690
> I am order'd by Mr. Johnston to send you the inclos'd letter from
> ye Bishop of Salisbury. He begs yr excuse for not writing, having
> done it last Post & Since that time nothing hath happen'd worthy
> yr Curiosity. Our Camp is still at Halle, 3 hours from this place,
> whither wee are returning this minute, tho there is little prospect
> of Action; nor can any good news be expected from these parts,
> till our affairs at Sea goe right. The Envoy presents his humble
> Service to yr self & family, & I beg they will be pleas'd to accept
> of the duty off [sic]
> Hon^d Sir
> Yr most humble & most
> obed^t Servant
> G.STEPNEY
>
> Sr William Colt
>
> This, & ye last
> letter are not inclos'd
> to Mons. Cordeman, but pass
> through Holland. But ye pacquets
> wch wee shall send from ye Camp
> shall be directed and sent as
> you desir'd.
> Yr favour is desir'd for ye inclosed.[10]

Stepney's first official letter is brief and to the point. The postscript reflects one of the preoccupations of any secretary: letters must reach their destination. Unlike Sir Peter Wyche, who had been helpless in such matters, Stepney was always aware of the dangers through which mail might pass, and he took what steps he could to ensure its safe arrival.

Johnston and his secretary returned to Halle. The next letter to Sir William Colt was written (by them both) under the influence of drink. Johnston had been entertaining the Brandenburg court and wrote that he had drunk so much he could not sensibly answer Colt's previous letter. Stepney's handwriting indicates that he too was *leicht beschwippst*. Johnston, however, wished to send the letter because he was indebted to Colt for an introduction to the Prince of Hanover [the future King George I – eldest son of Sophia], by whom he was received 'as the Emperor would have done.' The occasion was not only gratifying to Johnston himself but was a further testimony that the German Protestant princes were willing to accept him as a king's Envoy. Johnston repeated his thanks to Colt four days later, and admitted that Stepney had had to remind him of what he had previously written. In his drunken state Johnston had been fairly sure that the Elector of Brandenburg intended to give battle to the French. Now he withdrew that opinion,

> for our [i.e. the Elector's] resolutions are not like ye Laws of ye Medes & Persians; For now I know not when wee shall march, tho in a few days wee must do it for want of forrage.[11]

The campaigning season was coming to an end. Johnston and Stepney moved from Halle to Brussels and then to Cleves. Charles Montagu in London rebuked his friend for sending him a gift of wine – Stepney was treating him like a stranger – and in a later letter told Stepney the news that Matthew Prior was likely to go to the Hague to join the Embassy there. This was true: Lord Dursley, the Envoy, informed Colt that Prior was an ingenious young man, who had 'writ the mouse against Dryden which was polish'd by Mr. Montagu,' and added that Prior was 'wholly unacquainted with the business he is in.'[12]

During his stay in Cleves Johnston was granted a 'public audience' of the Elector of Brandenburg. This was an expensive and stately affair, involving fees to hired trumpeters, coachmen and footmen (£10) together with a banquet to the Elector, the Landgrave of Hesse and others at a cost of £35. The occasion was designed to reflect the affluence and dignity of King William. [It may be recalled that Johnston was paying Stepney £20 *per annum*.] Stepney himself in later life took care to avoid such extravagances.[13]

On 24 November (n.s.) Johnston wrote to Colt in irritation and perplexity because the Elector had announced his intention of departing from Cleves the next day for Hanover and Berlin. This decision had been taken despite the news of the intended arrival in Holland of King William, whom the Elector had been expected to meet. Moreover, rumours were circulating in Cleves that the French were making great preparations on the frontiers of Brabant and Flanders, despite the lateness in the season. Johnston himself was awaiting orders from England, whether he should accompany the Elector or await his own monarch. Presumably he received the latter instructions, for on 3/13 December he was still at Cleves. Then, happily, on 29 December Matthew Prior reported to Whitehall from the Hague:

> Mr Johnstone is at Utrecht and Mr. Stepney with Me at the Hague, He presents his humble Service to you this is all the news We could find here.[14]

So Stepney was free of Johnston (who was already referring to him as 'my Esquire') for some days, and doubtless he and Matt were enjoying such social life as the Hague could offer. Johnston himself arrived by 2/12 January 1691, and King William at the end of that month, having endured a fearful voyage from England, during which he and his immediate entourage (including Lord Dorset) were lost in an open boat in freezing fog for 18 hours.[15]

Fortunately for the Allies, the King came to no harm. Over the next month, the Grand Alliance was formally set up, and the Hague was full of the leading anti-French rulers: they included the Electors of Brandenburg and Bavaria, the two Dukes of Brunswick [i.e. Calemberg/Hanover and Zell], the Landgrave of Hesse-Cassell, Count Windischgrätz, representing the Emperor, and the Marquis of Gastañaga, who was then the Governor of the Spanish Netherlands. The congress continued until 9 March (n.s.) 1691, when the King went to his country seat of Het Loo to enjoy his hunting. All this time Stepney (and Johnston) were in the Hague. Their activity has never been precisely reported. It seems likely that Stepney was employed in the general running of the congress: he got to know Lord Dorset personally, and many of the great world at least by sight. And he had time, during the first weeks of February, to write in verse his 'Epistle to Charles Montague, Esq; on His Majesty's Voyage to Holland.' This poem was received with rapturous applause – partly, perhaps, for its propaganda value: it gave unstinted praise to King William. James Montagu (brother to Charles) wrote to Stepney from London, 'it is a non-pareille, i'faith.' Stepney himself circulated it to all the northern English embassies, and received congratulatory comments from Sir Paul Rycaut, Hugh Greg in Copenhagen, and Dr John Robinson, then secretary to the embassy in Stockholm, from whom it can be noted that Johnston had sent the poem to 'the Envoy.' Such publicity could do Stepney nothing but good. His discontent with his employer seems to have become known, because Rycaut's chaplain in Hamburg wrote to him to suggest that he might leave Johnston and take service with Sir William Colt at Zell, whither the chaplain himself was to transfer. Nothing came of the suggestion, however, and by 7/17 March both Stepney and Johnston were preparing to leave the Hague for Utrecht, Bremen, Hamburg and Berlin. They were travelling in the opposite direction to the King, who went to Halle to join his army. He was not in time to prevent the French capturing the town of Mons on 8 April. This loss gave rise to rumours of the formation of a 'Third Party' – i.e. all states who were opposed to the war. Johnston reported as much from Hamburg. The fear was that the Third Party would include the House of Brunswick.[16]

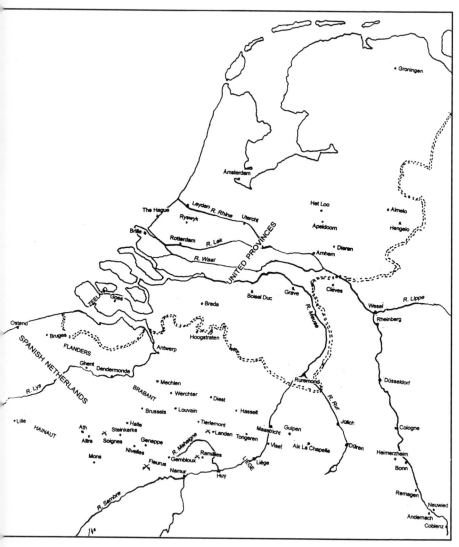

Map of the United Provinces and the Spanish Netherlands, 1690-1707.

Far away from the seat of war, James Johnston on arrival in Berlin lost no time in setting up for himself a visit to Carlsbad, in the seventeenth century as in the nineteenth a fashionable watering-place. Stepney went too. For him, this must have been a period of enforced idleness. Their stay at Carlsbad lasted six weeks. On return to Berlin Stepney was employed in sending news-letters, under his own signature, to Greg in Copenhagen and to Rycaut in Hamburg. During September he received a letter from Charles Montagu to tell him that the latter had left a 'Peruq' with Stepney's sisters, which he hoped would please the recipient; and hoping that Stepney would take part in Dryden's projected translation of Ovid's *Metamorphoses* – 'if you have time you will oblige the Town.'[17]

Of Stepney's private life in Berlin only little information has survived. He seems to have become involved socially with the community of Huguenot refugees who had settled in the city since the revocation of the Edict of Nantes by Louis XIV in 1685. At some time in 1690 one such refugee, Philip Plantamour, joined the English embassy, and became Stepney's secretary in 1692 – after Johnston had left – until 1699. One suspects that the excellent French in which many of Stepney's letters were written stemmed in the early days from Plantamour's pen. Both men were members of the Huguenot church in Berlin. Stepney later was in correspondence with the Pastor, Jacob l'Enfant (1661-1728), a distinguished theologian, whom Stepney invited to spend Christmas in Dresden, writing cheerfully:

> Soyez assure que si vous avez soin de nos ames nous n'en aurons pas moins de votre corps: Bon pain, bon vin, bonne viande, bon lict, et super omnia vultus.[18]

It is not, alas, recorded that the Pastor accepted the invitation.

Another divine of the Berlin church was a man named Polier. To him Stepney wrote, recalling their friendship and the fact that both were admirers of Sophie Charlotte (1668 -1705), Electress of Brandenburg and daughter of the Duchess Sophia of Hanover, '*cette adorable princesse*' as Stepney calls her. He wrote to Polier:

> J'avoue, Monsieur, que le Caractere d'un Amant et de Courtesan sont plus que sufficient pour excuser votre silence [these words scored through in the copy] – et sans parler des occupations d'un Courtesan le seul caractere d'un Amant suffit, pour vous justifier (quand vous scriviez que des billets doux) [bracketed words scored through] aupres d'un troc comme moy qui prefere toujours les amours aux amitiez, mais.

And Stepney continues with a comment on charges by the Catholic church relating to venal indiscretions on the part of Luther and

Calvin. He remarks:

> S'il [Calvin] avoit été d'un complexion aussi vigoreuse que l'autre,
> Pour ce qui est de vous et de moy nous n'en devons pas moins
> estimer ces grands hommes pour tout cela, puisque ce que leurs
> Ennemis traittent de foiblesse, peut bien passet pour une charité
> fort chrétienne.

And then he adds a P. S.

> Mr. Plantamour vous fait ses complimens et vous recommande
> Le Pain qui n'est pas sans Chair.[19]

This letter sheds a modicum of light on the way in which Stepney regarded the amours of himself and others: he was not unduly devout, and took a robust view of the sins of the flesh.

Of greater political use to Stepney was his acquaintance with yet another Huguenot, Mr. Couneau, who was private secretary to Eberhard Danckelmann (1643-1722) the then chief minister in Brandenburg, and with Peter de Falaiseau (1649-1726), a French refugee in the secret service of the Brandenburg government, who supplied Danckelmann with intelligence over a wide field.

As to living quarters, it is probable that Stepney lodged with a Mr. Vincent (who kept an inn) and whom Stepney later asked to forward not only letters, but also on occasion horses and equipage.

Although when he was transferred to Vienna Stepney used to express nostalgia for Berlin, at the end of 1691 he was by no means enamoured of the city. Johnston had taken to writing to Colt in his own hand: he was sick with a sore throat over Christmas, and had been at home for 15 days: he wanted Lady Colt to choose him table napkins. There is no word of how Stepney was employing his time. Nevertheless, with the New Year of 1692 came his release from his unloved chief: Johnston was recalled.[20]

V *Independence*
(Brandenburg 1692)

> the 30th of Jan 1691/2 Mr. Johnston took his leave of the Elector
> and at the same time presented me to his Highness under the name
> Sec^{re} du Roy, which is a title unusuall to us Englishmen, but
> nothing is more comon in the Northern and German Courts. This
> being done, Johnston decamped and left y^r Catt to shift for himself,
> without so much as leaving me one horse, servant or livery, nay
> without paying me the 82^{ll} [£82] which he owed me. But *Deus*
> *provedebit* was always my motto.[1]

It is clear that when George Stepney wrote to his friend Matt Prior
during the summer of 1694 he had a vivid recollection of the
circumstances under which he had been left alone to represent King
William at the court of the Elector of Brandenburg in Berlin.
Nevertheless, like the proverbial cat (his nickname), Stepney had
been confident of landing on his feet. But he was convinced that
Johnston, on reaching London, had never fairly represented his
services to the King or to Lord Portland, and he attributed this
omission to

> the true Genius of his Nation [i.e. the Scots], bashfull when he is
> to espouse an other mans interest, but egregiously impudent in
> pushing his own.[2]

In fact, Stepney was less than just to Johnston, who (according to
Richard Warre the Under-Secretary) had approached the King and
Lord Sidney on Stepney's behalf. But in the stress of arranging the
next summer's campaign King William had little time to consider
the difficulties of a young man left at a court which could be
presumed to continue loyal to the Protestant cause. Even Charles
Montagu thought that Johnston had stood up for his secretary in
Whitehall.

Interest was centred on the choice of an Envoy to succeed
Johnston. Two names were rumoured as possibilities: James Vernon
the elder (who had recommended Stepney to Johnston); and James
Cresset, (d. 1710), of age about equal to Stepney, but who was a
protegé of Daniel Finch, second Earl of Nottingham (1647-1730),
the Secretary of State, and also of Robert Sutton, second Lord

Lexington (1661-1723), an affable man, and rich, and a close friend of William III.

Stepney was in no doubt of his opinion in the matter, expressing himself to Montagu:

> If he [Vernon] be employ'd I shall think it my duty to give him the best light I am able into the affairs of these parts: but if his Majesty shall have chose the other I hope I may be allowed to know both him and myself better than to stay here 24 hours after his arrival.[3]

Where Stepney had first come across Cresset is not known: probably they coincided with each other in the Hague in the winter of 1691/2, when the Grand Alliance was being concluded. Stepney knew of Cresset's link with Lexington, and also that he had been refused a fellowship at Trinity College, Cambridge. Stepney described Cresset as 'a very pretty Gentleman, of good parts and behaviour . . .' but could not conceal his indignation that a man of his own age should be so soon favoured with the title and commission of Envoy.

And yet Stepney knew quite well, and admitted to his friends, that he himself was in no condition to support such a style. He was already in financial difficulty. Although Whitehall had agreed that a salary of £1 a day should be paid to him from the date of his introduction to the Elector of Brandenburg (30 January 1692), the order was not confirmed until 26 May, and for this he had to take out a Privy Seal (which of course had to be paid for) in order to convince the Treasury Clerks of his claim for reimbursement. He was therefore without apparent means of support during his first four months of independent life in Berlin. He managed by taking out loans, probably from his banker Francis Stratford, no doubt underwritten by Jane Stepney in London. During February 1692 George wrote without success to both Under-Secretaries (Richard Warre and John Pulteney) asking that his status should be clarified, and to be told what he might expect in the way of pay and allowances. He was comforted to learn that Charles Montagu was in touch with his family in Whitehall, and rejoiced at the news of his friend's appointment to the Treasury.[4]

It was of course Stepney's duty to report to the Secretary of State on the affairs of Germany, and indeed of the wider world, as soon as information reached him. At the turn of the year 1691-92 social and political life in Berlin was centred on the proposed marriage between the young Elector of Saxony, John George IV (1668-1694) and a cousin of the Elector of Brandenburg, the widowed Eleonore Erdmuth Louise, Marchioness of Ansbach. The

Matthew Prior,
ascribed to
Kneller.
Courtesy of the
Victoria and
Albert Museum,
London.

engagement was politically significant because John George had repudiated a marriage arranged for him with a princess of Denmark, which country was reputed to be a covert ally of France. Saxon ministers had been present in Berlin arranging the terms of the new alliance, and Johnston had lavishly entertained three of them the night before he left Berlin. The gaining of Saxony into the Grand Alliance was important because its Elector, in common with most of the princes of Germany, was only too ready to sell the lives of his male subjects, drafted into his army, to any state willing to pay for them in hard cash. The best paymasters were the Dutch Republic and the King of England. A more doubtful patron was the Holy Roman Emperor.

George Stepney began his official activity by writing to Pulteney on 1 March 1692, reporting the impending Saxon-Brandenburg marriage and providing lengthy detail of the state of Saxony according to the will of the late Elector (John George III) who had died the previous September. Stepney continued:

> I have a copy of the Demand which the Elector of Saxony has made to the States of Dresden tis 8 sheets in length but I shall have leisure to bring it to a few lines by next Post.[5]

Whether this promise was kept is not clear: but on 19 March the *Secrétaire du Roy* addressed to the Earl of Nottingham seven double-sided pages giving a full account of the Saxon repudiation of Denmark, and of the reported arrival in Dresden of two ministers from the Duke of Hanover, together with a French agent, in order to 'seduce the Elector of Saxony into the Caball of Peace Makers.' This scheme to lure Saxony into the ranks of the '*Tiers Parti*' [the Third Party in Europe which wished to bring about peace between France and the League of Augsburg] was anathema to William III, and to a lesser extent to the Elector of Brandenburg. The latter had been pressing the Dutch Envoy and Johnston to persuade King William to invest the new Elector of Saxony with the Order of the Garter, in the hope that this honour would divert him from a neutral stance. Stepney continued by describing the visit to Potsdam of John George IV:

> For 2 or 3 days the match seemed doubtful, the Marchioness having no person about her capable of managing an intrigue.

All however went well, and in Berlin eight days of feasting followed. Stepney added that the present Elector of Saxony (unlike his father) would not allow his troops to march without money.[6]

Stepney's sources for this first dispatch were, firstly, the secretary to the Marchioness, to whom he gave a *quid pro quo* in the form of permission to forward to London a box 'too big for the messenger to carry'; and secondly, those Saxon ministers who had been entertained by Johnston on the eve of his departure. Although George did not mention his own presence at the dinner, he was congratulated some days later on his capacity to survive drink. Sir William Colt's secretary wrote to him from Hanover:

> Surely you are a master in drinking, for that I can see not the least difference between your last of the 2d and your drunken letter (as you call it) especially in such a bout, wch I can easily imagine, wch I am sure would have laid me up for 3 or 4 days.[7]

This introduction to the Saxon way of life did Stepney no harm. He was later to complain of excessive drinking at many German courts, not from disapprobation so much as from a conviction that over-indulgence in alcohol was damaging to health.

The three Saxons whom Stepney encountered were all to figure in his future concerns. Hans-Adam von Schöning (1641-1696) was an able soldier who had transferred himself from Brandenburg to Saxon service, and who was reputed to be the *éminence grise* of the new Elector. He was also suspected of being in French pay. His name occurs regularly in Stepney's dispatches until his death in 1696. On the present occasion, in February 1692, he was in attendance on his young master during the state visit to Berlin, and was reported by Stepney to be keeping up a 'sullen humour' because he had not advocated the Elector's engagement to the Brandenburg princess. The other two ministers, Hans-Ernst Knoch and Ferdinand August Pflug, did not share Schöning's dominating personality. But they held senior positions at the Saxon court and Stepney was to have day-to-day contact with both men during his later appointment to Dresden.

Stepney had been enjoined by Lord Nottingham to make contact in writing with William Blathwayt (?1649-1717), Secretary-at-War to King William, who accompanied the latter during summer campaigns, which in 1692 began in March. Blathwayt had started his diplomatic career as secretary at the English Embassy at the Hague in 1668, and is said to have served later in Rome, Stockholm and Copenhagen. He was a good linguist. He had bought the Secretaryship-at-War in 1683, and at an opportune moment joined the cause of the Prince of Orange. Blathwayt has been described as a superhuman drudge. In fact he was more than this, for his was a position of power, since he could filter information (and introductions) to the King. To a certain degree, William trusted him. But it should not be forgotten that all the King's English ministers were in competition with the Dutch advisers to whom William confided the most delicate negotiations.

George Stepney had never met Blathwayt, and wrote diffidently:

> Not having the honour to be known to you, I shou'd [not] presume to trouble you with my Letters but by the orders I lately receiv'd from My Lord Nottingham

before repeating the account of the Brandenburg/Saxony affairs which he had already sent to Whitehall. Stepney then turned to his own problems, suggesting (with quotation of precedents) that he should receive an allowanced of 30s. or even 40s. *per diem*:

> besides extraordinaryes and something allowed . . . for equipage towards buying a Caleche and some Horses, wch I cannot do without, if I am to attend the Elr in his journeys to Saxony or to Cleves.

He begged for instructions whether or not he was to go to Torgau [north-east of Leipzig, in Saxony], to attend the state wedding; or to Cleves, where the Elector of Brandenburg was expected during the summer.[8] Blathwayt, at Het Loo, duly returned thanks to Stepney 'for the beginning of your Correspondency' and gave him permission to carry out both these journeys. But as to salary, Stepney was to receive 20s. a day from the date of Johnston's departure from the Brandenburg court; and nothing was said about equipage. A few days later Vernon, now also at Loo, wrote encouragingly to Stepney:

> I congratulate the care that I find has been taken of you and the

good dispositions I see in Mr. Blathwayt to doe you service, which you have much in your own power to improve; for as you have already recommended yourself to him by your Letters, so continuing to write frequently and with the same exactness, will encrease his good opinion of you.

This was true: Blathwayt told Charles Montagu that he found Stepney's letters ingenious, and that he was his friend: but he gave no hope of any allowance beyond the £1 a day, and discouraged any further approach being made to the King on Stepney's behalf.

Very soon after achieving independence from Johnston, Stepney wrote to William, Lord Paget (1637-1713), who since 1689 had been William III's Envoy to the Holy Roman Emperor in Vienna. Stepney introduced himself and reported, as was his duty, on the negotiations which were taking place in Berlin about the number of troops which the Emperor might expect from the Elector of Brandenburg for service in Hungary against the Turks. The result of this perhaps unusual flow of information from Berlin prompted Paget to offer George Stepney a post in Vienna as his own secretary, on the same terms as those which he had enjoyed under Johnston. Stepney however declined this suggestion with great politeness, confiding to Vernon:

The truth is, His Lop [Lordship] has the character of being difficult, and I shall be very careful how I engage a second time to such a man.

Moreover George was hopeful that after five years' experience as a secretary he might reasonably expect a settled post 'and not be a vagabond for the future.' Rather different was his comment to Matt Prior on a suggestion which Vernon had already made, that he might serve in Turkey, such a posting being (as Vernon put it) 'a ramble fitter for your years than mine.' Stepney's reaction was mixed: he wrote to his friend in the Hague:

I am not fond of such voyages, but had rather venture . . . than lye idle. The Salary (I think) is 40s. p.diem besides a Vest wch I shall gett at Audience, and the liberty of keeping as many wives as I can maintain. In your discourses with Mr. Vernon try to secure this employment either to me [or] yourself, which is all one for I wish you as well, If we come off with Life and Limb (as the seamen phrase it) we shall make a fortune for the rest of our days.[10]

The ramble to Turkey never materialised. But on 13 April 1692, Stepney set out from Berlin for Leipzig, writing cheerfully to Blathwayt that the Brandenburg Chief Minister, Eberhard von Danckelmann, had instructed the court *Fourrier* to provide him with quarters both in Leipzig and at Torgau, where the marriage of John George IV of Saxony was to take place. Stepney added that

Schloss Hartenfels, Torgau

Danckelmann's courtesy was to be regarded as a great honour, because such favours were not usually bestowed on secretaries. He had indeed come to Danckelmann's notice by a lucky accident: King William's Envoy in Stockholm, Charles Duncombe, had asked Stepney to find out who was Danckelmann's agent in the Swedish capital. Letters to Danckelmann which had been sent under cover to Duncombe had been opened, and he was worried. Stepney wrote to the Chief Minister immediately, in French, and took the opportunity to request quarters at the end of his journey, suggesting that he should give his name to the *Fourrier* as '*Secrétaire Résident pour S M B [Sa Majesté Britannique].*' This request was entirely successful.[11]

The wedding of the Elector of Saxony to the Marchioness of Ansbach was a glittering occasion. The bridegroom, at 24, was known to be devoted to his mistress, Magdalena Sibylla von Neidschütz, the daughter of a high-ranking Saxon officer and of a mother who delighted in intrigue. Sibylla at the time was 16. She was, Stepney reported, known as the 'young Electress' in comparison with the Marchioness who, at 31, had already been dubbed '*die Alte*' ['the Old One']. Stepney arrived on 20 April (n.s.) in Torgau where, at Schloss Hartenfels, the Electors of Saxony usually celebrated weddings or other state occasions. The same evening the Elector introduced his bride with an entry which was magnificent for the Saxon court. The following day a ball was held, and on the next a carousel, led by the Elector and his brother, both gorgeously attired in mediaeval costumes and plumes.

They completed exercises at menage [*sic*] with spear, javelin, pistol and sword. The Elector is very good at this, and so is his brother.

Castor & Pollux are nothing to these 2 Brothers.

The wedding was due to take place on 4 May (n.s.), but on 27 April the Elector sent for a minister and had the ceremony performed privately. Having bedded his wife, the Elector returned by 5.00 a.m. to his own apartments. Stepney noted that not only had the Elector seen his mistress the day the Marchioness arrived, but that Sibylla had been seated at the same table as the bridal couple at a banquet held at a 'Green House' which had been specially erected on the banks of the river Elbe, about half a mile below Torgau. This proximity of wife and mistress, Stepney remarked, 'confirmed the opinion that this match will not end well'. And he continued, with a measure of disgust, to describe the other celebration, which consisted, on 26 April, of:

> a Wolf, 2 Linces (or Wild Cats) 4 Bears and 19 Wild Boars [which] were brought in chests into the Court of the Castle and baited there . . . . Yesterday we had an Italian Opera, where Bella Margarita sung to Admiration. The night ended in Masquerade.
>
> This morning [29 April] the 2 Elrs are gone a hunting in a Wood hard by where 150 Staggs and some wild boars are Surrounded with Foils and are to be shot: this the Germans call a Royall hunt tho it be rather Butchery than Sport.[12]

Stepney was well aware that his master wanted more from him than social gossip, and he apologised for the lack of more important news from Torgau. Blathwayt had demanded of him

> as exact a Mapp as you can of the Court of Brandenburg – a List of all the Officers or of any other persons men or women that make any figure there, their age, quality and degree of favour, and more particularly for the Military part . . . a list of the Elector's Forces, Horse, foot & Drag[oon]s how commanded & disposed of at present & upon what terms & for what time, their Pay, method of subsistence, Arms & Clothing and of anything else relating to them which sort of acct would be no less welcome to me – of any other Court or Prince of Germany you can be acquainted with, but this is not a business of one day and therefore may be performed at Leisure. [13]

Stepney acted on these instructions throughout his career, and was meticulous in providing details of the society in which he lived. By 6 May (n.s.) 1692 he was again in Berlin and dealing with Danckelmann on what became known as 'the Golnau affair,' relating to territory which was the subject of dispute between Sweden and Brandenburg. He then settled to reporting on his experiences in Torgau in greater breadth for the benefit of both Lord Nottingham and Blathwayt. To Vernon he wrote more personally, again deploring the lack of any advance to cover his caleche and four horses, repeating with irony that he knew his case was 'particular.' He pointed out that Blathwayt 'has sett me a task which will make me very inquisitive', because Johnston had never left him with any precedent for reporting in detail on the court of Brandenburg. At Torgau, Danckelmann had asked him why he did not endeavour to become Envoy, adding compliments which made him (Stepney) blush.

> The truth is, when Mr. Johnston left me here, he promised to procure letters with some Character, tho I have profess'd both to him and Mr. Mountague that I desired no such thing, if I know my own mind, Ambition is not my vice, a quiet easy life is what I am fond of without want [and] with content, and such circumstances as may make those who are inclined to be my friends, not asham'd to own it. However this confession ought not to expose me to hard usage. . . .
>
> If I may speak my mind freely, his Majesty's interest and the credit of his Alliance with the Elector require an Individual of Fortune and Quality who may doe honour to the Character [i.e. of Envoy], for without these two Qualifications no Individual will be much regarded here.
>
> Mr. Rebenac (the last French Envoy at this Court) left behind him such a reputation of Generosity, that any Englishman who will not be undervalued, must have both Soule and Purse; and I heartily wish for the publick good, his Maty may make choice of such a person.[14]

This letter sets out with clarity one of the chief difficulties which beset Stepney throughout his career. He was not a rich man, but he was more ambitious than he admitted. The question of his 'character' – that is, the style (Envoy, Agent, Commissary) under which he presented his credentials to a foreign ruler – was of the utmost importance. An Envoy was expected to entertain lavishly and produce presents or bribes as appropriate. Such a life-style was impossible for Stepney, as well he knew. But he found himself repeatedly torn between his very natural desire to live up to the level of the court to which he was accredited, and the fear of plunging so deeply into debt that he might negate his career completely. For the time being, his credit was sufficient to cover the expenses of caleche and horses. The bill came to £96, plus £21 for liveries for the grooms.[15]

Brandenburg was not the centre of events in 1692, and on 21 May Stepney was writing to Blathwayt:

> You must expect little news from hence, all our hopes and fears are at sea and in Flanders, as if we were in suspense wayting for the great event which we think must soon decide the fate of Europe

... [The 'we' above, refers to the Elector of Brandenburg.]
    I put the best face I can on our affairs to balance against the
apprehensions of the Court.[16]

Thus George describes a state of mind so common to all diplomats:
the need to appear in public calm and serene, however much private
knowledge might justify nervousness. The cause of the anxiety at
the Brandenburg court was the successful French attack against
Namur. As Stepney wrote to Johnston:

You wou'd have laugh'd to have seen the posture of People at
Berlin upon the news of Namur. . . . I mean to have seen their
Figures, the Elector immediately call'd for his Armour, as if he
had been to engage within an hour: We had nothing to be seen but
black Cravats, Buff Waistcoats & Perriwigs in Baggs.[17]

The Elector left immediately for Cleves [close to the Dutch border],
and Stepney, following in his own caleche, was among the first to
arrive, on 13 June. He immediately wrote to Blathwayt to warn the
latter that one of Eberhard Danckelmann's six brothers (the
Commissary General of Brandenburg), with the Elector's Adjutant
General, were about to arrive in King William's camp to give notice
of the Elector's arrival and seek an audience. Stepney provided a
character-sketch of each emissary, and suggested that the King
should send someone to compliment the Elector, as was the custom.
No doubt George hoped that this pleasant and lucrative duty might
be allotted to himself. But King William was always reluctant to
waste time and money on a ceremony which he considered
superfluous. He did however notify the Elector, formally in Latin,
of the recent allied victory at sea [the battle of La Hogue]. The
Elector replied in kind. But this exchange was not carried out
through the *Secrétaire du Roy*, but through the Commissary General
of Brandenburg.

    Once settled in Cleves, Stepney found himself involved in two
unrelated matters which took up his time and his pen. The first was
consequent on the fact that at Minden, on his way to Cleves, he had
come across Joseph Augustus du Cros (d. 1728), and later shared
lodgings with him at Cleves. Du Cros was a roving diplomat of
uncertain background and loyalty. In 1692 he had seen and taken
great umbrage at an unflattering description of himself which had
appeared in Sir William Temple's memoirs. Stepney, apologising
to Sir William for writing to him without any prior introduction,
forwarded Du Cros' objections and mentioned that he had tried to
pacify him. Stepney also reported the matter to Blathwayt and to
Vernon, and did his best to extricate himself from an unproductive
correspondence.

The second episode which engaged Stepney's attention turned out to be detrimental to himself. On 10/20 June he wrote to Blathwayt:

> I ought not to conceal from you that Mr. Dankelman told me this day with great satisfaction how Mr. Duncombe had orders to continue in Sweden, and at the same time complained that Mr. Molesworth ruined by his briskness & Indiscretion what the other Gentleman built by his Prudence & Moderation. He had not time to instance what part of Mr. Molesworth's deportment gave occasion for this reflexion, but discovered [i.e. revealed] no great opinion of his Ministry.[18]

Robert Molesworth (1656-1725) was one of William III's supporters who had been rewarded with a diplomatic post, being sent in 1689 as Envoy Extraordinary to Denmark. His task was to counter French influence in Copenhagen, and to recruit Danish troops for the armies of the Grand Alliance. To be subjected to criticism from Eberhard Danckelmann was a serious matter which could, and did, cost Molesworth his job.

In mid-July Sir William Colt at Zell informed Stepney that Molesworth was just leaving him to go to Flanders to report to the King, and that he was very worried at the bad opinion which the Brandenburg court had of him. How this information first reached Molesworth is not known, but he found confirmation in Sir William Colt's study. Colt was reading a letter from Stepney which repeated the paragraph quoted above. Molesworth, standing behind Sir William's chair, also read the message, although at the time Colt did not realise this fact. Molesworth suspected that Stepney had fabricated the story, and this suspicion seemed confirmed when at Osnabrück he met a kinsman of Eberhard Danckelmann, who denied that the latter had ever denigrated him. Moreover, Molesworth was most upset that Stepney had never informed him of the adverse criticism, but had spread the rumour nevertheless. Sir William Colt was aghast that the Envoy to Denmark had read Stepney's letter in his (Sir William's) house, and wrote to Molesworth vigorously defending Stepney. Both Vernon and Blathwayt became involved. Eberhard Danckelmann (with some tact) refused to confirm his adverse opinion of Molesworth. Vernon advised Stepney to keep in with Danckelmann, rather than with Molesworth, who by August 1692 had been given his *congé*.[19]

Although this incident does not reflect well on George Stepney – he had, after all, circulated disparaging remarks about a colleague – a letter which he wrote from Dresden to his banker, Francis Stratford, some 18 months later, throws more light on the affair.

According to Stepney, Molesworth and his secretary, Hugh Greg, had written to Johnston warning the latter against Stepney, charging him with being an 'arrant Jacobite.' Stepney, furious, had written to Greg for an explanation, which had never been forthcoming.

> He [Greg] has several times promised me an answer, but has never kept his word; for in truth wt Recantation can be sufficient after such injuries? and to shew him thus evidently that his folly and malice are detected, 'tis satisfaction enough to me and mortification to him. So much for old Storyes.[20]

Throughout his career Stepney had a long memory for suspected slights against himself. At the outset of his service with Johnston any allegation of Jacobitism would have been highly dangerous. Johnston does not seem to have taken the charge seriously. But Stepney did not hesitate to revenge himself upon Molesworth as soon as opportunity offered.

Meanwhile in Cleves Stepney was preparing for a projected meeting between the King of England and the Elector of Brandenburg. The occasion was of particular importance to the *Secrétaire du Roy* because he had not yet been presented to his own sovereign. He wrote to Charles Montagu, asking the latter to communicate urgently with Blathwayt

> or any other of your friends about the King in fflanders, that they may present me after a handsome manner when I gett thither; wch may be a means of making me better known to his Maty. If I am to continue at the Court where I now am, you may easily imagine my Countenance [i.e. reception] that I receive at our own Court, will make good impressions here.

Whether Montagu exerted himself on his friend's behalf is not known. But Stepney travelled according to the timetable which he carefully copied into his letter-book:

> My Journey from Cleves to the Army at Genap and from thence to the interview at Wechtern

		hours
July 4	I set out from Cleves in Company of Mr.du Rosey The Elr Adjutant Genll at 8 in the Evening & came to Grave	6
5	To Boitleduc	6
6	To Hoogstraten	12
	To Antwerp	6
	To Brussells	8
7	To ye Camp at Genap	5
	Where I kiss'd the King's hand In all after dinner	43
8th	At 3 afternoon I left the Camp & removed to Brussells	5

9	to Wechtern	6

Where the King had an Interview with
the Elr of Brandenburgh on the 10th

The Elr went to Diest on the 11th, to Hassfelt [Hasselt] on the 12th and arrived at Liege the 13th.

Stepney wrote his thanks both to Blathwayt and to Montagu, confiding to the latter:

> Since I had the honour to write to you last, I have been at the King's Camp, where Mr. Blathwayt received me very favourably, and presented me to his Maty, who was pleas'd to ask me some questions, and heard me graciously, which has given me Life & Courage at this Court.[21]

During his visit to Genappe it was proposed to Stepney, and he accepted, that he should replace Hugo Hughes as English Secretary at the Imperial Diet which was held at Ratisbon [Regensburg] at regular intervals. Hughes was the brother-in-law of Dr Owen Wynne [Under-Secretary of State under James II] and, as already noted in Chapter III, had supplanted Stepney in 1685 as secretary to the then Envoy, Sir George Etherege. At the Glorious Revolution, Etherege had been displaced, and Hughes stayed on to represent the new regime. Now, he had misbehaved himself and on 18/28 July 1692 Blathwayt informed the Earl of Nottingham in London that the King wished Hughes recalled and Stepney appointed in his place. Vernon wrote to George that this was good news, 'since it was done without your sollicitation.' The kindly man also sent on to George the latter's precious seal which he had left behind him at the camp. Stepney was at pains to write to Wynne, saying that his sister had told him how Wynne had appealed to her regarding Hughes' circumstances, 'and what he will Suffer upon his Revocation,' and he continued at length to assure Wynne that Hughes' recall had had nothing to do with him.

> You will . . . give me leave to assure you I am not so greedy of Employment as to forget the Obligations and friendship I am under to you: and would rather choose to lye fallow the rest of my life than gain preferment by so dishonourable an Action as that of undermining another man; or so much as wishing his fall, tho it should prove a fountain to my good ffortune.

And George added that no date had been set for his appointment to Ratisbon, because he was still under orders to attend the Elector of Brandenburg until such time as an Envoy should be appointed to Berlin.

In fact, Stepney was always in two minds about the Ratisbon appointment. On the one hand it would have given him the stability he craved, time to write his poetry, and a tolerable allowance. On the other, it was the dullest of all possible appointments in Europe. The King of England had no voice in the Imperial Diet: his representative was there to listen and report only: he could have no influence upon events. In fact, Hughes stayed at the post at least until 1694, after which he led a precarious existence as a small-time trader. Stepney himself never did take up the Ratisbon appointment.[22]

On 15/25 July Stepney was at Mechlen, writing to Blathwayt

I have been unlucky ever since I left you. The Labourer at Antwerp whom I desired to send my Servants to Wechtern [Werchter] mistook the name of the place and sent em to Weert, a small village half a league from this place, so that ever since Monday Wee have plaid at hide & seek & hunted one another backwards & forwards betwixt Antwerp and Brussells, which has put me to great trouble & expence. But last night I found Em in this place and shall immediately set forward towards Maastricht and Liege.

Two weeks later, from Cleves, Stepney continued:

At Mastricht I found the letters of the 4th [August – n.s.] from the Camp which brought me the ill news of the death of many of our Brave Countrymen. His Highness [the Elector of Brandenburg] overtook me as wee were upon the march, and very passionately regretted this unfortunate attack: he told me he was certain the King would not have engaged with such disadvantage, but at the evident perswasions of the Elr of Bavaria & the Duke of Wirtemberg [Württemberg] to whose Councills wee impute this hazardous attempt.

The two men were discussing the bloodstained Battle of Steenkerke, which had taken place on 3 August (n.s.). Since the Brandenburg troops had not been engaged (although they were not far from the scene of the action) Stepney found the courage to comment to the Elector that

The Enterprise had been glorious if our men had been Seconded with vigour.

Blathwayt later commended Stepney's answer to the Elector. He also complained that George had not reported on a letter from the Elector to the King about reports that the Brandenburg generals had been backward in taking action on the Meheigne river. Blathwayt enclosed a copy of King William's answer, denying such reports. This prompted Stepney to point out that although he had known of the Elector's letter, he was not privy to it; and he could not complain of such 'usage' as he had no credentials at the Brandenburg court. Mr. Johnston, he added, had very seldom conveyed such letters. Danckelmann had used his brother as the channel for similar messages, or Dr. Ham [the Dutch envoy].[23]

Two weeks previously Stepney had written to Blathwayt of a matter which had come to his ears at Cleves: Blathwayt was reported to have used high words to the Danish Envoy to King William regarding the apparent reluctance of the Danish navy to clear the Baltic sea of French 'capers' [pirate ships] which were harrying English shipping. The Danish court had taken umbrage, and the incident had been reported at Cleves with the proviso that the Danish reaction should be played down if the Brandenburg court seemed alarmed. Stepney's source for the information was the local Danish secretary, 'my friend, whom I should be sorry to engage.' Blathwayt replied in due course: the expressions used had referred only to the possible provision by the King of convoys for English ships; no offence had been taken at the time. He promised that Stepney's message would go no further.[24]

Blathwayt also came up with a minor and tedious job for George: the errant Mr Hughes had written about a contact, a certain Madame d'Alencon, who insisted that she had information to sell concerning a projected attack on the King's person. The plot had been concocted in Paris, and a Jesuit was to be sent '*vers la Reine d'Angleterre.*' George was instructed to enquire carefully into the matter, which he did, over a period of weeks, before concluding that the whole affair was merely a ploy to gain money.[25]

Of greater importance to Stepney's career was the affair of Field Marshal von Schöning. Stepney had already met him briefly in Berlin. Now he was able to report the surprising fact that Schöning had been arrested by imperial troops at Teplitz in Bohemia on 13/23 June. The charge was treason, and the surprise was caused by the fact that the Emperor was not usually given to such decisive action. Schöning was suspected of treachery towards the Elector of Brandenburg during the siege of Bonn in 1689: of doing nothing to prevent French plundering raids into the Empire; and of corresponding with the enemy in the shape of Baron 'Hasfeld' [d'Asfeld] – a roving French ambassador who had been actively engaged in promoting the *Tiers Parti* among German princes. Also under arrest were two of Schöning's 'creatures' – Baron Löbel, his *aide-de-camp*, and Count Monceau, a French refugee of very doubtful loyalty. Both names recur in Stepney's correspondence.

The Brandenburg court was naturally delighted at Schöning's arrest, but Stepney correctly forecast that the Elector of Saxony (to whose service Schöning had transferred himself), would take a very different view and would support his general. Schöning himself by no means accepted his arrest humbly. In September Stepney reported that the general had tried to escape from his prison, but had got stuck in a window ('his great belly') and had been pulled back by the gaolers.[26]

In mid-September 1692 Sir William Colt was busy preparing a journey into Saxony in order to present the Order of the Garter to the Elector. The honour was designed (by King William) to ensure the Elector's adherence to the Protestant cause. Stepney wrote to Colt from Cleves suggesting that he too might join the party, frankly confessing that he 'would gladly come in for a Ring or Meddall,' but that he would forego these prizes if his presence would in any way embarrass Sir William. Stepney pointed out that he had had some share in a similar ceremony in Berlin, and therefore his presence might be useful; also that he already had some acquaintance with the Saxon court. Sir William might like to drop a line to Blathwayt for the necessary permission. But sadly for George, neither Sir William nor his secretary Schweinfurt was at all enthusiastic about accepting the proposal, and the matter was dropped.[27]

Stepney had heard of a possible further meeting between King William and the Elector of Brandenburg while the King was in residence at his palace of Het Loo in Holland. Although no meeting between the rulers took place, Stepney set off for Loo and had a meeting with Blathwayt during the early days of October. No direct account of this event survives, but subsequently Stepney was rebuked by 'Father' Vernon, who wrote to him from the Hague:

> I am sorry to find you surprised & uneasy that yo[r] privy seale for Ratisbonne is passing with an allowance of only 20s. per diem. I shall commend yo[r] endeavours to get it doubled, if you can prevayle. But I heard Mr. Blathwayt say before I came from the Camp that you mistook one another very egregeously, if you did not seem satisfyed at Turnhout to go to Ratisbonne with your present allowance for hee is positive hee never heard you mention any further summe. I must confess I don't remember any discourse wee had at Genap about 40[s] per diem but if this were from private chatt one can draw no consequence, upon the whole, as you have begun, I dont see but you may modestly press for an Augmentation, but you must give me leave to blame you if you do it with a design to resent a refusall for in the first place nothing will bee more apt to draw it upon you If that should be your humour. I am afraid you and I are too little to think of prescribing.

And Vernon continued with the advice that Edmund Poley (previously *en poste* at Ratisbon) had begun with 20s. a day and had later had it augmented. Anyway, Ratisbon was a cheap place to live.[28]

Whatever Stepney's feelings, he wrote formally to Blathwayt from Zell on 14 October, thanking for the favour shewn to him during his stay at Loo. He reported that he had arrived at Hanover on 10 October (n.s.), in pursuit of the Elector of Brandenburg, who had already left the Duchy for Berlin. But the Duchess of Hanover [Sophia] received George with great favour, and told him about the future meetings planned between the Welfs of Hanover and the Hohenzollerns of Brandenburg. And during this October visit to Hanover Stepney met, and was befriended by Gottfried Wilhelm Leibniz, with whom he corresponded for many years.

By 18 October Stepney was back in Berlin, only to leave the city a week later for Magdeburg, where the Elector was receiving the homage of his subjects. Perhaps the recollection of this episode was useful to Stepney when, 13 years on, he would formally receive the Principality of Mindelheim on behalf of the Duke of Marlborough. The visit to Magdeburg lasted only a few days, and then, the Elector complaining of toothache, the court returned to Berlin. Stepney could not resist recounting one incident to Blathwayt:

> I found Mr. Ham (the Dutch Resident) told Mr. Dankelman as he was at table with the Elr at Griningen (not far from Halberstadt) that his Maty was pleas'd to name me for Ratisbonne which gave occasion to Mr. Dankelman to ask what disgust I have received at this Court, that I should desire to leave it? and that I am mistaken if I think to leave it so soon, which I look upon as Caresses out of Season, and think myself but a Sojourner till I receive my Orders to remove to Ratisbonne. I cannot tell but he (Dankelman) may have writ to his Brother in England upon this occasion.[29]

At the beginning of December social life in Berlin flourished. The Duke and Duchess of Hanover were visiting their daughter, the Electress Sophie-Charlotte of Brandenburg. The formal entry of the visiting dignitaries to Berlin took place on 5 December, 'of which the details are too tedious to be repeated', reported Stepney. But he continued:

> I intended to pay my duty to the Dutchess in her apartments, but she perceived me in a Corner, and came directly up to me in the Elector's presence and offred me her hand, which threw me upon my knee before the Whole Court, a Compliment She affects as Princess of our Royall Family maintaining thereby her Title to ye Succession. . . . She was pleas'd to discourse with me in English very freely.[30]

The day following this incident Stepney wrote to Leibniz. He had already sent to the Duchess of Hanover, through her librarian, eulogistic verses in English and French, which fact may account for the favour shewn by the Duchess to this English secretary.

Leibniz had asked for Stepney's comments on a book recently received in Hanover, *The History of the Desertion*, by a Person of Quality, (published in 1689). In reply, George was at his most discreet. The matter was so delicate and secret, he wrote, that the only people capable of treating it properly were Lord Portland and Dr Burnet for foreign affairs, and Lord Sidney and Mr. Johnston 'for what concerns England.' The inclusion of Johnston's name in this context is surprising: but it indicates that Stepney was aware of the Scotsman's good standing with William III.[31]

Also on 6 December Stepney told Leibniz that he had just heard of his forthcoming posting to Vienna 'until Mr. Heemskirke returns from Turkey.' The posting came about because Lord Paget had been recalled from the imperial court: he was later to take up the important appointment of Ambassador to the Porte.

The news (from Blathwayt) seems to have reached Stepney too late for him to reply immediately, for he did not acknowledge the instruction either to Blathwayt or to Lord Nottingham until a week later. He also expressed himself rather more fully to Matt Prior in the Hague:

Sir,   Berlin, 11/21 December 1692
I received last night my Orders (that is, a very good passport) but for Credentialls, Instructions, and all other papers of that nature my Lord Nottingham has been pleas'd to put me of[f] with 3 lines, which I send you for the rarity of the thing. Was ever a ffellow sent to a strange Court without recommendations, or anything like it? You remember Moses his Question What shall I say to Pharao' when he will enquire who sent me? But I must take my ffortune and be contented till my Lord Nottingham is disgrac'd, and wee get a Secretary who understands fforain Business and has Bowells for those who drudge in em.
I am,[32]

And so, Christmas notwithstanding, George Stepney set out, in obedience to his sovereign's commands, on the first of the many journeys carried out during the cruel winter months, which eventually contributed to the decline in his health that became apparent after the turn of the century. But on this occasion he was to greet the New Year in Vienna with courage and hope.

VI *The Imperial Court*
(Vienna, January-October 1693)

Vienna <u>7 Janu</u> 1693
28 Dec

To the Earl of Nottingham

My Lord,

In obedience to his Ma^tics commands I have made wt diligence I
could by running Post day & night thro Silesia and Moravia, till I
got to Vienna the first day of the new year, NS, wch gives me a
naturall occasion of wishing yor Lp most heartily many happy
ones.

George Stepney's first dispatch to Lord Nottingham, quoted above,
does not reveal the date of his departure from Berlin. Before setting
off he had been at pains to provide himself with introductions to
prominent members of the imperial court, and the fact that he was
able to do this gives an indication of his good standing in Berlin:
he was, after all, only known in Brandenburg as the *Secrétaire du
Roy.*

His first letter of introduction was provided by Franz Heinrich,
Baron Fridagh zu Gödens, the Emperor's minister at Berlin, whom
Stepney had encountered while he was still secretary to Sir Peter
Wyche in Hamburg. The imperial posts passed through the city of
Breslau; Fridagh was acquainted with the Chief Minister of the
Duchy of Silesia, who entertained George, and advised him to seek
an audience of the Bishop of Breslau, who was a brother of the
Empress. George made a point of paying his respects.

One of Eberhard Danckelmann's many brothers was the
Brandenburg Envoy to the court of Vienna. The Chief Minister
gladly wrote an introduction. To Leibniz George owed his long-
lasting friendship with the imperial state-secretary, Caspar Florentin
von Consbruck, who was to become, both wittingly and unwittingly,
a source for Stepney's frequent accounts of the intrigues of the
imperial court.

Baron Fridagh gave two more letters to Stepney: these were to

Count Theodor Athlet von Stratmann (1636-1693), the Court Chancellor [*Hofkanzler*], and to Count Leopold Wilhelm von Königsegg (d. 1694) the Vice-Chancellor of the Empire. Both these men were trusted advisers of the Emperor Leopold I (1640-1705), and Stepney wasted no time before he presented himself. On 2 January, the day after he reached Vienna, Stepney requested an interview with both statesmen. Stratmann asked him to dinner on 3 January, which he promptly accepted, despite its being post-day.

> When wee rose from Table (ye Criticall minute when people, who have to do with him, are allowed to speak of Business), he drew me aside and told me he was very glad I was arrived, since it was absolutely necessary that some person should be here for his Maties affairs.

Stratmann then asked Stepney for his credentials, and George produced his passport, which Stratmann accepted. The following day Stepney saw Königsegg (who was laid up with gout) for two hours. This minister also asked for credentials, but conceded that, even without them, Stepney could attend a forthcoming conference to be held between the imperial privy counsellors, the Envoys of Spain and Savoy, and the other ministers of the Allies. The Vice-Chancellor then reviewed the state of Germany, and the war. He was doleful about the extravagance of the princes and their reliance on subsidies; about the lack of money in the Empire; and the alliance between France and the Turks. He was making a veiled demand for money from England and Holland.

> They are apt to conclude here, there is no end to our riches

warned Stepney, who ended his report to Lord Nottingham by quoting Königsegg's remark that the Emperor's grant of the Ninth Electorate to Hanover [intended to wean that state from the *Tiers Parti*] would create as many problems as it solved.[1]

Stepney continued at speed his round of official visits. By 9 January, he had seen both the Spanish and the Savoyard Ambassadors, and had had his first meeting with 'Prince Lewis de Baden', that is, '*Turkenlouis*' or the Margrave of Baden (1655-1707), at the time the best if not the only imperial commander of troops. Prince Louis in August 1691 had gained a great victory (Salenkemen) over the Turks in Hungary. Now, at the start of 1693 the threat to the Empire from France on the Rhine was deemed to be greater than that of the Turks in the East, and the Allies, prompted by King William, were pressing for the Margrave to be appointed to command on the Upper Rhine. Prince Louis desired troops, 40,000 or 45,000 men; but Saxon help, which was available, was

inimical to the southern German Circles of Franconia and Suabia;
and 6,000 men who were to have been provided by the Bishop of
Münster and by the King of Denmark had been withdrawn, owing
to the objections of those rulers to the grant of the Ninth Electorate
to the Duke of Hanover. Prince Louis' urgent desire was to visit
England or Holland early in the year to discuss his plans, without
loss of time, with the King of England.[2]

Meanwhile another influential friend of King William's had
made the acquaintance of George Stepney. This was Julius Heinrich,
Count Friesen (1650-1706), usually known by the French version
of his name, the Comte de Frise. Julius, whose family had long
been in the service of the Wettins [rulers of Saxony], had studied
law at the university of Utrecht, where he had become a favoured
companion of the Prince of Orange, whose exact contemporary he
was. He had accompanied William on campaign as early as 1672,
and from that time often preferred to be employed by the Prince of
Orange rather than by his liege lord, the Elector of Saxony. At the
end of 1692, however, Frise had come to Vienna on behalf of John
George IV of Saxony, to try to achieve a rapprochement between
the Elector and the imperial court. John George had been highly
incensed at the arrest of his general, Schöning; and he also wished
subsidies to be paid to him in return for Saxon troops. While these
negotiations were proceeding, Frise decided to keep the Earl of
Portland informed, and thus gave George Stepney his first good
reason for writing himself to Hans-Willem Bentinck:

> My Lord,
> I have long waited for a favourable opportunity of presenting my
> duty to yo' Lp and am at last obliged to the Baron de Frise for the
> occasion he has now furnish'd me by forwarding the inclos'd.

Stepney sent on not only Frise's letter but his own account of his
interview with Prince Louis, asking to know whether the King
wished the Margrave to command on the Upper Rhine (and if so,
whether arms and men could be provided), and whether the
Margrave's proposed visit to his allies would be welcome. Portland
(writing in French) replied affirmatively to the first and third of
these queries, but pointedly omitted mention of any addition to the
Margrave's forces.[3]

Blathwayt, from Whitehall, also wrote to Stepney, telling him:

> not to stick there [i.e. Vienna] so as to be useless to his Maty who
> is therefore pleased to give you a Title & Credentialls in the quality
> of his Agent or Commissary . . . Nor are you, I hope, to live by
> this air of dignity, but I will immediately proceed to gett your

allowance incrased [*sic*] or doubled that you may appear to act in
a style answerable to your Station.

This was something of a *volte-face* on Blathwayt's part. But the
news was no doubt very acceptable to Stepney, as was the King's
approbation of his dispatches written since his arrival in Vienna.
His new Agent's allowance of £3 a day was later confirmed, to
take effect from 11/21 December 1692.[4]

Before he had received this encouragement Stepney had sent
Lord Nottingham a lengthy account of the imperial conference to
which he had been invited by Count Königsegg. Besides the Vice-
Chancellor, the others present were the imperial privy-counsellors
Count [Ferdinand Bonaventura] Harrach and Count [Ernst Rüdiger]
Starhemberg, the Ambassadors of Spain and Savoy, the Envoys of
Brandenburg and Hanover, two secretaries of the court 'who took
the minutes or Protocoll' and finally G. Stepney and [Jacob Jan
Hamel] Bruynincx [d. 1738] who were described as 'Secretaries to
his Maty and the States General.'

Everyone spoke in turn, including Stepney, who was careful
not to commit William III to any expenditure. George pointed out
that the English treasury was not inexhaustible and that his country
was already supporting the common effort against France with
33,000 seamen and 52,000 land forces. Having recounted to Lord
Nottingham all the detail, Stepney ended his dispatch by remarking,

> The whole may be reduced to 3 points, a Million of Crowns which
> are wanting in Germany, half a Million in Pie[d]mont, and some
> Troops who may attempt a descent towards Provence.[5]

This conference, the first of many which Stepney was to attend
during the course of his career, established his position as King
William's representative, and his careful reporting strengthened his
reputation in Whitehall. Privately, he was now co-operating with
the Dutch representative, Bruynincx. This man was the son of a
more famous father, who had also served as Resident in Vienna.
Jacob Jan had arrived in Vienna only six weeks before Stepney.
The two became close friends, and drew around them other young
diplomats, including Florentin Consbruck, the imperial State-
Secretary, Ehrenburg the Swedish Resident, Baron Guillaume de
Nesselrode from the Bishopric of Liège, Baron Blumenthal of
Brandenburg, Hans Caspar von Bothmar from Lüneburg and
Christoph Dietrich von Bosen ('young Bose') from Saxony, with
whom Stepney wrote that he 'lived together in great friendship &
familiarity.' Under the guidance of Ehrenburg these men formed a
société des fumeurs for recreation and conversation. Stepney later

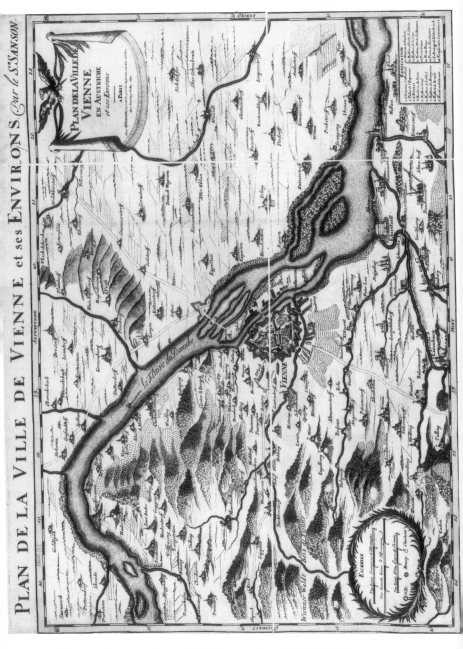

Vienna and its surroundings (1692). By permission of The British Library.
*28405 (9)

announced his intention of forming a similar group in Dresden, though there is no evidence that he carried out this plan.[6]

But the social life in Vienna was subdued. The court was in mourning for the death of the Electress of Bavaria [elder daughter of the Emperor]. There was no carnival, and it was already Ash Wednesday. George Stepney lamented:

> On a chatie une bande de Musiciens pour avoir joué hors de l'Eglise qui est le seul endroit ou l'on va pour se divertir. Ce que me rend plus Chretien qu'a mon ordinaire. Un jour à Berlin vaut mieux qu'un mois icy.[7]

War preparations continued, lethargically, in Vienna. Prince Louis had not been invited to participate in the imperial conference of 8/ 18 January (where Stepney made his *debut*). Now, Stepney had to inform him that the King, though passionately desiring that the Margrave should command on the Rhine, was unable to provide any troops. Stepney knew very well that under no circumstances must he commit his master to any expenditure of money, men or armaments without the most explicit instructions.

Regarding a subsidy for a campaign in Italy, Stepney had received only the vaguest orders, and he denied to Stratmann, Königsegg and to the Spanish Ambassador that he had received any positive commands from the King. He reported to London the general disappointment, as well as reports that the French were bribing the Savoyards to the tune of 150,000 Crowns, and that because the representative of the Bishop of Liège had been denied money by the imperial court, that prelate's troops might well defect to the French.[8]

News from Saxony was more encouraging. A treaty had been prepared by Sir William Colt with the Elector, who agreed to provide 12,000 men for the Allied cause against the payment of 400,000 Reichsthaler (or Dollars). This sum was to be provided by the Emperor, some of the German princes, the King of England and the Dutch Republic. The Elector of Saxony had so far failed to obtain the release from arrest of his general, Field Marshal Schöning, but had meanwhile 'borrowed' General Jeremiah von Chauvet from the Duke of Zell to command the summer's campaign. The Elector had also exacted from the Emperor a patent of nobility for his mistress, Magdalena Sibylla von Neidschütz, who was carrying his child. Stepney reported not only that Baron Frise was returning to Dresden on 12 March 1693 with the patent, but that Counts Stratmann and Königsegg had each received 4,000 Crowns for dispatching the business, which created Sibylla Countess

Rocklitz. Stepney was warned by Blathwayt in April 1693 that the King did not wish the Saxon subsidy to exceed 400,000 Dollars, of which England and the States General would contribute 150,000. George was also reminded that the success of this negotiation 'so farr as the scene of it may be laid at Vienna,' would depend on his own conduct and skilful management.[9]

At the end of March Stepney could send home but little news:

Wee are in the Holy Week which is so entirely taken up in holy Pageantry & devotions that I am not allowed to ask any of the Emp^{rs} Privy Councill what credit I ought to give to the report of Prince Lewis's being recalled to Hungary.

This rumour had arisen because Stepney's Dutch colleague Bruynincx had emphasised to the Emperor, at a private audience, news which he had received from the Dutch Envoy at the Porte, that the Turks were arming vigorously. Stepney thought that the report should have been played down, and told Bruynincx so. Writing to Blathwayt, Stepney added a paragraph dear to his own heart:

What Mr. Dankelman at Berlin ordered his Brother in England to move my Lord Portland to do in my behalf, is that his Maty wou'd give me the Title of Resident here: which is a shadow I am not fond of, being only desirous of a larger allowance; which is the good essential part; for which I am wholly oblig'd to your generous intercession and therefore as I am a thing of yr own making, it is but just that I shou'd be with all imaginable duty and respect. [End of letter.][10]

But Stepney never was appointed Resident, in Vienna or elsewhere.

By mid-April the King had arrived in the Hague for the summer campaign. Prince Louis had been too busy with his own preparations to have been able to make his proposed visit to Holland, but Count Frise [Julius] went to Het Loo to settle the operations of the Saxon troops. The King sent a formal letter to the Emperor, in Latin, announcing his arrival in Holland. This was delivered by Stepney personally at an audience on 19/29 April 1693. Stepney reported to Blathwayt:

I spoke in Latin slowly, & with as much of a Dutch [i.e. German] accent as I cou'd, to be the more intelligible: His Imp^{ll} Maty answered me likewise in Latin, & commanded me to assure his Maty of his brotherly affection, & to thank his Maty for the Notification of his arrivall. He promised Prince Lewis shou'd continue on the Rhine *secundem omnem possibilitatem:* I give you his own words, tho I am neither satisfied with the Latin nor the sense, since this *possibilitatem* includes some uncertainty;

> However I am fully perswaded Prince Lewis will not be recall'd
> but upon an Emergent necessity which (wee may normally
> imagine) will not happen.

And Stepney enclosed a copy of the '*harangue*' which he had composed himself and made to the Emperor, and which began: '*Invictissime Caesar, Imperator Semper Auguste*'.[11]

As soon as Blathwayt had taken up his duties once again as Secretary-at-War to the King, he invited Stepney to correspond with Lord Paget, the English Ambassador to the Turks, and with Coenrad van Heemskeerke, the Dutch envoy. Blathwayt wished to relieve himself of that duty. Stepney, soon after his arrival in Vienna, had written to Paget; and he had already transmitted to Lord Nottingham documents which had reached him from Heemskeerke and, meticulously, had kept copies of everything he sent, in French and Italian. Now throughout the summer Stepney continued to carry out this duty, at one moment complaining to Vernon:

> our correspondence [i.e. with Paget] has been hitherto like ye
> current of the Danube wch you know runs ever downwards without
> any return.[12]

However not long afterwards Stepney did receive a very friendly letter from Paget, acknowledging four of his letters and giving an outline of the Ambassador's mission in Adrianople, which was to propose William III's mediation in the war between the Emperor and the Turks. Paget did not attempt to hide his differences with Heemskeerke, nor his ignorance about the latter's plans. Was he, or was he not, about to leave? The result of this letter, and of others which reached Stepney from Turkey, was to put him in touch with Franz Ulrich, Count Kinsky (1630-1714), the Chancellor of Bohemia, and a formidable personality among the Emperor's advisers. Stepney had met Kinsky once only, soon after his arrival, and had not contacted him again, knowing the coldness which had existed between Kinsky and Paget. Now Kinsky, who had the management of all affairs relating to Turkey, sent his steward over to Stepney's house with the mail. Stepney at once called on the great man, and found him 'quite another man, affable, open & friendly almost to intimacy.' No doubt Kinsky found Stepney much easier to deal with than Lord Paget, and would have thought himself in no way in competition with him. He told Stepney the cause of his quarrel with Paget, which was over the routing, addressing and opening of mail to and from the Porte. This was a matter of concern, for letters took at least a month in transit from Vienna. The couriers travelled in great danger, and one at least was murdered *en route.*

But one can imagine Paget's annoyance at being invited to discuss what to him was a trivial affair.

Stepney offered to communicate Paget's letters to Kinsky, and received an assurance of information in the reverse direction. He wrote to Paget, telling him exactly which parts of his letters had been revealed to Kinsky, and sent him a copy of a Latin letter which Heemskeerke and his colleague Colyer had written to the Emperor, together with extracts from intercepted French diplomatic correspondence (all these papers obtained from Kinsky). This material was highly delicate, but Stepney had already arranged with Bruynincx that he could use the latter's cypher when writing to Paget; as Stepney informed Blathwayt:

> I have been up all night putting these writings into Cypher for my Ld Pagett's better information, and drawing up such Istructions (*sic*) for his Lordship as Count Kinsky told me the Emp^r thought most necessary upon this occasion.

Anticipating that Paget's mission might lead to a serious mediation between the imperialists and the Turks, Stepney had written to Blathwayt for permission to move to Belgrade if necessary. Now he told Paget of this bright idea – it should be remembered that all diplomats wished to be engaged in lucrative peace negotiations – and continued:

> 'Tis true there is some curiosity at the bottom of this request, not to say Vanity in contributing the little I am able to so glorious a work: at least the happiness of once more paying my duty to yr Ex^{cy} (if you shou'd think fit to come back that way) wou'd be a sufficient motive to an healthy rambling young fellow, as I am, to undertake such a journey. But this prospect is something remote & is to be submitted to what your Lordship shall advise and prescribe.[13]

But Stepney never did get to Belgrade.

In western Europe the war was increasing in intensity. On 17/ 27 May Stepney told Blathwayt that Prince Louis had reported the French crossing of the Rhine at Philippsburg on 6/16 May with 50,000 men and much artillery. They were making for Heidelberg, and there was little opposition. The Saxon troops had not arrived, having been refused passage through Franconia. Stepney correctly forecast that the French would offer the Circles of Suabia, Franconia and the Upper Rhine the alternatives of neutrality or destruction. The troops from Hesse had no provisions, owing to the negligence of the imperial commissary. Prince Louis' envoy to Vienna had returned empty-handed: there was no cash, only letters of credit on the Circles of Upper and Lower Saxony and Westphalia. Stepney commented that the Vienna Court was insensible, and would continue so until the Habsburg Hereditary Countries were in danger. According to imperial decree, the word of command was to be changed daily between Prince Louis, the Elector of Saxony and the Landgrave of Hesse-Cassel, which did not make Prince Louis' task any easier. By 13 June (n.s.) Heidelberg had fallen, and the destruction of the countryside was continuing. Meanwhile 6,400 Brandenburg troops destined for the Hungarian front were held up at Breslau owing to non-ratification of the treaty between the Emperor and the Elector, non-payment by the Emperor of the first month's subsidy, and the non-appearance of an imperial commissioner to take over the troops.[14]

Yet the Court at Vienna continued its daily life with unruffled calm.

> Yesterday [9 June n.s.] the Emp^r entred into the 53^d Year of his Age & his Birthday was celebrated at Laxenburgh with an Italian Serenade. The Court laid aside their mourning (to be in gala as they call it) but have resumed it today.

This prompted an urgent note from Stepney to Vernon when sending in his bill of extraordinaries:

> I must entreat you to let me know if my Lord Pagett reckoned nothing in his Extries for suits of Cloaths on ye days of Gala; here (as you know) they are very extraordry on these occasions and rather than be backward in my respect to the Emp^{rs} birthday I have put myself to 30^{ll} [£30] expence for an embroidered suit, without wch there was no appearing at Court and those who absent [themselves] are looked upon [as] disafected. However I dare not bring this to acct without having a president (sic) for it, tho you may be assured I should not have been so extravagant but to comply with the customs of ye country.

The embroidered suit was soon put to good use:

> On Munday night wee had an Italian opera in the Favorite, where the King of the Romans, the Arch Duke & all the Augustissima Casa entertain'd us with dancing. The Electrice of Bavaria's death had put a Stopp to all merriment, & this is the first divertissement wee have had since my coming hither . . .

And:

> I am now going to an Opera in the favorite; for today is Gala for the Empresses nom de Bapteme.

Then in great satisfaction at his increasing social success, Stepney told Vernon:

> Because you know the situation of Mr. Heemskerke's garden on ye Danube where Mr. Harboard lived, I must tell you an unexpected favour I received on Sunday last from Count Stratman,

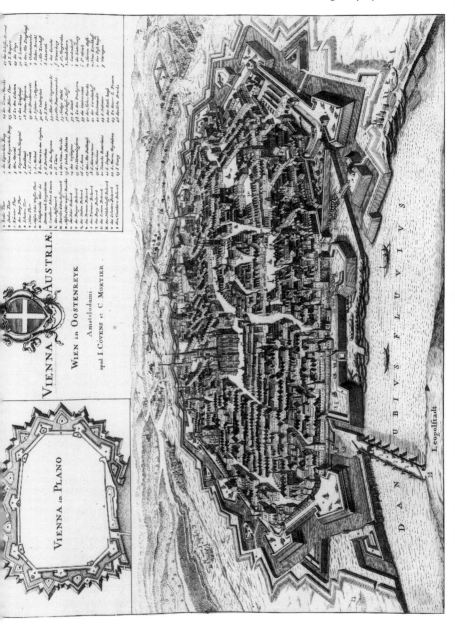

City of Vienna (c. 1710). By permission of the British Library. K. Top. XC. 41. d.

he did me ye honour to invite himself to dine with me and ye
Dutch Secry [Bruynincx] (since wee have taken possession of ye
house in Mr. Heemskerke's absence) & brought his lady & Count
Budiani, his son-in-law, who is lately declar'd Ban of Croatia:
Wee dined below in ye Grotto near ye fountains: & our mighty
guests were pleased to tell us at parting they were extreamly well
satisfyed: I would have put upon ym ye Compliment of Baucis &
Philemon: But they liked my sack, threaten to visit me frequently
before ye sumer [summer] is over & I leave you to judge how
saucy a little Agent is made by such extraordinary civilities.[15]

At the end of July, Kinsky again sent for Stepney to give him a
letter about the Hungarian dissident Imre Thököly who, being of
the reformed religion, had long been a thorn in the flesh of the
imperial Catholic administration. To Kinsky's annoyance, Thököly
was said to have had a meeting with Heemskeerke when the latter
travelled through Belgrade, and the Dutchman's reported comment,
that 'it was neither His Maty's intention, nor the States, *de le perdre*'
had been highly upsetting to the Bohemian Chancellor. Stepney at
once denied the report, and sent Kinsky's information to Paget and
to Blathwayt.

However, his own feelings on the matter were not in doubt:
I wish the unhappy man was safe in Persia or any where out of
their Clutches; for whenever he comes into their hands he may
expect no more Quarter than Monmouth had; for Count Kinsky is
of such a persecuting principle, that I believed he wou'd rather
the War shou'd last a Year or two longer, than that the poor Count
[Thököly] shou'd escape with Estate or Life.

Stepney was concerned about the persecution of Protestants within
the Habsburg dominions. He had already reported an incident which
took place on the feast of *Corpus Christi,* when a Swedish Lutheran
footman had been provoked into retaliation against a Catholic guard
who objected that the Swede had not removed his hat as the Host
passed by. Eventually the Swede was enabled to reach Hungary, thanks
to the intervention of the Envoy in Vienna from Brandenburg.[16]

The war did not go well for the Allies in 1693. The commercial
fleet from Smyrna had been sunk or captured by the French at the
end of June. Stepney heard the news from Blathwayt early in August
and wrote that he was trying to convince the court that the loss at
sea had not been so great or irreparable as the enemy would make
it. He missed a post-day because he was so busy with this task.
And he had to contend with the 'Italian faction' at court, who wished
to make peace with France. Then, hard on the heels of the losses at
sea came the news of the terrible battle at Landen/Neerwinden, in

Flanders, where the King after a four-hour struggle had had to admit defeat and save his remaining troops. Nevertheless the fact that William himself had escaped 'miraculously' was enough to give Stepney cause to hold up his head. He wrote, from the reports which reached him, a very clear and full account of the battle which he sent to Lord Paget.[17]

Blathwayt, who had become separated from the King during the chaotic aftermath of the affray, eventually came to rest at Lembecq (south of Halle). He begged Stepney to send by every post news of the siege of Belgrade, which was being carried out by imperial forces under the command of the Duke of Croy. The King desired the reports urgently; 'if you can find a more speedy conveyance for them, it will the more please the King.' Stepney had already written that the Vienna Court considered that the French were the greatest sufferers in the battle of Landen. In a religious ceremony the Emperor had vowed, in the event of success over his enemies [i.e. the taking of Belgrade] that he would rebuild all the churches which had been demolished in Hungary

> & lay the foundations of a new one on an Eminence not far from
> this City (called Calvenberg) on which side the Poles & the rest
> of the Confederates came down upon the Turks.

The Emperor was not immediately called upon to carry out his vow. The Duke of Croy raised the siege of Belgrade in mid-September, which prompted Stepney to compose a scathing epigram in Latin, judged by Sir Paul Rycaut to be 'very severe.' Severe also was Stepney's comment on a pilgrimage which the Emperor and his court made to the shrine of Our Lady at Mariazell in Styria, where they were to stay for 15 days:

> If this Journey of the Emp^r can have any effect upon the Turks,
> 'tis pity but he had begun it sooner, for then perhaps wee might
> have had the Miracle on our side. I know not what vertue may be
> in this expedition, but I am certain it is very chargeable tho wee
> [i.e. the Emperor] are in no very good condition to be at such
> expences at this time. A Pair of Candlesticks which are the offering
> cost 20,000 florins, & the expences of the retinue in this journey
> may reasonably be computed much more.[18]

In Whitehall Lord Nottingham had been replaced as Secretary of State by Sir John Trenchard, to whom Stepney addressed his first letter on 19/29 August 1693, describing French overtures for peace which were taking place at Ratisbon. Stepney had set up an excellent working relationship with the Spanish Ambassador to the imperial court, Don Carlo Emmanuele d'Este, Marques de Borgomañero, whom he had met for the first time at the conference of January

1693. His good standing with the Ambassador was a great achievement on Stepney's part, because the Marques was known to have the ear of the Emperor, whom he had persuaded to ally in the first place with the Protestant maritime powers against France. Stepney knew how to treat the great man, and rushed round to his house with a compliment when the Marques was appointed a Grandee of Spain. Only once did Stepney report a coldness between them, when at the request of Count Frise Stepney approached Borgomañero to ask him to obtain the release of General Schöning from captivity. Stepney found the Ambassador 'very stiff' on this occasion, and could not pursue the request. On at least one occasion Stepney was entertained by the Ambassador to dinner, and in 1695, when Borgomañero died, Stepney wrote to Lord Lexington:

> Wee have just now received ye news of ye death of ye Spanish Embass^r, wch I am heartily sorry for, he having been very useful to his Maty's service while I was employ'd at Vienna, & very much my Patron.

Now, in 1693, Stepney was active in briefing the Ambassador with documents to enable the latter to counter advice to the Emperor from the peace party. Similar proposals had been offered from France via Sweden in 1690, so Stepney made a copy of the details for the Ambassador, together with the King's reply. The whole was then reported to Trenchard.[19]

The rejection of the peace proposals by the Grand Alliance may be surprising to students of the twentieth century. But by the end of the 1693 campaign the Allies, though in a position of weakness, were not so debilitated as to make acceptance of the peace imperative. And the French were claiming the right to retain both Strasbourg and Luxembourg, which at the time seemed impossible for the Emperor to grant. The war was not fought in the winter season, and for hardened campaigners such as King William and Prince Louis, the year to come might always bring an upturn in fortune.

Prince Louis' command on the Rhine had fared no better than that of the King in Flanders. After the loss of Heidelberg Stepney reported in early July the sins of the Saxon troops within the Circles, and the endless disputes over the high command. [In this context it should be remembered that under the conventions of the time the high command was given, not to the most experienced general officer, but to whichever Prince could claim social precedence.] The Emperor, from a distance, was held to be the arbiter in such matters. He had just appointed a new envoy to Saxony in the person of Philipp Wilhelm von Boineburg (1656-1717) who was usually known by the French version of his name, (Baron Benebourg). This man was a close relative and friend of Lothar Franz von Schönborn (1655-1729), in 1693 Bishop of Bamberg, who two years later became the Archbishop and Elector of Mainz. Benebourg himself was a minor cleric, but did not behave with much piety. He was an able negotiator, and his task was to get the Elector of Saxony to support the view of the Emperor in such matters as the granting of the Ninth Electorate to Hanover and (more importantly) to achieve the readmission of the Emperor himself, as King of Bohemia, with full voting powers into the Electoral College of the Holy Roman Empire. Before Benebourg left Vienna, Stepney asked him 'accidentally' whether he had any instructions as to the Grand Alliance, '& I find he knows not one word of it.' However, in his next letter Stepney reported that this omission had been made good.[20]

Stepney's letters to Blathwayt or to Whitehall contain only rarely news of the Rhine campaign, but he was well informed of its progress from the series of letters which he received from Sir William Colt. The latter, who was under orders to accompany the Elector of Saxony on campaign, arrived in Frankfurt at the end of June. The Saxon troops had been too late in the field to prevent the destruction of Heidelberg, but Colt blamed the Franconians for delaying their passage and attributed this intransigence to French bribery. He also sent to Stepney a vigorous defence of the behaviour of the young Elector of Saxony, John George IV, whose presence in the field was resented by Prince Louis.[21]

At the beginning of July the French crossed the Neckar between Heidelberg and Mannheim, and it was urgent that the Elector of Saxony and his troops should leave Frankfurt. This they did, proceeding by way of Habitzheim [east of Darmstadt] towards Neudenau [a small town on the river Jagst] where the Elector of Saxony and Prince Louis actually met face to face, on 28 July (n.s.). The Elector had travelled at speed: the distance between Frankfurt and Neudenau as the crow flies is about 125 km [75 miles], which was covered in five days. Colt described the march as 'dreadful', and said that it shattered his equipage.

Four days later (1 August, n.s.) the Elector set up his headquarters at Sontheim, just south of Heilbronn, where Prince Louis was ensconced. But there was no action, despite the fact that a thunderstorm caused a fire in the French camp, and that the French decided to withdraw, recrossing the Neckar, on 13-14 August. The fact was that the weather was atrocious, horses and men falling sick. 'What with heat, flyes and fleas our camp is pleasant enough,' wrote Colt from Sontheim, 'but we have good wines this year to make amends for all.' But he was too optimistic: on 5/15 September, his secretary, Schweinfurt, wrote to Stepney from Frankfurt in great distress. Sir William had fallen very sick of a 'bloody flux' [usually dysentry] and had died on 9 September in Heilbronn.[22]

The report of Colt's death must quickly have reached the King's camp at St Quentin/Linnick, because already on 14 September (n.s), perhaps the same day as the news arrived, Blathwayt wrote to George Stepney telling him he was to be ready to replace Sir William as 'commissary' at the Court of Saxony, 'wherever it may be.' [This remark serves to remind us that in the seventeenth century diplomats were accredited on a person-to-person basis. That is, that it would be Stepney's duty to track down John George IV of Saxony, wherever he might be found.] Stepney was to take unofficial leave of the imperial court, explaining that he was going away on a temporary assignment. He would be paid all arrears of salary and allowances. If the Elector of Saxony was still at Frankfurt Stepney was to contact Prince Louis and the Landgrave of Hesse-Cassel and try to reconcile both to the grant of the Ninth Electorate to the Duke of Hanover. There is a final paragraph to Blathwayt's letter which is written-in to the Letter-Book in Stepney's own hand, and was probably taken from an enciphered paragraph sent to him separately by Blathwayt:

> The King does not give you ye title of envoy extr' because you are to return to Vienna, which you know is not intended for your residing place, because you are to return to Vien . . . [these last seven words crossed out by Stepney] but you may be assured that if His Majesty should think fit to have you stay with ye Elector or to employ you at any other court, you will not faile of ye character & allowances of envoy.[23]

Both Vernon and Montagu wrote to Stepney from London with congratulations. But the latter included a paragraph which would immediately have spoiled George's pleasure at his new appointment:

> Your friends here (particularly my Ld Godolphin) are a little concerned that Mr. Cresset should be sent to the House of Luneburgh as Envoye while you have the most troublesome employment without that Title. This has been represented as a hardship upon you, and wee will continue to say it is one till they raise your allowance to 5^l [£5] pp day and then let them dispose of you as they please.[24]

Meanwhile at Vienna Stepney had other tasks unconnected with the campaign on the Rhine. Before the court left on the pilgrimage to Mariazell, he and Bruynincx had been summoned to the Emperor's country house at Ebersdorf, where Leopold liked to spend each autumn, to enjoy the hunting and also to admire the beauties of the countryside, where rich cornfields bordered the river Danube. For the two secretaries, as for other ministers, no diversion was planned. A lengthy conference was held on 5/15 September, to discuss the affairs of Savoy. Stepney reported in detail to Blathwayt. He also had time to compose a dignified lapidary, in Latin, for the headstone of Sir William Colt's grave at Heilbronn. On 30 September (n.s.) he wrote to Blathwayt:

> This morning I have rec'd your 2d orders of the 8/18 Inst. to repair to Saxony for which I am ready & shall set out this evening or tomorrow early: I hope to be at Dresden in 4 days running night & day & I believe I shall find the Elector there.

As the Emperor had still not returned from his pilgrimage, Stepney said he would not take formal *congé* (as he might return to Vienna), but had taken leave of the ministers:

> I have found them in Generall very favourable to me, & have the Comfort of having left some friends, & no Enemies that I know of.[25]

Stepney could look back with some pride on his nine months' stay in Vienna. He had held his own in a strange court, where he had been accepted as a colleague by men of much higher social standing than himself. He had proved himself a most able reporter of the European scene. He had shewn himself willing and able to move at speed from one post to another. Before his move to Saxony he was at the peak of optimism about his future career.

VII *Romance, Death and Subsidies*
(Dresden, October 1693-July 1694)

> I writt to my mother ye Eve before I left Vienna acquainting her
> whether [i.e. wither] I was comanded & you may now assure her
> that after being a day & a night longer than Jonas was in ye Whales
> Belly I am at last thrown up at Dresden, almost in as filthy a
> pickle as he was at Nineveh,[1]

Stepney left Vienna on 1 October (n.s.) 1693. His hurried journey,
using the conveyances of the imperial post, took him via Prague to
Dresden, where he just missed the Elector of Saxony, who had
already left his capital for the delights of his hunting-lodge at
Moritzburg [12 km north-west of Dresden]. Stepney made no
attempt to follow, knowing that the Elector was due to go on to
Leipzig, where the autumn Fair, then as now, was an event of great
importance to the region. Moreover Stepney was awaiting the arrival
of his two colleagues, Baron Benebourg from the Emperor and Dr
Johann Ham, the Envoy of the States General. It was the duty of all
three diplomats to persuade the Elector to join the Grand Alliance
(which he had so far refused to do), and to bargain for his troops to
take part in the 1694 campaign. Stepney stayed in Dresden until
10 October, and during his first few days' residence he obtained
interviews – as he had previously done on his arrival in Vienna –
with the chief ministers of state. In Saxony he met the Grand Marshal
of the Court, Friedrich August, Baron von Haugwitz; Nicol, Freiherr
von Gerstorff (Director of the Privy Council); and another senior
minister, Hans Ernst Knoch. Stepney was as yet without credentials,
which caused him some difficulty with Gerstorff, who walked him
up and down an ugly long gallery for half an hour, talking about his
own foreign missions and refusing to say a word about Stepney's
assignment. The latter did not interrupt him, partly because he had
not yet seen his two colleagues of the Alliance, and also because
he did not wish to give Gerstorff the opportunity of raising the
thorny problem of subsidies, part of which, for the year 1693, were
already in dispute.

Meanwhile Stepney wrote to Blathwayt with his immediate

impressions of the court to which he had been so suddenly assigned:

> Wee [i.e. the Elector] are in ye height of frollicks & amours: The
> Mistress is ye Doll, & ye Electrice a figure not unlike Penelope,
> or good Queen Catherine in ye best reign of Charles ye 2d, so that
> it will be no fault of mine if my relations [i.e. dispatches] from
> this place look more like Romance & Mercure Galant, than letters
> of State & Politicks; since it is but reasonable that I take ye Aire
> of ye Court where I reside, wch I find are as different here from
> ye Devotion & Gravity wch reigns in Vienna, as Farce is from
> Tragedy.[2]

Before leaving for Leipzig George Stepney set about leasing a house
in Dresden, against his return. It is surprising to learn that in 1693
he had a cousin living there. This was Jane (née Stepney), a
granddaughter of the first Baronet Stepney of Prendergast in
Pembrokeshire. Jane had married a Major von Blauenstein – a name
variously rendered in English as Blew(m)stone or Bloysden – who
at one time had been equerry to Prince Rupert, from whom he had
learned 'much chymistry, particularly the secrets of founding
cannons.' After the Prince's death Blauenstein had come to Saxony,
where under the Elector John George III he had been commissioned
as a Major of Artillery, and was employed in making guns. How he
met and married Jane Stepney is not known. He had been acquainted
with Sir William Colt and with the banker Franc Stratford, and
even before George Stepney reached Dresden, Blauenstein
occasionally forwarded mail to him. In December 1693 George
wrote to his mother:

> My Cousin Blewmstone and his Lady give their Service to you.
> They are very good people, & very friendly to me.

There is no record of any very close intimacy between Stepney and
these relatives (although he tried, later, to help Blauenstein find
employment in Brandenburg). But the speed with which he found
accommodation in Dresden suggests that his family may have helped
him. He took up residence in the house of Frau Johanna Schröder,
opposite the Guildhall [*Rathaus*], where he rented the middle and
top floors for himself and his servants at a weekly rent of seven
Reichsthaler, from the day he moved in. Early on he had told Franc
Stratford that these lodgings were not far from those of the Grand
Chamberlain, [Ferdinand August] von Pflug, whose Lady

> (I know not upon what acct) has been very inquisitive of my
> Landlady if I am of a good family or not, by wt you may imagine
> wt a prejudice it is to me not to be a Baron for her sake .... The
> husband seems to be friendly enough to me. I knew him formerly
> at Berlin & here [Stepney refers to his visit to Saxony for John

George IV's wedding] & tho he is well in the Elr's favour he
cannot be much usefull, in our business, since he has no share in
the Ministry.[3]

When Stepney arrived in Leipzig he was joined by Schweinfurt
(secretary to the late Sir William Colt) who brought with him Colt's
papers for Stepney's use. These however were deficient: the copy-
book of Sir William's despatches from Dresden was missing, as
was any information regarding 'ye sprinkling of his Matyes bounty.'
Stepney at once told Blathwayt he was writing to Franc Stratford
> (who was ye Emissary in dealing about Corruption) how and whom
> he bribed.[4]

The Secretary at War confirmed to Stepney one of the latter's worst
suspicions: Blathwayt had told George that either he would remain
at Dresden with the title of Envoy Extraordinary, or return to Vienna,
or settle at Ratisbon. But then he added:

> The title of Envoy Extry to the Elr of Saxony on this Occasion wd
> have loaded you with a Quality more Expensive than usefull or
> agreeable to the designs which are most adequate to yr
> circumstances & intentions; wch should be rather to inform
> yourself for some time longer in the knowledge of the several
> Courts and affairs of ye Empire, than be confined by a Character
> to some thing that may be of less credit and duration.[5]

In part, Stepney agreed with Blathwayt's remarks, and told Vernon
so. But to Stratford he expressed himself very differently:

> You will perceive how yt worthy Gentleman [Blathwayt] labours
> to excuse my not coming hither with ye title of Envoy, & leaves
> me to my thoughts of when this expedition is finish'd.

The gravamen of Stepney's discontent was the appointment of James
Cresset as Envoy to the courts of Hanover and Zell. Colt had been
Envoy to all three courts, Hanover, Zell and Saxony. Now that the
duties had been split between Cresset and Stepney, it was apparent
to the latter that Charles Montagu's prediction had come true, and
that Charles had been unable to give his friend Stepney the same
support as that accorded by Lexington to Cresset. Stepney denied
to Stratford any feelings of jealousy; nevertheless his
disappointment is apparent in this as in other letters.

But Stepney's letter to his banker was not written solely to voice
his private concerns. His negotiations with the Elector of Saxony
and the latter's ministers would come to nothing if he could not
effectively produce the needed amounts in subsidies and bribes.
The subsidies which had been agreed with Saxony by the
representatives of the Emperor, the King and the States General
for the campaign of 1693 had been 400,000 Reichsthaler (Rx) in

exchange for a fighting force of 12,000 men. It was expected that this large sum would be provided as follows:

	Rx 000
The King of England	100
The States General	50
The Emperor, by Assignations	150
The Emperor, from the Habsburg Chest	50
To be shared between	
The Elector of Brandenburg	
The Landgrave of Hesse	50
The Dukes of Lüneburg	
Total	400

Stepney had known as early as August 1693 that the portion assigned to the last three donors shewn above was unlikely to be made good, and that the imperial court hoped that the King and the States General would supply the deficit. He had duly reported the situation to London, but now told Stratford that the problem had been simply ignored in all the instructions and letters sent to him. He reckoned that the missing 50,000 Rx was due at the time of the Leipzig Fair, that is, at the time of his letter to Stratford. He had also discovered that of the 100,000 Rx owed by King William, only two thirds had actually been handed over by Sir William Colt in May. The remainder was outstanding.

Stepney also desired from Stratford further information as to the bribery already practised, particularly in regard to 'the Fair One' [i.e. the Elector's mistress, Magdalena Sibylla von Neidschütz, now Countess Rocklitz], and to the Saxon ministers. Blathwayt was to advise Stepney to wait on the Countess as soon as possible, but George knew that etiquette demanded he should first pay his respects to the Elector. In both these duties he expected to be – and was – helped by Count Frise, who was distantly related to the Countess and was thought to be 'her Creature.'[6]

John George IV of Saxony eventually granted Stepney an audience at Leipzig on 15 October (n.s.) 1693. '[I] cannot much bragg of the manner in wch they treated me,' wrote Stepney to Blathwayt. Schweinfurt had taken a copy of the newly arrived credentials to the favourite minister, Knoch, and these two decided that Stepney's title should be 'Minister' although he himself always used the correct designation of 'Commissary.' The Grand Marshal had not wanted to importune the Elector during the Leipzig Fair.

Count Frise, however, had no such inhibitions, and the Elector agreed to a private audience at 12.00 noon. The Groom of the Chamber [*Kammerfurrier*] gave Stepney only 15 minutes, notice of the appointment. George went to the princely apartments, and was then kept waiting until 2.00 pm, by which time the Elector was dressed. Stepney made his compliment, and the Elector replied that he was obliged to the King and was ready to enter into a stricter alliance: however, things must wait for the arrival of the Emperor's Envoy. There was no civil word for Stepney himself, and no invitation from the chamberlain [*Hofmarschall*] to dinner, which George had expected, 'tho I am not of a constitution to bear many Saxon-Meales.' Stepney reflected that this cold reception possibly stemmed from the Elector's 'disgust' at not having an Envoy Extraordinary accredited to him. And the slight was compounded by the very different reception given a few days later to Stepney's Dutch colleague, Dr Johann Ham, who

> came hither ye 6th Inst [o.s.] in ye morning: at noon was admitted to audience, where he produced his Character of Envoy & dined with ye Elr.

On 22 October (n.s.), Stepney and Ham returned to Dresden, where three days later George was received by Countess Rocklitz. Not surprisingly, his mention of 'his Maty's Bounty' was well received, and the Lady promised to facilitate access to the Elector on any matter which could not be dealt with through formal channels. But negotiations for a new treaty were still delayed by the absence of Baron Benebourg, and Stepney could devote unaccustomed leisure to his private life, which he described more freely than hitherto in his correspondence.[7]

Whilst still in Vienna Stepney had received a letter from a friend of Matt Prior's, a Mrs Holmes, whose brother Mr Rickfeild was in Vienna in the service of Count Kaunitz. From Dresden George answered his correspondent in a charming manner:

> Fair Unknown wou'd sound too much like ye beginning of a letter in a Romance & as affected as those wth wch Mr. Welch has pleas'd himself to keep – therefore within ye bounds of ordry civilty
>
> Madame
> The distance betwixt London – Vienna is enough to remove all scandall for ye familiarity of Pen & Ink wch passes betwixt us; therefore you need not excuse ye nicety of yr sex for making such innocent acquaintance & are too liberall in yr thanks by so pleasant a letter, for ye kindness (as you are pleas'd to call it) my handling one letter backwards & forwards between you and yr brother; I only wish I had better opportunityes of shewing more effectually

how ready I am to serve you, or any whom you shall recomend

This letter was sent under cover of one to Prior, which allows a rare glimpse into George's student days:

> I have been long endebted to you for severall letters, as likewise to Mrs. Holmes; I knew none of yt name except ye Presbyterian Barrd who sold Ale and Oaster on ye Peese Market hill, & ye old woman at St. James's who was foster-mother to poor Ephraim Howard: But since I understand her maiden-name was Rickfeild, & that she is sister to that cath[olic] who 12 years ago [i.e. 1681] helped Ledger to cure my buttock when I was stob'd by George Man; Besides that I believe she may be yr familiar, & witty (as appears by her letter) m[ore]over to confirme betty in ye kind thoughts she has of me that I am Cavalier enough to answer all a Woman can say to me.[8]

In October-November 1693 Stepney carried on a light-hearted correspondence with two Catholic ladies, Frances Bellomont and her much younger sister, Ann. Frances had been the mistress of Prince Rupert, and had travelled to Vienna to make claims upon his estate. During her stay she had met Stepney and other members of his circle. He wrote to her shortly after his arrival in Dresden, repeating the comparison of his journey with the experience of Jonah in the whale's belly:

> My lady Ann, after having so long thum'd my Bible, cannot [but] be acquainted with ye Story.

George had lent money to Lady Bellomont and had underwritten one of her debts. Now he turned to the good-tempered Bruynincx to retrieve both the debt and the promissary note, as well as 91 florins which he had lent to one of the smokers' club, Baron Blumenthal. Another arrival in Vienna had been Lord Dartmouth, whom Stepney had missed, and to whom he now presented his services:

> & also to yr other 3 English Sparks who have only a thin wenscote betwixt ym & yr Lpps [Ladyships], wch (as Tom says) wou'd not have been a sufficient barricade for his Master while he was at Cambridge, so well is he acquainted with his constitution. Look to yrselves, make a quick dispatch in yr business & some time do me the honour to think of me.

Later, Stepney did run across Lord Dartmouth, together with Countess Münchhausen, with whom he (Stepney) had a passing amour – for not more than two Ducats. He wrote to an acquaintance:

> I . . . desire my Amours may be upon ye Square or if yt cannot be, my Purse Seldome reaches farther than a charitable relief of ye present necessities of ye Fair one. But my good nature never operates so far as to a Formall keeping wch is a foolish sort of

> fondness but one Digree [*sic*] from ye Madness of Marriage, from
> wch Good Lord deliver us.[9]

In fact, Stepney was bored during these first two months in Dresden. He was shut out from the court to a large extent, and there was little business to attend to in the absence of his imperial colleague. He took time to correspond with his mother, in a letter which illuminates both their characters. Jane had wanted to know how some of her son's augmented salary and allowances could be disposed of to advantage. George had to disillusion her: once his debts were paid there would only be a very inconsiderable amount left over. He gave her the details, and added that although Charles Montagu had offered to lend him £1,000, he had no intention of accepting:

> it is the last use any man should make of his friend, & wch I
> should be sorry to be reduced to.

He told Jane that Stratford was shipping some wine to England on his behalf, and he wished it to be given as a present to Blathwayt. He sent his love to his dear sisters. It is surprising to find that he allowed this quite intimate letter to be copied by a clerk into his letter-book.[10]

In the way of duty Stepney found time to complete a task which had been laid upon him by Blathwayt during his posting to Vienna. This was to provide character-sketches of the Emperor and of some of the latter's ministers. It so happened that this dispatch reached London soon after the death of the imperial court chancellor, Count Theodor Athlet Stratmann, and so should have been of interest to the Secretary of State, as well as to Lord Lexington, the newly appointed envoy to Vienna. For example, Stepney's pen-portrait of Count Ernst Rüdiger von Starhemberg runs as follows:

> Count Stahremberg [*sic*], famous for his Defence of Vienna, [in
> 1683, against the Turks] seems yet to live upon ye Credit of yt
> Action, has entrance into ye Counsell of conference but I believe
> does not much forward ye business. For he is one who does not
> usually stick to ye matter in hand, and has ye Talent of raising
> whipt cream upon wt ye others have said, without advancing any
> thing of his own, and abounds in words wch have no meaning.[11]

Despite Stepney's fairly good relationship with the Elector of Saxony's senior ministers, he did not know what to make of the rest of the court, nor they of him. Something had to be done, and despite the fact that no-one had had the 'ordinary civility' to invite him to dinner, he decided to celebrate the King's birthday (14 November n.s.) explaining to Blathwayt:

> I told you in my last, I intended to keep holyday for which I had
> several good reasons, as my zeal to his Maty, my being in a country

where good eating and drinking is much in vogue; besides a certain depit, in yt I have been here a month without having been invited either to the Elector's table by any of his ministers, and (to confess all) out of a secret pleasure in mortifying Mr. Ham (who never had the soul to treat any man) by shewing ye Towne a King's Commissary was not inferior to a Dutch Envoy. You will doubtless blame my extravagance when I confess this vanity cost me between 30 and 40 pounds. But I have had such satisfaction in the success of my entertainment that I would not for twice the value that it were left undone. I therefore think it reasonable to pay for my frollick, and am resolv'd never to impute it to an Extr Bill. I have thereby made a free acquaintance with all persons of any note in the Court, which (after their reserved way of using me) I shou'd never have done, if I had not layd hold of this publique occasion which countenanc'd my invitation, and made ym at a loss how to refuse me . . . .

Wee were 14 at Table without any dispute for Rank or healths, came to the Extravagance of Bruderschafft upon our knees, drinking under-Legg, & twenty other Antick postures which you must have seen in Dutch pictures; and I satisfy myself that I have not paid too dear for the familiarity which I contracted with some Persons that night, and the marks of distinction I have received since.

The guest-list, as given by Stepney, reads:

Baron Haugwitz (Gd Marschall)	Count Frize (Gen. Maj)
Mr. Knock – favourite minister	Mr. Ham – Dutch Envoy
Mr. Heim [Hoym] – president of finances	Mr. Reibold – Hof Marschall
	6 more chief officers

The Gd Chamberlain Mr. Phlugg of the Elrs court[12]

To Bruynincx Stepney admitted, two days after the debauch, that he was still feeling the effects. Ham had left early. The servants had also been entertained, and whilst the guests had drunk only 54 bottles, the servants had emptied 82 'potts' of *vin du pays*. But Stepney considered the evening '*la plus glorieuse de ma vie*.' He sent to Bruynincx, for the second time, a message to the man who probably had been his landlord in Vienna, Monsieur Pape. The previous month Stepney had complained that his valet had done dirt (*en fait de bouse*) by giving the housekeeper Stepney's coffee-pot and the coachman his boots. Both these pieces of property George wished returned to him. Now he sent a message to Pape that if his valet Godfride wished to join him in Dresden he could bring Stepney's horse, *tout doucement*, provided Pape had not sold the animal already. Bruynincx should please give Godfride enough money for the journey. Stepney explained that no-one had any recreations in Dresden apart from hunting or running at the ring.

The horse was just the right animal for these sports, and George reckoned he would have no difficulty in getting rid of it.[13]

To Blathwayt Stepney could not repress an explosion of jealousy and annoyance caused by the behaviour of his Dutch colleague, Ham:

> How can a man have patience to be made a meer property of, and be obliged to assist only as a zany to a Quack: I should be sorry any English Man but yourself shou'd know wee pay $\frac{2}{3}$ of ye Subsidies & ye Dutch have ye Merits of the Whole, but so it is, because Ham is an Envoy and I but a Commissary.

Johann Ham was no stranger to Stepney. He had been the Dutch Envoy in Berlin from 1692 ('Mr. Johnson and he were so-so') and had previously been employed by the Amerongen family. Stepney considered him awkward in his manners, mean, and unable to control his facial expression on hearing good or bad news. But one underlying cause of Stepney's dislike was that he knew Ham to be in correspondence with Lord Portland, and hence enjoyed a virtual direct line to the King. What Stepney did not know was that King William had a high personal regard for Ham.

A second factor which touched Stepney on the raw was – as he related to Blathwayt – that 'someone' had told the Elector he was no gentleman, and that it was this rumour which had prevented the Elector from inviting George to his table. Clearly Stepney suspected Ham of being the source of the slander. His riposte had been to write to Charles Montagu to persuade Lord Dorset (now Lord Chamberlain to the King and Queen of England)

> to gett me some Title of hangar-on, as Sir W. Colt had (Interioris Cubiculi Aulicus) wch will make a glorious appearance in the Instrument of ye Treaty, if ever wee come to sign; & I may be able to banter ye Germans with 3 Latin words, which in English signify nothing.

Charles Montagu once again came to his friend's rescue. Not only did he get Stepney made a Gentleman of the Privy Chamber, he also arranged payment of the quarterly allowance which was due on 8 December, plus another quarter in advance. Stepney wrote his thanks. Charles was 'ye good Angell at ye Brink of ye Pool' and Stepney enclosed his letter to Lord Dorset under cover to Charles.[14]

A diplomat could be of use to his friends in many ways. James Vernon had written to Stepney in September 1693, asking advice on the further education of his son (also James) in Germany, since France was closed to Englishmen by reason of the war. The boy was to study civil law. Stepney replied that James must learn High Dutch [i.e. German] but that there was nothing to equal the standard of Gievius or Bayle. Nevertheless Stepney recommended the new

University of Halle, founded by the Elector of Brandenburg (who got its charter from the Emperor in exchange for 6,000 men sent to Hungary), and especially Mons. Stryck,

> who teaches law, is reported to be the best man of this Age, & one
> who is the clearest in his method of instructing.

George had written both to Stryck, to find out if he took boarders, and also to Danckelmann in Berlin for a recommendation. Later, George recommended young Vernon to make a tour of the Empire, and said he would gladly receive him himself:

> Ye greatest pleasure you can do me will be, to lett us study some
> months together, during wch I can assure you, he will be exposed
> to no ill example.

(A rather necessary remark, since Stepney wrote this letter just three days after his debauch with the Saxon ministers.) In the event, young Vernon never did take up residence with George Stepney, but the latter received a similar request from Charles Montagu, on behalf of his stepson, Heneage. Stepney responded with two pages of advice: Heneage should visit not only Dresden, but the courts of Brunswick-Lüneburg, then Hanover, Berlin (with Stepney's introductions), Vienna over next summer; then Italy and home via Switzerland and possibly France. And Heneage Montagu duly came to Dresden, to witness the events of the following spring.[15]

How much the drunken party gave impetus to Stepney's social life is not entirely clear (he did at least receive an invitation from Count Frise). In the weeks before Christmas he wrote to Franc Stratford asking that claret, oysters and brawn should be dispatched to him 'when ye frost setts in.' By early December Stepney was in high spirits, writing to Prior:

> For me (State affairs apart) I am as happy as ye day is long, I have
> concluded ye Streight-Allyance with ye Fair one (who made me
> break of [sic – break off] my letter abruptly last Post) & [e]nvy no
> Monarch alive. There is a great deal of danger, expence & adultery
> in this affair; but the pleasure & vanity is wt I never expected to
> arrive in ye whole Course of my Life.
>
> Le[a]st you might mistake it will be necessary to tell you I do
> not mean ye Electrice but God dam me if I am 4 persons below her
> > With Pistoll & Pego both charg'd I advance
> > Prepared to encounter the Husband or Wife;
> > To breath out my soul in an amorous trance,
> > or to end the Intrigue with his or my Life
> I have another meeting this evening: & am so deeply engaged
> that I care not one farthing wt becomes of me adieu & prosper.

And the identity of the lady? About three weeks previously George had commented on his good relations with Madame Pflug, the wife of the Grand Chamberlain, that same lady who had inquired on his arrival as to his gentility. George had met her later at court, playing ombre with her (and losing his money). The romance continued over about 18 months, then died: as will be recounted in due course. And George continued from time to time a friendly correspondence with the husband.[16]

Officially, Stepney was now busy: the Danes had sent an offer of mediation to the warring powers, which was communicated by the Danish secretary in Dresden to Gerstorff, the chief minister. Stepney reported to London:

> soon after Baron Gerstorff had made his report to the Elector . . .
> . I had the honour & good fortune (for it has not happen'd often)
> to enter into Conversation with His Highness. . . . I was pleas'd
> most heartily to find in ye Elr such impressions as a Prince of the
> Empire ought to have.

That is, the Elector said it was no time to think of peace. He asked for Stepney's comments on the French propositions, and the latter replied that he saw no mention of Strasburg nor of Luxemburg, both of which were considered essential to the Emperor and the King of Spain. Stepney next had an interview with Gerstorff, whose Chancery 'being in no very good order', could not find the relevant papers on previous French offers of peace. Stepney therefore, at request, provided copies of the project which the Swedish minister had presented at Ratisbon the previous August, together with other papers which included a reply drafted by Lord Nottingham for the King in November 1690. Gerstorff shewed the papers the following day to the Elector (before the latter went hunting), and the King's reply of 1690 was used as the basis for the Elector's response to the Danish secretary.

There were repercussions: early in January 1694, Stepney received a letter from Nicholas von Danckelmann in Vienna informing him that the Danish Resident there, Johann Christian Urbeck, had accused Stepney of belittling the efforts of the Northern Crowns to achieve peace in Europe. Stepney replied that it was quite true that he, Ham and [Jobst Hermann] Ilten [the Envoy from Hanover] had all ridiculed the idea of the peace negotiations as proposed by Denmark, and they had got the Elector of Saxony to agree with them. True, Stepney had spoken freely to his old friend Bartholomew Meuschen, the Danish secretary in Dresden, but both were 'inconsiderable people,' and Stepney was not conscious of having said anything reproachful.[17]

The Electress of Saxony had for some time believed herself to be pregnant. Now, the pregnancy was declared to be false; 'for these 2 months wee have been praying to God Almighty to no purpose,' remarked Stepney. The Elector had rebuked his wife for ordering from Holland 4,000 Dollars' worth of lace for 'baby-clouts.' On New Year's Day Stepney called on the Electress, in her bedchamber. She was in tears. 'I pity her from my heart, & administered ye best Comfort I cou'd in such cases.'[18]

With the turn of the year political activity in Dresden was increasing. Stepney was still worried over the non-payment of the English share of the subsidies to Saxony. He had written repeated reminders to Whitehall on this subject and on the necessity of money for bribes to the Elector's mistress and to his ministers. The Countess of Rocklitz had been promised by Sir William Colt 6,000 Crowns *per annum* from the King of England, and the first instalment had been paid. But this sum was as nothing when compared with jewels worth 62,000 Crowns which, it was rumoured, she had been promised from France. The matter gained in urgency because Benoit Bidal, Baron d'Asfeld, France's roving ambassador, was expected to arrive in Dresden and to bestow favours. The Elector, however, remarked cheerfully that he would welcome d'Asfeld, and send him on to the King of England. John George IV was looking forward to the summer's campaign and was furnishing magazines of fodder and ammunition. For these preparations he naturally required money, and so had called a meeting of the Estates of Saxony to request supply. Saxony, wrote Stepney,

> might be powerful & flourishing if the Riches given were menaged with good husbandry, and the Taxes were lay'd more reasonably, for the greatest grievance is, ye common people pay all, and the Gentry are obliged to no contribution except that in case of necessity they pay a sort of Knight Service, by equipping out 2 Regimts of Militia Troops which in all consist of 1400 horse.[19]

At long last Baron Benebourg, Envoy of the Emperor, arrived in Dresden on 14/24 January 1694, to start the negotiations which, it was hoped, would persuade the Elector of Saxony to become a full member of the Grand Alliance. Benebourg told Stepney that the principal difficulties were the Elector's insistence on the release from arrest of his general, Hans Adam von Schöning; and the 50,000 Reichsthaler which were in dispute. Benebourg had indeed had a rough reception from the Elector at his first audience – a fact which comforted Stepney, who remembered the treatment meted out to him on his arrival in Dresden. Despite the fact that Schöning had been transferred from strict captivity in Brünn to more civilised quarters in Vienna the Elector insisted on complete liberty, and moreover said he would not treat with the Emperor on any other matter until Schöning was set free. Benebourg appealed to Stepney to back up his argument with the Elector by stating that King William and the States General did not wish Schöning's release. Stepney promptly refused: the Allies were not concerned in this affair.[20]

Meanwhile Stepney found time to compose a poem, in Latin and English, on the French King's offering the Netherlands to the Elector of Bavaria [see Appendix III]. This he sent round to several of his friends, including Vernon, Rycaut and 'young' Stratford [Franc's nephew, who resided in Leipzig]. It was purely a propaganda exercise, the action of the French King being compared with that of the devil tempting Christ upon the mountain. At the same time, Robert Molesworth's essay on the Court of Denmark had caused great offence. Stepney remarked to Stratford:

> Perhaps if it [i.e. the poem] ever reaches France it may fare as the present state of Denmark is likely to do in London, and Mr. Molesworth and I may be equally Martyrs for our disrespect of kingly authority. But wt will you have a man do, in a place where he has no business, can't sleep, & when a merry thought offers, wch will not let him alone till he has worked it into Meeter.

Sir Paul Rycaut received the poetic offering with delight, and had it copied for the benefit of John Robinson, the English Resident in Stockholm.[21]

Presently there was no more time for poetry. On 9 February (n.s.), Stepney reported a dressing-down which Ham had received from the Elector, who accused him and/or Stepney of writing 'that he [the Elector] had abandoned Schöning and thought no more of him.' Stepney at once attributed this accusation to a certain Holzbrink who was at the time in Vienna, not as one of the Elector's official representatives, but privately on behalf of the Schöning family. Since Stepney wrote frequently to his friend Bruynincx, the Dutch secretary in Vienna, he wondered if any of his mail had been intercepted, because he did not believe Bruynincx would have gossiped on such a matter to Holzbrink. The following day Count Frise had dinner with the Elector. Schöning's name was mentioned and the Elector – furious and with his hand on his sword – told Frise all that he had said to Ham. Stepney immediately went to court and demanded audience which, at the second attempt, he achieved. It was a Day of Ceremony, when the Elector dined in public with members of the States of Saxony. He put Stepney at his right hand. But there was no discussion of public affairs because

(as Stepney told Vernon but did not include in his official account of the incident)

> whilst we were at Table the Brother-in-law of the Countesse came and whispered to his Electoral Highness that the Countesse was fallen into ye fitts, which made an abrupt end to our dinner.

But the Elector decided to send his adjutant-general, Lt. Col. Carlowitz, to Vienna to seek Schöning's release.

Stepney wrote to London about the death of Count Königsegg [Vice-Chancellor of the Empire] in Vienna, concluding his letter:

> You will pardon this scrawl when I have told you where I have dined; and as in the Condition I am now in, wee use to speak what is at the bottom of our hearts, I cannot express mine better than by assuring you that I am with as much esteeme as man can be.

One feels that Sir Peter Wyche would have been proud of his pupil's ability, both for his capacity to write when drunk, and for the floridity of his expression.

More seriously, Stepney commented to Trenchard that one result of this 'Storm' had been to draw Ham and himself more firmly together. Stepney had also advised Benebourg to ask for a conference with the Saxon ministers.[22]

Three days later Stepney was able to announce to Trenchard that he had had the satisfaction of paying Holzbrink and the rest of Schöning's party in their own coin. Holzbrink had told Bruynincx, in the antechamber of the Emperor in Vienna, that he had received a staffetta from the Elector of Saxony to the effect that the Elector was dissatisfied both with Countess Rocklitz and with Count Frise over their attitude towards Schöning, and that he had sent for Ham and Stepney to rebuke them over the same matter. All this Bruynincx related back to Stepney, who shewed Frise the letter,

> and by his advice and Mr. Hams, I delivered the contents to the Countesse . . . that it was the impudence of Holzb . . . [sic] to say he had received a Staffetta from the Elr with news of what had happened, whereas it was Sch's family only that had dispatched these letters.

Stepney talked with the Countess Rocklitz for nearly an hour, in the sight of most of the Schöning faction at the Dresden court. He emphasised to her that Holzbrink, by making public in the Emperor's antechamber what the Elector had uttered in a passion and in private, could not but diminish her credit at the imperial court. Intriguers would be quick to dispatch a staffetta with news of the small mortification which she and Frise had suffered. The Countess thanked Stepney for his concern for her interest, and said she would ask the Elector to have Holzbrink recalled. Stepney's interview with the Countess took place on 13/23 February, in the evening,

> and at night, when she was in bed with His Highness she began her complaint, as her Valet de Chambre told me, who came by her order at Midnight to knock me up, to desire I might send her the letter I had received from Vienna, which could not be done for many reasons, but I sent her this extract of the passage which concern'd her with a line or 2 of excuse.

Both the Countess and Frise later told Stepney they had made their point with the Elector. Stepney continued:

> Count Frize is sensible I have done him no small service by lending him my Paw to pull the chestnuts out of the fire; nor could I in justice do less, since the Insult he had suffered was partly upon our account.

And during this entire incident, Stepney succeeded in withholding Bruynincx' name.[23]

Did the 'Storm' merely take place in a tea-cup? Not exactly, to a diplomat of the seventeenth century. In his following dispatch Stepney related how Emmanuel Willius, one of John George IV's secretaries who had resided in Vienna for some time, obeyed the Elector's express command 'to repair immediately to Dresden and give an account of his actions.' Two days later Willius found himself under arrest, and was confined either at the Castle of Pirne or at Königstein. 'Since that time we have heard no more of him.' Willius had been employed to solicit Schöning's liberty, but Holzbrink had accused him of lethargy.[24]

Worse was to follow: on 3 March (n.s.), Benebourg, Ham, Ilten and Stepney were all summoned to court to hear a statement from the Elector. This was delivered by the Secretary of War in the presence of most of the Privy Council, and was to the effect that since John George IV had been unable to obtain any reasonable satisfaction to his demands, he would recall his troops by sending a message to his commander, Lt. Gen. Neidschütz [the father of Sibylla], and the troops would begin their homeward march from the Rhine on 6/16 March, 'unless betwixt now and then he might receive contrary orders.' Everyone present was surprised. The Elector personally expressed his resentment at Schöning's arrest and two-year imprisonment, and continued that

> a certain minister there present had made him fair promises (meaning Baron Boyneburg) whereof he saw no effect, & therefore
> . . . he would no longer be *la dupe de l'affaire.*

Benebourg begged for a delay, until the response came to a staffetta which he had already despatched to Vienna. The Elector was sceptical, but agreed to wait for two more posts before sending away his order. The next day Benebourg, mortified, did not attend court. The other foreign ministers did. The Elector repeated his statement in milder form. Stepney intervened – and was told later by Frise that the Elector had taken it well – to point out that neither the King nor the States General had taken any part in the Schöning affair, and therefore although the imperial court had refused to give H.E.H. [His Electoral Highness] the satisfaction he expected, Stepney hoped he was too generous to let the other allies suffer by his resentment;

> and we had been waiting 6 months in hopes of concluding an Allyance & were now ready to do it. . . . The Elector said he had nothing against Ham or me, but wished witnesses to what he had said to Boyneburg.

After the meeting Stepney went round the Saxon ministers to see if anyone would approach the Elector to get him to retract his threat. None dared to do so. The ministers merely suggested to Stepney that his dispatch to the King might wait until a reply had been received from Vienna. Thinking out loud, Stepney continued to his Secretary of State:

> The Consequences of this Declaration are either, having no Saxons on the Rhine or having Schöning at the head of these troops, which are 2 points which many think equally desperate.

Should the imperial ministers stand on principle and not release Schöning, the Elector might well join the *Tiers Parti,* and a Danish minister might appear in Saxony. Stepney also complained that the warning given was too short: it was only four days before the courier was due to leave, and three weeks before the Lieutenant General was to begin the march. There would be no time for Stepney to receive an answer from England, and he would therefore be guided by the counsel given to Ham by the Grand Pensionary of Holland. Sending a copy of his dispatch to Vernon, Stepney voiced his fears as to his own future:

> You will see by my relation to Mr. Secretary that it is an even lay whether we sink or swim. . . . I shall think myself happy when I have once gott out of Saxony, where I have been very unlucky from the beginning, and fear their end still worse. . . . If there is no further use to be made of me for the present, I have been 4 years successively out of old England and shall not be sorry to visit my friends and wait for another vacancy.

Would Vernon please therefore inform Montagu, to whom Stepney had no time to write.[25]

On 9 March (n.s.) Stepney wrote officially to Trenchard to report interference with the post of himself, Benebourg and Ham. Letters had been kept

> 7 hours in their hands . . . ye marks . . . were too apparent on ye Seals; (for on mine there were yet remaining 10 or 15 grains of Quicksilver, wch they forgott to rub off after they had made ye false Impression).

All three ministers complained to Gerstorff and Knoch and wished the complaint laid before the Elector

> whom (wee were certain) was not capable of having given orders for so treacherous a Practice.

Such an act was not, after all, consistent with the Elector's public statements of wishing to entertain 'a good Correspondence and Friendship' with the King of England and the States General and with the Emperor. The three foreign diplomats absented themselves from court for two or three days, but could not continue to do so for fear of making a bad situation worse.

> The Fact, My Lord, is evident; The injury notorious & ye consequences might be dangerous. But wee are in a nice conjuncture when too high a Resentment is not seasonable but had better be dissembled, if wee cou'd gain our main point by bringing yr Elr into the allyance; of wch I can yet give no certainty.

In cypher, Stepney reported the violent behaviour of the Elector who, losing his temper, had attacked his mother, his brother and his wife. He had since been let blood.

A compromise had been suggested, whereby Schöning might regain his liberty but would not be allowed to participate in civil or military affairs until the war had ended. The Elector, not satisfied, decided to write to the Emperor again, but promised the allied diplomats that he would not recall his troops until he had received final advice from Vienna. Hence Stepney ended his dispatch to London in somewhat more optimistic fashion, although he related another intrigue: the Elector had received, via Holzbrink, a copy of a letter which Benebourg had written to Count Kinsky [now Court Chancellor at Vienna, replacing Stratmann] and which had been delivered personally to Kinsky by Lt. Col. Carlowitz, the Elector's own messenger to Vienna, but who, it was now rumoured, might be working against Schöning.

> There is nothing but intrigue and treachery in this whole business of Schöning's [complained Stepney] and it will be happy for us whenever wee get out of it.[26]

By mid-March Stepney had received news from Blathwayt and from his banker Franc Stratford that Whitehall had authorised the payment to the Saxons of the remaining subsidy for the year 1693.

This amounted to 33,333 Reichsthaler, 8 groschen, and had been due at the time of the Leipzig Fair the previous autumn. Stepney decided to pay over the money at once: it was of course the easiest course for him to take, and would ensure at least his temporary popularity in Dresden. He justified his action in a letter to Blathwayt:

> If the Elr sticks firme to the Allyes, for this year at least, (as I believe he will) it will be sufficient to justify wt I have done: if not I do not know if our homely Proverb of honesty is ye best Policy, will be enough for my excuse.

Luckily for Stepney the new Secretary of State, the Earl of Shrewsbury, wrote to him some days later that the King had approved his action. Stepney took the trouble to obtain an acquittance from 'young Bosen' that the sum promised by King William under the terms of the 1693 treaty had been paid in full. Shrewsbury also told Stepney that the King, having read his dispatch describing the Elector's threat to withdraw his troops from the Rhine, forbade Stepney to leave Dresden, whatever Benebourg's action might be in the matter. Stepney was to hold on, and do all he could to prevent the withdrawal of the troops. On 20 March (n.s.), Stepney had another interview with John George IV in order to present the King's formal reply to New Year greetings. It was a somewhat barbed encounter. The Elector complained that intrigues were still continuing, and Stepney knew that suspicion had by now fallen on Baron [Johann] Goertz of Hesse-Cassel, [d. 1699], who had been sent temporarily by King William to represent him in Vienna. The Elector assured Stepney that his troops were ready for the homeward march, and repeated his insistence that he would not be made a dupe.[27]

During the tense days at the end of March 1694, when the arrival of couriers from Vienna was so eagerly awaited in Dresden, George Stepney was involved in an incident which he did not at any time report to his superiors in London. It so happened that a private letter from an unidentified individual in Dresden (let us call him Mr X) fell into the hands of Johann, Count Clary & Aldringen, the Emperor's former Ambassador in Saxony. Clary had collaborated with Sir William Colt during 1693 in the abortive efforts to persuade John George IV to join the Grand Alliance. When these negotiations fell through Clary retired to his estates at Teplitz in Bohemia, where he appears to have been residing when he wrote a hurried personal letter to the Emperor (undated) enclosing the missive which had reached him owing to a postmaster's mistake, he claimed. The text seemed serious enough for Clary to have it copied by his eldest son (not by a secretary), because the handwriting of the original was difficult to read.

Mr X wrote in French to his correspondent in Vienna. The letter was written from Dresden on 12/22 March 1694 [see full text at Appendix IV]. Mr X acknowledged a note which 'Monsieur de Stepney' had slipped to him at the moment of his arrival [*réception* – presumably at Court]. The remainder of the text is confusing: Holzbrink, whom the writer had never met, had returned to Dresden for one day only, and left again. Mr X was expecting a package to be brought by Holzbrink, which had never arrived. The recipient of the letter was begged to make good this omission. Mr X then referred to the fate of the unfortunate Willius, imprisoned by the Elector; and to a parcel of books which he had been able to retrieve from the claws of those who wished to confiscate them, along with some Lutheran Bibles. He indicated that the recipient of the letter was Swedish; and concluded with a curious reference to the house (or firm) of Mr Lemmel, the Saxon Paymaster-General.

It is possible to guess at the identity of both writer and recipient. (The text which has survived is unsigned.) Count Horn was the Swedish Envoy in Vienna in 1694, and his Resident [i.e. the second-in-command] was Ehrenburg, who had become a close friend of Stepney's during the latter's stay in the imperial city. Stepney wrote to Ehrenburg at the end of 1693 that he would render him any service, even to a false oath. Ehrenburg had used Stepney to transmit letters to Count d'Hona [into whose family Frise had married] and Count Sinzendorf – and these letters had been delivered. George had also discussed with his friend their respective and passing love-affairs, with friendliness and good temper. Hence the recipient of Mr X's letter seems likely to be either Ehrenburg himself, or Count Horn, having written to Mr X via Ehrenburg and Stepney.

And Mr X himself? The most likely possibility is Count Monceau. This man was a Huguenot who had been recommended to Stepney in 1693 by Sir William Colt, who described him as being in prison and as having 'lost all in the persecution.' Stepney responded by telling Colt that he knew all about Monceau: his crime was that he wrote and spoke too freely. He was too zealous a servant of Field Marshal Schöning, and for that reason had been imprisoned in Prague when his master was sent to the Spielberg. The date of Monceau's release from Prague is not known, but by March 1694, he may well have been in Dresden. It is probable also that he was the recipient of a letter which Stepney wrote shortly after his (Stepney's) arrival in Dresden. It is copied in to the letter-book, but is undated and the recipient is not named. This correspondent was contemplating going to France, but Stepney warned that it was madness to do so:

> If you are caught, you hang: if you arrive, you starve, which is almost the same.

And Stepney indicated that he was breaking off the correspondence.[28]

Was Stepney creating an escape-route for himself, in the event that France should prove victorious in the ongoing war? This seems likely – and Stepney was not the only Englishman to take out such an insurance. Marlborough is a case in point. So is Edmund Poley who from Turin was suspected of holding correspondence with James II at St Germain. At the start of 1694 the prospects for the Allies were not particularly hopeful. True, there was famine in France, but the previous campaign had been militarily disastrous and the odds between success and failure must have stood, as Stepney would have put it, at even lay. All really depended, as many realised, on the life and energy of King William. Should he fall, either in battle or by assassination, the whole situation in Europe would change. So it is not surprising that Stepney should seek to render small services to a Swedish friend who might, if necessary, help him in time of trouble.

On 29 March (n.s.) 1694 Stepney and Ham were summoned to Court to be told by the Saxon ministers that the Imperial Court in Vienna had thrown all the blame for Schöning's imprisonment on to the Allies. Both were enjoined to reply at once and both demurred, saying they would seek instructions. Stepney introduced a *chicane* [a delaying tactic] by requesting that the protocol [the document prepared by the Saxons] should be presented either in French or in Latin, not in its original German. The reason for the Saxon ministers' manoeuvre was quite clear to Stepney:

> their drift is to extort from us a Solemn Declaration that the King and the States neither do, nor have any way concerned themselves in Schöning's case, which Testimonyes they will send to Vienna and from thence load ye Emp^r with being the only Prince who obstructs wt they sollicit, when the other Allyes have cleared ymselves of this Aspersion.

The ministers got their protocol translated into Latin by the following morning, and again asked for an urgent response. Stepney continued:

> I told 'em there was no hast, for that after having kept us 7 months without making any proposition, they might reasonably allow us a day or two before wee replyed to one so captious as this was.

And George proceeded to quibble at the Latin translation.[29]

While Stepney and Ham were thus engaged, Benebourg finally told the Elector that the Emperor would not concede his demands. John George flew into a rage, sent orders for his troops to be recalled, and as suddenly countermanded his order. Once again he despatched a messenger (from the Schöning faction) to Vienna, and once again delay threatened. The man would reach Vienna in the middle of Holy Week and would therefore be unable to gain audience. Time was pressing, for arrangements for the summer campaign should already have been in hand. Yet another conference was called: after all Schöning could be released on conditions, and the Elector was ready to enter into new engagements. He required m/400 Reichsthaler. Benebourg replied that if he would provide 12,000 men (as before) with proportionable artillery and other necessaries, he would receive, for the duration of the treaty (*durante hoc foedere*):

Rx

100,000	from Assignations on the Circle of Upper Saxony
50,000	from the City of Frankfurt
50,000	from the Emperor's own exchequer
200,000	hopefully to be made good by the King and by the States General

Ham said he had orders from the States General to pay 50,000 Rx; and Stepney agreed to 100,000 Rx in the name of the King. A debate followed over the remaining 50,000 Rx. Eventually Benebourg promised one third of 50,000 Rx in the name of the Emperor; but Ham and Stepney insisted they had no orders as to the remainder. The Saxon ministers accused the maritime powers of great riches, and the King with starting the war: what would be the effect on the Allies, they asked, if the Elector recalled his troops?

Stepney responded with warmth that the King had never besieged Philippsburg, 'which action was certainly the beginning of the Warre'; nor would the King 'be more or less King of England for their 12,000 men.' The meeting broke up without any resolution.

On 7 April (n.s.), Benebourg visited Stepney and Ham separately, trying to get them to agree to pay between them two thirds of m/50 Rx. Both refused anew, though Stepney wrote hurriedly to Blathwayt to find out what were the King's wishes in the matter. At the end of his letter he noted that the Elector's expected visit to the healthful watering-place of Carlsbad had been postponed, because the Countess of Rocklitz had contracted smallpox.[30]

No-one at first took this latter event very seriously. By now Stepney had been joined by Heneage Montagu, whose schoolboy writing appears from time to time in the letter-book. Stepney enjoyed Heneage's company, and in due course he received from Charles Montagu payments towards his stepson's board and lodging.

But from his private letters Stepney had learned the worrying news that the King had spoken to Lord Lexington 'as if he was to go to Vienna.' And so George Stepney opened his heart to Father Vernon in London:

> I am really of opinion that his Maty's affairs require at that Court [i.e. Vienna] a man both of ability and Quality and soe I shall gladly renounce any pretensions I had of returning thither. However I must confess it happens odly [*sic*] that Mr. Cresset and his Lord should out me from all places where I had any reason to expect footing. Mr. Cresset you know (at least I know it) was night and day at my Ld Nottingham to be employed at Berlin while I was actually there and immediately upon Sir W Colt's death (whom I might have pretended to succeed as well in his hon^ble and gainfull positions as in this vexatious commission) he stept before me to the courts of Luneburgh because he had the advantage of running post to Loo. If his Lord serves me the same Onion and while I am drudging here, excludes me from returning to a Court where I had orders not to take leave, being only called aside per interim. I do not say this [is] hard (because I am perswaded his Maty's affairs may be bettered by the change, to whose service I always am ready to sacrifice my interest) but I may be allowed to call it Fatall and wt does not happen every day . . . . I shall be glad to be once settled at Ratisbon where I hope I shall be out of my Ld Lexington's and Mr. Cresset's reach.

Poor Stepney! He was indeed to be outed from Vienna by Robert Sutton, second Lord Lexington, whose only two qualifications as a diplomat were that he (like Johnston) was a personal friend of King William, and that he was rich. News from the imperial court would be sparse in the extreme after his arrival there: what little we know was transmitted by Stepney, to whom Lexington occasionally wrote. But Stepney was nothing if not a pragmatist, and once his bitter disappointment had had time to die down, he took to corresponding with Lexington cheerfully enough. He also met Lexington in the late summer of 1694, when the latter was able to charm the bristling little diplomat into a more agreeable frame of mind. Later on, Stepney made his peace with Cresset. Both these men were dependent on their diplomatic salaries, and could not afford to bear a grudge for any length of time.[31]

By 16 April (n.s.) the Countess of Rocklitz was dead.

Aπ το α

commented Blathwayt, when he heard the news. The Elector of Saxony was distraught, and ordered the court into mourning, which was unprecedented. Stepney, Ham and Benebourg agreed between themselves to disobey the command, but Ham broke the agreement and put on black. Stepney eventually donned half-mourning, appearing in a black waistcoat and stockings as he went to console the Countess's mother.[32]

Baron Goertz in Vienna had told Ham that he and Stepney had been quite correct in refusing to contribute to the 50,000 écus (or Rx) in dispute; but that the Emperor really could not find the money, and unless the King and the States paid up he (Goertz) did not see any other way of bringing the Elector of Saxony into the Grand Alliance. Moreover, the Dutch Grand Pensionary Heinsius had made the comment that 'the rest will be found in one way or another.' The treaty seemed to be on the verge of signature. Ham had got permission from the States to pay one third of 33,333 Rx, and Stepney was prepared to make the usual contribution from the King of two thirds without waiting for further instructions. By the end of April the French were gathering their forces at Landau. The Elector knew this, but announced that he would send no help to Prince Louis unless Frankfurt was attacked. Two days after making this negative statement John George himself fell gravely ill of the smallpox which had carried off his beloved Sibylla. A week later he too was dead.[33]

At once court and society in Dresden were thrown into confusion. The heir to the Electorate was John George's brother, Duke Frederick Augustus (1670-1733), later to become known as Augustus the Strong. Stepney had already written of him that he was

> of a Mercurial Volatile spirit; who will content himself with his Women, his Wine, his Exercises, & his frolicks & in all appearances will leave the menagement of affairs to one Baron [Christian August] Haxthuysen ... who will govern as absolutely here, as Mr. Dankelman does at Berlin; and whereas this Gentleman has strong inclinations for Denmark and is no enemy to France, the prospect is not very agreeable.[34]

The new Elector lost no time. The day after his brother's death he received compliments, was proclaimed by the soldiery and put the mother of Countess Rocklitz under arrest. Stepney wrote:

> Certainly never men were engaged in so extraordinary (and as I may say fatal) a Negotiation as ours has been, and accompanied with such surprizing accidents in which the Divine hand has been very visible.

Schloss Moritzburg, Dresden.

For it was rumoured that John George had been twice married, and that his true wife had been Sibylla.

To Stepney, it now seemed as though the world had opened up to him. Diplomats were accredited personally to monarchs or princes, and the death of a sovereign negated all letters of appointment, which had to be sought afresh for the new ruler. Stepney immediately wrote to London, begging the character of Envoy, which had been promised to him. Also he suggested that the 6,000 Dollars (Rx) which had been assigned to him as a bribe for 'the Lady' should now be used by himself to cover the usual Envoy's allowance of £500 for equipage, plus a quarter's advance of his 'ordinary' [allowance]. He was at present in deep mourning 'with cloak & cap.' He did not know who would be appointed as Saxon envoy to the King, but Baron Eck had already been named to undertake the similar duty at the imperial court.

Stepney hoped to be allowed to present the Garter to the new Elector, because he had had experience in such a ceremony under Johnston in Berlin. He seemed to enjoy the favour of the new Elector, who had retired to the Moritzburg. When Stepney went there to compliment, he and two other envoys were invited to dine at the private table.[35]

But negotiations for Saxon troops to carry on the war were once again delayed. Frederick Augustus quickly appointed commissioners to treat with the foreign delegates. The same ministers, Gerstorff, Knoch and Bosen appeared as previously, together with Grand Marshal Haugwitz and the new Elector's favourite, Haxthuysen. Benebourg immediately began to make difficulties, saying he was awaiting fresh instructions from Vienna. Stepney intervened to point out that, the season being so advanced, if they could not complete within two or three weeks any treaty would be to no purpose, and money would be wasted. There was no progress, and a week later (25 May, n.s.) Stepney urged Gerstorff to hasten matters, claiming that the King, once arrived in Holland, would expect an account from him (Stepney) that all was completed and would be very angry if this were not the case. Stepney might even be recalled. All this was pure speculation on Stepney's part, but had the excellent result that Gerstorff told him the truth about the negotiations, to the effect that Benebourg together with Ilten (the Hanoverian envoy) had been undertaking private negotiations with Saxony regarding the granting to Hanover of the Ninth Electorate, and the re admission of the Emperor, as King of Bohemia, with full powers into the Electoral College. Benebourg had also made a new demand on Saxony, that 5,000 of the 12,000 men promised should remain on duty over the winter to guard the Rhineland at the Elector's own expense. Other conditions of the treaty were as before, it being assumed that the maritime powers would still share in the provision of the 'missing' 50,000 Rx.[36]

In England the Earl of Shrewsbury had been made a Duke. (Stepney at once asked for instructions how to address him.) Charles Montagu had been (unwillingly by King William) advanced to be Chancellor of the Exchequer and a privy counsellor. Blathwayt had written that all seemed set for Stepney's own promotion.[37]

Eventually the treaty with Saxony was concluded on 6/16 June 1694, (and Stepney got it back-dated to 23 May (n.s.), the date when Benebourg had signed on behalf of the Emperor the latter's treaty with Saxony). Stepney, in his own eyes, had succeeded in two points: together with Ham he had refused consent to the King's making up a proportion of the 50,000 Rx in dispute, because he knew the Elector had already agreed to join the Grand Alliance in the treaty which Benebourg had concluded. Secondly, Stepney had refused to commit the King to support the Elector of Saxony in internal disputes within the Empire. Stepney was referring to Saxony's pretensions to the Duchy of Saxe-Lauenberg, which in no way was the concern of the King of England. Within two days of the signing of the treaty, Stepney had had prepared by his secretaries a 63 page document containing 25 appendices, which he transmitted to the Duke of Shrewsbury to enable his Grace to follow the whole course of the negotiations with Saxony, from the year 1693 onwards.[38]

Yet despite this immense labour, and despite Shrewsbury's own warm recommendation to the King of Stepney's ability, the latter was once more to be a disappointed man. He thanked Vernon for his part in getting Shrewsbury to recommend him to the King (which

Blathwayt had thought might contribute towards his appointment as Envoy), but he added gloomily:

> I do not build upon it because I have a Dutchman to deal withall, Mr. Ham who without doubt has sollicited my Ld Portland that he may not be overtopp'd by me, and Mr. Keppel who has been named to make the compliment of condolence here, tho I am upon ye place, and the Elector has sent no person to his Maty with the notification.

Stepney's forebodings were fully justified. Within a few days he heard from Blathwayt:

> I have ventured to delay yr credentialls till I could have ye King's Determination concerning yr Title & Character, wch now I am sorry to tell you is not according to my wishes; for altho his Maty has expressed himself very kindly towards you, yet he has been pleased to say he did not think fitt to alter yr Title; so that I am forced to dispatch yr credentialls as they were before.

And in another letter Blathwayt had added:

> I was not mistaken in my apprehension that until Mr. Keppel be actually dispatched to ye Court of Saxony (wch will not be till we have a Minister from thence) his Maty would not be brought to give you ye Title of Envoy.[39]

Now, Stepney's one thought was to leave Dresden. He had no wish to meet Keppel, and part of his desire for a 'character' had been for its protection from Schöning's arrogance when the latter arrived in Dresden. Stepney also begged his superiors to excuse him from attendance on the Elector of Saxony if Frederick Augustus went to meet the Elector of Brandenburg. Without a character, Stepney would be 'oddly looked upon.'

In only one way could Stepney revenge himself on an unkind world. He had previously complained of being seriously out of pocket:

> I have not touch'd a penny these 9 months: I am a year in arrears for Extraordinaries and have not yet rec'd what should have been due upon the Tallyes which were struck upon my removing from Vienna; so that at this time [8 June (n.s.) 1694] I have near 1400ll [£1,400] owing to me, which is half more than I am worth.

Nevertheless three days later news came from England that

> the Treasury has pay'd me 956ll that was due to me and now owe me no more than one quarter of my ordry allowance and half a year's extries.

He confided to Prior:

> Since my Project of Envoy will not go Down, I will revenge myself by a Bill of Extryes wch shall be as long and as extravagant as a Taylors Bill.

And he planned to ask Montagu to get him the reversion of some employment in England which might become vacant.[40]

VIII *Hope Deferred*

(From Dresden to the Hague, August–November 1694)

<u>The Duke of Shrewsbury to Stepney</u>

Whitehall, 26 June (o.s.) 1694

I have received your very acceptable letter of the 8th inst. & am obliged to you for the paines you have taken to give me so full & clear account of the Rise & Progress of your Negotiations. . . . I don't doubt but his Maᵗʸ will bee very well satisfyd with your Care & Address in Executing his Orders, & that hee will not onely think you fitt to be continued in his Service, but . . . to be advanced to a higher & more advantageous Character Which (I assure you) I shall Industriously promote.[1]

For the time being, in August 1694, Stepney had to remain in Saxony. The signing of the treaty was not the end of the affair. Ratifications had to be sought by all parties. The Emperor and the Elector exchanged theirs very quickly: their two cities were after all only four days' ride apart. Schöning was to begin his journey home as soon as the Saxon ratification reached Vienna. The process took longer between Saxony and Holland or England. Stepney was anxious that the seals for the ratified treaty should be enclosed in silver boxes. This was to protect the wax from the heat of the summer. Needless to say, the London office took no notice of this advice – doubtless silver boxes were too expensive, and could have been adapted for private use – but when the ratified treaty turned up in Dresden not only were the seals damaged, but there was a mistake in the final drafting: Stepney's and Ham's names were omitted from the proper place and the Saxon ministers' names inserted instead. Stepney was furious about these errors, which he had to explain away to the Saxon officials.[2]

From his house opposite the Dresden Guildhall [*Rathaus*] Stepney could see '*la Générale*' – Countess Rocklitz' mother – being conducted there to answer charges of witchcraft. Stepney forecast that she would be tortured, and possibly executed as a witch. The process against her was made at the behest of John George IV's wife and mother, who set no bounds on their revenge.[3]

The funeral of John George took place in pouring rain. Stepney described the scene which followed:

> As soon as they came out of ye Church, the Soldiers and Officers turned their Swords and arms upwards & of a sudden the Scene changed from Mo[u]rning to Homage.

The crowds, repeating the oath, held up two fingers:

> wch here they cut off for Perjury, as they do ears in England.[4]

Stepney also wrote to Portland, from whom he had received an unexpected letter, since Portland usually corresponded with his fellow-countryman, Ham. However the latter was expected to return to Berlin, and Stepney would be left in Dresden as the sole English/ Dutch representative. Stepney answered the great man politely, but pointed out the various 'inconveniences' he had suffered, not enjoying the title of Envoy in Saxony, and having been exposed to the caprice of the late Elector, who had thought him an enemy of Schöning. But he (Stepney) had overcome his difficulties and finished the business he had come about. He told Portland that his character had not been increased on the death of the late Elector: therefore he had asked to be employed at another station. He repeated his complaint at having been given no opportunity to improve his circumstances, but said he would accept whatever the King should decide. He then sent a copy of this missive to Blathwayt, pointing out truthfully that he had not been 'meal-mouthed' in writing to Portland, but had spoken his mind freely.[5]

Bad fortune continued to dog Stepney during the summer. His relationship with Blathwayt was on the wane, as he admitted to Charles Montagu, to whom he wrote in thanks for the early dispatches to his affairs which had been given by the Treasury. No doubt Blathwayt was by this time weary of the stream of letters which he received from Stepney, usually pointing out how badly he had been treated. Nevertheless Blathwayt had not told Stepney that a vacancy had occurred in the Secretary's office in Whitehall. Had George known this, he would have expressed himself more forcefully in favour of a post in England.

A further disappointment occurred when Stepney's request for a secular fellowship at Trinity College, Cambridge was turned down by the Master. George had had visions, after his gipsy life,

> of finding within yr Walls *Otium cum dignitate*, and a quiet Retreat.

But it was not to be.[6]

On 19 August (n.s.), Field Marshal Schöning returned in triumph to Dresden, making his entry with 50 horse grenadiers as well as many supporters from his own party. He went briefly to his own house, and was then carried in a chair by four men to call on the Elector, where he stayed for an hour. Stepney, who described the scene both to Shrewsbury and to Count Frise, said that in Dresden 'everyone' was waiting to see what everyone else would do, *vis-à-vis* Schöning. Stepney asked for advice as to his own behaviour. He was told to be polite, but no more. His own business in the city was to distribute presents of up to m/12 or m/13 Rx, following the completion of the treaty, his own reward from the Elector being a diamond ring valued at 800 Crowns. He later habitually wore this ring, and eventually bequeathed it to his cousin and protégé Charles Whitworth (1676-1725).[7]

In mid-August Stepney was told he could go to Zell to meet Lord Lexington, who was on his way to Vienna, and then travel to Het Loo to report to the King. George hastily prepared to leave Dresden. First, however, he encountered Schöning, and told Blathwayt on 31 August (n.s.):

> This minute Feld Marshall Schöning has sent me a statle [stately] compliment . . . it consists in this: that I had [i.e. he had] sent 3 times to give me notice of his arrival, but he supposes either by the negligence of his servants or mine, the message was not rightly delivered: that the Character he has heard of me makes him desire my acquaintance . . . and that he would be the first to visit me if his Indisposition would allow of it.

And Stepney did go to visit the old man, sending a long account of the meeting to Blathwayt. Schöning actually returned Stepney's call, but not without an ulterior motive. This was to allay suspicion that he had caused a recent sudden withdrawal of Saxon troops from the Rhine, which had been ordered by the Elector on the advice of his commander, General Reuss, owing to lack of forage and provisions for the men. The incident caused a great furore among the Allies. Prince Louis had planned an offensive across the Rhine, in which Saxon troops were involved. Their sudden withdrawal towards Heidelberg wrecked his plans and he was understandably angry. So was the King. He expressed his wrath to Count Frise, who had joined him in Flanders for the summer campaign. Frise was charged to convey a regal rebuke to the Saxon Elector.

Stepney became involved in the matter because he had written from Dresden to Frise on 11/21 September, that the blame, in the Saxon court, was being fixed on 'young Bosen' who, as *aide-de-camp*, had presented orders for the withdrawal to the Elector just as the latter was leaving to go hunting. Frederick Augustus therefore had not had time to read carefully the paper he was asked to sign. Stepney remarked that 'others' had indeed charged Schöning with the orders for withdrawal. The Field Marshal was supposed to have signed an oath [*Revers*] in Vienna, preventing him from interfering in military affairs. Stepney had asked Count [Alois] Harrach, the new young imperial envoy at Dresden, to shew him a copy of the oath. Harrach claimed that the Imperial Vice-Chancellor had refused to let him have a copy, and that he (Harrach) was completely without instructions as to his behaviour towards Schöning. Stepney commented that he himself did not know what to believe about the matter.[8]

On 5 September, Blathwayt wrote to Stepney from the camp near Deinse [about 60 km west of Brussels] that Lexington was expected to visit Zell on 19 September. The King wished Stepney to meet him (Lexington) there. He should tell the Elector of Saxony and his ministers of this appointment. This letter was followed two days later by another command from the King, who wished Stepney to obtain audience of the Elector of Saxony and ask him about the disappearance of Count [Philip Christoph] Königsmarck, believed to be the lover of Sophia Dorothea, the Electoral Princess of Hanover [the wife of the future George I of England]. Königsmarck had left Hanover in order to take up Saxon service. His sister was the reigning mistress of Elector Frederick Augustus. But, mysteriously, the Count had vanished. King William's instruction to Stepney was that he should persuade the Elector of Saxony not to quarrel with Hanover over the affair.[9]

Stepney saw the Elector on 17 September (n.s. – a Monday), and spoke to his brief. The Elector told him he only wished an enquiry made into Königsmarck's disappearance, lest he should have fallen into the hands of private enemies. Stepney did not pursue the matter.

Indeed, he was itching to be gone, for he left Dresden on the evening of the 17th, and 'ran post' three days and nights to reach Brunswick. He was not the only traveller during the late summer month of September. Sir Paul Rycaut had written at the end of August that he hoped to meet Stepney, Lexington and Cresset at Zell, 'so that there will be the 4 of us together.' Now Cresset, who was accredited to the Duke of Zell, was not overjoyed at the prospect of any such meeting, and only hoped that the Treasury would enable him to entertain his visitors. In the event, Rycaut's happy expectations were not fulfilled. At Brunswick Stepney found a note

Palace of Het Loo, Apeldoorn (1689) shewing the Fountain of Venus. [Photo: E Boieijinga (no. 6f88045).] By kind permission of Palace Het Loo, National Museum, Apeldoorn, the Netherlands.

from him to say that he (Rycaut) and Lexington had been at Wolfenbuttel, but had gone on to Ebstorff [the Duke of Zell's hunting-lodge some 70 km north of Brunswick]. Stepney decided to follow, as soon as he had obtained fresh horses.[10]

Stepney passed through Zell, where he found Cresset on the point of departure for Holland. George was delighted to have confirmed the permission already given to himself to visit Loo. On 21 September he reached Ebstorff, and was pleased with his reception there both by Lexington and the Duke of Zell. He found time to write to a certain Madame Phlug, copying for her a little poem which, he said, he had found engraved on the window of the miserable inn where he had changed horses:

> *Souvenez vous de ma constance extreme*) *Le Rhime ne*
> *Souvenez vous de vostre engagement*) *vaut rien mais*
> *Souvenez vous de moy et de ma peine*) *le Coeur est*
> *Souvenez vous ne changer point d'Amant*) *tendre*
> *je suis resolu d'estre toute ma vie, Madame'*
> *Vostre tres humble et*
> *tres obeissant Serviteur.*

But there is no signature; and the letter was copied into the book by a secretary.[11]

On Tuesday 2 October (n.s.), both Stepney and Lexington were again at Zell. The latter – although he was en route to Vienna – had just received King William's permission to come to Holland. The two diplomats planned to set out early on 3 October, and travel via Hanover, where they hoped to be in time to dine with the Elector and the Electress [Sophia], and then continue to Hamlin where they should encounter Baron Goertz. All three would then continue towards Loo. Stepney included in his letter to Blathwayt the little news he had so far gathered about the unfortunate Sophia Dorothea:

> The French person who has been with the Electoral Princesse is returned and tells her parents that she is kept under very strict confinement and is mighty melancholy.[12]

For the rest of the month of October 1694 there is no word of or from George Stepney, or of any visit to Het Loo. According to Count Frise, Stepney was in the Hague on 16 October; but George's own letters do not resume until 2 November. By that time he knew that the King had refused him permission to return to England, telling him that he was needed in Saxony. Stepney at once set to work to gain an increase in character and allowances. But he was not consistent in his demands, claiming the title of Envoy (with appropriate allowances) from the Duke of Shrewsbury, but admitting to Charles Montagu that what he really desired was the allowance of £5 a day *without* the expensive title. This last wish was of course a chimera.[13]

Busily he was corresponding with his sister for items – periwigs and gloves – to be sent from England, together with the latest edition of the Book of Country-dances, destined to please the Saxon court. And he had ordered a 'Wastcoat' to be made for him, at a cost of £20, for he must dress according to his new status. Lexington, Frise and Goertz of Hesse-Cassel all promised to back Stepney's cause with the Earl of Portland, and Blathwayt too had promised to second the appeal to the King.[14]

The monarch was delayed in the Hague by unfavourable winds, so Stepney hoped that his request would be fulfilled in Holland, leaving only the Privy Seal to be drawn in England. He told Vernon:

> I look upon myself to be born under a very happy Planett, and cannot sufficiently admire ye strange hitts I have met with, wch farr exceed wt I deserve or wt I ever durst propose to myself.[15]

Meanwhile the King entrusted to Stepney the task of negotiating with Baron Goertz an agreement whereby the Landgrave of Hesse-Cassel committed himself to providing a contingent of troops, over and above those which he was already bound to supply to the Emperor, for use against the common enemy. The King, for his part, agreed to pay a subvention to the Landgrave of 25,000 florins a month, for 12 months in the year, starting in January 1695 (n.s.). The exact number of the Landgrave's troops was not stated, [see Appendix IV]. This contract, signed by Stepney and Goertz on 4/ 14 November 1694 at the Hague, was an agreement after King William's own heart: it was concise and simple, and required neither ratification nor expensive presents to the officials involved.[16]

But even before the agreement was signed Stepney understood that his high hopes of promotion were unlikely to be realised. He wrote to Charles Montagu that although Blathwayt had told him to apply to Lord Portland, the more he (Stepney) did so, the less effort Blathwayt made on his behalf. Eventually Blathwayt presented Stepney's new credentials to the King with the vital words '*ablegare – ablegatum*' [appropriate to an Envoy] left blank, and the King himself completed the document with the style appropriate only to a Minister, at the allowance of £3 a day.[17]

George was bitterly disappointed, and particularly because he knew that Frise had already informed the Saxon Court that he (Stepney) would be returning in the 'quality' of Envoy. Once more, on 9 November, George applied again to Shrewsbury, begging the appointment of Envoy at least for Saxony. He knew he must travel first to Hesse-Cassel, but that post was not so important to him as the one where he was already known:

This letter to the Duke of Shrewsbury crossed with one to Stepney written in Whitehall by Father Vernon, who even then, in ignorance of the King's decision, was busy drawing up a Privy Seal as befitted an Envoy. Then he added that he hoped Stepney would not have to return to Dresden at once:

> Mr. Secretary Johnstone told me yesterday that your mother was newly dead. I am sorry to bee the Messenger of ill News.

And three days later that Jane

> was buryed last night & that melancholy Ceremony was performed with great Decency.[18]

Of George's immediate reaction to this sad news no word has survived.

IX *Diplomat, Soldier and Country-Gentleman*
(The Hague and Dresden, 1695)

<u>Stepney at Wesel to Lexington 13/23 Febr. 1695</u>

> I forgott to tell yr Lpp how they have used me: I have not ye Title of Envoy (I suppose because Ham wou'd not have it so) but I have 4ll [£4] a day and 300ll allow'd for equipage with no other Title than that of Minister to ye Courts of Sax^s and Hesse: wch I am very well satisfy'd with.[1]

On hearing of the death of his mother George Stepney got leave to travel to England and probably crossed the Channel about 7/17 November 1694. He would have hastened to the 'Black Boy' at Charing Cross to comfort his sisters in their loss. His own grief was short-lived: he wrote a spirited account to Lord Lexington of a ball which was given in Whitehall, the letter being dated 21 November (o.s.) 1694. His professional status seemed assured, for he was accorded an hour-long audience of Queen Mary, shortly before she sickened and died; and during the mourning period which followed he described her illness and death in detail to Sophia, Electress of Hanover, from whom in due course he received an acknowledgement.[2]

King William, shattered by his wife's death, once more took up his war preparations. He had wished Stepney to depart as early as 15 December (o.s.). But the latter was still pursuing his application for the title and allowances of Envoy, which (as shewn above) was once more refused. To the Duke of Shrewsbury, as to Blathwayt, Stepney addressed a list of nine topics on which he requested firm instructions. For instance, was he to go first to Dresden or to Cassel? Would money be available for subsidies, or must he make excuses? If the Elector of Saxony wished his men to serve in Flanders (as had been proposed by the Imperial Envoy in London [Count Auersperg]), would this be agreeable to the King; and what if the Elector, and/or General Schöning, should wish to serve personally in Flanders? Finally (hopefully) was there any prospect of a return for the nine Polish horses given to the King by the Elector of Saxony last summer?

All this took time: Stepney got his instructions and took leave of the King at Kensington, where he also saw Portland. The Earl told him of a new project by the Elector Frederick Augustus of Saxony to serve, not in Flanders, but on the Middle Rhine and to command all troops there, including those of Hesse-Cassel.

At this time liaison between King William and the Emperor was confused. There was no English Envoy in Vienna: Lexington, the new incumbent, had only reached Ratisbon by 25 December (n.s.). Ham, in Dresden, was reporting to Portland. Count [Alois] Harrach, the Emperor's envoy in Dresden, had travelled to Vienna and waited there three weeks to hear the King's (negative) decision as to the Middle Rhine, which was conveyed to the Emperor via Count Auersperg in London.[3]

Stepney is next heard of at Wesel, on 11/21 February 1695. From there he wrote to Lexington an account of his travels. The King would not let him use the pacquet-boat, so he had taken the yacht *Centurion* which landed him at Ostend because the ports of Holland were ice-bound. Before starting the voyage he had been wind-bound at the Nore for 15 days, during which time he had enjoyed the company of a lady to whom he afterwards referred as 'my Duchesse' but without revealing her name. The crossing from Margate to Ostend, once started, took only 10 hours and he landed on 1/11 February. Then he went on to Bruges, Ghent, Antwerp (where he laid in some champagne), Bois-le-Duc, Gravellines, and so to Cleves, without incident. But at Cleves he had to cross the ice-bound Rhine (which he described as 'very frightening'), and then he had to wait at Wesel for two days until his own caleche arrived from Loo.[4]

Then Stepney continued 'post' over eight days and nights between Wesel and Leipzig. He had been instructed to travel via Cassel (as usual to discuss the provision of troops), but he found he had missed King William's friend Baron Goertz; and from the Chamberlain he begged to be excused visiting the Landgrave in person, pleading a 'defluxion of the eyes'. From Leipzig he admitted to Vernon that he had had bitter weather to contend with. Nevertheless between Wesel and Lippstadt he had written a poem on the death of the Queen; and he wished Vernon to send this on to his publisher, Jacob Tonson. The poem was acclaimed by his contemporaries. [See also Chapter XXIII.]

Stepney reached Dresden on 20 February/2 March 1695, but

the Elector was unable to see him, that Prince having his time taken up with tennis and Countess Königsmarck (the reigning mistress). However Stepney did make contact with senior Saxon ministers and with the Emperor's envoy, Count Harrach. He refused an invitation from Schöning, pleading still the cold in his eye. Although the Elector's project of a Middle Rhine army had been turned down by King William, Frederick Augustus had received from the Emperor the offer of the supreme command in Hungary. Schöning was blaming the Dutch Envoy Ham for not reporting the Rhine project in sufficiently attractive terms to the King; and a further messenger (Ruland) was sent to London, who left Dresden four days before Stepney's arrival, so that he was unable to stop him. By 26 February/8 March Stepney had seen the Elector, and reported accordingly to the Duke of Shrewsbury. The Elector wished to send 6,000 men to Hungary and keep 6,000 in reserve in Saxony, and be paid the full subsidy for 12,000 men. So Stepney's first weeks in Dresden in the spring of 1695 were taken up with the question of subsidies: how much should be paid for how many men, and where the troops should serve. Stepney had already told Count Harrach that only half the subsidy would be paid by the King and the Dutch if only half the agreed number of men arrived in Flanders. Schöning was doing his best to create bad blood between Stepney and Ham, by telling Stepney that Ham had tried to persuade the Earl of Portland to get Stepney sent to Ratisbon, thereby leaving himself (Ham) as the sole representative of the maritime powers in Dresden. Stepney already knew this, and ignored the general's insinuations. Schöning had also had the temerity to send back to Vienna six demands concerning himself: these included the annulment of his oath [*Revers*] not to take part in civil or military affairs, and agreement that he should have the high command of the imperial army, under the Elector.[6]

While Stepney was somewhat embarrassed by Schöning's effusiveness towards himself, he found the Elector Frederick Augustus a much easier man to deal with than his predecessor. Their good relationship was begun when the Elector discovered that Stepney had brought with him to Dresden two dozen bottles of champagne, stuffed into the caleche. The Elector promptly sucked Stepney dry, who had to order replenishments from Antwerp. But Stepney had been instructed to plead the cause of Count Frise, who had resigned his Saxon commission in order to stay with the King in Flanders. As soon as this subject was raised the Elector cooled visibly and snapped that Frise was expected to return to Dresden,

Het Loo, c. 1700, colour engraving. Published by Petrus Schenk (1600-1719). On loan from the Stichting Historische Verzamelingen van het Huis oranje-Nassau. Photo: R Mulder (no. 4f96104).

according to orders. Meanwhile Count Harrach was in difficulties in regard to Schöning. The latter was still under the Emperor's severe displeasure, therefore the Count was unable to meet him officially. The Elector invited all the Allied foreign ministers to attend a conference about the forthcoming campaign, and had included Schöning among his own representatives. Harrach countered by handing the Saxon ministers a 'protocoll' which required a written answer, and thus the conference was delayed.[7]

With Lexington, now in Vienna as Envoy, Stepney had started a lively correspondence (on his side) purveying reams of advice. He also told the noble Lord that he had received nearly incomprehensible instructions from the Duke of Shrewsbury, and these he set out, perhaps as much for his own edification as Lexington's:

> As far as I can comprehend they mean in few words, That the King is willing the Elr shou'd send 6 or 8,000 men to Hungary: but he expects the Empr should pay them, unless he sends back the Brandenburgers. 2/ly, as to ye remaining 4 or 6,000, the King is willing to pay for them in proportion to their number (whereby I understand after ye rate of m/12 for m/100 Rx wee are to pay, m/50 Dollars for 6,000 & m/33 for 4,000) provided they be sent

under Prince Lewis (which I despair of) & if it cannot be, between the Meuse & the Moselle rather than they should loyter at home.

And Stepney added his own comment on the foregoing:

The reason why ye Elr of Brand. is willing to leave his Troops under the Elr of Saxony's comand, is plainly this:

Brand. has contributions allotted him on the Dutchy of Luxemburg wch he is afraid the Saxons wou'd dispute with him if the[y] should chance to act between the Meuse & the Moselle . . . besides Saxy has pretensions on Berg, D. Juliers & Cleves, wch makes Brand. unwilling to see our forces in yt Neighbourhood.[8]

At the beginning of April, Stepney was convinced that the Elector of Saxony would accept the independent command in Hungary, but he had no intention of following him thither. Hungary was already well known as 'the graveyard of the Germans.' As soon as Count Harrach's treaty for troops was concluded Stepney's appointment to Saxony would come to an end, so he had to look further afield. True, he was also commissioned to go to Cassel, but there would be little work for him there once the campaigning season had begun, for the Landgrave would march his troops wherever King William required them. Somewhat surprisingly (considering his previous dislike of Lexington) he applied to that peer, 'Wt say you, my Lord, will you have me at Vienna?' and he went on to claim that he would maintain his own table, family and equipage, for his friends in London would see to it that his £4 a day would continue. But Stepney wished Lexington's approbation before continuing in the matter.[9]

In making this suggestion Stepney was correct in his view that the English embassy in Vienna provided enough work for two men, particularly when one of them was as lazy as Lexington. (News from the imperial city is sparse in the extreme until Lexington's cousin and successor, (Sir) Robert Sutton took over the writing of dispatches.) Yet, now that Stepney had become used to an independent command, it is difficult to believe that he would have settled happily into the rôle of 'underpuller.' Lexington did make an application on Stepney's behalf, but in such lukewarm terms that Blathwayt (who himself had his eye on Stepney's help) did not lay the matter before the King. And Lexington also wrote to Stepney in words which illustrate perfectly the difference in status between the two:

My dear Stepney, May 4th

I am just come away from Laxembourg . . . yr Treaty [he means Harrach's treaty] is not ratify'd nor can I get ye sight of it, but we

hope twill be on Friday but dare not press too much for fear they
shou'd [? dunn – word omitted] us for ye subsidys: I writt this
post to Mr. Blathwayt about yr coming to Vienna, and hope wee
may succeed, but to tell you ye truth, I dare not press too much,
for shou'd little Willy smoak that we have conceived it, and desire
it, he will never let it be, I know him so well. Deare Stepney I
thank you for your verses
Adieu
and without a compliment
think you really deserve a
medall.

Lexington's final comment was shrewd: but at no time would George
Stepney have committed the *lèse majesté* of referring to his
sovereign as 'little Willy', for George was dependent upon his
emoluments, whereas Lexington was not.[10]

On 10 May (n.s.) the Emperor's ratification of Count Harrach's
treaty reached Dresden, and was exchanged with the Saxon one
the following day. Eight thousand Saxons were to serve in Hungary
and 4,000 were to remain at home. None was to go to Prince Louis
on the Upper Rhine and none to Flanders. Both Stepney and Ham
had refused to release any subsidy for the troops destined for
Hungary, but they paid the arrears of subsidy for the year 1694.
Both took audiences of congé with the Elector on 11 May, for he
was on the point of leaving for Carlsbad and was not expected to
return to Dresden before going on to Vienna to take command of
his troops. The Elector made a compliment to the King, and
expressed the hope that the latter would be disposed to give a
favourable answer regarding subsidies. Stepney said he was
awaiting instructions and would go to Carlsbad if he had good news.
It is not clear what excuse he made to Frederick Augustus for not
accompanying him to Carlsbad: in fact he sent his secretary,
Plantamour, 'to patch up his health.' Stepney had already made a
further approach to the Elector on behalf of Count Frise, this time
via the Elector's favourite, Count [Christian August] Haxthuysen;
but the result was unfavourable and Stepney was advised to desist.
It is clear to the reader of Stepney's correspondence that his motive
in refusing to go to Carlsbad was to avoid the opprobium of the
Court for having refused the subsidies, and to escape the
disagreeable task of further promoting the cause of Count Frise.[11]

Despite Stepney's good standing with Count Harrach – they
were in and out of each other's houses in a joint attempt to help
Frise – he remained depressed and complained to Charles Montagu
that he felt abandoned by the English Court. At the end of May he

could not suppress a rebuke to Lexington:

My Lord, Dresden 20/30 May 1695

Out of the reall respect I bear yr Lp, I desired heartily to be with
you at Vienna, & did employ my best interest to obtain it: But I
find by ye answers I have rec'd to my letters, that your Lp has not
kept touch on yr side, & I have orders to keep ready for another
march: so that I must lose ye satisfaction I proposed myself of
being with you. You will know from Prior that ye King is arrived
at ye Hague: & I hope to be with him in Flanders within 3 weeks.
. . . Ehrembourg has been with me these 3 days: He goes away
towards Hann[ove]r this evening. Yr Post from Vienna is not yet
arrived; & ours is going away: so I must conclude, with my being
ever,
My Lord,
[etc.][12]

So Ehrenburg the Swede had been visiting with Stepney, and in a
private letter to an unidentified friend in Vienna George also
admitted to enjoying the company of the mysterious Monceau,
'*toujours le même Pelerin, Critique et Philosophe*', as he described
him. Nothing that took place in European courts during the Nine
Years' War remained secret for very long. Three months later, in
August 1695, Stepney's rival James Cresset was writing to John
Ellis [then Under-Secretary in London] of Stepney's known
friendship with Monceau who was 'Schöning's creature'; of the
known enmity between Schöning and Ham; and how Schöning had
flattered Stepney – 'ye little English minister'– into taking his
(Schöning's) side too vigorously. Cresset was referring to the events
of the previous year, when Schöning first arrived in Dresden on
release from captivity:

but this manadgement had like to have spoil'd Mr. Stepney, as I
found out last year at Loo by my Lord Portland and from ye King's
own mouth.

And Cresset had also sewn doubts in Ellis' mind as to Stepney's
friendship with the banker Franc Stratford, whom Cresset believed
to be a 'cunning and a dangerous fellow.'

Of course, Cresset was not a disinterested witness, but was
himself trying to ensure his future in an uncertain world.
Nevertheless rumours continued to circulate which were not
favourable to Stepney, and which may well have been the cause of
the King's reluctance to transfer him to another post.[13]

Meanwhile in London the Duke of Shrewsbury, owing to one
of his frequent periods of ill-health, had handed over the post of
Secretary of State to Sir William Trumbull (1639-1716), whose

Under-Secretary was John Ellis. Stepney wrote polite letters to
Trumbull to request patronage and also provided a very full account
of the situation in Saxony and of his own part in it. With Ellis,
Stepney was already on good terms, since the Under-Secretary took
up lodgings in Whitehall with George's sisters during the summer
of 1695. But with the King already in Holland, Stepney's taskmaster
was William Blathwayt, from whom he received a letter dated
10 May implying a rebuke from the King that he (Stepney) had not
accompanied the Elector to Carlsbad. Now George had no
alternative but to comply; but before he left Dresden two events
occupied his mind.[14]

The first was his pursuit of a debt owing to his banker Franc
Stratford by a Saxon gentleman named Planitz. Stepney chased the
defaulter by letter (in French). Whilst the detail is insignificant, his
tactics in the matter are interesting. He wrote that he was pursuing
the two-year-old debt in his capacity as a Minister of the King, on
behalf of one of the King's subjects. As soon as the debt was settled
[and it was!] he, Stepney, had no further interest in the matter. But
the Saxon had had the temerity to refer to Stepney as a 'scrivener'
(écrivain), thus implying he was no gentleman. This point Stepney
immediately seized on, pointing out that he was still in Dresden
and as a gentleman was ready to meet Planitz anywhere, at any
time. And, as he wrote to Stratford, should the matter be taken
further he (Stepney) would fight with pistolls, on foot, 'and the
Devills in it if I miss my mark.' Fortunately, there was no further
word from the Saxon and the debt was duly collected.[15]

Stepney's other and bigger concern, now that he knew he was
likely to be commanded to Flanders, was the matter of his equipage.
He sought the help of his friend Adam de Cardonnel (d. 1719)
whom he seems to have met for the first time in 1692 when he had
had his first audience of King William. Cardonnel was assisting
Blathwayt at that time, thus laying the foundations of his future
task as secretary to the Duke of Marlborough. Blathwayt was known
to drive his staff to the limits, and although Stepney had no wish to
offend the Secretary-at-War, he confided to Cardonnel:

> I must confess to so good a friend as you are, that I generally fall
> asleep before 3 in the morning and wou'd chuse to be his Servant
> at a distance, if that cou'd be compass'd without giving offence.[16]

On the subject of equipage, Stepney began a method of
correspondence which he was to follow throughout his career. That
is, he wrote an 'official' letter, which could be shewn to others,
accompanied by a fuller, private missive for the recipient's eyes

only. His plans for the campaign were lengthy and detailed, and accord a rare glimpse into his household arrangements. He proposed:

1) Myself with	3 Horses for my own riding
2) Mr Plantamour	1 Horse
3) Falconbridge	1 Horse
4) My little Dutch boy	1 Horse
5) My footman Morgan	1 Horse
Baggage	2 Horses
3 Grooms	3 Horses
8 people	12 Horses

Despite Stepney's assertion that he never wished to 'make a figure', his estimate above appears extravagant, and seems to have been reduced in practice. He was concerned about his secretary, Philip Plantamour, whom he wished to place with Blathwayt during the summer. John Falconbridge at the time was described as '*Maître d'Hotel et Valet de Chambre*'. and as a servant with whom Stepney did not wish to part. 'My little Dutch [i.e. German] boy' – another John – had been with Stepney for three years, could write an excellent hand and understood nothing of what he was copying. Morgan Price was a rogue, used to camp life and (unlike Falconbridge) no linguist.[17]

During the spring of 1695 Stepney was indulging in a little private trading. While he was in London at the end of 1694 Bruynincx had asked him to look for a beaver hat (Castor), and this Stepney now sent on to Bruynincx, noting that it had cost £3 or Rx 15. And via the former imperial envoy, Baron Benebourg, Stepney sent to Vienna a box containing four watches, two for Mr Huss from Brandenburg, one for Bruynincx and one for Ehrenburg. Each watch cost £11. Stepney's acquaintance from Hamburg days, John Storer, was now in Vienna with Lexington, and to Storer Stepney entrusted the distribution of the watches and the collection of the cash. He set out in detail the sums which Bruynincx owed him (in Reichsthaler): 21 Rx 8 gr[oschen] already owing; plus Rx 15 for the hat and Rx 55 for the watch, making Rx 91.8g in all. He pointed out that he was charging no commission![18]

By the end of May Stepney had his 'Loyns girt' and was prepared to liquor his boots for his impending move out of Saxony, but before leaving he could not avoid a call at Carlsbad to try to get the Elector to forgive and to reinstate Count Frise. Stepney arrived on 27 May/ 6 June, in time to attend a lavish masquerade which the Elector had commanded, in honour of his two mistresses, Countess Königsmarck and Fräulein Klengel. A building was erected at a cost of 2,000 Florins, designed only to endure for one day. It consisted of a large hall, with galleries, like an opera-house (as Stepney put it). The *retirades*, complete with beds, all favoured the act of love. Mirrors, torches and lights were sent from Dresden. The fact that during the preparations a floor collapsed, seriously injuring a workman, caused no diminution of the gaiety. A ballet was rehearsed, in which Countess Königsmarck took the part of Diana, and Madame Pflug was one of her six attendants.

Stepney did not neglect the object of his mission. He first saw Schöning and did his best to persuade the General to lay aside his persecution of Count Frise. Then George saw the Elector twice, and put as strongly as possible the King's case for wishing to retain Frise's services. All was to no avail. The Elector told Stepney firmly that Frise, in his disobedience and in resigning his command as [Saxon] Major-General, had defied his Prince. In honour he (the Elector) must demand his return. Stepney formed the impression that the Elector might well cause Frise to be kidnapped, in order to enforce his return to Saxony. 'Princes have long arms,' as Stepney put it to Blathwayt.[18]

On the day of his final audience of the Elector Stepney's mind was occupied by a more personal discouragement:

En partant de Mad^e Pl.[*sic*] Carlsbad le 8/18 juin 1695

Mad^e, Je suis assez bien ton homme pour souffrir de grand sangfroid qu'on me fasse Coeur, pourveu que cela soit avec meilleure grace et moins d'eclat que vous l'avez faite. Vous voyez Mad^e, par le plan cy-joint, qu'on monte à l'Amour avec difficulté et par plusieurs Degrez: mais helas le retour n'est pas de meme, puisque tout d'un coup on tombe dans le precipice. Me voyla, au pied de l'echelle, apres en avoir fait le rond. Je vous prievois, Mad^e, de ne plus songer à moy, mais cela n'est pas necessaire, puisque je voy trop bien que vous m'avez deja oubliée: De mon coté je tacheray d'eloigner de ma memoire tout ce qui me pourroit donner la moindre Idee de nos plaisirs et de vostre personne; Laquelle je rends sauve et saine et sans inquietude entre les mains du premier qui souhaitterez vous avoir: Car je ne suis plus tel que je l'ay été.

Vostre passionne serviteur

L'echelle de l'Amour[20]

On leaving Carlsbad (after the Elector of Saxony had departed for Vienna and Hungary) Stepney betook himself to Leipzig, where he lodged with *Bürgermeister* Steiger and enjoyed the company of the latter's two young daughters. There he received new instructions from Blathwayt. The commission to visit Hesse-Cassel had now

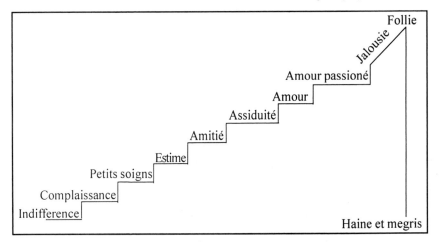

Echelle d'amour

been entrusted to Frise; and Stepney was told to prepare himself to travel by easy stages to Frankfurt and there await further orders. Stepney was disappointed. The steps he had taken to provide himself with an equipage had to be cancelled; and even his recreditif and the thought of a second valuable ring which he had received from Haxthuysen could hardly console him:

> To return home without an Employement (or at least the Prospect of one) will look very much like a disgrace in ye Eye of ye world and yt is next door to reall misfortune; wch I hope I have not deserved, because in all stations I have been in hitherto, I have had ye success to execute his Maty's comands, according to his mind, and therefore may expect not to be turned a-grazing.[21]

Indeed Stepney's prospects were bleak: if he returned to Berlin he would find his Dutch rival Ham already in residence, with the usual direct line to Lord Portland. There was Ratisbon: but that post was of little importance. The possibility of his becoming an underpuller to Lexington might be revived: yet Stepney did not now put any emphasis on this idea.

In fact Stepney remained in Leipzig until the beginning of July and used his days of leisure to write to his sisters and to his young cousin, Erasmus Lewis, about the latter's future prospects. He even carried on an amiable correspondence with Dr Johann Ham, about the disposal of the equipage. At last, on 22 June/2 July 1695, he received Blathwayt's definitive order to move, and set out for Frankfurt, travelling by way of Weissenfels, Naumburg, Erfurt, Gotha, Eisenach, Fulda and Hanau. He arrived on 1/11 July and

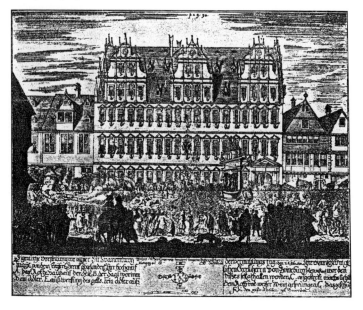

The Red House, Frankfurt am Main, c. 1688. From Die Baudenkmäler in Frankfurt am Main, 1914.Courtesy Stadtarchiv, Frankfurt am Main.

reported to Ellis that he had alighted into the famous 'Red House', one of the leading hostelries of Europe,

> where wee eat & drink chearfully & if ye King shall be pleas'd to allow me 4ˡˡ [£4] a day, for so doing (without cutting out other work for me) I think I have no great reason to complain.[22]

Immediately, Stepney found himself in the company of friends. An old acquaintance, Jemmy Sanderson, was travelling to Vienna in the company of Lexington's cousin and chaplain [Sir] Robert Sutton, who was later to succeed Lexington as a much more industrious Envoy in the imperial city. Then a lady arrived whose presence and favour gave Stepney adulatory pleasure: she was 'his' Electress, Eleanore Erdmuth Louise, the widow of John George IV of Saxony. Stepney hastened to pay his court.[23]

He was not completely idle in Frankfurt. He sent to all interested parties, that is to the Secretary of State, to Blathwayt and all the English ministers serving in Europe reports of war news concerning the activities of Prince Louis and of Count Lippe (the field commander of the Landgrave of Hesse-Cassel). A distinguished soldier then living in retirement in Frankfurt was General Jeremiah Chauvet, who had briefly replaced Schöning as Saxon commander during the latter's imprisonment. Stepney had previously met

Chauvet in Hamburg during 1686. Now, careful to respect the views of the older man, George found him a useful source of information on military affairs.[24]

At the end of July George was invited by Prince Louis to 'stepp over to ye Army at Heidelberg'. At the same time, however, another invitation arrived from the Landgrave of Hesse-Cassel for Stepney to join him at 'Menz' [i.e. Mainz] where the new Elector, Lothar Franz von Schönborn, had just assumed his office. Stepney chose to accept this second invitation and travelled overnight to reach Mainz at 10.00 a.m. on 4 August (n.s.) 1695.

Landgrave Charles of Hesse-Cassel (1654-1738) was the most loyal of King William's supporters among the German princes: and the new Elector of Mainz was brother-in-law of Stepney's old acquaintance, the imperial envoy to Saxony, Baron Benebourg. Both dignitaries received Stepney with great honour despite the fact that, since he was without credentials for Mainz, he insisted he was travelling as a private gentleman. He was delighted with his reception and begged from Blathwayt even the temporary style of Envoy, in order to compliment the new Elector from the King. (As usual, this courtesy was *not* accorded by William III.) It was a brief visit, but subsequently proved useful to Stepney since he was now personally acquainted with the Elector. On 6 August George returned to Frankfurt and on the 8th, in the evening, he received Blathwayt's command to accompany the Landgrave of Hesse-Cassel and the Hessian troops down the Rhine towards Flanders. In Germany, the imperial commanders were again at odds with each other, and the Landgrave's obedience to the King's request was as much to evade any cooperation with Prince Louis as it was to assist William III.[25]

Once Blathwayt's letter was in his hand, there was no sleep for Stepney. 'At 3 in ye morning' he was writing to Richard Powis, Clerk to the Treasury, who since 1693 had been handling (against payment) his affairs in London. Stepney's sisters would send on to Powis his Bill of Extries [Extraordinary Expenses] for the past three months. Stepney had stretched these as far as his conscience would allow, to compensate himself for the item of Exchequer Fees which, by order of Sir Stephen Fox, had been disallowed from his previous bill, to the tune of £79.

> I did not overreach myself with baggage: and indeed have no time to make myself an equipage if I would, for I am hurryed away at 10 hours warning: thank God I have a rambling-head otherwise such suddain orders might make me mad: I obey them

chearfully tho' they run away with all my ready money, and my
reimbursements come again but slowly by Tallyes.[26]

Stepney's last remark, above, was one which he would often repeat.
It was quite true that his hurried journeys had to be paid for, and in
cash: and the system of reimbursement of the overseas diplomats
by tallies – tokens upon various branches of the English revenue –
was one which caused great hardship. But by the summer of 1696
the English treasury was almost empty and Stepney's complaints
perforce went unheeded.

By '6 in ye morning' of 9 August, Stepney had completed his
acknowledgement of his orders to Blathwayt, and then he set off
by river to catch up with the Landgrave at Rheinfels. There, he
found that the Landgrave had already left, so Stepney too continued
until on 10 August (n.s.), he found the army at Remagen, '3 hours
above Bonn,' on the west bank of the Rhine. Already the Landgrave,
accompanied by Count Goertz and 300 men, was moving overland
to join the King before Namur. The main force of Hessians, under
Count Lippe, were to rest on 11 August. So Stepney travelled on to
Cologne, where he hoped to find fresh instructions from Blathwayt.
But the local banker/agent had rashly forwarded Stepney's mail
up-river to Coblenz. Stepney, fuming, sent for it, and at the same
time told his secretary Plantamour to stay with Count Lippe. He
wrote to Sir William Trumbull [Secretary of State] a two-page
account of the condition of Rheinfels, and as usual reported his
movements to Blathwayt.[27]

On 14 August (n.s.), the magistrates of Cologne kindly provided
Stepney with an escort of 25 men under a Lieutenant to take him
safely to Düren [about 40 km west of Cologne], where he joined
Count Lippe and both reached Aix [la Chapelle] two days later.
Stepney decided to stay with Lippe, who lent him horses and allowed
him a place at his table. At Aix, Stepney found time for his
correspondence and wrote among others to Matt Prior, discussing,
as ever, future prospects. George reckoned that he had by now saved
£1,000 which, together with the money left him by his mother, would
enable him to live 'above contempt.' Although he wished to stop
being a post-horse, he was not so mad as to throw up his salary of
£1,400 a year while he could keep it. He told Prior he was aware of
a bargain on foot between Cresset and Lexington, whereby Sir Paul
Rycaut should be persuaded to resign his duties in Hamburg in
favour of Cresset and Lexington should lend his influence to obtain
an employment in England for Rycaut.

In short, Mat, I see no footing for us – Berlin is not an Air for an

Englishman to breathe while Ham is there and Portland lives, For my part I really believe I shall come home this winter. If it be yr fate to be out of Place likewise (as Jane calls it) Wee'le clubb stocks, and write Satyr against thooes [sic] who have better fortune.[28]

At Aix Stepney did not neglect his social life. The same day (18 August) on which he wrote to Prior saw him during the afternoon calling on the Countess of Soissons [the mother of Prince Eugene of Savoy]. He commented to Heneage Montagu:

I saw her at the Hague in Splendour at the time of the Congress; she is now so miserably reduced that she moves pity: she left Brussels for Debt and grows uneasy here for the same reason.[29]

By 20 August the army had reached Liège, Stepney travelling with Count Lippe in the latter's coach. Lippe had taken to heart a message from the Landgrave, accusing him of not hastening sufficiently the march of the troops. But the weather had been foul, and Stepney averred that Lippe was not to blame. The final stage of the journey, the 65 km from Liège to Namur, was completed without comment from Stepney. He reached Namur on 23 August and wrote exultantly to Lexington:

My Lord,   At ye King's Quarters before Namur

16/26 Aug¹ 1695

You will allow me to magnify my merit in telling you that I have brought my Detachment safe & sound to joyne our army, just in time when wee have most need of them: I have been here 3 days, & expect to satisfy my curiosity in seeing both a Battle & a storm, for wee think wee shall have both within 3 or 4 days: Wee have 3000 Horse who have joynt Prince Vaudimont at Mazy [about 12 km WNW. of Namur] & 7000 foot who help at ye Siedge. The King is gone this evening to ye first of these places, & I follow toomorrow, wch you may certainly take as an omen of some great action. I never lead [sic] a more pleasant life; the King is very gracious to me, & continues my allowance for only attending him from one Camp to another on other people's Horses.[30]

And Stepney continued to enjoy an euphoric period in the company of his friend Adam de Cardonnel and of other civilians around the camp. He was in time to witness and describe the fall of Namur to the Allied forces, an event which is generally considered to be King William's greatest success by land during the Nine Years' War. Stepney wrote his piece on 20/30 August at the King's Camp at Maloigne. By 1 September, he was at 'The Camp at Ostin' writing to Ellis at midnight and confessing that he was very weary, both with riding and writing, having no-one to help him make copies.

Three days later he was at 'The Camp at the Cense of Bouquet', rejoicing that out of his £4 a day he only needed to spend 30s., sleeping in a tent. He also admitted to Ellis that on his first day at Namur a cannon-ball had missed him by six yards. But to Stepney all was redeemed by the best sight of all: the marching out of the French garrison.[31]

On 12 September (n.s.) Stepney was at the Camp at Limbecq, near Halle. The King, having reviewed his troops, was leaving the army and Stepney, too, departed for Brussels to take part in Ambassador Wolseley's celebrations of the victory. He left no description of that event, but wrote to Ellis from the Hague on 20 September. The King was moving from Breda to Dieren, so George slipped over to the Hague to rig himself out (as he put it), and was then running after his Majesty to Loo, 'where I believe I may have my dispatches for Dusseldorf.' This is the first intimation of Stepney's next appointment, though it was not to materialise for another three months.[32]

Once at Het Loo – that beautiful place in Gelderland built by William III for the enjoyment of himself and his wife – Stepney could write:

> You can expect not news from me, who (from a Soldier, as I have been of late) am now become a perfect Country-Gentleman: the Scene of my Life shifts so frequently, that I know not wt to make of myself.

And a few days later:

> I am still in status quo, santring about these fine Gardens, till some Deputyes (wee expect dayly from ye Electr Palatin) shall please to arrive, upon whose message my Instructions are likely to be form'd.

One can visualise Stepney as one of the small figures in the foreground of a contemporary illustration of Het Loo.[33]

Still Stepney longed for a settled appointment (like Cresset's) to bring an end to his gypsy life. Cresset had turned up at Loo, bringing with him the wandering minstrel, John Abel (1650-1724, who, in celebration of the victory, was to sing to Prince Vaudemont [one of William III's field commanders] verses composed by George Stepney, which began:

> Harmonious Strings your charms prepare
> to reach the Royall Conqueror's Ear;
> such is our Joy, as did inspire
> David's and Deborah's Lyre
> Be such our Numbers, while we sing
> The Praise of our Victorious King

Abel accompanied himself on the lute. The event was a success, and was repeated before the King on 3 October (n.s.).[34] Then the Court moved to the Hague, the King awaiting a fair wind for England. Stepney had still received no definite instructions regarding his forthcoming employment, and Portland was treating him with the accustomed coldness. Stepney was merely told to await further orders in the Hague. He could not conceal his loneliness at being left behind, writing to Lexington

> I saw yr Souveraign on bord yesterday by ten in ye morning, & since I make no doubt but ue fair wind and weather he has had since may have brought him to London by this time . . . I am thrown here like a fish upon ye shore, & shall not be fetch'd off till another tide serves, this time twelve months. I must confess to you, my Lord, it went to my heart to see everybody launch off, and myself left in ye lurch.[35]

And in the Hague, in Prior's house Stepney remained until the end of the year. He sent for his remaining goods which were still in Vienna; and wrote again to Ham (who had visited the Hague with the Elector of Brandenburg) about the disposal of the equipage which he had exchanged with Ham. He wanted not less than 280 ecus for his horses: if this sum could not be obtained he wished his old landlord in Berlin, Vincent, to have the animals conveyed *'tout doucement'* to Düsseldorf before the winter set in. Stepney's *calèche drappée* could be taken by Ham, in exchange for the Dutchman's, which was at Utrecht,

> *et vous pourrez vous servir de celle que vous m'avez pretee, vous la trouverez chez Madame Meyer a Cleves.* [36]

He took time to write to all his acquaintances, and to send a parcel of tea, 'the best I cou'd find in Amsterdam,' to Father Vernon in Whitehall, having discovered from Cardonnel that tea was Vernon's favourite beverage. As usual he wrote in detail to Richard Powis about his expenses. To Henage Montague he made the suggestion (to be passed on) that he (Stepney) might serve in Sweden, where John Robinson was said to be unpopular. Stepney put forward in his own favour the fact that he spoke High Dutch [i.e. German] which was the only language understood by the King of Sweden. Moreover he was

> of low stature, wch I have heard is a good qualification for an Envoy to ye King , who does not love to be overtopp'd.[37]

In Prior's company, life was not all gloom. The two friends often drank Lexington's health in champagne at the price of one Duccatoon a bottle, [about 25p]. And they were sending for a barrel of oysters, just arrived with the last pacquet-boat.[38]

Yet Stepney felt himself cut off from the mainstream of events, writing to Ellis

> I believe wee are treating for 3000 foot with ye bishop of Munster: I can only guess, you are to know ye certainty of these matters from My Lord Villiers, [the English Envoy in the Hague.]

At the same time, John Ellis in London received a letter from James Cresset, in Zell, which might have surprised Stepney:

> The Little man at the Hague is really capable, and I wish him wel with all my heart, he is wel back'd and probably will succeed in his designs but neither he nor I have any ground for great pretensions.

To Stepney's undoubted satisfaction – although he made no comment at the time – his credentials at last accorded him the rank, style and title of His Majesty's Envoy.

X *The Envoy to the Princes of the Rhine*

(1696)

> You may think perhaps I have linger'd here longer than I need,
> out of love of oysters, champagne and Prior. . . I must confess
> They were 3 powerful reasons. . . As soon as this is seal'd, I stepp
> into my Coach, in very cold weather,wch is always my Season of
> travelling: But I am pretty well furr'd & have a tough constitution.

As Stepney implied in his letter to Lexington (above), he had
deferred his departure from the Hague as long as he could, telling
Whitehall that an arrival at Düsseldorf over Christmas would be
inopportune, owing to the time spent by the Palatinate Court in
ceremonies and devotions. But it was true that during December
1695 he had received only minimal instructions from London as to
his mission. Blathwayt, in letters which may not have reached
Stepney before he left the Hague, had written brusquely that Stepney
was not to go to Sweden: he was posted to the Electors of the Rhine
with the character of Envoy Extraordinary; and his task was to
promote the prosecution of the war and get a train of artillery from
the Elector of Trèves. He (Blathwayt) declined to send an engineer
with Stepney: he would lend horses (to be kept in good condition).
Stepney's Instructions would follow, but as these had not passed
the Secretary of State's office, Stepney was to refer to them only as
'directions.'[1]

Unknown to Stepney, King William had had this new
commission in mind, ever since November 1695. The King had
written to his trusted friend, the Grand Pensionary of Holland
Antonie Heinsius (1641-1720) that he greatly desired a train of
artillery to be set up at Coblenz to facilitate a siege of the French
stronghold of Montroyal, and that he proposed to send Stepney to
the German Princes on the Rhine and the Moselle. However by
January 1696 William was urging Heinsius to send experts in
military supply on this mission, implying that Stepney alone would
be unequal to the task. Eventually Baron Goertz of Hesse-Cassel

became involved, though with as little success as Stepney himself.[2]

Stepney's Instructions, as composed by Heinsius, were clear. He was to call on the Electors of the Palatine, Cologne, Trèves and Mainz, and the Landgrave of Hesse [Cassel], to press for a firm alliance and unity during the coming campaign. The Allies should proceed with the recruitment of troops to obtain a force superior to that of the enemy. An army was envisaged to operate on the Middle Rhine, as well as the one on the Upper Rhine which was commanded by Prince Louis. Stepney was to emphasise the necessity for artillery, to which each prince – as well as the City of Frankfurt – should contribute. He must concert with all concerned the provision of magazines of food, fodder and ammunition; and he was to check that the decrees (*Placeats*) were being observed, which forbade transport of horses to and trade with the enemy.[3]

And so, on 27 December (n.s.) 1695, Stepney set out for Düsseldorf, which he reached on 3 January 1696, and he was granted an audience of the Elector Palatine the following day.

John William of Pfalz-Neuburg (1658-1714) was a Roman Catholic, brother to the reigning Empress Eleonore, the third wife of the Emperor Leopold I. In that the Empress could influence her husband in the matter of court appointments, so was her brother believed to exert at least indirect pressure on imperial councils; hence it behoved the maritime powers to treat him with civility. The Palatinate had been ravaged by the French during the course of the war – so the Court moved its seat to Düsseldorf in the County of Berg. The Elector was not a military man, but enjoyed the gentle arts of peace. Stepney described the situation perfectly to Lexington:

> I have been here these 9 days & am heartily contented with the Prince & his Ministers, as I hope they are with me: for wee pass our time very easily & merrily, in ye beginning of our Carneval . . . . [There are French comedies, balls, and an opera to come.] . . .But our hearts begin to ake when wee [i.e. the Elector] talk of business: our Palatinate is destroyed by friend & foe: wee pay contributions [to the French] for our County of Juliers; our Troops are turn'd upon our hands, & wee are left without subsidies, assignations, or Quarters: Wee had hopes our Brother in law ye Emp' wou'd have considered how much wee have done & suffer'd; That ye Circles (for whose safety wee left our own Country naked) wou'd have used us better; & lastly that the King of England who advised us to pay contributions to France, wou'd help us to bear that burden; But wee are neglected & as it were dispized on all hands.[4]

To Trumbull, Stepney wrote a less poetic letter, asking to be told precisely whether the King would agree to a subsidy being paid to the Elector Palatine; whether William III wished to use any of the Elector's troops, and if so, where they should serve. But on John Ellis's extract of this dispatch, carefully filed in Whitehall, are the notes:

Dusseldorf
Mr. Stepney 6 Jan 1696
The Elec's forces
no subsidy to be granted.[5]

Caught up as he was in the frivolity of the Elector's court, George Stepney did not entirely neglect his duties. He found *Placeats* against the exportation of horses into France: two or three fellows had been hanged for disobedience. The army of the Upper Rhine [commanded by Prince Louis] wished to remount its troops on horses from the neighbourhood of Düsseldorf. Nevertheless the trade into France was difficult to stop. Then he went round the walls of the town to see the artillery, and found 14 pieces bought recently from the Elector of Trèves. But the Arsenal had been pulled down to make way for a private house built by Count Hamilton [a Scot, and one of the Elector's close advisers]. The guns were exposed to the weather in the market-place. There was little ammunition. Stepney noted that the Elector's new opera house had cost 60,000 dollars. Hopefully, he submitted to Whitehall a list of the forces which the Elector supposedly had in pay. The grand total was 8,800 men.

Socially, the English Envoy was a success: Prince Charles, brother of the Elector, descended on Stepney accompanied by the chief officers of the court, to dine *à l'Anglais.* At one sitting they drank George out of the small quantity of choice wines which he had laid in for his winter provision. But an Envoy could not object to such treatment.

By 24 January (n.s.) Stepney had received a letter from Heinsius telling him that the Elector Palatine had no hope of a subsidy. Tactfully, George had to convey the bad news to that prince. Before taking leave of the Elector, Stepney (again prompted by the Grand Pensionary) suggested that Commissaries of the various German princes should meet to concert the plans for artillery and supply. At the request of the King's Dutch advisers in Holland Stepney also spoke to the Elector about the persecution of some Anabaptists in the Palatinate, and obtained a promise that the matter would be investigated.

Stepney's last dispatch from Düsseldorf contained one of his now regular pleas for money: the Treasury was £2,000 in arrears with him; and he needed cash for his continual journeyings.[6]

Moving on, Stepney was in Cologne on 22 January/1 February, but did not find the Archbishop/Elector. Nor was that prince in Bonn, where the Envoy had expected to find him. So Stepney decided to pursue the chief object of his mission, which was to raise artillery from the Elector of Trèves, who was reputed to have a better arsenal than any other German prince.

The castle of Ehrenbreitstein, over against Coblenz, was then (and remained through the nineteenth century) a formidable fortress. Stepney arrived on 3 February (n.s.) 1696, and took lodgings at an inn near the court. But the Elector of Trèves insisted that he should stay in the palace, sent coaches to bring him to an audience, came as far as the gallery to meet him and then seated him in an armchair. The cordial prelate (for the Elector was also the Archbishop of Trèves) was Johann Hugo von Orsbeck (1630-1711), who had achieved the Electorate in 1676. At the start of the Nine Years' War he had refused to accept a garrison of Swiss mercenaries which the French wished to impose on him. So Coblenz was bombarded and the Electorate was ravished. But the tide of war receded, and the Elector seemed content with the small subsidy given him four years earlier by the King of England and the Dutch. In Coblenz, as in Düsseldorf, Stepney was the first Envoy accredited by King William. Following up his good reception, Stepney inquired about artillery for the Middle Rhine. The Elector countered with questions about the army: who would command it and what would be its objectives? He feared that should a Middle Rhine Army come into being, all that would happen was that the French would take revenge upon his territory. In accordance with Heinsius' suggestion, Stepney put forward the plan that commissaries should be appointed by all the interested parties to discuss the practicalities of an artillery train. The Elector agreed. But as far as other supplies were concerned Stepney recommended to Whitehall that, once a military commander was appointed, that officer should send his own commissaries to negotiate for necessities. The Elector of Trèves' response had been lukewarm, and Stepney claimed in his dispatch that he had foreseen that no German prince wished to see a Middle Rhine Army in being, or would be prepared to contribute to it.

Baron Goertz of Hesse-Cassel was more optimistic. He had sent Stepney a project (*ébauche*) of what artillery each prince or state might furnish (complete with horses, servants and other necessaries for the train). The Elector Palatine was not included.

Stepney doubted whether any of Goertz' ideas could be realized. Nevertheless the new Envoy had already seen something of the Elector of Trèves' strength in weapons of war when he reported to Whitehall:

> About half a league from here I found Bombs in great quantity, they make them there, and are at present busy in furnishing a very great number wch have been bespoke by the States-General.[7]

A week later Stepney reported that he had completed his inspection, and had got the Elector of Trèves to promise to supply cannon, but not gunners or horses, for which ready money would be required. Stepney further suggested that Orsbeck should furnish his complete quota [according to Goertz] in cannon, leaving the horses, men and money to be supplied by the Bishop of Münster and the House of Lüneburg; and all such matters to be decided by the forthcoming assembly of commissaries.

Stepney was now making plans to leave Coblenz. His future movements were vague, but he was inclined to go on down the Rhine as far as Mainz, to find out if that Elector would send a representative to the proposed rendezvous, and then on to Frankfurt for a similar purpose. Before leaving, Stepney could report to Whitehall with some pride:

> All our letters from Trèves are full of what the French guess I am doing in these parts. They do me the honʳ to say I am disposing all things towards an attaque on Montroyall, and that wee [the Elector of Trèves] have already provided our artillery, provisions and ammunitions; I wish these fears were better grounded. However it is some satisfaction that they are so easily alarm'd.[8]

Stepney reached Mainz on 7/17 February, where he spent one night, and saw General Thüngen [deputy to Prince Louis] who provided a list of the artillery and stores available. This Stepney copied himself for the benefit of Whitehall. The next day he travelled to Frankfurt, whence he sent home a vivid account of the state entry of a Venetian Embassy which appeared, as he described it, more like 'a Turkish Caravan or an Embassy from Muscovy.' More seriously, he had to deal with a delegation from the city magistrates, who bewailed the sufferings of the city during the war, but nevertheless implied that they would be prepared to contribute to their own defence. They presented the Envoy (according to their custom) with gifts of oats and wine.[9]

The next call was at Cassel, where Stepney arrived on 23 February/4 March (1696 was a leap year). He stayed two days incognito, to avoid any dispute over precedence with two German princelings who were present at court. On 6 March (n.s.), the

Landgrave sent for Stepney and brought him to court with the usual ceremony, treating him as well as Sir William Colt, the former Envoy. Meanwhile an emissary of the Landgrave's, Colonel Tettau, had gone to London. Stepney got a sight of the Colonel's Instructions, on which he promptly commented. Tettau was to solicit for a payment of 104,000 Dollars to the Landgrave, because the King was in arrears with the promised subsidy. This sum would clear the debt up to the end of 1695, and Stepney asked Trumbull to urge payment. Stepney also recommended that when a peace with France was negotiated, the Landgrave should be left in possession of his 'darling fortress' of Rheinfels. The Landgrave had requested an augmentation of the subsidy, and the King had agreed, provided the number of the Landgrave's troops was increased. Stepney provided details of the troops available.[10]

To Lexington in Vienna, Stepney sent a copy of Goertz's *ébauche* with the urgent request that the Emperor should be asked whether he approved the establishment of a Middle Rhine Army, and if so, that he should approve it being under the command of the Landgrave. It was also desirable that the Emperor should urge the princes to supply troops, so that a body was raised which would be capable of acting; and also that the Emperor and Prince Louis should support the efforts to obtain artillery.[11]

Ten days later a *Te Deum* was sung and cannon fired from the walls of Cassel. News had arrived that King William had escaped an assassination attempt, and the Landgrave was expressing his relief. Colonel Tettau in London was instructed to make a compliment, and Stepney of course wished to be the diplomat who would make the reciprocal gesture. He had recently been honoured by an invitation to take the air with the Landgrave in the latter's coach, and had been asked his opinion of the 'Tyger-coloured horses' which drew the vehicle and which the Landgrave said he would like to present to the King.

> An humble Bow was all ye answer I made, for I wou'd neither reject nor take hold of ye offer till you please to inform me how his Maty may be disposed.

And Stepney suggested that the Landgrave would be gratified by a gift of English horses.

Then Stepney passed on the important news which he had received from Lexington, that the Duke of Savoy might make a separate peace with France.

In Whitehall the Secretary of State's office was having some difficulty in coping with the stream of letters which were arriving from Cassel. Trumbull, or his clerk, made notes on the reverse side:

> Landgraf of Hesse desiring 4000 men from Flanders, yt his troops shall go thither, if occasion be. If the Hanover and Munster troops joine, he proposes his and they may *rolle*, to avoid disputes about precedence . . . .
>
> Pr. L. desiring to take 2000 of the Munster and 2000 of the Saxon troops, the Landgr. desires the King to send him 4000 men out of Flanders instead of them. Cannot be.
>
> Mr. Stepney desires directions to go to Coblenz or F'furt to the meeting of Commissaries of the Princes about an army on the Middle Rhine.

On 2 April (n.s.) 1696 Stepney was able to report the numbers of troops available (at least on paper) for the Middle Rhine Army. They totalled 22,000, and contingents had been promised from Hanover, Zell, Münster/Paderborn and Ducal Saxony, as well as the core of 8,000 Hessians who were under the Landgrave's immediate command.

By now, Stepney had moved out of the Landgrave's palace and taken a house in town, partly to avoid abusing hospitality and partly to lessen any chance of a dispute over precedence with a Danish envoy, who was expected at court. In his new quarters he entertained the chief officers of the court, and even the Landgrave visited his house, unannounced, to drink the King's health.[12]

But the difficulties of preparing the campaign did not diminish. Who was going to pay for the magazines, and for boats to transport the troops, and for bridges? The King wished the Assembly of the Commissaries to take place at Coblenz; but Baron Goertz and most of the other delegates preferred Frankfurt. On 8/18 April Stepney was back there, having received from the Landgrave 'a Gobelet of Massy-Gold worth 600 Dollars.' Four days later he received from Trumbull the letter commanding him to return the Landgrave's compliment to the King: he never was lucky in such matters, and all he could do was to pass the command on to Baron Goertz.

By the beginning of May the expected Commissaries had arrived in Frankfurt; artillery had been promised by the Elector of Trèves and by the Landgrave of Hesse-Darmstadt; the Emperor had written to the Electors and Princes urging them to help with the artillery (but not, Stepney noted, to the City of Frankfurt, 'wch was more materiall than all ye rest'). Yet Heinsius was warning Stepney that the French were threatening the Low Countries with troops which had been brought from Piedmont and the Rhine. Stepney must hasten the preparation of the Middle Rhine Army, plus artillery, so that it could act. It was necessary incessantly to write to the princes

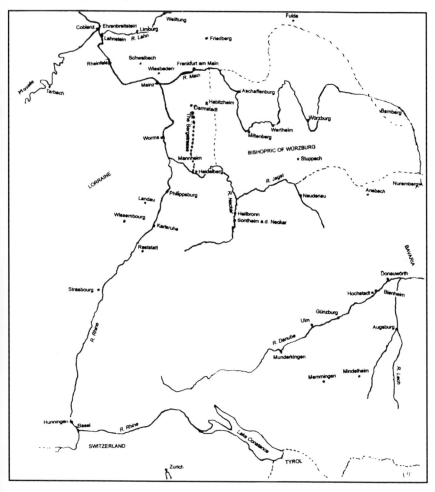

Southern Germany and the Upper Rhine.

to send their troops. Stepney was to concert his efforts with those of Goertz.

Again on 12/22 May Stepney began an optimistic letter to his Secretary of State. The Middle Rhine Army, on paper, now amounted to 26,960 men. Prince Louis had written obligingly to the Landgrave. The artillery count was 12 cannon and 5 mortars.

Then Stepney added a postscript: The French had crossed the Rhine at Philippsburg with 20,000 men, probably to destroy Prince Louis' forage. A week later Count Frise arrived in Frankfurt, to relate that Prince Louis' army was in reality much weaker than the paper projects: the French were stronger by 10,000 men, and, when Frise had left the Prince, the two armies were within one hour of each other. Urgently, the Margrave of Baden wished the Landgrave of Hesse-Cassel to march in his direction. But a similar request had already reached the Landgrave from the King in Flanders, and, as in 1695, the Landgrave chose to accept the King's orders rather than those of Prince Louis. Stepney, regretting that his efforts over artillery had foundered, awaited instructions.[13]

War-clouds notwithstanding, Stepney was by no means neglecting his social life. The King had arrived at the Hague and

I make at least 20 Ladyes drink his health this evening in an arbor
I have made for them about a Quarter of a Mile out of Town.

The guests included the Countess of Hohenlohe. The Count (who was at the time the imperial envoy in Frankfurt) had gone post to Vienna. Stepney added:

I wish you [i.e. Lexington] little of his Company, for he has tired
me out of my Life, with his intolerable chatt.[14]

Before any orders could have reached Stepney from Blathwayt (who as usual accompanied the King on campaign) another disaster threatened the Middle Rhine. Prince Louis had sent his deputy, General Thüngen, to visit the Landgrave who was then at Schwalbach [just north-west of Wiesbaden]. The General had travelled over the Bergstrasse, that German defensive line which ran along the hills between Darmstadt and Heidelberg. But a French raiding-party (known as 'Snaphanes') captured Thüngen and took him to Philippsburg. He was in no personal danger, for according to the conventions of the time general officers were exchanged or ransomed after a period of eight days (though Stepney noted that the French kept Thüngen for 15 days). More serious was the supposed loss of his papers. The result of this incident was that the Landgrave on 22 May (n.s.), wrote very politely to Stepney asking him to go to Steppach [Stuppach, 5 km south of Bad Mergentheim] where Prince Louis was encamped, to discover what instructions the Margrave had given to Thüngen. Stepney obeyed at once, travelling from Frankfurt by way of Miltenberg [well east of the Bergstrasse] to avoid any danger. He left Plantamour in Frankfurt.

Stepney reached Steppach on 25 May in the morning, and stayed with Prince Louis until the evening of the day following. He reported at length on his visit when he reached Schwalbach on 9 June (n.s.). Prince Louis had discussed (in French) the state of the war with his visitor. In writing to Blathwayt, Stepney was careful to stress that he had been very circumspect in relating to the Landgrave his interview with the Prince. Stepney saw it as his duty to try to preserve the best possible relationship between the two commanders, and not to foment discord as (he claimed) Colonel Tettau had endeavoured to do.

It appears from the wording of the Landgrave's letter to Stepney that Prince Louis had intimated – perhaps via an emissary of lesser standing than General Thüngen – that he would be happy to see Stepney employed on this mission. What prompted the Prince is not known: possibly in conversation with Count Frise he had been reminded that Stepney was now the King's Envoy to the Princes of the Rhine. In the event, Prince Louis chose an excellent intermediary, because Stepney carefully conveyed all the Margrave's hopes and fears to Blathwayt, and of course via Blathwayt to the King. The gravamen of the matter was Prince Louis' desire to lay siege to Philippsburg, so often the entry-point for French armies into German territory. For such a large enterprise he needed Hessian support and so was indignant at the Landgrave's decision to make for the Meuse and not for the Rhine. Prince Louis even threatened to desert his command in favour of one in Hungary, where he would find more troops at his disposal and be free from the vagaries of the German princes. What held him back was the trust placed in him by the Circles of Franconia and Suabia: he knew, if he left them, that they would immediately make the best deal they could with the French. All this, and more, Stepney transmitted to his superiors, and made a shorter, tactful report to the Landgrave. The latter asked him to reply to Prince Louis, and Stepney did so, writing from Frankfurt on 2/12 June.[15]

He was unable to send much comfort. The Landgrave was determined to carry out the King's orders and head for the Meuse. However he agreed to leave troops sufficient to cover the Bergstrasse, and made vague promises of assisting at a siege of Philippsburg when his army returned from the Meuse.

Stepney himself spent one day only at Frankfurt – presumably to collect his belongings and servants. Not without good cause, he complained to Lexington that he was 'hattering about like a Courier.' He added:

> I return toomorrow to Schwalbach & am ordered to march with ye Landgrave, & so hope to see my Souveraign before Dinant one of these days; wch is ye only consolation I have in ye world, for it is a sad case that I must have 40 mouths in family (counting man & Horse) & have no hopes of being pay'd this entry otherwise than by tallyes wch will not be ready money these 2 years.[16]

These remarks were only too true: Stepney's anxiety would only have increased had he known that, three days later, his sovereign would write to the Grand Pensionary of Holland in the following terms:

> *M. van Geldermalsen doit vous avoir informé hier de l'indispensable nécessité de procurer quelque avance aux entrepreneurs de vivres, pour qu'ils fournissent du pain à l'armée du Landgrave qui vient se cantonner sur la Meuse. Si j'étais moi-même en état de le faire, je n'importunerais pas les Etats; mais vous savez qu'il s'en faut de beaucoup, et que je suis réduit à une telle pénurie, que je ne sais comment me tire d'affaire plus longtemps.*[1-]

By the end of June Stepney was in Cologne. Lexington had been teasing him by letter about his semi-military function, so he replied to that peer:

> My myrmidons were to pass the Meuse at Viset this morning: I am going to Düsseldorf to take hold of some Rogues. But I hope to overtake our Army before they have joined the King. I have no orders to make any ouvertures to ye Elr [of Cologne] & I believe his heart is too [?hid] to be ye first to speak to me.[18]

In fact, a somewhat incoherent letter from Blathwayt had reached Stepney two days earlier when he (Stepney) was at Gulpen, between Aix and Viset. The King's camp had been alarmed by a report from the Dutch Resident in Düsseldorf that conspirators involved in the plot against the King's life were to be found in the territories of the Elector Palatine, and that one of them, named Tilly, was under arrest at the castle of Juliers [Jülich]. Stepney was to go to Düsseldorf, ostensibly to inquire about the Elector's troops, but in reality to insist that Tilly, who was the King's subject, should be handed over to his army for examination. Blathwayt thought that Stepney already knew something about Tilly. This was true, for Stepney responded to Blathwayt's letter:

> I make no doubt but to be Master of Tilly, as I have a Servant in my family (whom I shall have secured under a Guard till my return) who knows something of the matter and will serve to confront Tilly when wee have him.

It is not known which of Stepney's servants was involved. But Stepney did go at once to Düsseldorf and saw the Elector, who told him Tilly was under strict confinement, but was sick of the pox, and when he had recovered he would be sent to the King. Meanwhile Stepney requested for himself an army commission from Blathwayt, to protect him in case he met the same fate as General Thüngen. The King promptly refused to give him one, but ordered Blathwayt to tell his Envoy to be wary in his marches. Blathwayt was also to add:

> You will take care that the prisoner be treated better or worse as you find he deserves, but without any other hardship than of safe custody.

This was in keeping with King William's practice – unusual in his day – of shewing mercy to his opponents.[19]

Stepney stayed in Düsseldorf until 6 July (n.s.). While he was there he wrote to his sisters a surprisingly frank letter which conveys to a twentieth-century reader the uninhibited *mores* of the late seventeenth century:

Düsseldorf, 21/31(*sic*) June 1696

Dear Sisters,

> I expect you shou'd thank me heartily for a very good acquaintance I am about to procure you by sending this Letter after Mad⁰ Steingens, an English-Italian German Lady for whom I have all imaginable esteem, the rather because she is an agreeable lively little Creature not unlike yrself. I am certain you will be contented with each other at first sight, therefore I need not many words to bring you together. I wish it may lye in yr power to contribute any thing to her Service or satisfaction, and I beg you to do all you can towards it, wch will be but a small return for the many civilities wch I have received both from her and her Husband, when I was last in Düsseldorf, and wch are increas'd at present by Mr. Steingens having received me under his Roof and given me possession of her Bed, wch you must allow is the Highest Civility. I leave you to retailliate it by yr best service both by Mrs. Steingens to [he means 'and'] Mrs. Campbell, another very good-natured Gentlewoman who is generally with her, and whom I likewise recommend to yr acquaintance as an instance of ye affection with which
> I am, etc.[20]

The Tilly episode took Stepney from Düsseldorf to Maastricht and then to Liège, whence he joined the King's camp at Gembloux by 6/16 July 1696. At Maastricht he had taken Tilly's deposition, and then found himself in complete charge of the man, even having to redeem some of Tilly's clothes from pawn. Tilly remained at Maastricht, but the expenses of maintaining him were borne by Stepney personally until the end of the year. The prisoner was allowed five or six shillings a day for his food, which was usual for a man of his rank. Stepney put in repeated claims for reimbursement, all of which were ignored by King William's government.

Stepney had hardly been a week at Gembloux when the King

came up with the idea of sending him to mediate at Pinneberg [north-west of Hamburg] in a dispute between the King of Denmark and the Duke of Holstein. This was *not* at his own request, as Stepney was quick to point out to Sir Paul Rycaut.[21]

The volunteer-Envoy had however picked up some useful information. His *valet de chambrè* (un-named) had been captured by the French when he was en route (on Stepney's orders) to Liège. The French treated the man well, and released him. And told him that the French had made peace with Savoy and that a general peace was expected soon.[22]

For the war was deadlocked. The camp moved to Nivelle, and Stepney filled in time by writing to the Reverend Richard Hill, who at the time was paymaster to the army. For the next ten years Stepney was to maintain a partly friendly, partly exasperated relationship with Hill. In 1696 they were on good terms:

> Sir,
>
> According to yr desire I send you ye little news we have . . . Wee have layne still this day & I am not a Politician or Soldier enough to know Why wee did so; Toomorrow wee march forward to Soignes, & when I learn any thing worth yr knowledge you shall have it. In ye mean time I comend yr choice of ye Idlest man in ye army for yr Correspondent.[23]

When the camp moved to Attre on 6 August (n.s.), Stepney's future changed again. The Pinneberg negotiation was entrusted to Cresset (which was sensible, as he was in the neighbourhood), and Stepney was told to be ready to wait on the Elector of Brandenburg at Cleves. Meanwhile he was worried that the outbreak of peace would lose him his foreign employment, and, at Blathwayt's suggestion, he wrote to Charles Montagu to ask him for help in obtaining the post of Secretary to the Commissioners of Trade, because he had heard that the incumbent William Popple, was said to be unsatisfactory. The job in Cleves did not materialise, being given (as usual) to a Dutchman. The court (and Stepney) moved by degrees to Breda, Dieren and the Loo. There was talk of the King himself visiting Cleves, partly to look over a princess of Brandenburg who was of marriageable age, and partly to maintain a good relationship with the Elector. The King had his objections. Stepney related that, when a courtier told his Majesty of the gossip about the princess, William replied that 'if they might have so soon forgot the Queen, he had not'. And there was a difficulty in arranging any meeting between the King of England and the Elector, owing to the matter of the armchair [*fauteuil*]. According to English custom no-one was allowed to sit in the King's presence. William insisted on that etiquette with the Elector of Bavaria and saw no reason to change it for the Elector of Brandenburg. Eventually the visit took place, and Stepney – as an eye-witness – described it to Trumbull. On arrival, the King was entertained by the Electress and the Princess for four hours to the card-game of ombre. The Princess was not allowed to sit, although Keppel was provided with a chair. Meals were not taken in common: the King dined with the Electress and the Elector ate in his own apartments. However on the second day of the visit the King did walk in the park with the Elector. The King returned by boat along the Rhine, and two days later the Electoral prince (aged eight) returned the visit.[24]

Towards the end of September a Swede, a certain Baron Muller, turned up at Loo claiming to have knowledge of intrigues with France. Lord Portland, who was busy, turned the man over to Stepney, who discussed Muller's claims with him during the journey from Het Loo to the Hague, Stepney asked for all the information in writing, and this Muller provided, although he carefully handed over copies to be made by a secretary, not wishing to allow his handwriting to become known. The substance of Muller's information was that Count Vehlen, one of the Elector Palatine's ministers, was carrying on a secret negotiation between his master and the French government. Stepney merely handed copies of the report to Portland and to Heinsius. But a year later he had to warn Lord Villiers (then the English Envoy in the Hague) against Vehlen when the latter represented the Palatinate at the peace negotiations. The incident indicates that Portland, although he never in any way furthered Stepney's career, was not averse to using the younger man as occasion required, on confidential business.[25]

By 1 October Stepney was once more in the Hague. Heinsius told him there might be work for him in Germany, so once again George forbore to ask leave to go to England, describing himself as:

a Ghost on the brink of the river, who would gladly get over, but cannot.

A month later he wrote drearily again: he needed a post at home and recompense for the £3,000 he had had to find during 1696 to satisfy his bankers. He was paid in tallies for timber; and later complained that his £5 a day was reduced to about 50s., owing to the discount on tallies, the exchequer fees and the expenses to which Envoys were put.

He found some relief within his own family. His cousins,

Lancelot and Joseph Stepney (brothers) were from the elder branch of the Stepney family based in Hertfordshire. The two were traders, with a correspondent in Rotterdam. Lancelot very generously gave George permission to draw on Gerhard Steenlack and thankfully George did so, at first to the value of £100. By the end of the year this figure had increased to £400, and a page of the letter-book (in Stepney's own hand) shews that, including the £400 he had borrowed from six other lenders – among them Cardonnel – a total of £1,990. It was certainly necessary for Stepney to remain in the King's service.[26]

Signals which could lead to the ending of the war were emerging from all the participants. In Vienna, the ultra-Catholic party, guided by the Court Chancellor Kinsky, favoured the conclusion of a peace with France to be mediated by Savoy. This was to be kept secret from the maritime powers. However in late seventeenth-century Europe a secret was the hardest thing to preserve. Stepney was keeping up his correspondence with Lord Lexington who, on behalf of the King, was officially opposing any idea of peace with the French. Stepney congratulated Lexington on his negotiations in Vienna, and continued:

> I always looked upon [?old] Leopold to be wiser than all his privy-Councill, & infinitely more honest to the cause wee serve. I hear he dash'd out with his own hand the Clause wch deferr'd ye mediation to ye duke of Savoy.

And Matt Prior added to the same correspondence

> His Excellency Stepney is here still [i.e. the Hague] but going towards Frankfort to hinder broken heads, for winter-quarters, & to stand between the Hessians & Palatins to see fair-play, like Vinegar in the ring at Lincoln's Inn Fields. He does not like the simile, & I told him I would see if you did or no.[27]

Prior was right in that the would-be participants of the Middle Rhine Army, the Hessians under Count Lippe and the Palatins under Comte d'Autel, were at loggerheads, and separated only by the river Main. Stepney described it as a *petite guerre* between them, with bastonades and fists used by the men. For the commanders, the problem of finding winter-quarters for the armies was a perennial cause of dispute. Stepney was once again under the *de facto* direction of Heinsus, but this time he was writing his own Instructions, to be discussed with the Pensionary before departure. One result of his new commission would have been pleasing to Stepney: when he left the Hague the affairs of Tilly were to be handed over to the English Envoy, Lord Villiers. By 11 December (n.s.), Stepney had talked over his task not only with Heinsus, but also with Baron Goertz of Hesse-Cassel. Stepney was to renew his search for artillery. He knew, in advance, that Prince Louis wished to have nothing more to do with any Middle Rhine Army and had threatened that, if all dispositions were not completed to his liking by the end of January 1697, he (the Prince) would not act at all during the coming year. [28]

On 11 December (n.s.) Count Frise turned up in the Hague en route for England. He was held up for a week by contrary winds, but then crossed the channel. He had come from Vienna, and brought news from that city as well as of Prince Louis. Stepney heard from Trumbull that his memorial concerning his Instruction had been shewn to the King, who only commented that Stepney would receive orders shortly. But William on 15/25 December was writing to Heinsius that he was so short of money he found it impossible to contribute to any troop levies, and for that reason he had no idea what Instructions he could give Stepney.

And so the year 1696 came to an end. Christmas Day was spent in devotions. Stepney sent a letter to a young cousin of Blathwayt's, Harry Watkins, whom he had met among the hangers-on of the camp, describing his comfortable life at Prior's house:

> My humble service to your Brother, and to any of our Oxford friends who are so kind to enquire after me. The best account you can give [of] me (if you tell truth) is that I am over a good turf fire with our friend Mat, roasting chestnuts and drinking Lamb's-wool for his Maty's service.

And as Stepney regarded the periods of idleness at the end of the year as relief from his rambling employment, he was for the time being content.[29]

XI *The End of the Nine Years' War*
(January-September 1697)

> Friese und Stepney erhielten Auftrag für die Durchführung der Association [von Frankfurt] und für die Vereinigung aller deutscher Streitkräfte unter dem Kommando des Markgrafen zu wirken.[1]

No diplomat in the service of King William could expect to remain idle for very long. Even in winter the war situation could change, and no-one was sure of the intentions of the French, whether they favoured peace or continued war. From the Hague Stepney reported on 28 December 1696 that the enemy had crossed the Rhine at Andernach and raided Neuwied, a small town on the opposite (east) bank of the river. This happened just before a fair was to take place, so the robbers' booty was high. Both these places lie about 15 km downstream of Coblenz. The next major town on the Rhine in that direction is Bonn, and Stepney feared for the loss of that city to the French, for then communications with Coblenz would be cut.[2]

Lexington wished to leave Vienna and had his eye on the rôle of commissioner to negotiate the peace. (As usual, the King havered over this appointment.) It was conjectured that Stepney might replace Lexington in Vienna, but though George was flattered at the rumour, he realised that his financial state would make life difficult in the imperial city. Prior seemed to have his future secure as Secretary to the Peace Commission. Blathwayt had had his eye on Stepney for that appointment, but the latter commented:

> My age and proffession of forraine ministry would justify some curiosity I have to see a new show, and how people live at such a mission: but to be sincere with you, I do not like the Company of 3 Stoicks with whom I shall have no manner of conversation: if there had been any sociable good fellow among them, like Ld Lexington, 2 or 3 months wou'd pass merrily at such an assembly, but these honest Gentlemen are too rebarbatif for me, and I believe wee should much differ in our humour and Politicks.[3]

However, Stepney had heard of the possibility of a Treaty of Commerce being negotiated with the French. In this he was very interested; he told Blathwayt he would like to conduct it, and thereby gain pretension to be Secretary to the Commission of Trade. As for the purpose of his forthcoming journey up the Rhine, which was concerned with military matters, he felt that either Count Frise or Lord Galway could better serve the King.[4]

During January 1697, the Hague suffered under *pénible froid.* Stepney occupied himself with domestic affairs: he wrote to John Ellis about his cousin, Joseph Stepney, whose papers relating to a Power of Redemption for lands in Ireland were stuck in the Secretary of State's office: would Ellis please secure their release. And George found time to acknowledge, in Latin, a letter from '*Nobilissime Juveni G. Villiers*', son of the English Envoy to the States General, Lord Villiers. Matt Prior got permission to visit England. Stepney, jealous, once again approached his patron, Charles Montagu:

> I see no certainty, nor can take any satisfaction in this vagabond
> life which is full of care and I fear will end in nothing but debts.[5]

Then a letter came from Baron Goertz of Hesse-Cassel about a new development in Germany. Since the autumn of 1696, the six Circles of the Empire which lay closest to France had held an Assembly in Frankfurt, with the purpose of creating a standing army for their own defence. The force envisaged was 40,000 men in peacetime, and 60,000 men in time of war. Stepney reported on the project to Trumbull early in January 1697; the King already knew of the scheme because emissaries from the Circles had seen him at Loo the previous autumn. Heinsius had recommended that Stepney's main task in Frankfurt should be to support the project. George, of course, wished specific instructions. Now, according to Goertz, the Conference of the Circles had already ended and a decision had been made to provide the force. George had learned that Hesse too was recruiting, and that Lüneburg would contribute 9,000 men, but that neither of these contingents would serve under Prince Louis. The same caveat applied to any Saxon troops. Goertz wished to know when Stepney was leaving the Hague.[6]

Count Frise had spent Christmas in England – that is, with access to the King. Stepney, knowing that the wind was in the east, sent him a copy of Goertz's letter and told him that Heinsius wished him (Stepney) to await Frise's arrival in the Hague before setting out for the Rhine. Once again George applied to Blathwayt for instructions. By 1 February, he had learned that Frise now held the King's commission to replace Lord Galway as commander of the Protestant troops which were returning from Piedmont. Stepney was uneasy at the thought that Prince Louis and Count Frise should between them have charge of the King's subsidy.

Charles Montagu, Earl of Halifax, by Kneller (c. 1703-10). Courtesy of the National Portrait Gallery. London.

To Lexington (who had now achieved the appointment of Plenipotentiary for the peace negotiations) Stepney commented wryly on some of the King's other appointees:

> another Dutchman made an English Earl, a French-man made an Irish Govr. & a German-English Envoy made Gen[ll] over our French troops on the Rhine.[7]

Now Stepney havered about his credentials, writing in opposing sense to Blathwayt and to Ellis, first denying that he needed credentials and then requesting them. Eventually he was provided with Instructions and had a meeting with Heinsius and with Count Frise. Then he got some cash from his bankers, and set off for the Rhine, travelling in the same coach as Frise, on 13/23 February 1697.[8]

Stepney provided full details of his travel and its cost between 23 February and 27 May (n.s.) 1697 (see Appendix VI). In effect he found himself repeating his task of the previous year, and indeed Heinsius had advised him to refer to his 1696 Instructions, in so far as they could be applied to the 1697 conjuncture.[9]

At Düsseldorf Stepney met his secretary, Philip Plantamour, his servants and his baggage. His reception by the Elector Palatine was not cordial. John William was upset at the King's accusations (which had reached the Elector in a roundabout way via Vienna) that he – John William – had been negotiating with King James. Stepney felt the coldness as the Elector denied the charge, and wrote to Heinsius that he (Stepney) felt it to be his duty to re-establish the correspondence between His Electoral Highness and the King.[10]

On 4 March (n.s.), Stepney, arriving at Coblenz at noon, saw his friend the Elector of Trèves the same evening. Here he was met with the news that King William had refused to lend any troops for the defence of the city. Now, the Elector did not know to whom to turn for help. Stepney reported the situation the next day to Heinsius, remarking at the end of the letter on the Elector's pretensions to the Abbey of Stablo, over which claim the Archbishop hoped for Heinsius' support.[11]

At 'Wisbaden' (where he seems to have had no public business) Stepney took time to write privately to Lexington, concluding his letter with a singular postscript:

> I saw at Dusseldorf ye fat Princesse to Saxe-Lauemburg (widow to ye Prince Palatin) who is to be re-married after Easter to the Prince of Florence: Balls, fireworks & operas are preparing, wch (I fear) will be her best divertissements, for an Italian Philosopher will be but a poor play-fellow for a Lady of her complexion: a female friend of mine shewd her ye other day wt she woud come to (the jealous Instrument) wch (scandall says) she applyd to her orifice, & does not much like yt Muzzle: However it will be her fate, & yr Count Zinzendorf & Abbe Montaculi are labouring to bring her into ye Noose, tho she shews great reluctancy agst living in Italy: the Instrument was finely lined with crimson velvet, *mais jamais il n'y eut de belle prison.*[12]

Stepney reached Frankfurt on 8 March (n.s.), and was happy to be there: at the end of the month he rented his own house. First however he had to travel on to Mainz, and this short journey he undertook in company with Comte d'Autel, a Palatinate acquaintance of the previous year. In Mainz, where he stayed two days, Stepney presented letters to the Elector from King William and, on instructions, tried to further with the Elector the claims of Hanover to a Ninth Electorate. This was a matter of continuing importance: Hanover, Protestant, was capable of providing men and money for the war against France. The Elector of Mainz, as Chancellor of the Holy Roman Empire, wielded influence within the Electoral College, but as a Catholic would not wish to see disturbed the preponderance of that religion amongst the Electors. Stepney reported his discussions to London and wrote also to Frederick William Goertz of Hanover [brother to King William's friend from Hesse-Cassel] urging three separate and necessary actions:

> 1) that Hanover should send troops without loss of time;
> 2) that the consent should be gained of the Elector of Bavaria to the Introduction of Bohemia [to the Electoral College – the Emperor himself being King of Bohemia];
> 3) that the Imperial Court should explain itself regarding the satisfaction promised to Electors and Princes [for their agreement to the Ninth Electorate].[13]

Socially George had the pleasure of a short visit from his friend of Vienna days, Jacob Jan van Hamel Bruynincx, who had been recalled from Vienna to the Hague to be secretary to the Dutch Plenipotentiaries at the peace negotiations.

At the end of April, when Frankfurt was full of rumours of French troop movements, Stepney fell ill of a quite serious fever. He was bled, purged and made to sweat, and at one point feared to lose his hearing. Possibly his malady was caused by a rushed journey to the spa of Schwalbach to see the Landgrave of Hesse-Cassel. This nobleman, usually such a staunch ally of the anti-French cause, had become involved in a dispute with his neighbour, Count Weilburg, over the repayment of a debt. The sum of money was trivial, but the Landgrave had sent a captain and 100 *fantassins* into the Count's territory in order to settle the matter. Weilburg was outraged. Stepney tried to mediate, pointing out the pettiness of the matter and the greater danger which threatened both parties. But since Weilburg was in the service of the Elector Palatine, and that Prince was also at odds with the Landgrave, the prospects for the campaign did not look hopeful. Stepney referred himself to instructions, dated 19 March, which had reached him from Blathwayt. In consultation with Baron Goertz of Hesse-Cassel, he was to put the two princes [the Landgrave and the Elector Palatine] *en bonne intelligence*; and persuade the Landgrave not to command his own troops, but leave them under Prince Louis.

The Landgrave had been at Rheinfels, seeing to the repair of fortifications. Stepney knew he would be at Schwalbach on Sunday 5 May (n.s.), so he went there on purpose to see him and spent the day with him. Tactfully, George did not advance the matter as set out in Blathwayt's letter, but he did discuss the forthcoming campaign. The Landgrave said his troops were ready and waiting, but no-one had asked them to march; and moreover, if he was not with them, they would '*Manque de bonne volonté ou de bonne conduite*'. Despite George's compliments and tact, nothing would induce the Landgrave to allow his troops to serve under Prince Louis. All Stepney could do was to hope that Baron Goertz might have more success with his master. But Goertz too had been ill, and was losing ground visibly owing to his bad health, which prevented his regular attendance on the Landgrave. Stepney asked Blathwayt whether he should not now suggest to the Landgrave that his troops should march towards Brabant.[14]

From his sick-bed, Stepney wrote to Comte d'Autel on a more intimate matter:

> J'ay taché de m'aquitter dignement de la commission dont vous m'avez honoré de bouche à bouche, mais je me suis attiré une disgrace en voulant executer vos ordres au pied de la Lettre; et en effet j'ay trouvé à trop bonnes enseignés que la bouche était fort succulente; par ou elle me paroit moins belle: pour vous dire naturellement les choses la dédaigneuse par une fierté malhonnete répondit à mon baiser par un crachet qui n'étois gueres à l'honneur de la Prosopée . . . . Vous jugerez par là que mes amours vont comme les Ecrivisses.[15]

As usual, when he was comparatively idle, Stepney's thoughts turned to his future and he set out his ideas to Blathwayt, who had invited him to Het Loo. But if this invitation were accepted, what would happen next? All such speculations came to an abrupt end when orders arrived that Stepney was to go immediately to Cassel to persuade the Landgrave to bring his troops forthwith to the Meuse, as he had done the previous year. Count Frise was to break this news to Prince Louis, and seek his agreement. Neither Stepney nor Frise was given any reason for King William's request.[16]

Stepney received these commands on 15/25 May. One day later he was at Friedberg [30 km north of Frankfurt] on his way to Cassel, which city he reached two days later. Immediately he sought out the Landgrave. Charles made excuses: the consent of the Emperor would have to be gained before he moved his troops and (more materially as far as he was concerned) the Estates of the Upper Rhine would probably withhold the subsidy which they had promised. The Landgrave wished the King to provision his troops, once they reached the Meuse, as he had agreed in 1696. Baron Goertz was quick to remind Stepney that of the last year's assignations to the Landgrave, less than half had actually been paid. And the Hessians were complaining of the losses they suffered by the rate of exchange. In his own hand Stepney worked out a troop count for Blathwayt (copying his letter to the new Earl of Albemarle and to Trumbull) [17]

Turning to his own affairs, Stepney addressed Mr. Chanc[llr] of the Exchequer [Charles Montagu], pointing out that he had £4,120 lodged in tallies; £2,857 were due to him in arrears; that he owed £3,000 and did not know to whom to turn for credit. All winter he had kept 12 horses in his stables, ready to execute the King's orders. Probably he would now have to march to Brabant.

> But unless some Methods may be taken in the Treasury for my
> Relief . . it will be hard for me to subsist.[18]

Back in Frankfurt, war preparations continued. Stepney had to guide the Hessian troops towards the Meuse, without allowing them to come into conflict with their supposed allies from the Palatinate. To this end he attended a conference, held on 6 June (n.s.), with Count Frise and the Emperor's Envoy Baron Benebourg to try to prevent Count Weilburg taking revenge on the Landgrave's raiding-parties. That same day Stepney took coach again for Friedberg to try to get Baron Goertz to preach peace (as regarded Count Weilburg) to the Landgrave. After one night only spent in Friedberg Stepney was back again in Frankfurt, and expected to leave the following day (8 June) by river for Bonn. But this last departure was delayed owing to the slowness of the march of both Hessian and Lüneburg [Hanoverian] troops.

> They [the Hessian cavalry] rested 4 days in Count Weilburg's
> estate, wch is a mean revenge.

Meanwhile the Hanoverians had taken a route via the territories of Hesse, and stayed there eight or ten days. Only two baillages were untouched.

> This is the misery of our German forces [wrote Stepney] who
> have no regular Etappes (as ye French have) but eat up one another
> as if yt was all they have to do in a warr. . . . My equipage will be
> up with the Hesse horse this evening near Limburg and I myself
> go tomorrow for Mentz [Mainz].

This was to take leave of the Elector, whilst at the same time urging him to agree to the Ninth Electorate. Stepney proposed to call next at Rheinfels to find out from a Hessian officer, Colonel Tettau, what was happening to the Hessian infantry. At Coblenz, Stepney would call on the Elector of Trèves. Then he would go to Bonn.[19]

In the event, George did not get away from Frankfurt until 12 June (n.s.). The Landgrave now wished to reduce the number of those troops which were to obey King William's commands. Count Weilburg had encamped his contingent on lands belonging to Hesse-Darmstadt. There was no news from Prince Louis. Stepney commented that the Margrave's inactivity might stem from the fact that he was bidding to become King of Poland. Could the French have espoused his interest?

Stepney carried out his planned visits. He joined two of the Landgrave's senior officers inspecting the fortifications at Rheinfels, and wrote a description, while awaiting the arrival of the commanding general, Count Lippe. The latter arrived during the evening of 3/13 June, and as soon as Stepney heard orders given for the shipping down the Rhine of three battalions of Hessians, he returned to his boat and set off for Coblenz, leaving Lippe and the troops to follow. Arrived at the fortress of Ehrenbreitstein, he was greeted by a lieutenant with the news that the Elector of Cologne had refused passage to Hessian troops, although the Lüneburg infantry had been given permission to cross his domains. Stepney continued immediately for Bonn, where, on the afternoon of 5/15 June, he added to his letter to Blathwayt:

> This Postscript will tell you that the Elector of Cologne has bethought him and . . . has given us passage at Bonn, so our Horse begun their passage at 2 this morning and will be over with baggage etc before ye Day be pass'd.

However, the Elector's change of heart does not appear to have resulted from any appeal to him by George Stepney, who only added that he would, before he left Bonn, compliment the Elector if possible.[20]

The troops were now moving towards Maastricht. The weather was foul, being at first unduly hot, and then plaguing the troops with violent thunderstorms and rain. At Heimerzheim, 'three hours from Bonn', Stepney found a hint from Blathwayt that he was to be included in the new Commission for Plantations and Trade, at a salary of £1000 a year. On 8/18 June this good news was confirmed, and four days later he composed a letter of thanks to the King:

> Sir,
> It is with the deepest sense of gratitude and devotion that I now beg leave to lay myself at your Majesty's feet and return the most dutifull thanks that a Soul can be capable of, for your Majesty's

Royall grace & favour, and having not only bore with my weak performances for severall years that I have had the honour to be employ'd in your service at the Cheif Courts of Germany, but now for having been graciously pleas'd to confer on me an Employment in England in the Commission of Trade; which I shall zealously endeavour to execute with the greatest fidelity and Industry, in the hopes thereby to attone for my want of other Qualifications, and that your Majesty will be graciously pleas'd to accept of the remaining part of my life wch I am always ready to sacrifice to your Maties service being with the highest veneration Sir Yr Maties

most obedient, most dutifull &
most loyall Subject & servant

GEORGE STEPNEY
Gulpen
12/22 June 1697

Continuing his way westwards, Stepney passed through Tongern and joined the King at the camp at Cocklenberg, near Brussels. He was graciously received. His pride in his new commission was somewhat tempered by the fact that he discovered he was expected to pay the whole fee for the renewal of the Commission. He expected this, commenting to Ellis:

for from those who have not, must be taken away even wt they have, wch I have often thought a nice expression, but wt has frequently been applicable in my Circumstances.[21]

At camp Stepney came upon Richard Hill, also with little to do. The two took to promenading together. But serious business was also afoot. The official peace negotiations were languishing. The King authorised Lord Portland to talk to the French General Bouffleurs. On 10/20 July, their third meeting took place, in an open field, 'half a league' from Halle. Twenty gentlemen were in Portland's train, Stepney and Hill included. All the entourage were presented to Bouffleurs; then the two 'Cheifs' retired behind a hedge for their private conversation, and the followers on either side entertained each other. Stepney remarked that the French troops were badly clothed and mounted, and looked dejected. He recommended that the whole allied army should see them, as being the best remedy against desertion.[22]

From Cocklenberg Stepney wrote to his banker. He wished to dispose of a 'Basin imperiale' and of a diamond-studded snuffbox. It is not known where or when he acquired these gifts, although the snuffbox may well have been presented to him when he left Dresden, for Frederick Augustus, Elector of Saxony, was known to have a *penchant* for diamonds. George desired a modest price for the first item, which he hoped might be sold to craftsmen in Augsburg who would refashion it. As for the snuffbox, he would accept any price for the diamonds which the banker thought reasonable. It was important that the diamonds should be sold separately from the box, lest such a gift should be traced back to him. There is no further reference to this transaction, so we do not know its outcome.

By 10 August, Stepney was again in the Hague, having travelled round Zeeland in company with Lord Westmorland. In the Hague he was entertained both by Villiers (now Earl of Jersey) and by the Earl of Pembroke. He called at Amsterdam to view another visitor to the Dutch Republic who at the time was causing much comment. This was the Czar Peter the Great of Russia; but despite his efforts, Stepney could not be sure he had actually set eyes on the great man, who was incognito in the city. But Stepney could and did describe the entertainment which the city fathers had organised: fireworks caused the death of two spectators, but a mock sea-battle went off without casualties.[23]

Stepney was waiting for a convoy to England, and meanwhile hoped 'to discover still more of this mystery of Peace.' He also took pains to provide for his secretary, Plantamour, who had been left behind in Frankfurt, and to whom he mentioned that he had heard nothing from Madame Steingens. But Stepney was never noticeably successful in his *amours*. As long as he remained in the Hague he continued commenting at length on the treaty which was being prepared at Ryswyck, but in which he had no part.

On 7 September (o.s.) 1697 Narcissus Luttrell included in his bulletin:

> Yesterday Mr. Stepny his Majesty's envoy to the princes in Germany, arrived at Whitehall, and says 'tis believed in Holland that peace will be signed the 10th instant.[24]

XII *Brandenburg and Poland*
(1698-1699)

William R.

Our Will and Pleasure is that you forthwith prepare a Bill for our
Royal Signature for passing our Privy Seal containing our Warrant
to the Commissioners of our Treasury . . . to pay, or cause to be
paid, unto our Trusty and Well-beloved George Stepney Esq
(whom we have appointed our Envoy Extraordinary to our good
Brother the Elector of Brandenburgh. and other Princes of Germany)
. . . the Sum of Five Hundred Pounds for his Equipage, and the
further sum of Five pounds by the Day for his ordinary Entertainment
and Allowance to commence from the Date hereof . . . .

Given at our Court at Kensington,
the first day of January 1697/8.
In the ninth year of our Reign.

To the Clerk of the
Signet attending By His Ma^{ty}'s
Command
Ja: VERNON [1]

King William's reasons for despatching George Stepney to Berlin
(less than four months after his return from the Hague) are not
precisely known. The excuse for getting rid of the little Welshman
lay easily to hand: he was by now the most experienced of diplomats
who dealt with the German-speaking world; and from Brandenburg
news had recently arrived of the dismissal from office of Eberhard
von Danckelmann [President of the Council of Brandenburg],
always a good friend of William III. There is little information as
to how Stepney passed his time in England, other than what relates
to his appointment as Commissioner of Trade, which will be
examined in a later chapter. The King had no affection for Stepney.
He could and did use the man – when he thought about him at all.
But such thoughts may well have been suspicious rather than
benevolent. Stepney was the known *protégé* of Charles Montagu,
and a persistent Whig. On both these counts the King would have

been glad of his room, rather than of his company. But the thought of sending Stepney to Berlin, to intercede for Danckelmann, seems to have come from the King's great confidant, the Grand Pensionary of Holland, Antonie Heinsius, to whom the King wrote from Kensington on 24 December/3 January 1697/8:

> Je suis aussi très-peu edifié des proces dures entamées contre le pauvre Danckelman, et j'ai resolu, conformement à votre avis, d'envoyer sans tarder Stepney à cette cour; il delibera avec vous sur la maniere dont il devra s'y prendre.[2]

Stepney's Instructions were dated the same day as the precious Privy Seal. George was immediately to embark on board the ship appointed to carry him, and with what speed he could repair to Berlin (or to such other place where the Elector of Brandenburg might be found), and having notified his arrival as usual, he was to request an audience as soon as possible, deliver his Letters of Credence and accompany these with 'such expressions of our Friendship and the Esteem we have for the Elector's person and Allyance' as he should think proper.

He was then gently to insinuate the King's concern for President Danckelmann. The King reminded the Elector that he was dealing with an ancient servant, who had had a great hand in his education, and although the King had no wish to appear officious, he wished to use his good offices in mitigation of extremities, and hoped that the charges against Danckelmann were the result of mistake, misinformation or defect of judgement.

Stepney's further Instructions were more general and traditional: he was to maintain good relations with the Court of Brandenburg and inform himself of their 'inclinations and designs.' He was to declare the King's approval of the Association of the Circles and Princes of the Rhine, and [vaguely] to hope that such associations might be more general. Should he be approached on the matter of hemp from Königsberg, he was to listen and relate – but not enter into discussions without further instructions.

He must promote the Ninth Electorate. He must maintain a good correspondence with the ministers of other Princes residing at the Court of Brandenburg, and 'penetrate into the private designs of their masters.'

There followed the usual clause (dating back to the time of King Charles II), that Stepney should not 'insist to have the hand' of any Ambassador in his own house.

He was to assist the King's subjects; correspond with the King's Ambassadors and Ministers in foreign countries; write a report on his return; and observe any further instructions which might be sent to him.[3]

But within a week of receiving this new commission, an event occurred which surely delayed his departure, although no reference to it occurs in any of Stepney's surviving papers. This was the fire which occurred in the Palace of Whitehall during the night of 4/5 January (o.s.) 1697/8. There is no means of knowing how the blaze affected George's two sisters, who lived so close to the court. The next news of Stepney appears in a letter which he wrote on 28 January from Whitehall to his Secretary of State, James Vernon, expecting to leave for the Continent the following day. Meanwhile Stepney had not been idle: one of Eberhard Danckelmann's six brothers was at the time in London, and had told Stepney that the cause of the President's disgrace was the intrigues of the house of Hanover. The London Danckelmann was about to suggest to the King that Stepney should call at Hanover, and George told Vernon he would wait at the Hague for one post, so that he could receive instructions on this point, after which he would consult the Pensioner. Meanwhile Lord Portland had told Stepney that he (George) might be given the commission on 'the affair of Neufchatel.' Further, George had heard that the Elector of Brandenburg might visit his domains in Prussia. Should he accompany him?[4]

The winter was hard, and the Envoy had matters other than diplomacy to occupy his mind. From Rotterdam, on 1/11 February 1698, he wrote to John Ellis:

> This is to acquaint my good friend that I have made as happy a voyage as cou'd be expected in a Winter-season, Wee put out from Margrett-road [i.e. Margate] the 30th of Jan. [o.s.]: abt 8 at night with ye wind at N W wch our Capt thought pretty hazardous considering wt a sea it makes on this Coast; but wee were resolv'd to venture because wee had lost very much time by ye frost; & last night wee gott happily within ye Booms of this City, without receiving any damage from ye Ice.[5]

There were friends in the Hague: Lord Lexington, on his way home from Vienna, was waiting to pick up the yacht which had brought Stepney over, as was Count Frise. Stepney duly called on Heinsius, and learned of the recent death of the Elector of Hanover, husband of his patroness Sophia and father of the Electress of Brandenburg. Hurriedly Stepney wrote home, wishing to convey the formal compliment of condolence, because that office might procure him presents. He received no reply from England, and a week later wrote a personal letter of condolence to Electress Sophia, regretting that it was obviously not a seasonable time to pass by Hanover. Sophia replied very charmingly, saying that his conversation would have consoled her more than his obliging letter.[6]

The journey, over Amsterdam towards Bremen and Hamburg, was not particularly pleasant:

> I am got into the deserts of Westphalia [Stepney was at Haselünne, '4 hours from Lingen'] and am waiting only till I can get fresh horses for myself and baggage, wherewith wee may jogg on all this night, which I esteem a less hardship even in this cold Weather, than to bear the Stench of these nasty habitations.

Stepney continued that he hoped to reach Bremen the following day. [1 March, n.s.] but that the route to Hamburg was doubtful because of the ice. However he arrived in Bremen as planned, to be greeted by the magistrates bearing flagons of wine and compliments. Despite floating ice on all the rivers he pressed on, and was in Hamburg on 5 March. Again he was among friends: the city magistracy too donated presents of wine, and the English Company invited him to become a member. Stepney accepted with alacrity, and wrote immediately to Vernon asking the latter, as Secretary of State and Member of Parliament, to promote the interests of the Company.

In Hamburg he found awaiting him Eberhard Danckelmann's eldest son. From him Stepney heard of the plight of the father, and of all relatives of the Danckelmann clan. Stepney discovered that Eberhard's rudeness to everyone, including the Electress, was the cause of his downfall. The President was now a prisoner at Peitsch, a garrison town on the Oder. Prospects for his reinstatement seemed very bleak.[7]

Arrived in Berlin on 14 March (n.s.), Stepney found himself plunged into difficulties – so trivial to a twentieth-century mind but so real to one of the seventeenth – regarding the ceremonial of the Brandenburg court. Everything hinged on the way the Elector would receive the representative of a reigning monarch, (and Stepney knew perfectly well how much the Elector resented the fact that King William had never allowed him (Frederick III) to sit in his presence). Now, the Elector had introduced a step up to his chair in the audience-chamber. And George Stepney was the first Envoy to be received under this new arrangement. Letters which Stepney had picked up on his arrival were not much help to him. Vernon had written that the King did not care one way or the other about the ceremonial at Berlin, provided Stepney was treated in the same way as other envoys.

In the event, all went well. The Elector sent three coaches, each drawn by six horses, to collect Stepney for his first formal audience, together with the Chamberlain, the Master of Ceremony, two *Kammer-Junker* and two Gentlemen of the Chamber. Long cloaks were worn by all, in mourning for the Elector of Hanover. A Guard was provided at the entrance to the Palace, and Stepney was conducted on his way by various courtiers. The Elector stood on an *Estrade* (a 'sopha' about a foot high and 12 feet square), but advanced to the door of the audience-chamber to greet Stepney, who made a reverence and then accompanied His Electoral Highness [H E H] to the elevation, whereupon the privy counsellors withdrew. Stepney made his compliment in French and presented the King's *Lettre de cachet.* The Elector was neither seated nor covered (as Vernon had feared he might be), but stood on the sopha level with Stepney, without distinction.

Such ceremonial was not provided free of charge. In his own hand Stepney carefully noted the fees he had paid, in Reichsthaler (Rx):

To Trumpetts	20 Rx
To Hautbois	6
To Camer Furrier	12
To Footmen	24
To Coachmen and Grooms	18
	80

To the particular footmen 4[8]

Ten days after his first ceremonial audience Stepney decided that he must carry out his Instructions and approach the Elector on behalf of Eberhard Danckelmann, having heard meanwhile that further steps were planned against the President's family. This second audience took place on 6/16 March and lasted two hours. Stepney began with the argument that it behoved the Elector to deal generously with an old servant, and the Elector heard him with more patience than Stepney had expected. But with the details of the case Frederick grew angry and cited all the reasons which had led him to put Danckelmann under arrest: in any case he was well treated at Peitsch, having two castles and a town for his prison. But he was there for life. All that Stepney could do was to beg for mercy to be shewn to Danckelmann's family, and that their houses and estates should not be subject to confiscation.

One of Stepney's difficulties lay in the fact that he could not approach the Electress – '*cette adorable Princesse*' – about the Danckelmann affair, because Sophie Charlotte considered herself to have been insulted by the President, and was no longer his friend. But Stepney on 6 April (n.s.) saw the Elector again on behalf of Danckelmann's wife and children, and pleaded that any clemency shewn to them would be taken as a mark of friendship for King William. The Elector replied that Danckelmann's estate was forfeit because he was believed to have acted dishonestly; and he regretted that the King should have made the one request with which he could not comply. He added:

> Et vous, Monsieur, vous me ferey grand plaisir si vous ne
> m'en parlez plus.

So Stepney concluded that the matter was closed.[9]

The fact that Europe in 1698 was enjoying a period of peace (following the Treaty of Ryswyck the previous October), did not mean that the English Envoy was idle. The world was waiting for the death of King Charles II of Spain, who had no son, and whose empire was likely to fall apart. Stepney reported on 6 April (n.s.) that a Madame Berlips from Brandenburg was in attendance on the Queen of Spain and might well persuade that lady, on the death of her husband, to marry the Dauphin of France and thus become Queen of France and Spain. Now the Queen of Spain was sister both to the Elector Palatine and to the Empress Eleonore. Stepney's comment was that the Empress' family would be enhanced by such an alliance, and that the Elector Palatine would promote the advantage of his sister 'by the Interest he has been making for many years in France.' In London, King William was already in correspondence with Heinsius about the Spanish Succession; no doubt he studied Stepney's remarks with great care.[10]

For the first time in years, a French Envoy was expected at the Court of Brandenburg. Stepney confided to Ellis:

> There is one thing that I must desire you, that if his Ma^{ty} sends me
> orders to stay at this Court some time, you will give notice to my
> sisters that they may send me a good chariot, for if I am to bear up
> against a French Envoy (as the Pensioner thinks I should) I must
> stretch my Purse not to be inferior to the figure he shall pretend to
> make here.[11]

It is not known whether the Stepney sisters succeeded in this task.

The Elector was due to visit his domains in Prussia. He had also planned a meeting with his neighbour, the Elector Frederick Augustus of Saxony, who at the end of 1696 had bribed his way to the elective crown of Poland as King Augustus II ('the Strong').

He was of course well-known to Stepney (who occasionally and ironically used to refer to him as 'my hero'). King William had already instructed Stepney to accompany the Elector of

Brandenburg to Prussia, and now provided his Envoy with credentials for the Polish king. Stepney, although he complained to Charles Montagu about the expense of this journey, was not unwilling to undertake it:

> I must confess I have some Curiosity left still to see the Fag end of the world, before I return home again.[12]

For Stepney had indeed written both to Vernon and Blathwayt of his wish to be recalled to England, owing to his lack of success with the Elector over the Danckelmann affair. This earned him a sharp rebuke from Blathwayt:

> Perhaps a little sacrificing of your Interest and Credit with the Elector and his Court on this occasion may recommend your Zeal and Ministry to the King whatever the success of your Negotiation may be. . . . Another thing I am to add by way of Caution to you [is] that it is look'd upon even by Mr. Secretary that you make a shew of abandoning yr business too soon in supposing it already dispatched, so as to excuse you from the necessity of attending the Elector to Prussia.

In general, Blathwayt was correct in his comments, for he had perceived Stepney's over-sensitivity to his popularity – or lack of it – at any court to which he was assigned. However in this case Stepney had undoubtedly persevered in his task. He replied to Blathwayt with dignity, ending his letter:

> I know very well I am plac'd here as a Sentinell, and must neither desert my Post nor desire to be relieved; at least I am resolv'd to stand my Ground and struggle as boldly as I can for the time I stay here.

Blathwayt later apologised for his letter.[13]

Stepney left for Poland on 29 April (n.s.), travelling by coach. He left in Berlin his faithful secretary Plantamour, with instructions to do what he could to help Madame Danckelmann. The President's successor, Johann Kasimir von Kolbe (later Count Wartenberg), had wished to have the Elector's arms displayed over the door of Danckelmann's house, thus indicating to all that the estates were forfeit. This unkind gesture was delayed as long as Stepney remained in town, as disobliging to the King of England. However as soon as Stepney's back was turned, the persecution of the Danckelmann family continued.

It took Stepney a week to reach Danzig, where he was greeted with enthusiasm by the English merchant community, 'not to mention the Scotts who seem a people to themselves', commented the Envoy. The Englishmen desired an augmentation of their privileges, in competition with the French. They produced a document dated 1638, which Stepney did not think was a title or contract. But he asked Mr Secretary Vernon to have the Paper Office in Whitehall search for the original. Apart from comforting the merchants, Stepney spent a day watching cannon-casting, for King Augustus was preparing for his summer campaign.

The stay in Danzig was marred for Stepney by news which reached him there of the death of his first *protégé*, Heneage Montagu. Stepney was still thinking about it when he wrote a condoling letter to Charles Montagu, and to the young man's mother. To Ellis, Stepney continued:

> He [Heneage] lived with me a year at Dresden and was a very sensible companion, & one whom I loved heartily; but wee must all follow in good time.

After four days in Danzig (6-10 May, n.s.) Stepney set off for Warsaw. His comments to Charles Montagu are revealing:

> The wretched accommodation I met with on the road between Dantzig and Warsaw 7 days together, made me almost repent of the curiosity I had to see the Country. For notwithstanding the soil is the best in the world, never greater misery was seen among the ordinary people, The nobility being so tyrannical as not to suffer their subjects to enjoy ye fruits of their Labours in any reasonable proportion.

He arrived on 16 May, and one day later was able to give an account of the position of the various factions in Poland, beginning with the Cardinal-Primate [Michael Radziowsky]. It had taken two years for King Augustus to establish himself; (the former King died on 17 June 1696). Nearly all the Polish noblemen were at odds with each other: Stepney commented that hitherto King Augustus had taken no sides in this feuding, it being in his interest to allow everyone to weaken himself by war. The King however wished to 'signalize himself' by warlike means, and had his eyes on Wallachia and Moldavia. Stepney achieved his (private) audience, partly through the good offices of his old friend Baron Phlug (no mention being made of that gentleman's wife, of whom Stepney had been so enamoured four years previously). The audience took place at 10.00 a.m. on 19 May. Stepney travelled in a coach drawn by six horses ('for ordinary visits are never made at Warsaw with less'), the vehicle having been lent to him by a friend. It is likely that the friend was Baron Blumenthal of Stepney's first Vienna posting. Stepney certainly found him in Warsaw, but failed to collect the 91 florins which the Baron had owed him for many years.

During his stay in Warsaw Stepney was present at the ceremonial submission of the Cardinal Primate to King Augustus. (Stepney was careful to compliment both men – separately). To his surprise, George encountered an 'honest Jesuit.' This was Father [Carlo Maurizio] Vota, an Italian who had been confessor to the late King and continued in the same office with Augustus. Stepney discovered that

> The good man is known to be an irreconcilable Enemy to France, and an honest well-wisher to the prosperity of Poland without entering into the dangerous intrigues of his Society.

This was enough for Stepney to recommend that King William should award Father Vota a medal, and indeed this was done, a few months later.

While Stepney was in Warsaw Lord Paget was beginning his mediation to conclude a peace between the Emperor and the Turks. Stepney complained of his lack of information on this topic. However he made contact with the Emperor's Envoy (Count Sedleminsky) in Warsaw, who kindly provided no less than eight separate documents about the peace negotiations, all of which Stepney sent back to London. King Augustus was highly suspicious of these proceedings: he wished to continue the war against the Turks, in the hope of adding territory to his own dominions. Stepney assured him that King William's mediation was not intended to prevent this aim. Meanwhile the meeting between King Augustus and the Elector of Brandenburg was arranged to take place at Joansburg on the southern shore of Lake Spirding , about 150km north-north-east of Warsaw, on 24 May (n.s.). Stepney however made no effort to be present (not wishing to pry into the secrets of the two rulers), took leave of King Augustus, and left to rejoin the Elector of Brandenburg in the far-off city of Königsberg, on the coast of East Prussia.[14]

It seems extraordinary that Stepney avoided the meeting between King Augustus and Elector Frederick, because his Instructions told him clearly that he was to do his best to inform himself about the 'inclinations and designs' of the Court to which he was accredited. Stepney excused himself to Vernon, saying that neither the King nor the Elector wished him to be present. Dr Johann Ham (still in Berlin as Envoy from the States General to Brandenburg) did not attend either, but sent a secretary as an observer. Stepney obtained news of the meeting from a friend (possibly Baron Blumenthal), which he sent back to London. He noted wryly that Ham was reporting directly to Lord Portland.

Stepney reached Königsberg on 8 June (n.s.) 1698, and reported to Vernon two days later. He arrived four hours after the French

Envoy, Mr Des Alleurs, who gave notice of his arrival, so Stepney
called on him.

> He seems an honest plain man with whom I may hope to live
> easily and friendly enough.

But a curious incident took place. Stepney had already noted the
presence in Berlin of a Frenchman named Tristan, who was well
received in society. This man seemed to have been given the task
of preparing the ground for the new Envoy. Now, when Stepney
made his call, he was surprised to find that Tristan followed himself
and the French Envoy into the reception-room, and seated himself
behind Des Alleurs. Stepney however felt he could not object.

On 12 June, Des Alleurs returned Stepney's call, in company
with Tristan.

> To put a stop to too great Familiarity, I desired Three English
> Gentlemen who live with me to carry him into another Chamber
> and entertain him there, which he declined, and continued with
> them in the Hall, near half an hour that the Visit lasted.

Apart from noting Stepney's insistence upon privacy, one's interest
is immediately drawn to the fact that he now had three young
diplomats in his household: they may be assumed to have been
Harry Watkins, placed with Stepney by Blathwayt; and Charles
Whitworth and Erasmus Lewis, both first cousins of Stepney's, the
first on his mother's, the second on his father's side of the family.
All three contributed to Stepney's later career.[15]

The stay in Königsberg was not rewarding. Stepney had a four-
hour audience of the Elector on 10/20 June, but could glean no
information on the topics which were of interest to him: the result
of the princely meeting at Joansburg; Danckelmann; the possible
negotiations carried out by the Danish and French Envoys; or even
of the possibility of the Elector making a journey to Cleves.
Depressed, Stepney wrote privately to Vernon, requesting
revocation, and proposing that his secretary Plantamour should stay
on in Berlin as the King's representative.

During these dog-days of near-idleness Stepney found time to
request instructions on a matter of etiquette which troubled him:
his French colleague, Des Alleurs, had complimented the Elector
of Brandenburg by attending him to dinner, and standing behind
his chair, much like a servant. The Court was surprised, the Elector
delighted, and was likely to ask the English Envoy to follow suit.
Sure enough, two or three friends were sent to discuss the matter
with Stepney,

> to which I have only answered in generall, that I have the Honour
> to serve a Master who is to give Examples and not to follow them,

and that in a matter of so high a Nature, I am not Master of my
own action, but am to be guided by positive Orders.

Unhelpfully, King William declined to give Stepney any further
guidance on this tricky point, merely remarking that if Stepney (in
company with other Envoys) decided to pay the Elector such a
compliment, it should be on an occasion when the Electress was
present. In fact, George never did wait behind the Elector's chair,
and in later years was critical of Lord Raby when the latter did so.

Another matter troubled the English Envoy. Should he refuse
any present offered to him by the Elector when the letters of
revocation arrived? While he obviously hoped that London would
allow him to accept a gift, George's conscience told him that any
proffered present should be refused, because the Elector had refused
the King's request about Danckelmann, but this might look like a
Huff.[16]

The return from Königsberg to Berlin, via Danzig and Stolpe,
was not pleasant. On 16/26 July Stepney sent a circular letter to his
friends from the Brandenburg capital:

> I arrived here last night and tho' my constitution is tough I must
> own it has suffered no small breach by this terrible journey in
> excessive hot weather, wch will oblige me to rest for some days.

And the Envoy did not attend court until 1 August, although Kolbe
and various foreign envoys called on him at his house. He was
happy to learn that the Danish Envoy had received instructions not
to compliment the Elector of Brandenburg by waiting behind his
chair at dinner.

Then a letter arrived from Blathwayt (who was still in Whitehall)
raising for the first time the possibility of Stepney's being sent to
Vienna to negotiate affairs. But on 2 August (n.s.) Blathwayt, who
as usual accompanied King William to Holland, wrote to tell
Stepney that he was to remain in Berlin. A week later George wrote
a long dispatch about the strong possibility of the Elector of
Brandenburg entering into a firm alliance with France and listing
five heads, under which the Elector felt himself misused by his
former allies, the maritime powers. Four days later Stepney was
claiming that his arguments with the Elector had turned the latter
away from the French enticements. And, typically, George could
not suppress the comment:

> My worthy colleague Mr. H- [Ham] has kept in his morning-Gown
> all these days of difficulties, and has not had the Courage to appear
> once at Court, or to make a visit to one minister, tho our greatest
> interest lay at stake.

Yet, George was convinced, Lord Portland would attribute to Ham all the success of recent days, which had been George's own work. To Vernon, in a private letter, Stepney trumpeted:

> If ever it be allowed to do onesself justice, I may venture to tell you, as my best friend, that what I have now done is the chief piece of work, and the most dextrously menag'd of any service I have done his Ma⁺ˢ since I had the honour to be employed.

What a pity that these remarks did not come from London, rather than being addressed to the Secretary of State! However it is fair to note that the King took over Stepney's dispatch about the Elector of Brandenburg's complaints, and kept it by him to read and re-read. [17]

A week later Stepney was writing on another matter, ever dear to his heart: he had heard of a rumour flying around the Hague that the Elector of Brandenburg was dissatisfied that he was not sufficiently 'dignifyed' – high-born – to be employed at the Court. The Elector, however, denied any such attitude, and caused Stepney to be told that he [the Elector] would rather have Stepney in Berlin than any other minister. George asked Blathwayt to find out the source of the rumours, and hoped that the intriguer was not Mr Hop (then the States' representative in Vienna) who might wish for another colleague. [18]

But two events enlivened the days of the English Envoy. The first was a letter from Blathwayt telling him of the King's intention to visit the elderly Duke of Zell, probably at Ebersdorf [Ebstorf – about 50 km north-north-east of Celle, on the Lüneburger Heide] to which meeting Stepney would be invited and a decision taken as to whether he should be sent to Vienna. The second agreeable happening was the arrival of a diamond ring, sent to George by the King of Poland, containing one large diamond valued at 1,500 dollars, and really worth £250 sterling. Stepney was delighted, and promptly asked that a similar courtesy should be shewn to Christoph Dietrich Bosen, then King Augustus' Envoy with King William. [19]

The meeting-place between King and Duke was eventually fixed at the Duke of Zell's hunting-lodge at Goer. Stepney awaited his call there which, he wrote, 'will quicken me like the voice of an Arch-Angel.' Erasmus Lewis then takes up the story:

> Mr. Stepney left Berlin last Tuesday and came hither [i.e. to Goer] on Friday: we are lodg'd in a little wooden tent, where we have so small conveniency of writing, and He desires to be excus'd to you [Ellis] till he has either some business or opportunity. He has already had severall discourses with his Ma⁺ˢ, the result of which, He thinks, will be, that he shall be condemned to return to the place from whence he came, perhaps before the King leave this Country.

This was true. The Elector of Brandenburg had declined to attend the meeting, owing to the unfortunate difficulty of the armchair, in which he was not permitted to sit in the King's presence. The Elector of Hanover [later King George I] did attend, but took dinner in his own apartments, for the same reason.

Stepney, attended by his two cousins Erasmus Lewis and Charles Whitworth, reached Goer on 3 October (n.s.), half an hour after the King's arrival. He was graciously received in three audiences, when he reported on the situation in Berlin. Owing to the absence of Elector Frederick, it was decided that Stepney should return after one week and convey to the Elector the terms of the First Partition Treaty (agreed between England, France and the Netherlands) for the peaceful division of the Spanish Empire upon the expected death of its king, Charles II. On 9 October, Lord Portland read the text to Stepney, and allowed him to take notes.

> I must confess upon ye opening of ye Scheme, the Scales fell from my Eyes, & I ever own ye depth of yt Councill to be one of ye greatest Miracles of his Maties Life.

The following day Stepney took post, 'big with ye Secrett and honoured with letters from his Ma^ty both for the El^r and Electrice.' But he was given no copy and did not see the contents. Reaching Berlin on 12 October, Stepney had audience of the Elector the next day in the latter's bedchamber, where he used an atlas to explain to the prince the details of the partition. Tactfully, Stepney added that Frederick was the first Elector to be informed of the treaty, ahead of those of Bavaria and Brunswick.

Frederick accepted the announcement calmly, and made two perspicacious comments: that the French were probably not to be trusted, and would wish by degrees to assume the whole monarchy; and that no provision had been made by the drafters of the treaty in case the Electoral Prince of Bavaria (who was designated as the future king of Spain) should die without issue.

Stepney himself, reflecting on the matter, attributed the conception of the First Partition Treaty to Robert Spencer, second Earl of Sunderland, 'for I know no man upon Earth but himself capable of such a Project.' And already George was contemplating the possible adverse consequences for himself, for he expected to be sent to Vienna to break the news of the treaty to the Emperor Leopold, who hitherto had been kept in ignorance of it.

In the short term George was allowed no rest. The Elector of Brandenburg immediately ordered him to travel back to Goer, to inform the King his master of the Elector's intention to mount a surprise attack on the Polish city of Elbing [62 km east of Danzig]. Stepney was scandalised at this plan and remonstrated with the Elector that such an attack would break the recently-achieved friendship between Frederick and King Augustus, which had been celebrated at Joansburg. And George was even more horrified to learn that a secret agreement had been concluded between the two princes, whereby King Augustus would receive private recompense for acquiescence in the plan:

> wch however will not justify ye proceeding, & notwithstanding my Diamond Ring I may take leave to inferr from this accident, that there are some cases when Sovereigns may be and are Traytors to their People.

Stepney left Berlin again early in the morning of 14 October (n.s.), this time taking Plantamour with him. The King's court had moved to Celle, and Stepney lodged with his one-time rival James Cresset (who was accredited to the Duke of Zell), and the two men drank to the health of John Ellis and Richard Powis in Whitehall in a bottle of admirable Burgundy.

By this time Stepney was well known for his collection of European treaties over the century, and for the ease with which he could produce them as required. On this occasion he told King William that the Elector of Bavaria [Max Emmanuel] had under his contract of marriage with the daughter of the Emperor Leopold, renounced for himself and his heirs the whole Spanish monarchy except the Netherlands, 'of wch Contract I presented his Ma^{ty} [with] ye first Copy he had ever seen of it.'[20]

By 25 October (n.s.) Stepney was back in Berlin. He was soon to write to Ellis:

> I have my head full of Masquerading-habit, furnishing 5 rooms, treating 45 people at 3 Tables & practising Country-dances agst ye Kings Birth-night when I am to have ye Electrice & the whole Court at my House, *nolens volens*; you know Mr. DesAlleurs and Mr. Ahlfeld [the Danish Envoy] began ye frolick wch I could not forbear imitating without sneaking; therefore to colour ye extravagancy I chose ye King's birth-night, wch I hope will sound well at Loo, notwithstanding it may afford an article in a future Bill of Extry^s to be submitted to ye ordeal-fire (as you call it) of ye King's approbation.

The party, held on 14 November (n.s.) cost £300 and was a huge success. Two entertainments were necessary, because the Elector wished to dine and retire early; the Electress to sup and dance. The Elector effectually invited himself, because after Stepney's return to Berlin he had asked him whether there was not a large hall in his house? Stepney took the hint, and set about arranging the event.

The Court was ordered to lay aside mourning [for the late Elector of Hanover] and to appear in gala. The Elector arrived in a new coach drawn by eight horses with magnificent harness, used for the first time on this occasion. The suite included all the officers of the court, 24 footmen and the horse and Swiss guards. At table His Highness was accompanied by the Electoral Prince and most of the foreign ministers, who were seated by Stepney so that 'no difficulty could arise on account of Ceremony.' The Elector began by drinking the King's health standing, with drums and trumpets sounding at each glass, 'which is our high German serenade.' The Elector had had the idea of bringing cannon up to Stepney's door, 'but I found means to prevent yt disorder.' When the Elector rose from table and retired into an apartment, he and Stepney drank *Brüderschaft* (Stepney representing the King).

In the evening the Assembly, which was usually held on Friday nights, took place at Stepney's house. The Electress and her ladies attended, as well as the Margraves [the Elector's brothers] and the gentry of the town.

> Wee divided ourselves into Basset and Ombre Tables, till the Electrice was disposed to sup. . . . Wee had 20 Ladys at the table with the Electrice, and the rest were furnished in proportion, and I may venture to say wee were well served and without disorder. Supper ended wee fell to dancing and the Margraves with other of the gentlemen appeared in Masquerade.

Dancing continued until 2.00 a.m. And after the Electress had returned to court, a courier arrived with the news of the surrender of Elbing to the Brandenburgers. Stepney was gratified at his success. He claimed that the point of the exercise had been to demonstrate that the English Envoy was quite as capable of lavish entertainment as his French colleague. Through Ellis, Stepney arranged that an account of the entertainment should be given in the *London Gazette.* And the King gave his approval to the event.[21]

The gaiety of the Brandenburg court did not extend until the year's end. The Elector, in hard weather, prepared for a journey into Prussia, partly for political reasons and partly because there was a near-famine in the countryside around Berlin, so the court would be obliged to move. In the event, a thaw set in, which made the trek eastwards impossible, although in January 1699 the court did move to Magdeburg, so that the Elector could meet the Landgrave of Hesse-Cassel. King William travelled to England,

and never did give Stepney any firm instructions to betake himself
to Vienna. Blathwayt commented to Matthew Prior:

> Friend Stepney does not hasten to Vienna, but entertains himself
> with the lesser affairs of Elbing and Poland.[22]

But the implied criticism was unfair: Stepney had already made
one journey from Berlin to Vienna in the depths of winter, and
would have had no desire to repeat the experience without explicit
directions. Besides, the King of the Romans [the eldest son of the
Emperor] was about to be married, and, according to Stepney, a
'person of quality' would be required to make the usual compliment.
Meanwhile it was likely that King William's mediation might be
sought in the dispute over Elbing, in which case Stepney's presence
in Berlin was still necessary.

At home the King was faced with an unruly Parliament and
hostility to his foreign policy. The Whigs were in trouble. Stepney
had no doubt of his own views:

> Being out of reach [of] ye danger of being call'd to ye Barr of the
> House of Comons, I make no difficulty of censuring their vote for
> ye breaking of our army as the most unreasonable, violent and
> pernicious resolution that wise men ever took: & I cannot
> sufficiently wonder how it is possible for us to have forgotten so
> soon the dangers wherewith we struggled nine years, so as to
> relye entirely on ye goodwill of our Neighbours.[23]

Reluctantly, Stepney accompanied the Elector of Brandenburg to
Magdeburg. The visit was a short one, but one of George's main
objects was achieved, which was to ask the Landgrave to intervene
in favour of the Danckelmann family. For George had been in secret
communication with the former President, knowing that the
Landgrave was his friend. These efforts were unavailing. But the
stay in Magdeburg included a dinner given by the Elector for the
Landgrave and for the Duke of Wolfenbuttel, who had joined the
party incognito. Stepney, as well as the French and Danish Envoys,
was invited: and George felt honoured at the opportunity to sit at
the same table as three sovereign princes.[24]

As soon as the Magdeburg visit was over, Stepney's mind turned
again to the subject of his recall. He wrote about it both to Lord
Portland and to Charles Montagu. This wish was strengthened when
the news reached Berlin, about 16 February (n.s.) 1699, of the death
of the Electoral Prince of Bavaria ten days earlier. Stepney revelled
in 'I told you so' to his London correspondents: but the prophet of
this event had not in fact been Stepney, but the Elector of
Brandenburg.

However the affair of Elbing was rumbling on. Stepney

considered that the Elector of Brandenburg had fair pretensions to the territory under a treaty signed at Velau in 1657. Although King Augustus might well have connived at the Brandenburg invasion, the Polish nobility had not, and were threatening hostilities. The Emperor had offered mediation, and wished the King of England to participate, probably by sending Stepney for the task. And most European rulers wished to be represented at any conference, including Denmark, the Netherlands, France and Sweden. Stepney remarked to John Robinson [English Envoy in Stockholm]:

> I have begged for Revocation, but by the last letters I am commanded not to think of it. However to comfort me his Ma^{ty} has promis'd to turn Sollicitor for me in ye Treasury. I hope he has some Interest there.[25]

But although George reckoned his appointment to Berlin had cost him £1,200, after all his Treasury bills had been paid; and that he was 'indifferent where I am to linger out my life', in fact he later looked back on this second year in Berlin with great pleasure. At Goer, the King had agreed that further remonstrances about the treatment of the Danckelmann family would be useless. So George had been received back again into favour by the Elector of Brandenburg, and more particularly by his wife, the Electress Sophie-Charlotte. Already on 31 January (o.s.), he told Ellis he had missed a post-day because he had been 'on a ramble' with the Electress, and throughout 1699 his cousin Charles Whitworth quite often was asked to complete the outgoing bag of mail and to excuse the Envoy for diverting himself.

For Stepney had found an agreeable companion at court. Mlle Pelnitz [or Pöllnitz] was First Lady-in-Waiting to Sophie-Charlotte. She was something of a blue-stocking, was interested in Plato and was described by Sir Andrew Fountaine (who was making the Grand Tour about 1703) as 'pritty and witty.' Thus it comes as no surprise that Stepney took an interest in her, for he had been attracted to a previous *amour*, Mme Steingens, for the same reasons. He corresponded with Fräulein Pöllnitz for at least five years. Now, in Berlin, Stepney enjoyed the friendship of both the French and the Danish envoys, Mr. DesAlleurs and Mr Ahlfeld, with whom he joined in the entertainments provided for and by Electress Sophie-Charlotte. The princess was in the habit of amusing her friends with news of her French 'aunt.' [This lady was in fact Elizabeth Charlotte of Orleans, daughter of the Elector Carl Ludwig of the Palatinate, and therefore Sophie-Charlotte's much older first-cousin.] Writing in 1704, when DesAlleurs had been sent to Prince

Franz Rákóczy in Hungary and had adopted a moustache and the clothes of the Hungarians, Stepney recalled that the outfit must have made him such a

> *figure autant grotesque pour lui, que celui qu'il avoit après minuit à Berlin lorsque nous donnames la Masquerade à l'adorable Princesse dans Son apparte^mt où ma tante Francoise fit son Entrée. Il ne manque que ma flute et le violon de Mr. Ahlfeldt pour rendre la représentation complette.*

And Stepney added that these thoughts were fresh in his memory, and he regarded those days as the happiest of his life.[26]

In Berlin in March the marriage was celebrated between one of the Elector's brothers and a daughter of the Princess of Anhalt. For once Stepney was told to make the formal compliment from King William. The Latin letter was drafted in London by John Ellis, to whom George wrote complaining that (i) the Margrave's name was Philip, not William; and (ii) that Ellis had wished him a numerous issue:

> whereas if he has more than one or two Wee shall be tempted to use them as wee do Kittens![27]

About the same time George received a letter from his first diplomatic chief, Sir Peter Wyche, now living in exile in Lisbon at the age of 71. Sir Peter wanted help in collecting his arrears, and pointed out that he had waited for the end of the war before making any application. It is pleasant to record that Stepney responded to the old man with a kind and friendly letter, wishing to repay the obligations which Sir Peter had heaped on him in his youth. At the same time George asked Charles Montagu to arrange that Wyche should be accorded the same generous treatment which Edmund Poley and Lady Sylvius had obtained.[28]

By mid-April the King's offer of mediation in the Elbing affair had been turned down; but Stepney became involved in another matter which will be all too familiar to twentieth-century readers. Refugees were leaving the Catholic cantons of Switzerland and were making their painful way to those parts of Europe which would accept them. Six thousand were expected to come to Brandenburg. Their Deputy in Berlin visited Stepney and handed him a memorial. This he immediately sent to Mr Secretary Vernon, asking that it should be passed on to the Archbishop of Canterbury, and that the Bishop of London might be reminded to remit to Berlin part of the collection which had already been made in England. This indeed was done, and by the end of May Stepney received £1,500, for which he was asked to account. He lost no time in delegating the day-to-day administration of the fund to Philip Plantamour, and in writing to his friend Franc Stratford (now a Governor of the Hamburg Company in London) for advice on how best to deal with the matter, so as to give the least possible trouble to them both!

However George was not heartless about the plight of the refugees. He was soon to take up direct correspondence with the Archbishop of Canterbury; he insisted that the allocation of money to each fugitive should at least be enough to cover the cost of the journey to Brandenburg; and he undertook to advance part of the £1,500 from his own private credit, to avoid any delay in disbursement.[29]

Another theme which recurs during Stepney's 1699 correspondence was the exchange of gifts of horses between the rulers of England and Brandenburg. The Elector had decided to establish a breed of carriage-horses at Potsdam. His newly appointed envoy in London, Count Christoph D'Hona, had instructions to look for stallions in England in order to enhance the stud. Stepney had mentioned the matter to the King at Goer; William had offered to make a present of the animals to the Elector, and asked Stepney to see that he was reminded of this promise. George duly did so, and sent back specifications. However the King's 'jockey', Harry Ireton, complained that Stepney was asking for cart-horses, and that the colours required were 'whimsical'. This was not the first time that Ireton had criticised Stepney's choice of horse-flesh, because he had taken exception to the 'tyger-horses' which the Landgrave of Hesse-Cassel had previously presented to King William. George disclaimed responsibility, but had to take up direct correspondence with Ireton because the reciprocal gift from the Elector to the King was already *en route* to Holland. He urged Ireton to continue with his efforts:

> the Dimensions I own are something monstrous, but such might be found if wee wou'd search in earnest. . . . The little black Nag you saw at Goer I have presented to the Elector, and he has given me two of the best coach-horses I have seen; I have pick'd up a 3d, and will try if I can form a sett of ye same; wch I intend to bring to England with me.[30]

In mid-May the court moved to Potsdam, and on the understanding that it would be in residence there for some time Stepney took accommodation for his complete 'family.' Scarcely had he done so when the Elector changed his mind, left suddenly for an unknown destination, and ordered the Electress and her children to return to Berlin. Stepney did the same. He was encouraged by the King's annual visit to Holland, which began in June, and at Blathwayt's hints that he (Stepney) might be allowed to visit the King at Loo. But at the same time the Secretary-at-War was also referring to the importance of Stepney's reporting on the Polish Diet in Warsaw, and so once again cherished thoughts of Loo and of the journey to England had to be postponed. Dutifully Stepney set out what he knew of the Diet; and reported on the celebrations of the Elector's birthday (1/11 July). That prince had reappeared from Oranienburg. He was entertained by his wife at her private house then known as Lützelburg, half-way between Berlin and Spandau. 'Our Poetasters' were set to compose epigrams, to be placed over the door on this occasion. Stepney's was chosen – four Latin lines – which he submitted to Blathwayt, together with a variety of translations

> whereof I send you the best partly for entertainment and folly, that you may see how hardly Wee are put to it to do anything tolerable in this country.[31]

For Stepney never forgot his Westminster education!

Blathwayt approved the epigram and opined that Stepney would be sitting at 'our Board' come November. He must send news of the Diet in Poland being concluded and copies of his credentials and instructions so that these could be adapted for use with other rulers on the way home. Stepney complied at once: his head was full of a probable call on the Bishop of Osnabrück on the way home, and of a ramble as far as Paris. Yet his departure from Berlin was still a long way off. 'Rambling Abell' – a travelling musician and singer who was a favourite at the English court – had turned up in Berlin, and Stepney was pleased to capture him for a concert which he gave 'to some Ladyes.'[32] And rumours as to Stepney's replacement had leaked out. The emissary chosen by King William was none other than Stepney's German colleague Count Frise. Officially, Stepney welcomed the choice: privately he wrote that a worse choice could not have been made, although he declined to give his reasons. Blathwayt kindly told George that he could choose his own method of leaving Berlin: either he could first visit Loo and then return to Brandenburg to take leave, or he might be able to travel to England directly from Loo. Now it was Stepney's turn to haver. Having urged his own departure for so long, he now seemed to be in no hurry.

> My design in the main as I have explained to you is to spin out my comission till both I and his Maty get to the other side of the water.[33]

Of course, it must be remembered that in the seventeenth century there was no contract between a diplomat and his master to ensure that his journey home would be met from public funds. In practice, this was usually the case, but the expense account had to be submitted *post facto*, and was subject to approval. Stepney would cross the channel free if he accompanied the King.

First there was yet another matter on which Stepney wrote at some length to Blathwayt:

> On the 17/27 [August] the Elr wou'd have a frollick and gave us a general invitation to a Masquerade where were about 20 couple, all in religious habits, both men and women, of different orders; and wee were treated at supper at a long table with litte Messes by way of Pittances: how this humor came abt I know not: and only wish it may not be ill-taken at Vienna where the bigottry yt reigns may not be a little scandaliz'd at the unseasonable Mockery; wch may be interpreted as a sort of violation of the peace of Westphalia, whereby no religious ought to be insulted. Mr Desalleurs declined making his appearence for fear of giving scandall to ye devout Court of France; but I made no difficulty by bearing part in ye Frollick (tho' underhand I endeavoured Censurer of his pleasures and more scrupulous than the whole Court and ye other forraine ministers.

And Stepney added that what scandalised him most was that the party was held in Eberhard Danklemann's confiscated house.[34]

The foregoing well illustrates Stepney's general attitude towards matters religious. Although no-one could doubt his Protestantism, he was always tolerant and understand towards those Catholics who, he considered, were undertaking charitable acts of piety. Instances of these views will recur during the second period of his diplomatic career.

A week later (15/25 August) Stepney at last received permission from the King to depart: yet still formalities remained to be completed, and the Brandenburg court required a formal letter of recall. Even these plans did not immediately materialise. On 5 September (n.s.) Blathwayt wrote briskly to Stepney that owing to a 'little Devil' of dissention in the North, Stepney was to remain where he was and transmit instructions and views to and from the Elector. Even Lord Jersey (who did not like George) found it in his heart to exclaim 'Poor Stepney!' in a letter which he wrote to Matt Prior.

The trouble in the north of Europe had been caused by the death of King Christian V of Denmark and the succession of the unknown Frederick IV. The young King of Sweden, Charles XII supported his brother-in-law, the Duke of Holstein, in the latter's perennial quarrel with Denmark, particularly at a time when the new Danish King was establishing himself. George Stepney resigned himself to another winter in Berlin.

A little more than a fortnight later the King had relented, and the precious Letter of Revocation arrived. Stepney presented it at once, and was relieved to find that the Elector was not going to insist of a formal audience. But again Stepney's actual departure date was postponed. The Electress was making a journey to Dessau and Leipzig, and invited Stepney to accompany her. He could not refuse, particularly as the French and Netherlands Envoys were also invited. The occasion was the Leipzig Fair, (to be attended by King Augustus of Poland) as well as a visit to the Princess Anhalt at Dessau. The entertainment included German opera, French comedy, masquerades, redoutes and balls. At Leipzig the party included Sophia – Electress Dowager of Hanover.

Stepney described the meeting of this lady with King Augustus, which pleased the latter:

> for the good old lady has the gift of doing all she undertakes with a very good grace, and told me her chief aim on this occasion was not to lessen the honour she has of being allyed to his Majesty. I was the only forreign minister who had the honour to be of the party.[35]

Once again Stepney returned to Berlin to take final leave, and pack up his affairs. Blathwayt sent a final plea (too late) that Stepney should look out for a 'Stone horse [stallion] for my Dun mares'. George at last took leave of all the electoral family on 28 and 29 October (n.s.) and received the Elector's 'Pictor' set in diamonds to the value of 2,200 dollars. Endlessly writing letters, Stepney finally tore himself away on 23 October/2 November, and made for Hanover, where he found Sophia 'all alone at Herrenhausen'. She insisted that her visitor should not leave before 10 November (n.s.).

By 17 November George was again in the Hague, and after a 10 day stay in that city announced that he hoped to travel to England with Lord Selkirk in the yacht *Catherine* from Rotterdam.

One reason for Stepney's stay in the Hague may have been that the King was endeavouring to complete the Second Partition Treaty with France, but there had been continual delays, partly caused by the Netherlands and partly by delaying tactics on the French side. On 10/20 November 1699, William wrote from Kensington to Heinsius

> *J'espre aussi que vous serez bientot d'accord avec Lilienroth, et*

que le traité pourra être signé: je trouverai bien de mon côté
quelqu'un pour le faire, quand même Stepney aurait quitté le
Haye.[36]

But on 7/17 November, Vernon had written that the King was awaiting Stepney's return with impatience, so that the Envoy could brief his successor.

Of course Stepney was held up by contrary winds. No particular notice seems to have been taken of his eventual arrival in Whitehall: but on 7 December (o.s.) the Board of Trade & Plantations were considering regulations and methods in relation to the issue of passes. A letter was drafted to Mr Secretary Vernon, asking for copies of letters lately received from the Government of Algiers in this context. The last of the seven signatories (who included Lexington and Blathwayt) was George Stepney.[37]

XIII *The Commissioner of Trade*
(September 1697 – January 1698 (n.s.)
and until the year 1700)

> For my part I am laying in to wait upon ye King at Loo or Cell, &
> am employing all my thoughts how to make my Retreat, & go
> home to look after my Trade – For I must confess to you the 5
> months I passed lately in England were worth ye 9 years I have
> rambled in Germany.[1]

So wrote Stepney to Richard Hill from East Prussia in June 1698,
and indeed he always took his responsibilities as a Commissioner
of Trade very seriously.

The Commission had been revived by William III in 1696 with
the task of promoting and advancing the trade of the kingdom;
considering the proper methods of employing the poor; looking
into the administration of the [overseas] Plantations, with particular
regard to the provision of naval stores 'from thence' and the
prevention of any staple, manufacture or trade being developed
which might be prejudicial to England. Further, the Commission
was to examine the Acts of the Assemblies of the Plantations and
to report on 'the Usefulness or Mischief thereof to Our Crown,'
and to hear complaints of oppression or maladministration. The
Commission was empowered to examine witnesses on oath, and
could consult the Attorney or Solicitor General as necessary about
points of law.

Yet the Commission for Trade and Plantations (or Board of
Trade, as it came to be known) had no executive authority. It could
advise or initiate only. Instructions – to Plantation Governors or
others – were issued by the King in Council, though often these
followed closely the advice of the Board.

The members of the Commission included the Great Officers
of State (including the Chancellor of the Exchequer). However these
dignitaries attended only rarely, and usually at request. The First
Commissioner (or President) was John Egerton (1646-1701), third
Earl of Bridgewater. He had voted for William and Mary in 1688,
and became a Privy Counsellor. His Presidency of the Board of

Trade seems to have been his first tangible reward, for it is to be noted that all members enjoyed a salary of £1,000 *per annum.* His team included Forde Grey (d. 1701) Earl of Tankerville, a Whig with a very chequered past, but who did not attend often. A much more responsible member was Sir Philip Meadows (1626-1718). He had been Envoy to Denmark under Cromwell and was considered an authority on Scandinavian affairs. His knighthood was conferred by Cromwell in 1658. Eclipsed under the Stuarts, he now had his reward from King William. His son – also Sir Philip (d.1757) – would under Queen Anne succeed Stepney as Envoy to the Imperial Court.

William Blathwayt has figured frequently in Stepney's life. He was conscientious in his duties at the Board of Trade, as were the other members: John Pollexfen (b. 1638 – date of death unknown) was brother to the lawyer of that name who had defended the seven Bishops accused of treason by James II. John was a merchant and writer on economics. John Locke (1632-1704), philosopher, requires no introduction. However his presence at the Board of Trade has perhaps been underestimated by his biographers. Despite ill-health he was in 1696 and 1697 regular in his attendance at the meetings. Finally Abraham Hill (1635-1721) well-to-do business man, scientist and linguist, also took an active part. He was related to Abigail Hill (of the Bedchamber, under Queen Anne), but was no relation to Richard Hill, Stepney's companion in diplomacy. Stepney replaced John Methuen (?1650-1706), the King's Envoy to Portugal since 1691, but who had in January 1697 been appointed Lord Chancellor of Ireland. The Board held its meetings in rooms in 'the Cockpit', Whitehall.[2]

It is not known exactly when George Stepney left the Hague for England in September 1697, but Narcissus Luttrell was correct in reporting that he was in Whitehall on the 6th (o.s.) of that month. That day he attended, for the first time, the Commission for Trade and Plantations, doubtless being introduced by Charles Montagu who, in his capacity as Chancellor of the Exchequer, took part in that day's meeting. The others present were Meadows, Pollexfen, Locke and Hill. These four, without Charles Montagu but together with the newcomer, continued business the following day.

At once Stepney was precipitated into a New World (both figuratively and on the map). The matters under consideration included the Laws of Barbados, on which the opinion of the Attorney General had been asked; a letter from John Parker, Consul at the Groyne, about the progress of woollen manufacture [backed by English merchants] at Sada in Spain; draft Instructions for the Government of Bermuda; the General Trade of England; the Poor Tax; Counsellors for Barbados – the original commission had been lost at sea. Hence it was thought the names should be inserted into the new Governor's Instructions. But there was a difficulty: 15 new men resulted in a Council of 22. Only five were needed for a quorum. The Board ordered that:

> the original constitution of the Council be looked into, in order to their Lordships' further deliberation upon that matter.

There was a further development of this case because, at the end of October Stepney 'moved the Board' on behalf of Edward Russell (1653-1727) Earl of Orford. This was a political matter, for Orford as a member of the Whig 'Junto' would have had no difficulty in commanding Stepney to do his bidding. Orford wished the Board to represent to the Lords Justices [the King being still absent in Holland] that four persons should be included by mandate in the Council of Barbados because this had been allowed by the King in 1695. The Board, however, continued to insist, in their Representation, that the number of Counsellors in Barbados should be limited to twelve. This opinion was transmitted to the Lords Justices the same day. On 8 November, an Order in Council was issued, based on the Board's recommendation. There is no record of the reaction either of Orford or of Stepney.[3]

It was not necessary for all members of the Board of Trade to attend every session, so Stepney took the next day off. He was in his place on 9 September, but then took a week's leave from Friday 10 through Friday 17 September.

On his return he found himself busy: the problem of the poor, and more specifically the Poor Tax, had been exercising the minds of the Board. On 23 and 27 September Stepney produced two papers which had been drawn up by his acquaintance Gregory King, Lancaster Herald, who was engaged in his pioneering work on social statistics. King's papers comprised

> (i) A Scheme for the Inhabitants of the City of Colchester . . . as a specimen of what might be done of that kind upon occasion; and
>
> (ii) A Computation of the Endowed Hospitals and Almshouses of England.

On 23 September, after the receipt of the first of these studies (which the Board ordered to be copied), it was decided that each member of the Commission should draw up a scheme for the employment of the poor, for consideration the following week so that 'such things may then be agreed upon as shall seem most proper'. Abraham Hill took this resolution seriously, and produced his paper on 30 September. He was asked to continue, and make his draught 'more particular'. Locke contributed his views much later, at the end of October. His paper was discussed, 'but a debate arising, the matter was postponed'. Pollexfen's remarks were added on 17 November, when all three papers were debated, but any decision again postponed. There is no word of any personal contribution on this subject from George Stepney.[4]

In the early days of his new employment Stepney was used as a link between the Secretary of State's office and the Board of Trade. The first instance of this activity was when John Povey (d. 1705), the Clerk to the Privy Council, gave him a letter from the Governor of Jamaica addressed to Blathwayt, who at the time was still in Holland with the King. Presumably Blathwayt sent it to Whitehall: the subject was the disbandment of soldiers in Jamaica. Now that the war was over, this topic was of importance in England as well as in the Caribbean.

Edward Orth [secretary to Sir Paul Rycaut in Hamburg] wrote to Trumbull twice during September 1697 reporting the activities of the Scottish East India Company, who had plans for establishing themselves in Chile, where a gold mine had been discovered. Stepney acted as messenger in bringing these papers to the Board of Trade.

Two other matters arose which were of more direct concern to a diplomat who had been employed in Europe: Both related to the wool trade. The first was the attempted establishment, by English merchants, of a wool manufacture at Sada in Spain. The English were concerned that there should be no interference from Dutch competitors. Lord Villiers in the Hague obtained a letter from Heinsius to this effect, and the correspondence was delivered to the Board by Stepney.

The second case – carefully filed by the Board's staff under 'Trade Domestick' – reads

Copy of Lre [*sic*] from an unknown hand to Mr. Sec^{ry} Trumbull, dated at Rott^{dm} ye 11th Inst n.s. relating to the Exportacion of Wooll out of Scotland into Holland
Brought to ye Board by Mr. Stepney
Rec'd }
Read } ye 8th Octo^{br} 1697

The writer stated that the wool was actually produced in Northumberland, but was carried into Scotland and thence to

Holland, to the great disadvantage of the English trade. The subject was pursued by John Locke, whose correspondent from Elsinore in Denmark confirmed that smuggling was taking place. By November Stepney, acting as Trumbull's courier, provided

> Particulars of 982 great Bags of English and Scotch Wooll arrived at Rotterdam in ye beginninf of Octr last.

And a table listed nineteen ships, named their masters and shewed the number of bags carried by each.[5]

At the end of the year the Board produced for the government a 'Representation relating to the general State of Trade of this Kingdom.'

The report covered trade from 1670 onwards. The increase of trade at the end of the Dutch war, from 1673 to 1688, was noted. But during the last nine years there had been difficulties. The Board tried to distinguish between 'good' and 'bad' trade: i.e. between exports and imports. For example, the imports from the Baltic – metals, hemp, furs and wood – had increased; while the duties imposed by Sweden on English wool were so great that the merchants had retreated. And only about half the trade was carried in English bottoms.

French trade was adverse; but that with Spain, Portugal, Italy, Turkey, Barbary and Guinea was considered positive. Trade from the [American] Plantations, particularly those in the south, was beneficial, and much was re-exported.

Hamburg trade was considered good. The City accepted English wool, and the commodities sent in return were necessary goods, and not luxuries.

Trade with Holland and Flanders had increased during the recent war, but the balance was considered to be even, particularly if the laws prohibiting the import of lace from Flanders were observed. (But here a note was recorded, that the laws about lace had been repealed.)

The Russian Company was considered to be too small: it consisted of only 13 persons. More people should be admitted to the Company, against small fines. The fisheries had been reduced, and were now open to foreigners. But, noted the Board

> those more used to hard labour and the dyet get a greater share of this trade.

The Board recommended the encouragement of Irish linen, and the importation of flax and hemp so that sail-cloth could be made in 'this Kingdom' [i.e. England].

A further recommendation was that 'Catts' – the ships used for the bulky Norwegian and Danish trade – should be naturalized: because 'we cannot build such ships.'

Duties on French goods should not be reduced; and [one can hear the sigh of regret round the table] brandy should be totally prohibited.

The report continued with paragraphs on the East India trade; fisheries; manufactures (including wool); linen; and paper.

A new book of rates was thought to be needed; and more honesty in the transfer of bonds. Finally, the by-laws of various corporations needed revision.

Perhaps with relief, the Secretary to the Board of Trade, William Popple senior, noted that 'Nothing was ordered upon this report.' Later, Blathwayt wrote to Stepney when the latter was on his way to Berlin:

> Our Gen[ll] Report of Trade has gain'd applause in the world. That of the Poor is less approv'd of.[6]

At the end of the year 1697 George Stepney received three letters from his colleague Dr. John Robinson, the English Resident in Stockholm. One of these letters included a paper on Anglo-Swedish trade, together with a draft treaty (in Latin) between the two countries. Blathwayt and Stepney kept the Board of Trade informed of this project, and Stepney

> translated it into the Mother Tongue for ye benefit of some of our Gentlemen who do not delight in learned Language.[7]

When Stepney took up his appointment as Envoy to the Elector of Brandenburg he did not cease to be a Commissioner of Trade. We have seen how he was greeted with enthusiasm by the merchant community as he passed through Hamburg. His compatriots who were further afield were equally keen to see him. In March 1698 he had an obliging letter from [John] Scarlett, an English trader in Königsberg, who told him that both the English and Scotch merchants in that city were anxious to greet King William's Envoy. The chief concern of the expatriate community was the confirmation and extension of its privileges and immunities. Stepney helped his countrymen in Königsberg, as he did those based in Danzig, by writing to London for copies of relevant documents. He firmly refused to be drawn into any internal disputes within the English community. However such assistance to the King's subjects was part of his normal duties as Envoy, and was not directly consequent upon his appointment as a Commissioner of Trade.[8]

More closely connected with the Cockpit was a minor dispute with Brandenburg over the island of Tertolen. This was situated (according to Vernon) in the 'Caribees'. [It was actually in the Leeward Islands.] Apparently the Brandenburg African Company had bought the island from English people who probably had no right to sell it. The island now lay under English domination. The Danckelmann brother who was resident in London and the Brandenburg Envoy, Count d'Obrzinski, wished to see the island restored to their Elector. Vernon suggested that the Brandenburgers should be repaid the purchase price and that English sovereignty should be confirmed, to prevent frauds in customs and goods. He sent Stepney a report from his 'brother Commissioners,' and instructed George to support the English Government's case. In the event, the negotiations about the island were carried on in Whitehall. In August 1698 Stepney told the Elector of Brandenburg that King William would notify him as to the results of enquiries in England. The Elector was not impressed. Stepney commented to Vernon that the Minister – i.e. Count d'Obrzinski – was more eager than the Prince:

> and the reason is plain, He [d'Obrzinski] was unwilling to return without seeming to have done something.[9]

Both Blathwayt and Popple kept Stepney informed of Board of Trade affairs during his assignment in Berlin. The former had written about the Board's Report on the state of the Plantation in Virginia. Stepney commented that the report was too eager, and

> tho' abuses are certainly to be reform'd, it is not decent in a commission to censure peremptorily as wee seem to doe in the project I saw before we left England: I am for moderation in all things, for violent changes are dangerous and difficult and ye attempt against all the officers of a Plantation will certainly draw a general odium upon us.[10]

To Popple Stepney reported the gossip he had heard in Warsaw about the establishment of a Colony at Heliginau, at the far end of the Baltic. Some Scots had obtained privileges there from the former king of Poland, and these were likely to be confirmed by King Augustus. The Elector of Brandenburg viewed this development with suspicion, since he was anxious to build up the trading potential of both Königsberg and Memmel. For this reason Stepney recommended both the Brandenburg outposts as fertile ground for English adventurers, who would be likely to be granted all reasonable privileges.[11]

In August 1699 Blathwayt passed on to his friend an enquiry from the Board of Trade regarding the price and quantity of foreign tin. Stepney responded at length, giving details of tin production in Brandenburg and Saxony, and basing himself on a three-page report from a French engineer which, for good measure, was also forwarded to Whitehall. And in September Stepney provided another report, from the Inspector of Mines in Saxony.[12]

There is no record of any further activity on Stepney's part in connection with the Board of Trade until he joined his colleagues at the Cockpit on 7 December (o.s.) 1699.

XIV *The Turn of the Century*
(The year 1700)

> The Board [of Trade], taking into consideration the Earl of Jersey's letter of the 2d of the last month, inclosing the French Ambassador's Memorial about Tobago, as also an Order of Council of the same date, referring the Settlement of that Island and St. Lucia to the consideration of the Board, Mr. Stepney was desired by their Lordships to Look over the Papers in this office and Draw up a State of His Majesty's Title to the Island of Tobago.[1]

When George Stepney reassumed his place at the Board of Trade on 7 December (o.s.) 1699 it was to find that a new President had taken over from the Earl of Bridgewater. The new incumbent was Thomas Grey, second Earl of Stamford (1654-1720) who had supported the Whig cause ever since the days of Anthony Ashley Cooper, first Earl of Shaftesbury. All the other members of the Board were unchanged since 1697. But during the two years of Stepney's absence the sessions of the Board were increasingly taken up by the problems of the Plantations in America and in the Caribbean, less and less time being devoted to the trade of England or the employment of the poor.

The request to Stepney to look into the King's title to Tobago was perhaps linked to the fact that it was disputed by the Duke of Courland [modern spelling *Kurland*], territory in the eastern Baltic under the protection of the Elector of Brandenburg. The Board took a short Christmas holiday between 22 December, when Stepney was allotted his task, and 2 January of the new century 1700. The following day Stepney presented the draft of a representation to the Privy Council about the King's title to Tobago, which was immediately 'agreed upon and ordered to be transcribed fair.' Stepney pursued the matter and investigated both the Duke of Courland's title to the island (which dated back to a contract with King Charles II in 1664), and the claims of the merchants who possessed a contract with the Duke to settle the plantation.[2]

Although he attended Board meetings regularly, there seems to have been no other specific work allotted to Stepney. But in June he was listed, with his colleagues, to form a Commission to treat with the French regarding the territorial boundaries relating to Hudson's Bay in Canada. The people most concerned in the matter were of course the members of the Hudson's Bay Company, whose representatives attended the Commissioners' meeting on 12 June. The Lord President of the [Privy] Council also attended, as did Mr Secretary of State Vernon. The Commissioners of Trade quickly passed all the papers to Vernon, and there is no record of any further intervention on their part.[3]

On 28 June 1700, John Locke told the Board that owing to ill health he had had to resign his place, and that the previous day he had waited on the King to ask leave to do so. On 17 July, the new Commission was read, which shewed Locke's name omitted and that of Matthew Prior inserted. Prior attended the Board on that day, for the first time. During the year his good relationship with George Stepney cooled off: but there is no word as to how Stepney viewed this new collaboration with an old friend.[4]

At the end of June the King left England for his annual visit to Holland, taking Blathwayt with him. He stayed abroad until the beginning of November.

Although there is little record of any initiative taken by Stepney during his attendance at the Board of Trade, it has been possible to establish with great accuracy the dates when he was present, and hence the periods when he took leave and therefore could have travelled beyond London. He had a long weekend (Thursday, Friday and Monday) between 4 and 8 January inclusive, followed by two weeks between 22 January and 2 February. It is not known where he went, or how he spent his time. The King was at Hampton Court. Charles Montagu had succeeded in reserving for George a little room there, as he had once been asked to do. But no Stepney letters from Hampton Court have survived.[5]

There is news of Stepney's next holiday: he was absent from the Board between Thursday 11 April through Tuesday 16 April. With the Lords Stamford and Lexington, he was at Newmarket. The King was expected to attend the spring race meeting, but in fact he did not do so. Parliament had just caused his Dutch guards to be withdrawn. However on 13 April Stepney wrote from Newmarket to his friend John Ellis in Whitehall, asking the latter to forward two [unidentified] letters. He added:

> Wee have had very good sport, & sett out too morrow for Cambridge. I hope to kiss yr hands by Tuesday night.[6]

Of more significance for Stepney's reputation among historians –

at least in footnotes – is his correspondence during the year 1700 with Sophia, now the Electress Dowager of Hanover. This exchange of letters has wrongly been ascribed to the following year, 1701, after Stepney's appointment as Envoy to the Imperial Court. In fact, Stepney wrote to Sophia after the death' of Princess Anne's son, the 11 year-old Duke of Gloucester, which took place on 28 July (o.s.) 1700. The date ascribed to this letter by the eminent nineteenth-century German historian Onno Klopp was 11/21 September 1700. [The text is available in Klopp's edition of Leibniz's correspondence with Sophia, but the original manuscript letter seems to have been lost.] Sophia replied in an undated letter turning down Stepney's suggestion that she should accept the succession to the crown.

Klopp averred that Stepney would never have put such an important proposition to Sophia without King William's direct instructions. But the King was in Holland at the time of the Duke of Gloucester's death, and from the evidence of the Board of Trade Journal Stepney could not possibly have accompanied him there.

On Tuesday 13/23 August Stepney wrote to his friend of Vienna days, Jacob Jan Hamel Bruynincx, that he was in the country, 11 miles from London, and without any news because the King on the other side of the water was leaving everyone in ignorance. George added that by the death of the Duke of Gloucester the house of Hanover had come nearer to the crown of England. He indicated that he was staying at 'Bushy Park.' At the time this country house, close to Hampton Court, was inhabited by the Earl of Macclesfield, a Whig peer, who had entertained the King to dinner on 19 June. The names of the other guests are not known. Stepney attended the Board of Trade on 19 and 20 June. He was also at the Board each day from Tuesday 13 August (o.s.) through Friday 16 August. It seems likely that Stepney's letter to Sophia was consequent on his meeting with Macclesfield (and possibly with other Whig leaders, although there is no direct evidence of this). After receiving Sophia's reply, Stepney wrote to her again from Whitehall on 11/22 October 1700:

Madam,
I return most dutifull acknowledgment to yr Electorall Highness for the honour of your letter, by which I do not perceive your Heigness [*sic*] is yet so far determinet in the great affair as to give any direction in it; I hope the Second Interview with His Ma^ty may lay a foundation in our Councills this Winter, in which tho my part be but small I dare promise it shall not be inferior to any in zeal and application; for I am with an entire devotion,
Madam . . . .

If Stepney's first letter had been written in mid-August 1700 (as opposed to September) there would have been appropriate time for the exchange of letters by horse and sailing-ship. The 'Second Interview', to which Stepney refers, took place between Sophia (accompanied by her daughter) and the King at Het Loo at the end of October 1700. No contemporary account of their meeting survives. But in 1701 the Earl of Macclesfield did lead a delegation from England to present the Act of Settlement to the Electress.[7]

After the King's return to England in November 1700 George Stepney may well have hoped for a court appointment to augment the income which he earned as a Commissioner of Trade. He was taking part in the social life of the day. Some of his poetry was being re-published. But, as he wrote from Vienna years later to the Duke of Buckingham, he was indiscreet enough to comment adversely on King William's foreign policy. He said he had *opposed* the partition of the Spanish Empire because of the evils it would bring to the Habsburg family. He continued:

> that has always been my opinion, and for owning it in a private company near 3 years ago I had a severe reprimand (the only one I had in 14 years that I have served) from his late Ma^{ty} by Mr. Secretary Vernon, and perhaps had been sacrificed upon that account, if I had not chose to beg for transportation.

Now, John Sheffield, first Duke of Buckingham (1648-1721) was a Tory and it was he who, writing to Stepney from St James' in the reign of Queen Anne, had criticised the original Treaty of Partition. Stepney's sentiments, as quoted above, were certainly not those which he had entertained at the time of the treaty [see Chapter XII]. Later by another three years, in 1706, Stepney's recollection was somewhat different. This time he was writing to James Vernon the younger about the Danish/Swedish quarrel:

> your Father can tell you the message he brought me at Hampton Court from the late King above 5 years ago when I ventured to say in a private conversation that Sir George Rookes' Expedition before Copenhagen was a little too severe, and our engagements at Travendal more than appeared at that time.

The man who betrayed Stepney's private conversation to King William was probably James Vernon (senior) himself. George anyway thought so, and in 1701 shewed coldness towards him. The King of course was an autocrat who would not tolerate from an English servant any stricture upon his handling of foreign affairs.[8]

Stepney did not leave England on his next foreign assignment until March 1700/1701, and before he left he had probably completed his only surviving prose work, *An Essay upon the Present*

Interest of England. This is Whig propaganda, advocating the renewal of the war against France and explaining the impossibility of accepting any king whom Louis XIV might wish to impose on England. But despite praise of King William's 'sublime genius' and condemnation of French policy, Stepney's essay did not redeem the disfavour in which the King apparently held him.[9]

XV *The Grand Alliance*
(March 1701-March 1702)

William III to Antonie Heinsius

le 1 Avril 1701

J'ai oublié de vous dire dans ma lettre précédente que j'envoyais Stepney à la Cour de l'Empereur en qualité de mon Envoyé. Je n'ai pu lui donner que des instructions très générales par rapport à l'état des affaires dans ce pays-ci; mais il devra en receuvir successivement de plus particuliers, suivant la marche que prendrent les negociations à la Haye.[1]

George Stepney's posting to Vienna, in the spring of the year 1701, can be seen as a watershed in his life. He had achieved much: he was now well known among the luminaries of the Whig party – his portrait by Kneller was included with those of other members of the Kit-Cat Club. Before his departure there was now no doubt but that his allowance for equipage would be paid, and a yacht put at his disposal for the Channel crossing.

It is also evident to the reader of his vast correspondence that the tenor of Stepney's letters had also changed. Gone is the scattering of private correspondence which evaded the destructive hand of Erasmus Lewis and survived in previous Letter Books. Now, the detailing of public affairs is almost overwhelming. Hints as to George's private life are meagre.

His Instructions were dated 2 March (o.s.) 1700/01, and contained the usual preamble and paragraph that he was to hasten towards the Emperor. William III wished to negotiate, with the States General, an alliance against the overgrown power of France. Stepney was to ascertain the Emperor's thoughts on this matter. He was to report on the condition of the imperial court and its forces; promote the Ninth Electorate; and inform himself as to the disposition of the princes of the Empire. Then followed a paragraph which, at this date, although it may not have surprised the Envoy, he could not have foreseen that its consequence would be the increasing ill health of which he would complain in years to come.

> You shall as you see a fitting occasion, take notice to the Ministers of that Court, of the ill Condition (We are informed) the Protestants of Hungary are in, in relation to the Exercise of their Religion, and the Severities used to Them on that Account, which you will insinuate We should be glad They were freed from and the Liberty thereof allowed Them, so long as They behave Themselves peaceably and obediently under the Government.[2]

Stepney's involvement with the Hungarian uprising will be discussed in due course: it is important however to realise that a duty in this regard was laid on him from the very outset of his second posting to Vienna.

On 19 March (o.s.) 1700/01 Stepney was 'on board the Henrietta Yacht at Sheernesse' and writing to his Secretary of State, Sir Charles Hedges:

> I am sorry to acquaint you that hitherto I have made but little Progress on my Voyage, the wind having been both violent and contrary for a whole week that I have been aboard: Wee tumbled for 2 nights in Margaret [Margate] Road, but were oblig'd for our safety and ease to go up into this Harbour on the 15th and have not been able to stir abroad ever since. Toomorrow Wee have a new Quarter of the Moon, when Wee hope for a change of Weather. You may imagine I am under no small uneasiness to be thus detain'd from executing his Majesties commands. I must endeavour to recover the time I have lost at Sea, by more than ordinary dispatch when I get to Land.
>
> I am with respect, etc.[3]

The enthusiasm of the Envoy was somewhat dampened when he reached the Hague on 2 April (n.s.) 1701. He called on the Grand Pensionary Heinsius the evening of his arrival, and was ready to proceed quickly by way of short visits to the Electors on the Rhine, as the King had indicated to him verbally at his last audience before departure. But Heinsius thought there was no need for Stepney to be in violent haste to reach Vienna, and that the visits on the Rhine might be more useful in the present conjuncture. Heinsius promised to make Stepney's excuses to the King, and recommended that credentials should be sent over to him, as formerly, for the Electors of the Palatinate, Cologne, Trèves and Mainz, and for the Bishop of Würzburg. The Envoy of the Emperor in the Hague, the Comte de Goes, seconded Heinsius' opinion, and so Stepney wrote that he would spend three or four days in the Hague to inform himself of the state of affairs; and to see the English Envoy, Alexander Stanhope, as well as to have further meetings with Heinsius and with Goes. Stepney was impressed by the resolution of the Dutch in their 'struggle for life,' and wished that a similar fervour had been evident in England.[4]

Privately to Hedges Stepney confided that Count d'Avaux, the French Envoy in the Hague, had been 'talking high' and shewing everyone the orders he had had from his Foreign Minister. Stepney thought these instructions might well have been forged by d'Avaux himself, because the Frenchman was much less forceful after Heinsius had received him very calmly. The Dutch had already recruited 100,000 men – a prodigious effort – outside their naval strength. Stepney recommended that the Royal Navy should intercept the 22 Men of War held by the French at Brest. This would be an Act of War, but 'surely wee want not provocations to justify such an attempt.' Moreover, d'Avaux was spreading false rumours, such as that the Elector of Bavaria [then Governor of the Spanish Netherlands] was likely to head a party within the Empire 'to stand Neuter.'[5]

The respite from travelling which Stepney enjoyed in the Hague was short. On 8 April (n.s.), he wrote from Leyden that he had left the Hague that afternoon and was now in a yacht on his way to Utrecht, expecting to proceed the next day to Arnhem and thence to Düsseldorf. And in a postscript to this letter he made the first reference to the man who, above all others, was to become the *bête noire* of his diplomatic life. This was Count Johann Wenzel Wratislaw (1669-1712), the recently appointed Envoy from the Emperor Leopold to King William. In fact, the Emperor's decision to send Wratislaw to London was made just two days after the news reached Vienna of the death of Charles II of Spain. Wratislaw was a man of charm, ambition and high intelligence. He was known to most of his contemporaries as 'the Elephant' because of his huge size. There is no record of Stepney's first meeting with him, but it must have taken place between Wratislaw's arrival in London at the end of December 1700, and Stepney's own departure for Vienna in March 1701 (n.s.). Now, writing to Hedges, Stepney noted that both Goes and Wratislaw had been given full powers to conclude a treaty with the English and the Dutch either in England or in the Netherlands, 'and to come to an application of that [1689] alliance.' Stepney, of course, had been given no such powers and he continued to suffer from the fact that he was excluded by the King from the negotiations which were to be undertaken by the Earl of Marlborough. Indeed Wratislaw conveyed to his master the Emperor King William's advice *not* to trust Stepney completely '*weilen ein Engellander der Nation alles kundt machet*' – that is, no Englishman could be trusted to hold his tongue.

Whether King William really expressed himself in this way to the Emperor's Envoy cannot be verified. Wratislaw's mission to London was his first, and he was anxious to keep the threads of diplomacy in his own hands. He was not particularly popular with the King: in March 1701, William wrote to Heinsius that Wratislaw's lack of moderation did not help the cause of the Emperor. [This was in the context that the English and the Dutch, by a secret clause in the alliance of 1689, had promised the Emperor to support the Habsburg succession to the Spanish crown.] But William was firm in his intention that any negotiations must take place under his own guidance either in Holland or in England, and this fact gave Wratislaw a considerable advantage over Stepney.[6]

At Arnhem Stepney found all in alarm. General Coehorn had been organising fortifications, and the common people were transporting movables to Amsterdam. George repeated – possibly as his own propaganda – that the Dutch believed a peace would be more ruinous to them than a war at the present time. The journey proceeded by 'ye worse road to Wesell' – that is, north and east of the Rhine, to avoid French raiding-parties. On 18 April, Stepney was in Bonn, without credentials. He had been kindly received at Düsseldorf by his old acquaintance the Elector Palatine, whose court was committed to the Emperor's cause. However he gave Stepney disquieting news of his neighbours: the three ecclesiastical electorates [Cologne, Trèves and Mainz] had recently sent representatives to meet at Lahnstein [near Coblenz] to discuss their possible neutrality. According to John William, the meeting had been arranged by Max Emmanuel, Elector of Bavaria, and his brother the Elector of Cologne. And Max Emmanuel was by now entirely in the French interest.

At Bonn Stepney saw the Elector of Cologne and his chief minister, and then ran across his old colleague DesAlleurs, now the French Envoy to Cologne. Many French officers wished to take service with the Elector of Cologne. Stepney sent home a list of these men, and, via Alexander Stanhope, a copy of a Project of a Treaty between the King of France and princes of Germany for their neutrality. This was for Stanhope to have translated, and distribute further. This letter and the papers attached to it gave great satisfaction to Hedges. King William, however, refused to believe Stepney's allegations against the Elector of Bavaria. For his part, having seen the proof of French diplomacy on the Rhine, Stepney was now inclined to believe d'Avaux's high-handed behaviour in the Hague.[7]

Briefly Stepney visited a disconsolate Elector of Trèves at Ehrenbreitstein: the prelate had been promised, but had never received, the Abbey of Stablo, for his support given to the Allies in the late war. A French envoy had already visited him. Travelling at night via Bauerach [Bacherach] Stepney was hastening on to Mainz. That Elector, Lothar von Schönborn, was away hunting in the forest of Spessart, in company with one of the imperial commanders, Count [Leopold Joseph] Schlick (1663-1723). Stepney found them both, and discussed with them the new Association of the Circles which had been formed at Frankfurt. This was a defensive alliance, as much against the depredations of German contingents from Brandenburg and Lüneburg as it was against the French. Stepney thought the Elector had reasonably good intentions towards the Emperor, and only wished to protect his lands from war.

At Nuremberg on 25 April, Stepney had an unexpected stroke of luck. He found Prince Louis, Margrave of Baden, at his 'Garden-House', within the gates of the city. Stepney reported to Whitehall the attitude and complaints of the Prince, who had never been consulted by the imperial court during all the four months he had recently spent in Vienna. Neither had Prince Eugene been consulted, who was to command the imperial force in Italy.

On 27 April, Stepney took to a boat on the Danube at Ratisbon [Regensburg] and reached Vienna on 1 May.[8]

Eight years had passed since Stepney's first appointment to the imperial court. Although the ceremony continued as before (and had even increased now that the Emperor's eldest son Joseph, King of the Romans, was married and had his own establishment) the society which King William's Envoy now enjoyed had greatly changed. Former ministers had died – Kinsky, Königsegg, and the renowned elder Starhemberg – the *société des fumeurs* was no more: but at least Jakob Jan Bruynincx was installed as Envoy from the States General to the Emperor, and with him, as with Robert Sutton [cousin and former chaplain to Lord Lexington] Stepney expected to drink to the health of absent friends on the night of his arrival. But before that small celebration took place Stepney had been present in the evening of 1 May, when the Emperor reviewed a regiment of foot which was about to leave for the war in Italy.

Officially Stepney was very busy. It took him only three days to arrange his first audience of the Emperor, via the Grand Chamberlain, achieve an interview with Dominik Andreas Kaunitz (1655-1705), now Vice-Chancellor of the Empire, give notice of his arrival to all concerned and send back to London a long list of the chief ministers at court, and foreign envoys.

Yet already Stepney's mission was being by-passed. In his first letter (written on 4 May) to Hedges he remarked that the first two articles of his Instructions had already been carried out. Count Wratislaw had sent an express courier from London to Vienna to ask for the Emperor's view of the proposed new Grand Alliance, and Stepney reported:

> The Emperor has ordered Count Goes to enter as a party into the Negotiations begun at the Hague: and has likewise by Count Wratislaw's courier (who was dispatch'd the day before I arrived) open'd himself to his Majesty by letting him know of the Proposalls He has to make, and what terms and conditions he expects.

The underscoring above is Stepney's own. Not without irony he continued that he could not be expected to give a perfect account either of the King's overture to the Emperor or of the latter's demands, since neither had been communicated to him. Privately to Hedges Stepney asked whether the overtures brought by Wratislaw's courier came from the Secretary of State, or had been conveyed merely by word of mouth from the King to the Count. If the first, he (Stepney) could hope to have some information by the next post; but if the second, *Nil ultra quero Plebeius*. Hedges later told Stepney that no intimation had been made by the King to Wratislaw, either officially or verbally. Stepney suspected hidden channels, later referring to the Earl of Albemarle and 'Mr. Sec^ry' [James Vernon, Secretary of State, Southern Department] in this context.[9]

Stepney's first audience of the Emperor took place on 5 May. It was a friendly occasion. Both men spoke in Latin during the official part of the interview: after that they probably used Italian, which was the Emperor's favourite language. Leopold confirmed that he had given orders to his Envoy at the Hague to attend the Anglo-Dutch Conference; and that he had immediately ordered one army to Italy, while another destined for the Empire was in preparation. He would appoint a Commission, headed by Count Kaunitz, to confer as necessary with Stepney. George was pleased at his reception, not only by the Emperor but by the Court. He noted with satisfaction that the French Envoy, Marshal Villars, was under a cloud because his correspondence with Hungarian rebels had been betrayed to the imperial court. In fact, Stepney's arrival in Vienna coincided with the arrest and imprisonment of Prince Franz (II) Rákóczy (1676-1735), the leader of the rebels; but he could not have foreseen at this time how far his future career would be influenced by that of the Prince.

The round of official visits, obligatory for any newly-arrived diplomat, continued. Stepney dined with Marshal Villars, just before the latter's departure. Prince Eugene of Savoy was of the company: Stepney had indeed already seen him, and had been told that there would be immediate military action in Italy, because the troops could not subsist for long in the mountains which divide Italy and Austria. The King of the Romans (aged 22) answered in 'High Dutch' [i.e. German] Stepney's opening compliment, which he made in French. Conversation continued in German. Stepney had been warned of Joseph's liking for that language by his friend Count [Leopold Joseph] Lamberg (1654-1706) who then held the appointment of Imperial Ambassador at Rome. But the word 'friend' was a curious one for Stepney to use in describing the Count, for the two men had never met. However Stepney was engaged in leasing the Palais Lamberg from the Count's wife [who came from the family of Sprinzenstein] and so George may have had the information from the lady. It would not, of course, have been proper for him to admit such a thing in official letters.

The Palais Lamberg was near the Imperial Court [*Hofburg*] on the site now occupied by No. 3 Wallnerstrasse in the First District of Vienna. It was across the road from the Palais Esterházy and further down the street was a convenient inn, *Zum grünen Baum*. Stepney paid a large rent of £270 a year for the house, unfurnished. He found himself a close neighbour to the wife and sister of Prince Franz Rákóczy. Stepney stayed in the Palais Lamberg until just after Marlborough's visit to Vienna in November 1705, when he was displaced as a tenant by Count Schlick. It is not known whether Stepney took the house over from his immediate predecessor, Robert Sutton. The latter left Vienna on 7 May, leaving no papers for Stepney's guidance.[10]

If Stepney was suspicious of Wratislaw's 'secret channels' in Whitehall, he was not slow to set up similar lines of enquiry for himself in Vienna. At the start of his mission he set up a good relationship with Count Kaunitz; and he renewed his previous friendship with Caspar Florentin Consbruck, the Secretary of State, from whom he received a copy of King William's official reply to Wratislaw over the question of the Grand Alliance. The King, as usual, had omitted to keep his Envoy in Vienna fully informed. Consbruck continued to be very useful to Stepney throughout the latter's stay in Vienna. This is not to imply that Consbruck was in any way acting dishonourably: he simply passed on information which, in the midst of a court which was renowned for its intrigue, he judged suitable for the English Envoy's ears.

Throughout the whole of Stepney's first summer in Austria he was chivvied by his master over one theme of great importance: this was the provision by the Emperor of an army to act on the Rhine. Jakob Jan Bruynincx received the same instructions via Heinsius, and the two Envoys of the maritime powers were urged to act together in pressing the Emperor on the subject.

During May the Court moved to Laxenburg, the Emperor's summer residence [about 16 km south-east of Vienna]. On 9 June, Leopld's birthday was to have been celebrated by an opera, but a hurricane carried off the scenery, so the performance had to be postponed. Stepney made 12 journeys to Laxenburg between his arrival and the end of June, for which he charged £2 a time in his 'extrys'. He also wrote to Hedges with a round-up of affairs: the French threat to the Rhine; Italian military operations; the mediation in the quarrel between Sweden and Poland; the death of the Duke of Orleans; the plague in Constantinople, which had caused the death of Lord Paget's secretary and of his interpreter. Paget himself had retreated to a garden three miles from the town. Finally, Count Styrum had informed Stepney of the state of the army on the Lower Rhine.[11]

At the end of May Stepney had received the news from London that Philip of Anjou, now the Bourbon King of Spain, had announced his succession to King William, and the latter had acknowledged the fact. To his Envoy in Vienna, William carefully added that this diplomatic move would make 'no alteration in the measures of affairs now taking, in relation to the Emperor or otherwise.' Nevertheless Stepney was circumspect in his visit to Laxenburg to observe the 'countenance' of the various ministers on receiving the news. The Court was downcast. However better things were in store: on 6 July, Stepney heard of the resolution of the House of Commons to support 'such alliances as the King should think fit to make in conjunction with the Emperor and the States General for the Preservation of the Liberties of Europe and the Prosperity of England, and for reducing the exhorbitant power of France.' This, remarked Stepney, was the most agreeable news he had received since leaving England: the Court had reacted with joy, and Stepney's task was now to prevent them making too presumptuous demands for the assistance which they expected from England. He at once wrote to Prince Eugene in Italy to let him know of Parliament's Resolution; and he urged Blathwayt, Hedges and Stanhope to get a fleet sent to the Mediterranean.

To his friend – or rather his ex-friend – Matthew Prior, now addressed as 'Dear Sir', Stepney revealed a little more of his situation in respect of the dissensions in London. He already knew about the impending trial of his Whig friends (including Charles Montagu, now Earl of Halifax) for their complicity in the Second Partition Treaty. George told Prior that during his present appointment he had resolved to write only to his Secretary of State [Hedges]:

> not being able at this distance to distinguish between friend and foe, and being unwilling that any of my letters tho' never so innocent should be lyable to false constructions, as my discourses were. . . I grow every day less in love with my own Country, and had I my health here would never think of solliciting my Revocation, as I believe I shall, if I hold out this Summer and next.

For George had complained to Paget that a 'defluxion in his eyes' prevented him from writing in his own hand to that nobleman. However, serious deterioration of Stepney's health apparently did not begin until he had to make exhausting and repeated journeys in Hungary when the revolt there was renewed in 1704.[12]

During the heat of July, Count Kaunitz visited his estate in Hungary, the court was at Laxenburg and Stepney in Vienna remembered that he was still a Commissioner of Trade. He had been approached by English merchants in Vienna to try to get suppressed a flourishing factory at Linz which was producing serge cloth. Stepney commented that such a move might be possible: the same had been achieved by English influence both at Sada in Spain and in Languedoc. However George was not altogether in favour of the idea:

> all princes are not only at liberty to use all honest arts towards advancing the interests of their subjects, but are obliged to do it both in Prudence and Conscience.

The quicksilver mines at Idria near Trieste were another matter. These were profitable, and an agreement was about to be made with Holland for their exploitation. George suggested that the Austrian banker involved could just as well deal with England, and that possibly a monopoly could be achieved. Another project was one in which [Zachary] Sedgwick 'Lord Nottingham's man' was involved. This related to the transport of Hungarian wines across Germany to England; and possibly to exchange raw silk from Turkey and Persia with woollen cloth from England – again overland.

The English Envoy's official entertaining had begun: he made arrangements to entertain [Ferdinand Bonaventura] Harrach, (*Grand Maître*) of the Court, Count Wallenstein (*Grand Chambellan*), Count [Heinrich Franz] Mansfeld (President of War), and Count Dietrichstein (*Grand Ecuyer*), 'and some young men who are their creatures.' Stepney esteemed their presence as an extraordinary favour [but he was, after all, a king's representative, and few noblemen refused a free dinner!]. Kaunitz and friends were not invited, Stepney being by this time very much aware of friendships and enmities at court and knowing that Kaunitz and his cronies would mix with the others as 'Oyle with Vinegar.'

The dinner was a success: for liquid refreshment Tokay and *Eau de Barbados* was provided, and a singer named Webb performed very well. The next day the guests – described by George as 'the old Gentlemen' – entertained the Emperor with the song in which all had joined:

Wee swear no more by Blicks
Nor by the Gods that made us
Nor by the River Styx
But waters of Barbados.

And Stepney wrote at once to Blathwayt for further supplies of rum.[15]

Stepney continued to be concerned at the lack of information from the Hague. The King, accompanied this time by the Earl of Marlborough, had arrived in Holland. The Earl was now both Commander-in-Chief of the 'succours' – the help to be given to the Dutch and to the Emperor – and Ambassador Extraordinary and Plenipotentiary for such negotiations as were to be carried on in the Hague. Stepney wrote a polite letter to His Excellency, offering service but pointing out that he had no knowledge of the proposals for an alliance which had arrived in Vienna with Count Goes' secretary at the beginning of August. Stepney had already made contact with Marlborough through a third party, this being Hugh Boscawen, later the first Viscount Falmouth, who had been placed with Stepney to learn diplomacy, probably by Lord Godolphin, whose nephew and *protégé* he was. 'Mr. Buscowen', as Stepney called him, had a hot temper, and the relationship between the two men was not as happy as that which Stepney enjoyed with other students. However when Boscawen left Vienna on the offer of an appointment as aide-de-camp to Marlborough [which in fact he never took up] he was at least proficient in French 'and in the knowledge of men and business.' Before his departure John Ellis wrote that Hedges was anxious to send a 'young gentleman to you for Education at the feet of Gamaliel.' The youth was in France learning the language. After some delay, Joseph Addison (1672-1719) duly sojourned in Vienna, to Stepney's pleasure, for both were poets.[16]

The King had been asked to mediate in the ongoing quarrel between Sweden and Poland. Sir Charles Hedges at once suggested Stepney as capable of undertaking the task. George had no objection, provided his salary was increased by the £3 a day which was usual for a plenipotentiary. The proposal came to nothing, because the King feared the French would become involved.

At the beginning of September Stepney made the only visits outside Vienna which – as far as is known – he ever undertook purely for pleasure. As he explained to Blathwayt:

> My first start was to Count Kaunitz at Oesterlitz [Austerlitz] in Moravia where he is laying out m/300 Dollars on house and gardens which will hardly turn to account. I then removed to Brunn [Brno] the capital of that Province, and was lodged by the Governor Count Breiner in the high castle of Spielberg, in the same room where Gen[ll] Schoning was so long a prisoner. The Prospect is not inferior to that of Windsor. In my return I visited the Prince of Dietrichstein at Nicholsburg, and the Prince of Lichtenstein at Feldsburgh. This last is I believe the richest subject in Europe having near m/400 Dollars yearly income. He show'd me his Harras of horses which is esteemed the best in the world; he has at least 4,000 horses of all sorts and his stable when finish'd will be little inferior to Chelsea College. My last *Gite* was with Count Zinsendorff [sic] at Ernstbrun who has made a lake and a canal at the bottom of cornfields in which he keeps a Man of War of 40 Guns, a Galley with 40 oars after the Fabrick of those at Malta, and 3 or 4 Gondolas after the Venetian mode.[17]

Stepney's tour lasted a week, between 10 and 17 September 1701. No sooner had he returned when he received an outburst from William Blathwayt, who was then with the King at Loo:

> The Pensionary and Lord Marlborough have been here some days and I have discovered that Count Kaunitz has given an account to the imperial ministers at the Hague of some conference you have had with him about the Treaty, and declarations he made to you that they are not satisfied with it, and have desired him to be more reserved another time in the business of the Treaty wherein they know you have no share. This is an advertisement I give you that you may know better how to contain yourself in time and place. I may already let you know that this Treaty of Alliance is intended to be kept as secret as possible and that our negotiators think you have no copy of it. The best use you can make of this mistake is not to own your having it, and above all not to communicate it to

any Person alive, not to yr best friends upon any account whatsoever. I conjure you again to follow my advice herein, and not to oblidge any body with what may turn to your prejudice and mine that is not to send a copy of the treaty or extract of it or any criticisms relating to the West Indies or otherwise to any person alive. You know Acteons fate, and tis best to be blind on the present occasion.[18]

Stepney replied in cypher on 24 September. On the 21st he had already informed Blathwayt of the arrival on the 17th of a courier from the Hague with the Alliance signed, and that the fact would not be kept secret. Count Goes himself had reached Vienna on 21 September, and had immediately sought audience of the Emperor. Before his tour to Moravia Stepney had 'picked up' the introduction to the Project of Alliance, and got to know much about the treaty from the flow of gossip at the imperial court. Marlborough had already excused himself to Stepney, for not keeping him informed, and implying that his silence had been imposed by the King. The Earl added that he had no objection to receiving Stepney's comments on the attitude of the imperial court, from time to time.

Stepney was aggrieved at the whole matter. He had corresponded with Hedges as usual, and in accordance with his instructions. He did not fear any betrayal of his actions from that source: but he was worried lest the matter should come to the ears of the senior Secretary of State, James Vernon, for it was he who had revealed Stepney's former criticisms to the King, and was now in a position to do Stepney great harm.

The affair blew over, but not before Stepney informed Blathwayt privately (and in cypher) that reports on Marlborough which had reached Vienna from the imperial representatives were not much to the Earl's advantage. Blathwayt told the King that Stepney had had no copy of the treaty sent to him from the Hague. William then authorised one to be sent, and added that Stepney was to be told that no other English foreign minister had received a copy. Stepney was mollified by this action.[19]

World affairs moved on. News reached Vienna of the death of King James II in France. (Stepney enquired as to what he should do about mourning.) The event was important, because Louis XIV took the opportunity to recognise James' son as the rightful king of England, which eventually caused the English declaration of war against France. In Vienna, the eyes of the imperial court were fixed on Italy. A revolt in favour of the Habsburgs took place in Naples, and was quickly suppressed by the French authorities. The

Emperor's advisers blamed the English, for neglecting to send a fleet to support the insurgents. Hedges wrote to Stepney, providing him with arguments in justification of the English decision. And Stepney responded with the suggestion that 'pilots' should be sent overland to sound out the depth of ports in the Adriatic, which might be suitable to receive an English fleet. This request foreshadowed the visits of Edmund Halley to Vienna and the Adriatic two years later.

In the west of Europe the Earl of Macclesfield had been commissioned to visit the Electress Sophia with further pleas that she should accept the inheritance of the crown of England. This mission eclipsed the hopes James Cresset might have had of carrying it out, he being the English Envoy to Hanover. And earlier in the year Lord Raby had been assigned the pleasant task of congratulating the Elector of Brandenburg on assuming the crown of Prussia. Stepney growled to Blathwayt:

> Wee may slave 20 years without picking up 6,000ll [£6,000] Sterl' in our vocation and a lord at Hannr or Berlin getts a fortune by one jobb.

Yet life in Vienna was not too onerous: Stepney had occasion to write to the Dutch representative in Berlin:

> La Vie de Vienne est assez douce et sociable. Nous frequentons les Ministres le Matin et leurs femmes le soir, Sans que le Souverain ou les Maris apprehendent que nous allons corrompre les unes ou les autres; Car si on a la Volonté d'etre mechant, la jalousie et la defense ne servent que pour exciter la Curiosité et donner du goût aux Crimes.

Stepney did not dare mention the name of Pellnitz

> car il y a un Siecle qu'Elle ne songe plus à moi, et je ne scay pas par quel endroit j'ai pû avoir merité sa disgraces.

By now Stepney had augmented his wardrobe by a black 'imperial habit' (obligatory when he had audience) at a cost of £70, and three embroidered suits for the gala occasions of the court at £50 each. During the winter he was 'hooked in' to give a ball, explaining that this frolic was against his will and inclination, because his shape prevented him from taking any delight in dancing. [Had he already put on weight since his Berlin days?][20]

More seriously, at the request of the States General Bruynincx and Stepney jointly presented a memorial to Kaunitz urging greater efforts on the part of the Emperor to provide an army for the Upper Rhine. The court, as usual, held conferences on the matter. Prince Rákóczy succeeded in making his escape from his prison, of which the Commandant was promptly arrested and later executed. Stepney gave another dinner-party on the occasion of the King's birthday; and was successful in recommending that his cousin Charles Whitworth, who had accompanied him to Vienna, should be promoted to be King William's representative at the imperial Diet at Ratisbon. This post was only intermittently filled, but at the end of 1701, any way of exerting pressure on the German princes to provide men and money for the war was sure to be pursued.

The health of both Emperor and King was causing anxiety. Leopold made a good recovery, and was told by his physicians to be more regular in his diet and not to take his final meal so late at night. Blathwayt may have had a presentiment about the future, for he ended his last letter from the Hague to Stepney on 4 November (n.s.) 1701, with the words, 'Adieu from hence, perhaps for the last time.'

Nevertheless King William reached England safely and settled at Hampton Court for the winter. Parliament was obstreperous, and Stepney's friend Sir Charles Hedges lost his job because he would not support the King's choice of a Speaker of the House of Commons. The incumbent chosen was Robert Harley (1661-1724). James Vernon once again resumed responsibility for the Northern Department of the Foreign Office, while Lord Manchester took over the senior (Southern) Department.

The last messages from the King to Stepney, conveyed by Vernon, continued to stress the urgency of getting imperial troops to go to the Rhine.

On 30 March (n.s.) 1702, the news reached Stepney of the King's death. He opened his heart to his colleague, and the King's known friend, Count Frise:

Mon pauvre Frise, en quel embarras la Providence nous a-t-elle jette par la mort du meilleur des Rois et des Maitres! J'en suis tout desole et je m'imagine que vous ne le serez pas moins, mais il ne nous reste que constance pour tout remede. L'empereur qui comme vous savez, parait assez indolent pour les affaires de ce monde, a pourtant temoigne beau-coup de chagrin de la perte qu'il vient de faire de notre grand Roy. Je suis trop afflige pour vous pouvoir dire d'avantage.[21]

XVI *The New Reign*
(April 1702-December 1703)

> As I have not the honour to be much known to her Majesty by reason of my long and frequent excursions I have recourse to your goodness in representing me to her Majesty in such a manner as my service may be made acceptable to her: at least my Duty shall never be wanting.[1]

So wrote Stepney to James Vernon senior (Secretary of State, Northern Department) on learning of the death of King William III. He had reason to be worried as well as grieved. Queen Anne's Tory inclinations were well known, and the new monarch was under no obligation to employ the servant of her predecessor, or to pay his debts. In fact, she did continue to employ Stepney, whose new credentials were sent off by Vernon just five days after his letter which announced the death of the King. Stepney was to put himself, his servants, his house and equipage into the deepest mourning. (For this, he later charged £240.)

Money was a different matter. Stepney claimed that just before he left for Vienna in 1701, the King had promised him a greater 'ordinary' allowance owing to the cost of serving at the imperial court. Certainly in February 1701/2, Vernon had received from Stepney a list of expenses, but had not yet 'moved' the King about them. There is now no evidence that King William ever approved a larger allowance for Stepney, and knowing the monarch's parsimony, one may conjecture that Stepney was indulging in wishful thinking.[2]

Meanwhile Marlborough, still Ambassador Extraordinary and Plenipotentiary to the States General (and newly-created Knight of the Garter and Captain-General), had been sent to Holland to assure the Dutch of the Queen's stedfast resolution to adhere to the Alliance and of her continued support. Stepney was ordered to correspond with the Earl and to obey his commands. George readily obliged, and on 9 April (n.s.), transmitted a Summary of the State of Affairs, containing details of troops available in Italy and in the Empire. The next day he officially and in Latin informed the Emperor of the death of the King, the new Queen's accession, and that he (Stepney) had been reaccredited to the imperial court.

At the same time George wrote his commiserations to Blathwayt. The latter had commented on the unspeakable loss to Europe by the death of the King, and had counselled Stepney to keep in close correspondence with Marlborough and with Godolphin – also with Lord Rochester, Tory uncle to the Queen. Blathwayt knew that his own circumstances were somewhat changed; but, he wrote, only by his staying at home which, after 10 years abroad, he would not mind. Stepney responded at once:

> Your letter of the 10th of March which I received by last Post is
> so full of Courage and friendship, that I cannot sufficiently thank
> you for the assurances you give me of an happy Government and
> the direction to what objects my Devotions are to be addressed.[3]

On 22 April (n.s.) 1702 Stepney wrote a private letter to Vernon to protest, gently and politely, against letters from the English foreign ministers (including himself) being read by a Committee of the Council. This was on the grounds of security. Stepney was aware – as was Bruynincx – that reports were coming to the ears of Wratislaw or Goes and by them being relayed back to Vienna, 'which is not very agreeable.' He attributed the leakage of information *not* (of course) to Vernon personally, but indicated the possibility that some of the Queen's other counsellors might not always be on their guard.

Stepney had good reason for his concern. At this date he did not know that Wratislaw had succeeded in gaining access to the Queen to compliment her on her accession on the very day of that event; but he did know from Vernon of the good relationship which existed between Wratislaw and Marlborough.

The Empress' young relative, Prince George of Hesse-Darmstadt, had visited England and left with the King a written memorial suggesting a 'Descent on Spain.' This was a highly controversial matter, favoured by the English who wanted to acquire the port of Cadiz, but less agreeable to the Austrian Habsburgs, who now thought of Spain as a 'mere carcase' and preferred to bend all their efforts towards the establishment of their rule in Italy.

Prince George, a former Viceroy in Catalonia, knew Spain and its peoples, was Catholic, and was prepared to represent the Emperor in any expedition which the English might make. But the Commander in Chief, the Duke of Ormond, declined absolutely to agree to the Prince's presence.

During his stay in England, Hesse-Darmstadt had not brought

the Emperor's Envoy, Wratislaw into his confidence. Wratislaw however had got to know of the Prince's mission and of his Memorial to the King, and had adversely reported on both to the Emperor. According to Stepney, the Duke of Ormond's animosity against the Prince could be attributed to Wratislaw.

Stepney became involved, because the Empress (who was no cypher in imperial politics) requested him to write directly to the Duke of Ormond, to explain that the latter's supreme command was never in doubt. Stepney did so, adding as a post-script that, just in time, Wratislaw had changed his tack and was now supporting Hesse-Darmstadt, so that hopefully all difficulties would now be removed. The Prince was eventually sent in a separate ship to Lisbon, where he was active in persuading King Pedro of Portugal to join the Grand Alliance; and it was Pedro who, later in the year, was to insist that the Habsburg Archduke Charles (the second son of the Emperor) must show his face in the peninsula as King of Spain.

English politics paused for the coronation of the Queen; and in Vienna Stepney enjoyed an occasion dear to his heart:

> This morning [13 May n.s.] 8 horses arrived which were sent by his late Majesty to the King of the Romans. The Prince of Dietrichstein is Master of the Horse and has been to visit them in my stables; after they shall have rested a day or two he has promised to give me notice where and when I shall have the honour to present them.

And on 16 May, the presentation took place, in the plain near Laxenburg:

> Mr. Ewen and the English grooms who brought them [the horses] coursed about in their hunting equipage.

The animals were well received.[4]

Changes at Whitehall took place: Vernon, Manchester and Ellis were out; Lord Nottingham and Sir Charles Hedges were in. Although Stepney did not learn for some weeks who would be his new 'provincial' – and addressed his dispatches formally to 'Right Honourable' – he was content with the change, since Hedges was both conscientious and fair to him. England's official declaration of war on France reached Stepney on 20 June (n.s.). Preparations for the summer campaign had already begun, with Marlborough arriving in Holland and the King of the Romans (accompanied by an enormous baggage train) setting off for the Rhine and the siege of Landau. Another important visitor arrived in Vienna from the east: Lord Paget had relinquished his appointment at the Porte and was returning overland, together with a staff of 100 people, and

140 horses. In late June Stepney went to Raab [now Gyor,] in Hungary – about 110 km east-south-east of Vienna – to meet him. George did not stay long: in three days he was back in Vienna to prepare for Paget's arrival, and succeeded in having him put up in 'Starhemberg's garden, half way to the Favorita.' Paget remained in Vienna until mid-August, so that Stepney's expense account was augmented by his presence, although George did not of course have to bear all the costs of the retinue.

At the imperial court Stepney was encountering the usual difficulties of intrigue, indolence and ignorance. Prodded by the Empress, the Emperor decided to appoint his brother-in-law, the Elector Palatine, as Governor of the Spanish Netherlands when that country had been re-conquered for the Habsburgs. The court kept this decision entirely to itself: Stepney discovered the situation from his friend Consbruck, and wrote to Hedges:

> I took occasion of telling Count Kaunitz (as from myself) that since her Ma^{ty} and the States General were put to all the Expence both of Blood and Treasure in wresting those Provinces out of the Enemys hands, it would have been a point of ordinary Decency and Civility towards 'em to have asked at least their consent and approbation as to the Person to whom the Government thereof might be entrusted. I proceed no further till I know your pleasure.[5]

But the Council in England was not likely to take offence, and indeed was havering as to the best way of prosecuting the war. Among other measures they hit on the idea of sending Stepney to Ratisbon to replace Whitworth (who in turn would serve as a secretary in Vienna) in order to achieve a declaration of war against France from the Empire [as opposed to the Emperor], and to obtain a prohibition of commerce, letters and all other things with France. And before leaving Vienna Stepney was to bring the Hanse towns [in northern Germany] into a prohibition of commerce!

The Envoy claimed he was always ready to obey orders, despite inconvenience. Of course, he pointed out, he would need credentials and *money* – for his arrears were now around the £3,000 mark. Moreover, there was in fact little point to the journey, for Vienna was the place where the 'cheif dispositions' were made. As regards the Hanse towns, at the beginning of the former war the representative of the States General in Vienna had tried and failed to prevent the trade with France. But Stepney would do his best. The next day he prepared a seven-point memorandum for Kaunitz. The maritime powers wished steps to be taken to bring Portugal and Denmark into the Grand Alliance; and to cajole the Elector of Bavaria to do likewise.

The Emperor held a Conference on 24 July (n.s.), to discuss the propositions. Directly it was over, Kaunitz made his escape to his estates 14 [German] miles from Vienna, without telling Stepney anything about the outcome. Stepney collected news from his other sources: included in the discussion had been the possibility of the Archduke Charles going to Spain to assume the crown, but the Emperor could not make up his mind on that point.

Eventually the idea that Stepney should go to Ratisbon was shelved. Proclamations were made by the Emperor against any trade with France. And once again an emissary was sent to Max Emmanuel, Elector of Bavaria, to try to win him for the allied cause. All was to no avail, and on 8 September, to everyone's consternation, Max Emmanuel invaded the imperial free city of Ulm.

The Elector's treachery overshadowed the victory on the Rhine: Landau had fallen to the Emperor's forces, and Stepney's former colleague Count Frise had been appointed its governor. Meanwhile Stepney received a letter from Hedges instructing him to 'interpose' himself to get negotiations going between the Emperor and the King of Prussia whose dispute was believed to be about ceremonial. Stepney was to inform himself of the details and report. George did just that: the Brandenburg pretensions were more serious, and were concerned with arrears of subsidy and conquests in the West Indies. It appears that Stepney had no wish to become involved in this affair, for he countered with a suggestion to Hedges that because he was within five days' journey of Charles XII of Sweden (who had invaded Saxony) he should instead be accredited to that monarch for a mission of mediation.

Just at this juncture Stepney may have been surprised to receive a message from Count Wratislaw, who was still in England. The Count was well aware that one of the bribes offered to Max Emmanuel was that he should be given command of all or part of the Emperor's forces in Italy. Of course, such a commission would displace Prince Eugene. Wratislaw warned Stepney, via Lord Nottingham and Sir Charles Hedges, to be careful how he supported Prince Eugene (known to be the choice of the English government) for the command in Italy. The warning was necessary because Kaunitz was a particular friend of the Elector of Bavaria.

Amid vague and belated instructions from London, and at the end of the summer campaign – Prince Eugene had defeated the French at the battle of Luzzara – Stepney decided to write to that Prince:

Vienne, ce 11 d'octobre 1702

Vostre Altesse aura sans doute appris par les Correspondences avec Mr. le Comte de Wratislaw la haute estime que Sa Ma^{te} Brittanique fait de vostre personne, de vostre merite, et de vos services: Et jusqu'à quel point la Nation Angloise s'interesse en ce que Vous regarde, Je dois y ajouter qu'il a plu à la Reyne de me donner ordre de solliciter Sa Ma^{te} Imp^{ll} et ses Ministres a fin qu'ils secondent vostre Altesse autant qu'il sera possible par les secours nécéssaires pour l'execution de ses desseins. A fin que j'y puisse mieux reussir, je supplie vostre Altesse de me faire savoir sur quels points et par quelles voyes je pourrois luy étre de quelque utilité; Je m'y employeray avec beaucoup de plaisir, tant pour obéir aux ordres de la Reyne, que pour vous temoigner avec quel zèle et que respect je suis, Monseigneur,[6]

On 23 October, the Prince sent his reply from Luzzara, which reached Stepney by 1 November. The needs were for men, money and remounts for the cavalry; more money for provisions and for regular and prompt payments to the troops: without such an effort to finish the war, added the Prince, its continuation would be extremely difficult.

Meanwhile Stepney had, by 'irregular means' learned of negotiations with the Duke of Savoy being carried on by a servant of the Duke's Ambassador, in great secrecy. In order to change sides once again, Victor Amadeus had demanded the alienation of certain imperial lands in Italy. The Emperor was said to have agreed, and Prince Eugene to be about to conclude a treaty. Stepney kept his knowledge from the imperial ministers with whom he normally dealt. Nothing came of this *démarche*, but Stepney was to become involved with Savoy the following year.

As regards the proposed visit to the King of Sweden, that monarch had just (incorrectly) been reported dead. In any case, Marlborough, to whom Stepney's suggestion had been sent, disapproved of the expedition because – as he put it officially – Stepney's residence at the Court of Vienna would have been a disadvantage to him. George, although quite relieved at being excused another winter journey, correctly attributed Marlborough's decision to the interference of the Swedish Envoy Lilienroth [Lilieroot], against whom King William had often warned his ministers. But George also admitted, privately to Ellis, that his main reason for proposing himself for the mission had been to get his arrears paid.

These latter were still a worrying fact of life, and the more so when Stepney in December received a letter from his agent in

Whitehall, Richard Powis, who had discussed with Ellis and Tucker, Stepney's emoluments and the late King's promise of £800 or £1,000 in consideration of the expenses of Vienna. The civil servants had been fearful of creating a precedent. Powis proposed that the Queen should give Stepney a boon, by way of the Treasury. Halifax had spoken to the Lord Treasurer, who ordered that half a year's ordinary should be paid to Stepney out of the Queen's money, and his first three bills [of extraordinaries] should come out of the arrears of the King's money. But this last fund was not as great as had been expected, and Stepney was not the only candidate. Ellis and Tucker always told Powis that Stepney's bills would be passed immediately, but this was not the case, and the two scrupled over the amount claimed for mourning, which was more than Stanhope or any other envoy had submitted. Moreover, Powis added, the opinion of all Stepney's friends was that

> seeing the change of Ministers and turn of states, and the small thanks you have for spending your money so largely, that you should tye your Purse strings a little closer, for it has been replyed to me not a few times, nor by a few Persons, *what is Mr. Stepney that he cannot live on the Queen's allowance,* and save money as well as others that have gone before him?

Yet there was one comforting fact: the Privy Seal for George's Trade Commission was being renewed, and the half-year's salary from Lady Day to Michaelmas would soon be paid.[7]

Now Stepney found himself in grave disagreement with Count Kaunitz, Imperial Vice-Chancellor and the official with whom foreign envoys normally dealt. Stepney had had no answer to the proposal which he had made in writing a month previously (in accordance with instructions received from Whitehall) regarding the means of bringing Portugal into the Grand Alliance. The Count had neither given a written reply, nor allowed Stepney a suitable occasion when the matter might be discussed.

Knowing from other ministers that a conference about Portugal had taken place, Stepney wrote a note to Kaunitz in the morning of 18 November to find out whether the Vice-Chancellor was ready to explain the Emperor's pleasure before the post went away.

George then went to court at the usual time, and as he was getting out of his coach in the courtyard he saw Kaunitz on the point of leaving.

> As soon as he saw me he stopt and made signs whereupon I sent my Page to know what he meant, for I could not imagine he could forgett himself so far as to call me to his Coach-side without getting out to speak to me, which usage I should not have bore as a

> Gentleman in my private capacity; however he continued to make
> signs both to me and to the Secretary of State [Consbruck] (whom
> I chanced to meet in ye passage, coming from a Conference), and
> cry'd out he shou'd tell me the state of the matter; which he did
> (continuing in the passage), after the abrupt manner wherewith I
> related it to you by last post.

Stepney then wrote formally to Kaunitz, requesting either an answer
in writing regarding the Portuguese affair, or a suitable time and
place where the matter could be discussed seriously.

The Vice-Chancellor took offence, and wrote back immediately
that he was not accustomed to receive notes such as Stepney had
sent. However, he agreed to see Stepney again, if the latter would
request an interview in the usual way.

The affair blew over, thanks to the intervention of Count Schlick,
who accompanied Stepney when the latter travelled to Guntersdorf
[c. 55 km north-west of Vienna] to bid farewell to Paget who was
en route for Prague. Stepney bore no ill-will towards Kaunitz, and
recognised that he was an honest and well-meaning man. But the
quarrel caused comment at court, as reported by the eighteenth-
century Swiss historian, Guillaume de Lamberty, according to whom
'Stepnei' had sought an interview with Kaunitz in the usual way,
but was late in keeping the appointment. The Count waited for a
quarter of an hour, and then left. Meeting Stepney in the street, he
told him he would send someone to him, and did indeed send his
secretary, who informed the English Envoy that owing to the missed
appointment, the Count considered that the audience had taken
place. If Stepney wished another, he could apply in the usual way.
At this (the report continued) Stepney, annoyed, wrote a letter to
the Count full of bitter remarks, that his standing as a gentleman
had been violated, and that he would complain to the Queen his
mistress. Despite Kaunitz's moderation, Stepney had indeed written
to the Queen. Eventually the Court decided that Kaunitz had been
over-punctilious; and that Stepney had been too quick with his anger.

It is now not possible to decide the rights and wrongs of the
case: but it is noticeable in Stepney's correspondence at this period
that he was never averse to putting other people right, sometimes
in a tactless way. About the same time as the quarrel with Kaunitz
he had occasion to write to Lord Nottingham who was temporarily
standing in for Hedges at the Northern Department. Stepney wrote
a long letter explaining the late King's strategy for the forces on
the Rhine and in the Netherlands, as well as the importance of
keeping the Circles of the Empire in heart. The way this letter was

expressed – as a schoolmaster to a pupil – would hardly have endeared the Envoy to the Secretary of State.[8]

After a not over-successful summer, news of the English/Dutch fleet's success in capturing the Spanish silver fleet at Vigo reached Vienna just a month after the event. Writing on 29 November, to Hedges, Stepney let him know that a *Te Deum* was to be sung in celebration, and that festivities were planned. Stepney had wished to be host himself, but was overtaken by the Prince of Liechtenstein, tutor [*Ayo*] to the Archduke Charles, who insisted that George, and nine English gentlemen who were in Vienna should dine with him. Subsequently the party was invited to the court, where the *Augustissima Casa* was entertaining itself, to which 'family' occasions outsiders were only rarely present. Against custom, the Archduke spoke to Stepney to congratulate him on the victory, and George neatly turned the compliment, assuring the Archduke that his personal interest was of no less concern to the English. Stepney's guests were Lord Scudamore; Mr Lake (nephew to the Earl of Scarsdale); George Montagu (nephew to Lord Halifax); Mr Dashwood (eldest son to the then Lord Mayor of London); and Mr Addison. Others unnamed were on their travels to or from Italy. Of those listed here, George Montagu was staying with Stepney together with a tutor, a Mr Gougain; and young Dashwood and Addison had also been placed with Stepney to further their education.[9]

The year ended with the holding of a conference, to discuss the allied prospects in Spain and Portugal. The elder Count Harrach presided, and the other participants were Counts Kaunitz and Mansfeld, together with Stepney and Bruynincx, and Consbruck acting as secretary. Stepney sent home a dispatch consisting of six double-sided pages. He also summarised the results for Stanhope in the Hague: the treaty with Portugal had been referred to the imperial envoy in Lisbon [the young Count Wallenstein], together with 'the Amirante' of Castile, who was an old Habsburg supporter. Whitehall had wished the Emperor to give the Queen's representatives a free hand in the negotiations, so this decision of the court was negative. The Emperor was pressing for a fleet to be sent to the Mediterranean, and particularly to the Adriatic. During the year the Queen and the States General had been willing to provide cash to bribe the Elector of Bavaria to adhere to the allied cause. Now, the Emperor desired that this money should be made available to reduce Max Emmanuel by force. It was also suggested that a Dutch contingent should go to the assistance of Prince Louis, to enable a two-pronged attack to be made on the Elector. (The other imperial army was to be commanded by Stepney's acquaintance, Count Schlick.) Stepney admitted he had been forced to propose that the Queen should give a sum of money to the Emperor, although he recommended that a loan should be made, perhaps against a cautionary town, for example Ostend. In a letter which crossed with this dispatch, Hedges informed the Envoy that the Queen desired a peaceful solution of the Bavarian problem. Stepney thought there was no hope of such a thing, and therefore did not declare the Queen's intention.[10]

On 8 January (n.s.) 1703, Prince Eugene reached Vienna from Italy. Stepney entertained him to dinner a week later, in a carefully chosen company. George described the Prince as an honest, plain man, who was distressed at the condition of the army he had left behind in Italy, and particularly at the state of the horses, who were suffering from an obscure disease. At this time the relationship between the two men was good. But the Prince later became disillusioned at Stepney's failure – in his eyes – to obtain anything more than promises from the maritime powers.

Another illustrious visitor to Vienna was Captain Edmund Halley, mathematician and astronomer, who was sent as a result of Stepney's request for an expert to recommend which Adriatic ports might be suitable to receive a fleet. Halley arrived on 10 January. Stepney took him to court the following day and was scandalised to find that news of the mission had already appeared in Dutch prints. During the course of 1703, Halley made two visits to Vienna and the Adriatic, and provided careful reports, particularly on Buccari. Despite his efforts, no allied fleet arrived.

At the start of the year 1703, Stepney's own situation was not comfortable: his health was beginning to give him trouble, although he was not specific about the cause. He was also the target of detrimental rumours which were circulating in London and in the Hague. Stanhope confirmed George's suspicions of the Swedish diplomat Lilienroth. As he put it:

> Ye Swedish Intelligencer informed you right, I have seen a letter by chance from Stockholm that Mons Liliroot had orders from his Court to object against you, tho' tis not unlikely he sollicited those orders, tis certain he executed them effectually here, and the business did not stop there neither, wch leads me to the other point you desire to have explain'd concerning Comte de Goes who being questioned by a great man I need not name [i.e. Marlborough, presumably] whether the Court where you are be satisfied with you, or had rather have some other, wherein they

should be gratified, answered as became an honest man to his
master and the friendship and esteem he professes for you. This
is to be inter nos for yr own sake and mine . . . only in general as
to Party-business. I believe . . . you are a humble servant to our
friend whom I have often mentioned to you . . . [Lord Halifax]
. . . if there be, [*sic*] pray be cautious for the future.

Stepney vigorously defended himself: he had never been a party-
man, and would like the report traced, if possible. He wrote of his
diligent and impartial service in Vienna, but commented that he
could not escape the scandals and imputations which 'lay at the
door of mankind.'[11]

The objectives of the maritime powers on the one hand and the
Emperor on the other continued to differ widely. Stepney described
the situation both as to Bavaria and to Portugal in two long
dispatches to Hedges dated 7 and 10 February, respectively. He
also sent a welcome present of Tokay to Lord Godolphin, who, in
acknowledging the gift, told Stepney succinctly the requirements
of the English government from the court of Vienna. These were,
full details of the prospects of the war in Italy, because the Queen
had decided to send a fleet as far as Naples and Sicily, and it would
be inexcusable to send a squadron to no purpose; and the pressing
need for the Archduke to go to Spain. The fleet was due to sail two
months from the date of this letter – marked by Stepney, 'The last
of December 1702, rec'd the 2 of Feb 1703 s.n.' – so Stepney
must act quickly.

George responded by sending an edited version of the Italian
troop count which had been given him by Count Mansfeld, the
President of War; and continued by bringing Godolphin up to date
on the court's views on Portugal, which were couched in general
terms only. As far as the Archduke was concerned, Stepney stated
that it was impossible for him to go to Spain: The King of the
Romans had no heir, and his Queen was unlikely to bear more
children. Ominously, Stepney ended his letter by forecasting French
support for the Elector of Bavaria. And to Hedges, four days later,
he attributed the indolence of the Emperor towards the Bavarian
threat to the fact that Max Emmanuel was Catholic, so that the
Pope and the Jesuits might well be pleased if he reduced Ulm and
Memmingen, both Lutheran cities.[12]

Count Wratislaw in London had not been idle. He had put the
imperial point of view on the Portuguese treaty to the English
government (as was his duty) and reported their reactions by courier
to Vienna. Perhaps because of Stepney's heightened standing at

Vienna, following his dispute with Kaunitz, that nobleman invited him to hear the court's reply to Wratislaw, which had been composed after no less than three conferences had been held on his information. Fair words were made to Queen Anne about Portugal, together with complaints about Methuen [the English Envoy in Lisbon] being too reserved, and the Amirante being a proper person. At which point Stepney interrupted to protest against an imperfect answer which, if repeated without any improvement, might cause 'disgust' against the imperial court. Moreover, he added, the Emperor should consider the distance between Vienna, England and Portugal, so that frequent communication of projects was not possible; and England had a long correspondence with Portugal. Stepney requested Kaunitz to stop the courier to Wratislaw, until the Emperor had had time to consider these objections.

Stepney won his point. Kaunitz gave him a formal answer to his objections (which was read to him in German), in which the Emperor promised that his envoy in Portugal would not create difficulties in opposition to what the Queen should judge reasonable to be granted to Portugal for the common good. Stepney added his own comments in transmitting the document home, which he described as a direct translation of Wratislaw's instructions. Stepney had reason to be pleased with himself, for Hedges later approved of his action. And Wratislaw had asked for his recall from England – according to Stepney to get married. But here George's information was incorrect: Wratislaw was given leave for some months to attend to his private affairs, and later returned to England.[13]

In March the imperial expedition against Bavaria began unluckily. The Elector surprised a contingent near Passau, and defeated it roundly. Stepney, when he sent home the prints about the battle, noted on them in his own hand:

270 kild
<u>289</u> wounded and prisoners
559

At the start of April, Prince Louis' representative arrived in Vienna to plead his master's desperate state, with his lands at Rastatt ravaged; with no money and with few troops. And Prince Eugene had offered his resignation to the Emperor. But more serious for the Emperor than either of his generals' complaints was the death, reported by Stepney on 2 May, of 'our rich Jew, Oppenheimer.'; and, a month later, that the Jew's son was likely to be made bankrupt for want of ready cash. The result of this disaster, Stepney continued, was that the Emperor, who was indebted to the Oppenheimer family by about 15 million florins, would not be able to make his remittances or provide for his armies either in Italy or in the Empire. The only good aspect of the general confusion at the Vienna court was that Prince Eugene was likely to become President of War. On 29 June (n.s.), the Prince's appointment was announced, Stepney reporting it to London the following day.[14]

Stepney took the initiative in one episode which related to his former service in Germany. On 19 April, he wrote obliquely (lacking a cypher) to Adam de Cardonnel, who was now established as Marlborough's secretary. This was to introduce to Cardonnel Daniel Steingens, of the Palatinate, now resident in Cologne, and who was known to the merchant Bilderbeck (a man who had been used by Stepney and other diplomats for forwarding mail). It is quite obvious that Stepney thought Steingens would be useful to Cardonnel as a spy, and Cardonnel did indeed take up the introduction.[15]

On 16 May, the Duke of Moles called on Stepney. This man, Neapolitan by birth, had been Ambassador in Vienna for King Charles II of Spain. Now, he had declared in favour of the Emperor, who had made him a Privy Counsellor and one of his confidants. He told Stepney that he was empowered by Leopold to impart to the Envoy the details of the negotiations which were taking place with the Duke of Savoy. Stepney was of course delighted to be let into any secret, and more than happy to report on the 16,000 men which the Duke of Savoy might put at the Emperor's disposal. What Moles did not mention (but Stepney discovered later from the Savoyard secretary who was still in Vienna) was that the maritime powers were to be asked to provide a subsidy for the Duke.

The Savoy treaty was supposed to be an affair of the greatest secrecy, but when the imperial envoy, Count [Leopold] Auersperg [d. July 1705] left on 8 June, for Turin, Stepney remarked that there had been so much whispering about his journey that the French were bound to know about it.

Badgered by London to persuade the Emperor to allow Archduke Charles to travel to Spain, Stepney had audiences of the Emperor on 22 May and 14 June, and also with the Empress, the King of the Romans, and the Archduke himself. Bruynincx had had no instructions from the States General to add to this pressure, although later he was permitted to join Stepney's pleas in general terms. The Emperor's ministers all wished the Archduke to try his fortune first in Naples.

While the Portugal treaty was being examined by the Emperor

and his ministers, Stepney reported:

> after Midnight we had a general allarm here upon 40 Huzzars
> having been seen in a body within twice Musquet-shot of the
> Favorite (the country house where the Emperor now resides) and
> it was suspected these men were come hither on an ill design
> against the imperial family, who use to be so slightly guarded that
> perhaps twice that number of resolute fellows might be able to
> execute some desperate attempt. As many of the Emperor's and
> King's Trabants as could be gathered at that dead Season, sallyed
> out with a resolution to encounter the Visitors, which upon their
> near approach, they found to be a guard of Hungarians belonging
> to our Palatin Prince Esterhasi, who had conveyed a large parcell
> of bad wines which were following him hither from that country.[16]

Such alarms were later to become more serious.

Count Wratislaw arrived in Vienna on 4 July (n.s.) 1703, and
had audience of the Emperor and the King of the Romans the
following day. Forty-eight hours later Stepney received a letter from
Marlborough at the Camp at Hanneff, praising Wratislaw's
contribution in England to the public good and advantage of the
Allies, and instructing Stepney to inform the court at Vienna that
the Count was extremely acceptable in England. Stepney did as he
was told.

Although the Portugal Treaty had been received in Vienna
(despite the Emperor's Envoy to Portugal having been captured at
sea by the French on his way home) Stepney was left to deal with
one matter still outstanding. This was the demand of the maritime
powers that the Emperor and the Archduke should agree to refund
one third of the expenses of the expedition, and sign a promissary
note to this effect. On 3 July, the Emperor had reluctantly agreed to
ratify the treaty in all its parts. But the route to be taken by the
Archduke towards Spain had not been agreed, and was the subject
of more lengthy conferences, in which Wratislaw (but not Stepney)
took part. Nevertheless Stepney, as usual, managed to inform
himself as to what passed at the conferences, and he was the channel
through which the imperial views on the treaty were transmitted to
England. On 20 July, Stepney wrote to Marlborough that the
approximate date for the Archduke's departure had been put at the
end of August. and that Wratislaw had represented to the Court of
Vienna that 'wee' [the maritime powers] could not be ready sooner
with the agreed forces and fleet. Moreover the Emperor had not
answered the demand that he should share in the expenses. Stepney
continued:

> Count Wratislaw bestirs himself at a great rate, but I believe the

business might be done better by less violence, though I own that
would not have so great appearance of merit and sufficiency and
it would be vain to perswade people to change an humour that
has been too much indulged.[17]

And to Hedges Stepney defended his own handling of the Portugal
Treaty – a gentle and gradual application – without which he would
have received a flat negative from the imperial court.

During the summer of 1703, Stepney had been quite keen to go
to Italy, partly because he thought the climate might improve his
health, and partly for the reason that since the death of King William
the interest of the English government had been turned towards the
campaign in Italy rather than towards the Rhine. Prince Eugene
had even invited Stepney to visit Italy and take a tour of the army.
All this George had reported to London, adding that he would not
wish to undertake the Italian journey unless the £50,000, which
had been half-promised by the Queen, was actually paid before he
left. However the Envoy's first choice was to accompany the
Archduke to Holland – if such an event came to pass – and then be
allowed to take leave in England. By August the proposed Italian
trip had been laid aside, but Stepney found himself involved in two
other cisalpine matters. The first was a signal from the Venetian
Republic that it might contemplate joining the Grand Alliance.
Stepney had two sources for his information, one being Count
Lamberg, the imperial Ambassador in Rome, and the other the Duke
of Shrewsbury, now retired from English politics and living in
Rome, with whom Stepney carried on a friendly correspondence
for several years. Since the Venetians were about to send two
Ambassadors Extraordinary to England to compliment the Queen,
George had moments of dreaming a similar appointment for himself
to the republic.[18]

More serious, as things turned out, was the breaking of the Savoy
treaty with the Emperor. Count Auersperg had begun his
negotiations with optimism, although Stepney continued to regard
the Duke of Savoy as having a 'slippery temper.' Victor Amadeus
had pitched his demands high: 6,000 horses and 20,000 troops from
the Emperor, and a subsidy from the Queen of England, without
being at all specific as to what he would provide in return. He was
also, rightly, worried about French knowledge of these (to them)
treacherous negotiations. Stepney had had no reply from Whitehall
to his own first report on the Duke's likely change of heart, though
he knew in early August that Richard Hill had been appointed Envoy

to Turin. At first Stepney had news from Auersperg that owing to
Savoy's extravagant demands, the conclusion of the treaty would
be transferred to Vienna. Stepney at once wrote to Hill (then in the
Hague) to stop short, wherever he was, lest his arrival make the
secret public. And since the negotiations were being transferred to
Vienna, Hill should travel there, and not to Turin. By 8 September
Stepney knew that the treaty was broken; that the Duke of
Vendôme's secretary had been in Turin negotiating a treaty between
Savoy and France; and that Auersperg was on his way to Austria.[19]

On 12 September (n.s.), the Emperor proclaimed his second
son King Charles III of Spain in a splendid ceremony, of which
Stepney transmitted all the details to London. The young man was
to make a pilgrimage to the shrine of Mariazell [130 km west of
Vienna] before setting off for Holland via Prague, Leipzig and
Düsseldorf. This final departure took place on 19 September, and
Stepney congratulated himself on the event:

> you will have seen with wt success I obtain'd that Resolution.[!]

Wratislaw, who was one of the numerous *entourage*, left Vienna
on 29 September; but Stepney had by that time received instructions
that he was to wait there, as the official document put it:

> to conclude and sign a Treaty between Us [i.e. Queen Anne], the
> Emperor and the States General on one side, and the Duke of
> Savoy on the other.

And he was also to handle any negotiations that might take place
with Venice.

On 10 October (n.s.), Stepney reported the trap set by the Duke
of Vendôme for the Savoyard generals on 29 September, who,
having accepted an invitation to supper, were seized and put under
arrest, while six battalions and twelve squadrons of Piedmont troops
were made prisoner by forces from the State of Milan. The
whereabouts of the prisoners was not known, but their horses had
been distributed among the French regiments. This action was no
doubt intended to frighten the Duke of Savoy into submission to
France, but instead it had a quite opposite effect.

Stepney was concerned that lack of security about Savoy's
negotiations with the Emperor had prompted this move; and more
particularly that it might have been triggered by a letter which
Richard Hill had written to a Savoy official, Count de la Tour, who
was known to have French leanings. The originator of these
suspicions was in fact Count Auersperg, but Stepney did not hesitate
to pass them on.[20]

The Envoy's prolonged stay in Vienna caused him to be the

butt of complaints against English behaviour from the Court. Although Prince Eugene was confident that his cousin the Duke of Savoy would eventually join the Allies, his anxiety about the war situation both in Italy and in Austria was great. True, the Elector of Bavaria had suffered a surprising setback in Tyrol, thanks to the resourcefulness of the peasant army of the valleys. But there had been a defeat for imperial forces under Count Styrum at Höchstädt in Bavaria – the same area where later the Battle of Blenheim took place; and the Hungarian rebellion was steadily gaining strength, always connected with the louring possibility that the Turks in the Balkans would take their part. As far as Italy was concerned, imperial plans hinged on an advance towards Naples, for which Prince Eugene had prepared 1,600 troops at Buccari (the port which had been surveyed by Captain Halley), to await transport by the Allied fleet. But, for perfectly good logistic reasons, the fleet under Sir Cloudesley Shovell only reached Leghorn and then returned to its base in Spain. Prince Eugene

wonders he (Shovell) came so far, since he could go no further.

And Stepney wrote a clear and forthright account of the grievances of the imperial court against the lack of support they had received from their allies for the operations in Italy.[21]

On 3 November 1703, the Savoy Treaty arrived in Vienna, not by the hand of Count Auersperg its negotiator, but brought by the Duke of Savoy's Master of Ceremonies, Count Tarini. It needed, of course, ratification. And now a new problem developed: although Stepney had full powers to sign a treaty, if he thought fit, on behalf of the Queen, his colleague Jacob Jan Bruynincx had only just received instructions from the States General, who insisted that they must see the full treaty before they committed themselves further. Stepney refused to commit the Queen to any subsidy, but suggested to the Emperor that he (Stepney) should personally explain matters to the States General – an offer which was gratefully accepted. From Aglionby [Queen Anne's representative in Switzerland] Stepney learned that the Duke of Savoy was now ready and willing to receive Richard Hill as the English Envoy, and George took care to arrange to meet him on the road home. He also left with Charles Whitworth an Act to enable the latter to be his substitute in case the States General unexpectedly agreed to the signing of the three-party treaty in Vienna. From all appearances, Stepney invented this 'Act' himself.

Count Tarini allowed Stepney a copy of the treaty, with the proviso that it was secret. Stepney had it copied in duplicate, and sent one to Hedges, in case of accident to himself on the road. He expected his journey to the Hague would take two weeks, because of the state of the roads. On the evening of 10 November, he left Vienna.[22]

By 24 November, Stepney was in Cologne, having travelled via Pilsen, Bayreuth and Aschaffenburg, calling on notabilities on the way, most of whom were by now his friends. Three days later he was in the Hague, in time to greet the King of Spain, who had got no further. He also found Richard Hill, against whom Cardonnel had sent a warning, partly in cypher:

> I must not omit to acquaint you that 184 [Hill] has complained to me more than once of the freedome of yr writing, and he takes particularly ill what you mentioned formerly of President la Tour so that you will not take amiss if I advice [sic] you to be a little causcious in what you write on this subject.[23]

However it is improbable that Stepney received the warning before he left Vienna.

On 28 November Stepney went to see the Grand Pensionary Heinsius, taking Richard Hill with him. Hitherto Stepney had not told Hill that he had with him a copy of the Savoy Treaty. In the presence of Heinsius he had to admit the fact, although he truthfully stated that the copy he had with him was imperfect, having been copied in a great hurry by four different hands. When Stepney continued his narration of the events surrounding the treaty, Hill not only interrupted somewhat rudely, but commented that he did not pretend to receive instructions from Stepney. George replied that there was not much more; probably Hill's further Instructions and the necessary remittances might reach him before he could get to his journey's end.

> He snap[t] me up again with his usual good nature by asking me why I did not then save him the trouble of going so far, by concluding [the treaty] myself at Vienna, since I was authorised to do so?

Stepney answered that his instructions were, not to sign until Bruynincx could do so too. Hill persisted in preventing Stepney telling his story, until

> at last I could bear no longer, but desired him to let me explain quietly some points which I thought I might understand, and wch I presumed he did not. . . . He fled from his Chair, and so the conversation ended very abruptly and I was obliged next morning to convey my thoughts in writing to the Pensioner, not to trouble him so soon with a second visit.

Despite this unhappy encounter, both men calmed down sufficiently for Stepney to shew Hill, the following day, all his correspondence with Hedges. And two years later the two corresponded without rancour. There is no doubt but that Hill had reason to feel aggrieved at Stepney's behaviour, but it is significant that no word of the interview with Heinsius appears in his printed correspondence. And Stepney sent his full account, not to the Secretary of State, who might produce it in Cabinet, but to his friend John Tucker the Under-Secretary.[24]

Once again Stepney found himself spending a month in the Hague. One major cause of delay for all who wished to cross to England was the dreadful storm which swept the channel and all neighbouring coasts on 10 December (n.s.). The fleet which was supposed to take the King of Spain to his new realm suffered dispersal and loss, particularly of HMS *Vigo*, which went down with all hands and with considerable baggage belonging to the officers who were to accompany the King. These men were left in a destitute state, and the Dutch disclaimed responsibility for them. The Dutch Envoy in London proposed that someone should make a particular application to the Emperor – and Heinsius, not, one feels, without a lifted eyebrow, proposed to Stepney that he should, in the public interest, forego his leave in England and travel post to Vienna to see what he could do. Stepney talked himself out of any such mission, claiming that if the Emperor were pressed too hard, it would diminish the esteem in which he was held in the Empire. George was, after all, hoping to embark for England the next day. This conversation with Heinsius took place on Christmas Day (n.s.). On 20 December (o.s.) Stepney, in London, was submitting his expenses for the previous quarter, which included:[25]

	££ s. d.
For Gala-Cloaths when the A-Duke was proclaimed King of Spain	50 00 00
For my Journey from Vienna to England	140 00 00

XVII *The Hungarian Mediation (I)*
(January-August 1704)

Leopold I in Vienna to Count Wratislaw in London, 13 February (n.s.) 1704

Uebrigens habe auch aus Eures obberührten Schreiben ersehen, was für Motive der Stepney gehabt hat, so unversehens dorthin eine Reise zu thun, und nehme ich Allegnädigst, dass Ihr Euch befleisset, dergleichen Sachen zu penetriren, welche für's Kunftige grosses Licht geben können. Von diesen werdet Ihr auch erstgedachten Grafen Goess informiren, auf dass er bei Dorthinkunft des Stepney im Haag behutsam mit ihm umgeht.[1]

There is no direct information from Stepney about the short time he spent in England at the turn of the year 1703/4 (n.s.). He attended the Board of Trade five times between 20 December and 10 January 1703/4. The composition of the Board had changed (although William Blathwayt was still a member, as well as Prior) but there is no record of any initiative taken by Stepney.[2]

His leave turned out to be less than the six weeks which he had requested. Even before he arrived, Marlborough was writing to Heinsius that he should be sent back to Vienna as soon as possible, and asking the Pensionary's advice as 'to what princes Mr. Stepney may be made use of in his way to Vienna.'

To a certain extent, Stepney was treated with honour. He attended a Cabinet Council (although no minutes of that particular meeting survive). He met the Duke of Marlborough for the first time, and in mid-January travelled with him back to the Hague.

But, as Stepney later complained to Tucker, all was not well. As may be seen from the Emperor's letter quoted above, Count Wratislaw had reported badly on his counterpart, and the Emperor was uneasy at George's precipitate departure from the Vienna court the previous November. At the time, George knew nothing about this correspondence, though later he suspected it. The cause of his immediate disquiet was the rumour circulating in London that he had written privately to his friend Charles Montagu, now Earl of

Halifax, about an audience he had had with the King of the Romans, whom he had advised that the Emperor was being served by incapable and disaffected ministers. Prince Joseph was said to have replied that it was still worse in England, where the present set of ministers were known to be Jacobites. Stepney utterly denied the existence of any such letter, unless it were a forgery. But he mentioned that he was also suspected of having revealed the Savoy Treaty negotiations to Halifax, because the latter had mentioned it early on. Upon enquiry, it was found that Halifax had had the news 'from Sr Harry Furnese.'(who was not one of Stepney's correspondents).[3]

Any irritation at Stepney's behaviour in London seems to have dissolved by the time he reached the Hague. He was charged not only with new negotiations with the Elector of Bavaria, but also with the proposed mediation in Hungary. In the event, it proved impossible to pin Max Emmanuel down to any meaningful exchange of views, and Marlborough (who with Wratislaw was also furthering the military solution to the Bavarian threat) took over in July the authority to negotiate with the Elector. But Stepney was involved, together with Heinsius, in the preliminary counsels at the Hague at the end of January (n.s.) 1704.[4]

Stepney became intricately involved with the Hungarian situation over the next two-and-a-half years. It may therefore be helpful to the reader to look briefly at the history of that unhappy country, before describing the state of affairs at the beginning of the year 1704.

For centuries during the middle ages Magyar horsemen had terrorised western Europe by hit-and-run tactics during the summer months. They developed a kingdom – an alliance of the greater nobility, which succeeded in imposing on King Andreas II in 1222 a 'Golden Bull' whereby the aristocracy lived tax-free and were permitted to revolt against the monarch if he abrogated any of their fundamental laws. But the Turkish victory at Mohacs in 1526 caused part of the nobility to seek an alliance with the Habsburgs of Austria; hence the election of Ferdinand I as King of Hungary on 17 December 1527, he having accepted the terms of the Golden Bull. At this period in the sixteenth century a Magyar counter-king appeared, who was in alliance with the Turks. He was firmly suppressed by Ferdinand. But the Habsburgs lived with the fear, which more than once became a reality, that a Magyar leader would find support from the Turks, from France, or from Sweden.

During the long reign of the Emperor Leopold I, which began

in 1658, his relationship with his Hungarian subjects varied from the oppressive, when he could afford it, to the conciliatory. In 1681, before the Turkish siege of Vienna, he had attempted conciliation: the Hungarian Estates were allowed to elect a Palatine (Prince Paul Esterházy), their liberties were confirmed and the Protestant religion was permitted. Later in the seventeenth century the imperial government was successful in its struggle against the Turks, thanks to the military skills of – among others – Prince Louis of Baden and Prince Eugene of Savoy. And Lord Paget (then English Ambassador in Constantinople) had brought to pass the Treaty of Carlowitz (1699) which excluded the Turks from Hungary and Transylvania.

Yet the Magyar population simmered. They were largely Protestant, to the *chagrin* of the devoutly Catholic Leopold and his Jesuit confessors. The revolt however was not fought on religious grounds, for the leaders, including Franz Rákóczy, were mostly Catholic. The grievances against the Habsburg rule lay in attempts to impose taxation and on the behaviour of the Germanic troops which were used to enforce government decrees during the periods of oppression.

Franz Rákóczy was the stepson of a Magyar 'freedom fighter' and had inherited a large estate in north-eastern Hungary. He had been educated (by the Jesuits) outside the kingdom, and before 1700 would have been content to exchange his Hungarian estate for lands in Austria. But this suggestion came to nothing. When a Magyar revolt flared up in 1697 Rákóczy fled to Vienna, but his estates in Hungary were not ravaged by his countrymen, and for this reason he was distrusted by the Court, many of whom possessed lands which had suffered badly.

When Franz returned to Hungary in 1700, he found a friend in Count Nikolas Bercsenyi (b. 1666), who was a most determined leader of the Magyar people. The two men decided to write to Louis XIV of France, hoping to obtain a subsidy for a revolt which would be as useful to France as it might be to the Magyar. The letter was entrusted to a certain Captain Longueval, who betrayed it to the imperial court. Both conspirators were arrested and brought to Wiener Neustadt (30 km south of Vienna). Stepney reported the Vienna gossip to his friend Lord Lexington, that Princess Rákóczy (who was born Charlotte-Amélie von Hesse-Rheinfels) was the mistress of Longueval, and would have had no objection to seeing her husband executed. However both Rákóczy and Bercsenyi escaped from captivity.

Magyar discontent led to raiding parties into the Hereditary Countries of the Habsburgs. On 4 October 1703 the Emperor wrote to Prince Louis.

> dieses Rauberisches Gesindel auch bis hieher vor Meine Residenz durchbrechen und streyffen.

And during Stepney's absence on leave Charles Whitworth reported the growing menace from the Hungarian borders of Austria.[5]

When Marlborough and Stepney arrived in the Hague at the end of January 1704 the situation of the Emperor had worsened because his son-in-law Max Emmanuel, Elector of Bavaria, had recently occupied Passau. There was a real threat that with the support of the French the Bavarians could join hands with the insurgent Hungarians, and that Max Emmanuel might displace Leopold as Emperor. Stepney had reported the outbreak of the revolt in Hungary in June 1703, and voiced at once the danger:

> Care must be taken to shutt this back Door, or the Diversion joyned with what we have already suffer[ed] by the Elector of Bavaria, will hinder the Emperor from continuing the war, as he ought to do.

And it became a principle of the maritime powers, that the Emperor should make peace with his rebellious subjects, in order the better to pursue the war against France. In the Hague, Stepney discovered that Charles Whitworth had proposed that he (Stepney) should be given powers to mediate in Hungary, and at the same time Bruynincx received instructions to support any offer of the Queen towards mediation. Stepney signified his willingness to act, provided he was given suitable powers, suggesting that these should be drawn up in a form identical to those provided by the Dutch for Bruynincx, without any mention being made of religion. And Stepney added that a separate letter should be drafted for the Queen to send to the Emperor, to say that he, Stepney, would not use his powers except as His Imperial Majesty (HIM) should direct. This last was of importance, because Stepney was well aware of the reluctance of the imperial court to undertake any negotiation with the rebels, because to do so would derogate from the Emperor's authority as sovereign lord of Hungary.[6]

On 12 February (n.s.) 1704, Stepney left the Hague (by yacht, as far as Utrecht), and from there he continued to Leyden and Hanover, where he arrived on the 19th. His stay was brief, because his '*adorable Princesse*', now Queen of Prussia, invited him to accompany her to Berlin. Sophie Charlotte had arranged for 174 horses to be available as Relais at every Post, so that the journey to Berlin was completed in 50 hours. However Stepney, by special invitation, stopped at the Queen's own palace of Lützelburg [later Charlottenburg] outside Berlin. This respite only lasted one night, for Stepney recorded his meeting with King Frederick I and his chief minister Baron Kolbe the next day (24 February). Stepney carefully requested that his second successor in Berlin, Lord Raby, should attend a conference with the Prussian ministers. His relationship with Raby was prickly. During his stay the two discussed poetry, in particular verses written by Stepney's fellow-member of the Kit-Cat Club, Sir Samuel Garth. Raby later complained to Brigadier Cadogan that Stepney had criticised Garth's poem too stringently; and that he (Raby) did not enjoy meddling with poets, lest he should find his name in the next lampoon.[7]

Continuing his journey via Breslau, Stepney reached Vienna on 6 March (n.s.) 1704, and had much to report to Hedges two days later. He discovered that Whitworth and his Dutch colleague Bruynincx had set up a good correspondence with the Hungarian leader Bercsenyi, although no-one knew whether the latter was sincere, or was only trying by negotiation to gain time enough for the grass to grow sufficiently to feed his horses on their raids. However Bruynincx, armed with his power to negotiate sent to him by the States General, had decided to go to Pressburg and there try to agree preliminary matters with the Hungarians. Stepney was ready to follow: but his first duty was to be received in audience by the Emperor and the Empress, and this took place on the evening of 8 March. The Emperor told Stepney that he was satisfied with the Queen's using her endeavours in Hungary, provided it might be done with due regard to his 'Sovereign Authority and Decorum.' (Stepney's underscoring). The Emperor raised his voice at this point, and so did the Empress.

Five days later Stepney recorded in his Letter Book, in French and apparently for his eyes only, a mistake which he had made.

On 12 March, between 7 and 8 p.m., he was busily engaged on his dispatches, when Kaunitz's valet interrupted him to ask for the return of a Latin paper which the Vice-Chancellor had lent him. This was folded in the same way as another, and Stepney gave the wrong paper back. Next morning, arranging his letters, he realised the mistake and rushed to see Kaunitz. The latter's valet had however already taken the paper to a certain Monsieur d'U. Stepney was horrified at his own carelessness, and felt himself at the mercy of a man to whom he would not like to confide any delicate affair. Kaunitz, who saw Stepney's confusion, got into his carriage and together they went to find U, whom they discovered in a courtyard of the palace. Stepney asked for the paper, which U admitted having received, but said it was in his lodging. At Stepney's insistance, U joined him in the coach [Stepney does not reveal what happened to Kaunitz at this point] and on the way U pulled the paper from his pocket, and swore that he had made no copy. This assurance however was not good enough for George Stepney, who asked for a written and signed statement that U had made no copy, or, if he had, that it was destroyed.

Not surprisingly, U refused this demand, saying his word was as good as his bond. Stepney apologised for having transgressed the rules of behaviour between gentlemen, but threatened to take the affair to the Emperor to get him to exact an oath of secrecy from U. The latter admitted that Stepney was quite capable of taking the affair to the monarch, but assured him that such a step was unnecessary; and on reflection Stepney admitted to himself that it would be unwise to stir up further trouble. He resolved to *ménager cette homme* for a month or two, by which time the matter should have blown over.

This whole affair is puzzling: there is no clue as to the content of the paper about which Stepney was so anxious – except that it touched the Emperor – or as to the identity of Monsieur U. Stepney had two acquaintances whose names began with that letter: one was Major-General Count Uhlfeldt, who at the end of 1703, was attending King Charles III of Spain. The other was the Danish Resident in Vienna, Johann Christoph v. Urbeck. It is possible that the missing paper may have been relevant to the negotiations with the Elector of Bavaria; and because Denmark was frequently thought to act in the French interest, this would justify Stepney's anxiety over its loss.

The affair reveals Stepney at his most vulnerable: he had once previously, in 1695, insisted on a written note of indemnity from a merchant to whom he had consigned a jewel belonging to the widow of Sir William Colt, and which had gone astray. But such a procedure was foreign to the imperial court.[8]

It cannot be claimed that Stepney hurried to join his friend Bruynincx in Pressburg. The latter had at first wished him to hasten his steps; but on 12 March, a depressed letter arrived from the Dutchman, who had got as far as Schinta [east of Pressburg], to say that Stepney should await his return to Vienna, as nothing further was to be achieved in Hungary. And by 15 March, Bruynincx himself arrived, tired and indisposed, but bringing with him a manifest distributed by Franz Rákóczy a year earlier. Stepney read this over, and reported that the Prince wrote as a patriot, asserting the liberty of his country which he alleged had been violated; but shewing resentment of past injuries rather than any disposition to come to terms or an agreement. A few days later the immediate demands of Nikolas Bercsenyi were listed by Bruynincx more clearly:

1 To have the Malcontents [the insurgents] treated as Free States;
2 Immediate application to be made to Rákóczy as their Chief;
3 Sufficient security and guaranty to be made for performing what should be agreed to.

Stepney commented that the imperial court would never treat with the rebels as a free state. Nevertheless he recommended that he should be sent fresh powers, drafted in a way suitable for use with the rebels, and that in future he and Bruynincx should address themselves directly to Rákóczy.[9]

On 12 April, Stepney wrote a private letter to his Secretary of State:

By an extraordinary accident an Original letter from Ragoczy [sic] is fallen into my hands, and which I do not intend to produce for fear of exasperating; for therein it appears that the Elector of Bavaria and He had formed a design of besieging Vienna this Spring. The latter has provocation enough to undertake anything, for besides all the ills he has formerly suffer'd, he has lately discover'd that people have been hired to assassinate or poison him.

Stepney never revealed how he came by Rákóczy's letter. He was later criticised by nineteenth-century historians for his failure to hand it over to the imperial court. In fact, the information it contained was of no material value, because (as Stepney wrote a week later) any convergence of Bavarian and Hungarian forces had been made impossible by the success of the imperial army under General Heister 'this side of the Danube.' And other discussions were taking place between Hungarians and imperialists, which, it was hoped, might at least lead to an armistice.

Now clouds of disapproval were gathering over Stepney. He received a warning from his friend Alexander Stanhope in the Hague, that

Count de Goes saies he had a letter from a friend in Vienna, who writes he heard you argue in a publick Company as warmly to justify the cause of the Rebels, as if you would put yourself at their head, and that it was much wonder'd at.

And at the same time Stepney was warned by Bruynincx, who had heard from the Hague that Count Wratislaw had been complaining against him, such strictures having doubtless already been made by the Count to the Emperor. Stanhope confirmed Bruynincx's warning, adding that Stepney's vigorous defence of the rebel cause had encouraged them to demand of the Emperor a new election of a king, who would displace the King of the Romans in that function. Stanhope had yet another charge to convey:

> the letters I mentioned to you attribute your great concern for the cause of the Rebells to the passion you have for a Lady your Neighbour, Sister to Prince Ragotzy; with whom you are continually. You may be sure that this with all the rest is writt into England and may take yr measures accordingly.

Stepney defended himself: yes, he had argued at court in defence of the rebels, because no-one else did so. When he was with the Malcontents he would argue on the other side; and this was his function as a Mediator. As for his friendship with Rákóczy's sister [Juliana, Countess d'Aspremont], this dated from the time of his arrival in Vienna. Despite her brother's activities she was well known and liked by both Court and Town, and

> [I] do not find in any part of my Instructions that the Conversation of Ladyes is forbidden me.[10]

The campaign of the imperialists in Hungary was brutal. They were supported by the 'hawks' of the imperial court, amongst whom should be counted Prince Eugene. In mid-May a Deputy from the Reformed churches of Transylvania arrived in Vienna to tell of a massacre of students and professors at the university of Engodin. Writing to Hedges about this incident (which he did not report until he had received some confirmation of the truth of the matter) Stepney continued:

> Mr. Bruyninx happen'd to light upon Prince Eugene and complained a little of this hard usage, and of the Imperialists having burnt 200 villages in that Province; His answer was, He wished it had been two thousand, for as much as that whole people was Rebellious.

So the Prince did not look favourably on the mediation; and on quite another matter Stepney, through no fault of his own, fell from grace. As in the previous year, the allied fleet was being prepared to go to Lisbon, and at the beginning of May Stepney was instructed to inform the Emperor that the ships would continue into the Mediterranean. Offers of service were made, and the ship-to-shore signals of 1703 were repeated. Stepney gave the news to Prince Eugene, who immediately wished to know how many ships were involved, and how many land forces they had on board. Having received no information, Stepney could not reply.[11]

The Envoy however was now let into the secret of Marlborough's plan to march his army to the Danube, and not merely to the Moselle, as had been originally believed. Stepney was to inform the Emperor secretly, and also the Elector Palatine who, since 1702, had become a displaced person at the Emperor's court. Not that, at this stage, Marlborough seems to have set much store on secrecy, since he sent similar news to his friend Count [Philipp Ludwig] Sinzendorf (1671-1742).[12]

Since Count Wratislaw's complaints about Stepney had indeed reached the imperial court by mid-May 1704, the Envoy decided to object in writing to Kaunitz. His defence was that he had arrived in Vienna on his return from leave after Bruynincx had already left for Hungary; and the only communication which he (Stepney) had had with the Malcontents was one letter which he wrote to Bercsenyi on 7 March, with which the latter was *not* pleased, because it was too partial to the *Augustissima Casa.* After Bruynincx had returned, Stepney had called on Sinzendorf, where he also found the Duke of Moles, and had told these two Court officials that the claim of the Malcontents to be regarded as a separate state was inconsistent with the oaths which they had already sworn to the House of Austria. And Stepney had also told Bruynincx that it was impossible to treat with the Hungarians as a free and sovereign nation.

Stepney sent copies of all these papers to Marlborough on 21 May, in a bitter letter which accused Wratislaw of having been the cause of his (Stepney's) exclusion from the negotiations of the Grand Alliance in 1701; and of casting aspersions on his friends and interest in England during the summer of 1703:

> And to crown all, by this latest act he has used his best endeavours
> to destroy me in a point where I was in hopes to have acquired
> some merit. [i.e. as a Mediator.]

And Stepney ended his letter by pointing out that Wratislaw's powerful position depended on his friendship with Prince Eugene and the 'Countenance' which Marlborough had been pleased to shew him.

Both Marlborough and Cardonnel sent comforting replies to Stepney, though the former regretted that George had allowed his resentment 'to go so far.' And the Duke added the (to Stepney) unwelcome information that he had requested Wratislaw to stay with him on his march east, towards the meeting with Prince Louis.[13]

As so often in times of stress, Stepney turned to his friend Lord 'Hallifax.' He did indeed report the arrival in Vienna of Halifax's nephew, George Montagu, together with a tutor. By now, Stepney was weary of Vienna:

> I have been at this expensive Court above 3 years without any
> consideration more than what is allowed to Her Majesty's Envoys
> at Lisbonne and in Switzerland, where a man may live as privately
> as he pleases. I have lost the best of my age, am deprived of my
> friends and Relations and see no prospect of bettering my fortune
> tho' I stay here 3 years longer.

But he stipulated that he would like to be redeemed with a good
air, and with the appearance of the Queen's satisfaction with his
services.[14]

The usual celebrations of the Emperor's birthday [9 June] were
marred by the appearance of the Malcontents within two English
miles of Vienna, attacking the Emperor's autumn residence of
Ebersdorf. The imperial menagerie was kept there. The Hungarians
destroyed many animals and mutilated the eagles. The Emperor
was very upset.

Stepney also wrote privately to Hedges (and partly in cypher)
his anxiety that the Catholic church was using the disturbances in
Hungary as an excuse to have the Protestant religion extinguished
there. One of his reasons for this view was the fact that General
Heister, in command of the imperialist troops, was known to be an
adherent of the Society of Jesus. Stepney had not wished to make
this charge as part of his official report, so as not to 'affect the
Alliance.' He ended his letter:

> However in duty and conscience I cannot but give you this
> account, that you may see what unsuitable returns are made to
> Her Majesty by destroying the Protestant faith (whereof she is
> the Defender), at a time when her Armies are on the march towards
> the Danube as the onely means left for preserving this family [the
> Habsburgs] from utter destruction.[15]

In England changes had taken place in the Department of State which
later became the Foreign Office. Lord Nottingham had retired; Sir
Charles Hedges moved to the Southern Department; and the newcomer to the Northern Department was Robert Harley, who still
retained his appointment as Speaker of the House of Commons.
Harley came to be known as 'Robin the Trickster'. Be that as it
may, he was a good psychologist, and his handling of the Queen's
touchy Envoy in Vienna was masterly. But he did not provide the
clear and unambiguous instructions which Hedges usually sent to
Stepney. Upon Harley's appointment Stepney wrote a polite letter:

> By my being long abroad I have scarce the honour to be known to
> you.

And saying he still had hopes of his task in Hungary:

if our military men and our Jesuits do not still defeat ye Empr's good intentions.

Two Deputies from the Malcontents (though with no authority from Rákóczy) were in Vienna, and desultory talks continued. Stepney suggested that Rákóczy should designate a place where a congress could be held of deputies from both sides. He and Bruynincx could assist, if they were accepted as Mediators by the insurgents, as they had already been by the Emperor.[16]

By 19 June the Deputies had been given the Emperor's official response, couched in general terms. To Harley, Stepney commented that the imperial ministers should have shewn

more clearly and plainly what the Nation [Hungary] has to trust to, whereas these obscure and general terms seem design'd as a snare to induce the people and their Cheifs [*sic*] to lay down their arms and disperse, which is little better than leaving themselves at discretion to be treated as wrongfully at the next Diette as they pretend they were at the two last.

The Emperor's offer of an armistice was turned down by the Malcontents, unless the Emperor withdrew his forces, in which case the rebels promised to withdraw from Austria and Moravia. Stepney and Bruynincx immediately applied to the Elector Palatine, to get the Emperor to agree. The Elector would listen to no such suggestion, and told Stepney that when the 'blow' against the Elector of Bavaria was over, m/15 or m/20 regular troops would be available for Hungary. The two Mediators did not argue, not wishing to be thought too partial to the Malcontents.

The English government, and Marlborough, continued to press, through Stepney and also through Wratislaw, for an accommodation with the Hungarians. And before the news of Hedges' change of department had reached him, Marlborough wrote to Sir Charles:

I am altogether of your opinion that Mr.Stepney takes the difference between him and Comte Wratislaw too much to heart, and so I have told him; the sense of his own innocence and integrity, which is so well known, should make him slight it.[17]

News of Marlborough's victory at Donauwörth reached Vienna on 9 July (n.s.). A *Te Deum* was ordered, and Stepney basked briefly in the glow of approval from the imperial court. The King of the Romans decided to 'make the campaign,' preferably with the English army. A few days later Stepney was approached by Count Sinzendorf (probably on instructions) to find out if Marlborough would like to accept the dignity of being created Prince of the Empire, and further, what would be the best means of 'managing' the sense of obligation felt by HIM. Stepney admitted to freedom in his reply:

> to give reasonable terms to the Hungarians, and to find means of prosecuting the war against France with more vigour than had been done of late.

However, he was not invited by any imperial minister to celebrate the victory; so

> I follow Fanshawe's Maxim, of having my own Shoulder of Mutton and my own Flatterers.

And Stepney promptly invited to his celebration Bruynincx and all others whose masters had had any share in the glorious action, together with the Prince of Lobkowitz, who first brought the news to Vienna.[18]

Wratislaw was trying (without imperial instructions) to negotiate a peace with the Elector of Bavaria. The project quickly got into the press – Stepney sent Cardonnel a copy of the *Nuremberg Gazette* – and told Marlborough that, from the Elector's point of view, these talks were merely a blind. The Court had intercepted letters from Max Emmanuel to Louis XIV on the subject.

At the beginning of August Stepney fell ill of fever, and was at home for eight days. 'It brought me very low.' He also commented to Cardonnel, sadly, on the ravishing of Bavaria by the English troops.

There was soon news to cheer him. On 17 August 1704, he was conferring somewhat gloomily with the Marquis de Prié, considering what help it was possible for the Empire to spare for the Duke of Savoy [now firmly engaged on the side of the Allies]:

> When Count Altheim pass'd by my window with ye news of our wunderfull Victory [i.e. the Battle of Blenheim], wch made us throw away our papers.

And to Marlborough, on the very day of Altheim's arrival, Stepney continued:

> I take leave once more to congratulate yr Grace and the English Nation for so signall an advantage wch still heightens ye reputation of her Mat^{ies} armies, so useful to Her Allyes and formidable to Her Enemys.[19]

XVIII *The Hungarian Mediation* (II)
(August-December 1704)

Marlborough at Sefelingen to Stepney

27 August (n.s.) 1704

I have received a great many letters from you, most of them at the same time. . . but I am sorry to tell you they bring me very little satisfaction in the business I am most concerned for. You will easily guess I mean the treaty with the Hungarians. . . .

Mr. Cardonnel has communicated to me the desire you have of making us a visit before we leave Germany; and though I cannot but be concerned at your taking so long and tedious a journey, yet I propose so much satisfaction to myself in your company, that rather than want it. . . I could meet you part of the way. [1]

Already on 9 August (n.s.) 1704, Stepney had written suggesting that he should visit the camp, and pay respects to Marlborough, without specifying any other necessity for the journey. It could be assumed that he felt the need for personal encouragement, and the companionship for some days of his particular friends, Adam de Cardonnel and Harry Watkins (who, although officially Judge Advocate to the army, acted as assistant to Cardonnel as required). Stepney had recovered from his fever, and cheerfully concluded his letter:

Pray consult yr friend Brig^r Webb and look ab^t for 2 or 3 pretty sizable padds [horses] for me wch perhaps may be had at reasonable rates when you break up yr Camp. [2]

Before the news of the Blenheim victory had reached Vienna, the situation in Hungary had worsened. Hopes for a truce seemed to have evaporated: General Heister had renewed his operations, and the rebels were carrying out their usual tactics [the word *guerilla* had not yet become part of the English language] of exhausting the imperial army by sudden raids and swift retreats. Stepney and Bruynincx then applied to the Emperor, by a memorial delivered to Kaunitz on 27 August, to get orders sent to Heister to suspend his operations, and that an officer should go to Buda to regulate an armistice. The memorial was accepted, but three days later Count

Kaunitz suddenly left for his estates in Moravia, for a stay of six weeks, and the Mediators did not know to whom to turn. However on 3 September they achieved a joint audience of the Emperor and asked him directly to restrain his general. The Mediators then called on various ministers who were about to participate in a conference to decide on suitable advice for the monarch. Stepney was pleased to find that the president of the conference would be Prince Adam von Lichtenstein (in whose castle he had once been a guest). The Prince had large estates in Moravia (as did Kaunitz) and, since these were very vulnerable to Hungarian raids, he might wish the negotiations well. One result of the conference was that the imperial court decided to change its own go-betweens with the rebels. More seriously, the court was suspicious of any congress called by Rákóczy, since he was suspected of wishing to use it to announce his self-assumed title of Prince of Transylvania.[3]

Stepney left for his visit to Marlborough on 11 September (n.s.) 1704. He had left detailed instructions for his steward, James Fury, who reported:

According to yor hon^{rs} Commands, I had the Silver Trunks carry'd up into the room with ye 2 Iron doors, whereof Mr.Whitworth keeps the keys and I those belonging to the Truncks, before I lock'd them, I took an inventory and found all as should be.

Then there was Tyrolean wine to be bought and bottled. The white wine was pure and clear, but the red tasted of 'ye barrill which was foul'; but George Montagu thought the wine would lose the nasty taste, and then Stepney would be creditably stocked with Tyrol wine. The sale of some horses had not gone forward.

Fury also undertook the detail of an exchange of money which Stepney had arranged with Wratislaw's successor as imperial envoy in England, Count [Johann Wenceslas] Gallas (1669-1716). The Count had not yet left to take up his appointment, and found it convenient to supply Stepney with florins in exchange for sterling. Fury reckoned the rate of exchange at 8.3 florins for each pound sterling, and Stepney's expenses (in sterling) at £180 per month.[4]

The route which Stepney took towards Marlborough is not known. The Duke did not come to meet him, but on 19 September (n.s.) George arrived at the small town of 'Cron Weissembourg' [now Wissembourg, just inside the French border, 48 km north of Strasbourg]. His arrival was noted by Prince Eugene, who was not pleased and wrote to his *confidant* in Vienna that having spoken with Stepney he (the Prince) was determined to obtain from Marlborough orders that the Mediators were only to proceed with their work in a manner which would be agreeable to the Emperor. A fortnight later Prince Eugene repeated this view, but asked his correspondent to keep the information to himself.[5]

The King of the Romans also reached the camp on 22 September, to be received by Prince Eugene and the Duke. Stepney wrote to Whitworth:

> Next morning his Grace visited ye Trenches and returned hither [to Wissembourg] last night [24 Sept.] I follow as close as a shadow everywhere, and am extreamly satisfyed with ye Excursion I made.

And having insisted on accompanying Marlborough to the town of Landau, now once more under siege by the Allies, George could add:

> from whence returning alone in the Coach with my Lord Duke I had an opportunity of entertaining him with my own small concerns, to wch he gave a very favourable ear and I hope some months hence to find ye benefit of yt moment.

The 'small concerns' were about Stepney's wish to be transferred from Vienna to the Hague (as soon as Stanhope retired). At the same time George was dreaming of his appointment as Third Ambassador at the time of any peace treaty with France, and, more immediately, of an increase in his allowances to bring him up to the usual standard of Plenipotentiary [£8 a day]. What the tired victor of Blenheim thought privately of his little Welsh companion is not known.[6]

More serious than Prince Eugene's privately-expressed doubts as to Stepney's behaviour were Count Wratislaw's dispatches to the Emperor himself. The Count repeated the imperial distrust of Stepney and the fear of his possible influence over Marlborough. The Emperor answered him on 4 October:

> On my part I would fain have gotten out of the Hungarian affair long ago, but these turbulent people demand such insolent and audacious things, have also sought ways and means [*manier*] to promote their ends, that it is impossible blindly to assent to them. About these circumstances I charge you accurately to inform Marlborough, and to assure him that I will willingly do all which is possible to facilitate this work, but Stepney has always shown too much passion in the matter.
>
> While I really cannot say what cause he has had, I can say that at certain times and occasions he has gone and been carried too far in his expostulations, that it almost seemed as if he would inflame [*aufhezen*] the rebels instead of helping to bring them to reason.[7]

During his stay at Wissembourg Stepney occupied himself in preparing for Marlborough (in French) a reasoned paper entitled

Burger's House in Wissembourg, built 1599. By kind permission of the Archives Municipales, Hotel de Ville, Wissembourg, France. Photo: Ch Muller.

Réflexions sur les affaires d'Hongrie, in which he set out the damage to Austria and the Allies caused by the rebellion, and the necessity of ending it as soon as possible by an amicable accommodation. He argued that it could not be denied that the Emperor had *not* been entirely motivated by his usual clemency. He had nominated various commissaries to treat with the Hungarians, but had changed these officials too often to allow any of them to understand fully the Malcontents' desires, and to advise what steps should be taken to get out of the affair. The Emperor himself had accepted the mediation by the maritime powers; but his generals had done all they could to destroy the idea.

Yet there were some signs of improvement: the Emperor had generously agreed to a provisional armistice until the end of September. Rákóczy had sent the Court eleven articles on which he hoped a truce of three months might be concluded, during which time he proposed that Commissaries from both sides should meet and work towards a general peace.

These articles seemed to Stepney reasonable. However, that Prince had *not* agreed to the mediation, and insisted on guarantees, which the imperial court was unlikely even to discuss because in its opinion they were incompatible with the respect due to the Sovereign. Unless the Hungarians could have a positive assurance on which they could rely for the future, they were unlikely to lay down their arms. If this difficulty could be overcome, Stepney recommended that the truce should be well observed by the imperial generals; and that moderate ministers should be chosen by the Emperor as his Commissaries.

It was impossible, wrote Stepney, to separate the people from their chiefs. Regarding the people, the Emperor had already expressed himself favourably regarding the reform of finances, and on the free exercise of the Reformed religion. But without a guarantee, it was difficult to believe that these promises would be executed. The treatment of the chiefs was difficult. Amnesties had been promised to them, but none had availed himself of the terms. Equally, some imperial ministers objected to clemency being shewn to rebellious subjects.

Finally, an event had taken place which was likely to retard the accommodation which ought to be made: this was the acceptance by Rákóczy of the title of Prince of Transylvania, which the Emperor would not allow. Stepney suggested that Rákóczy should be placated by land in another country which would be equivalent to the value of the goods and estates he would leave behind in Hungary: but where such a territory should be found, the English Envoy did not presume to advise. He listed for Marlborough the imperial troops in Hungary, regiment by regiment. The total came to 23,800 men.[8]

According to Wratislaw (who duly informed the Emperor) Stepney left Cron Weissembourg on 15 October (n.s.) 1704, having been strictly commanded by Marlborough *not* to involve himself in the Hungarian unrest save with the greatest caution and requisite moderation. And Wratislaw added that the Duke had promised him to arrange with the Lord Treasurer as soon as he (Marlborough) reached England he would recall Stepney from Vienna and accommodate him elsewhere. Marlborough wished this information kept secret for the time being.

Meanwhile in Vienna, Charles Whitworth had been keeping Secretary of State Harley as well as Stepney up to date with the latest news on the Hungarian mediation. After some difficulty over passports, Jakob Jan Bruynincx together with the senior imperial negotiator, Baron [Johann Friderich] Seilern had left on 5 October, for Pressburg, with the intention of continuing to the northern Hungarian mining town of Schemnitz [Selmeez], where the conference of the two sides had been set up.

George Stepney took a week over his journey. Probably he was able to travel by river as soon as he reached the Danube, for Bavaria was now under the control of the Allies. He reached Vienna on the morning of 22 October, and went straight on to Hungary the following day. In Pressburg Stepney was greeted by Count [Sigismond] Lamberg, Master of the Horse [and a brother of George's landlord]. This officer was *en route* to Vienna with a packet from the imperial commissioners. Bruynincx, in Schemnitz, had already been to visit Rákóczy, but had found little disposition among the Malcontents to come to an accommodation with the Emperor. And Bruynincx suspected that the Hungarians were using the armistice merely to gain time to re-arm. Nevertheless Stepney, after one night in Pressburg, proposed to continue his journey and hoped to to join the conference before it met to do business.[9]

Despite an accident *en route* (of which he gave no details) Stepney reached Schemnitz on 27 October, in the evening. On the way he met a Commissary from the Malcontents, who told him that their army was moving, and that he had heard nothing of any prolongation of the truce, which was due to expire at the end of the month. Bercsenyi greeted Stepney coldly, and referred him and Bruynincx to Rákóczy, who was taking the waters at Bad Eisenach 'two Hungarian miles from Schemnitz.' The Mediators visited the Prince the following day and urged him to agree to a prolongation of the truce. After time for consultation, he gave a flat refusal in the name of the Hungarian Confederacy. The cause of this denial was the Confederates' reaction to an entirely new demand only recently made by the Imperial Commissioners, requiring the cession of 100 Hungarian miles of territory. Previous requirements from the imperialists had been more reasonable; Stepney had discussed some of Rákóczy's amendments with Prince Eugene and others at Landau, and all had agreed that it should be possible to create a foundation on which to build further. Now, Bruynincx pleaded with the imperial commissioners for a modification. This was refused, and an answer was demanded from the Hungarians. Rákóczy and his deputies maintained that the new demands deserved none. However at the Mediators' insistence, something like an answer was promised. This arrived on 30 October, but again was rejected. The verbal battle continued until 1 November, neither side wishing to give an absolute negative, lest it be accused of causing the breakdown of negotiations. Stepney commented

> We have run round in a Circle, and might have done so till dooms
> day if the Imperialists had not given out first by informing Count
> Bercseni that they intended on the 5th inst. [5 November (n.s.)]
> to remove from hence by way of Gran; and soon after Mr. Bruyninx
> and I shall return to Vienna by way of Pressburg.

But before leaving Stepney and Bruynincx visited the mines near
Schemnitz:

> They are the richest in gold and silver of any in Europe; we had a
> curiosity to go down an hundred and fiftyeight fathoms, and have
> seen ye progress of these metalls from ye Quarry to ye Mint.

Stepney added that the chiefs of the Hungarian Confederacy enjoyed
the benefit from the mines; but the army was paid in copper coin.
He sent a sample to London.

The Mediators, after a slow journey, reached Vienna on 12
November (n.s.). That very night Stepney set to work on his
dispatches. Although both the warring parties were only too ready
and willing to continue hostilities, at least the insurgents, in the
person of Bercsenyi, claimed to be still willing to negotiate a peace,
and suggested the town of Tyrnau as a suitable location, for the
safety of all negotiators.[10]

Three days later [15 November (n.s.)] Bruynincx and Stepney
had meetings with Counts Harrach and Kaunitz, and reported
accordingly to their respective governments. They told the Austrian
ministers that they intended to complain against particular persons
(meaning Seilern), but would wait until the Court called a
Conference about Hungary; then, if they were asked, they would
explain the sense of the Hungarian Nation and what steps might be
taken towards an agreement. Until that time, or until their own
governments sent a further application to the Emperor, by letter or
otherwise, not to let the negotiation fall to the ground, the Mediators
would reserve themselves. Writing to Harley, Stepney added:

> I know very well that a letter to this purpose will be imputed by
> this Court, as having been procured by my suggestion, and they
> will be apt to suspect I have represented the Imperial Ministers
> not to have been so hearty in this good work as might have been
> expected: but I am indifferent what they either say or think of me
> on this account, since I am satisfied in my own Conscience that I
> act upon no other principle than that of justice and what I think to
> be both for Her Mat^yes service and indeed for the Emperor's own
> Interest, if rightly understood.

So much for Stepney's official stance. But on 19 November, he
admitted to Harley that he was perfectly aware of Rákóczy's
correspondence with Louis XIV, Max Emmanuel and possibly with

the Turks. Stepney excused the Prince on the grounds that men in his circumstances looked everywhere for succour, wherever they could hope to receive any assistance. However, they might still wish for an accommodation:

> tho' the conditions be never so just and advantagious [*sic*] since it is certain this last End is the ultimate scope of their desires, whereas the other extremity ought to be reputed as the last efforts of their despair, which this Court should try to prevent by applying suitable remedyes.[11]

It is not surprising that later historians, particularly those of the Catholic persuasion, should have found Stepney's argument specious.

Rákóczy had entertained Stepney and Bruynincx with delectable Tokay. Both Mediators wrote to him from Pressburg to thank for their reception. The Prince acknowledged these letters from his camp at Neuhäusel and asked that the negotiations should continue under the same mediation.

On 21 November, Stepney had an audience of the Emperor, and asked him not to give too much credit to the reports current in Vienna, that the Hungarians were averse to any sort of agreement, Stepney humbly submitting the opinion that the negotiation might be retrieved if more suitable proposals could be made by the Court. Leopold replied that he would do what he could to reclaim the Malcontents, insofar as might be consistent with his honour. The Emperor's amicable response to Stepney should not be taken at its face-value: on 5 November, he had written to Count Wratislaw that he had heard from the Savoyard minister in Vienna that in Hungarian affairs Stepney was causing much damage ('*hirein viel geschadet, und zu schaden continuere*'). During the last months of his life Leopold's suspicions of the English Envoy never diminished.[12]

In Vienna after his travels, Stepney again took up his ordinary duties as Envoy. Charles Whitworth left him, having been allotted the hazardous appointment as Queen Anne's representative in Russia. Wratislaw (who was expecting an appointment in Bohemia) returned to Vienna, as did Prince Eugene. No official Conference was held immediately on Hungarian affairs, and neither Stepney nor Bruynincx was asked for an opinion. Instead, General Heister left for Hungary at the head of 11,000 men. Stepney described him as the Angel with the flaming sword that drove poor Adam out of paradise.

Instructions from London arrived requiring Stepney to get the Emperor to intervene with the Republic of Venice to prevent that state joining others in Italy in a pro-French alliance. Stepney was sceptical, and commented to the Duke of Shrewsbury [then residing in Rome] that the fate of the Dukes of Savoy and Modena gave but poor encouragement to other Italian states to join the Grand Alliance.

The City of Exeter and boroughs in the west of England had complained to the Queen about the duties on woollen manufactures which were imposed by the Emperor. Stepney was asked to resume his efforts – he had been through all this in 1701 – to obtain relief. Meanwhile he had 'picked up' and sent to London and the Hague a copy of a treaty between the King of Prussia and the town of Danzig, to which the Dutch objected. And he recorded the death of his landlady, Countess Lamberg [Katherina Eleanora, *née* Sprinzenstein, b. 1660] together with her sister the Countess of Hoyos and her son-in-law Count Roggendorf, all from smallpox and within three days of each other.[13]

From his visit to Cron Weissembourg Stepney had returned with a task, entrusted to him by Brigadier [William] Cadogan (1675-1726), to compose a Latin inscription for a plan or monument of the Battle of Blenheim. Stepney was gratified by this commission.

I believe it [the Latin text] is too long but it may be put into a little letter and crowded into any corner of yr design. If you have any room to spare, you may fill up with Decorations: Two fair women, naked up to ye knee, with flying Petticoats and loose Breasts may represent Fame on both sides of ye Monument with a Trumpett in one hand and a Lawrell in ye other.[14]

He sent his composition to various friends for comment and correction. However once again George was unlucky in his undertakings: the inscription on the map of the battle which is preserved at Blenheim Palace is not his work. True, his text is to be found in the British Library in a booklet published in 1705 entitled *The Inscription Appointed to be fix'd on a Marble Pillar. Erected at HOCHSTADT In Memory of That Glorious Victory – The Latin Written by Mr. Stepny, and English'd by a Gentleman of Oxon.* but, alas, no marble monument was ever erected in the months following the battle.[15]

The Duke of Marlborough had need of Stepney's help over another matter: the great commander had travelled to Berlin at the end of 1704 in order to buy 8,000 men from the King of Prussia for service in Italy to help the Duke of Savoy. Although the subsidy for the troops was to be paid by the English and Dutch governments, Marlborough had had to agree that provisions for the army, whilst it served in Italy, would be at the Emperor's expense. Of course the Duke had no authority to make any such commitment but, as he wrote to Stepney, without it the deal would have fallen through, and he left it to the Envoy to make apologies and excuses to the Emperor as best he could.[16]

At the end of the year Harley in Whitehall transmitted to Stepney the Queen's command to press the Emperor to renew the Treaty and make peace with the Hungarian Malcontents. At the same time Sir Charles Hedges forwarded a similar instruction, that the Emperor, now that Bavaria was within his power, should settle a constant allowance upon his son, the King of Spain.

On the second point Stepney sent a memorandum to the Duke of Moles, because the Emperor was indisposed. As to the first, Stepney was already dealing with the King of the Romans, who was taking over from his father much of the direction of affairs. Eventually, on 26 December, a Conference was held in Kaunitz's house, those participating being Prince Adam of Liechtenstein, Seilern, Consbruck, Stepney and Bruynincx. The two latter spoke as one man, and contradicted Seilern's account of events. Stepney emphasized that he had told Rákóczy explicitly that he would never be acknowledged by the Emperor as Prince of Transylvania, and Rákóczy had not raised the matter again during their conversation which had lasted seven hours. Privately to Harley Stepney claimed that he and Bruynincx had justified themselves to Seilern's face, and in public, and had been thanked by Kaunitz [Vice-Chancellor of the Empire] for their work. Stepney hoped Kaunitz's compliments were sincere; but he suspected that the meeting had been held purely *par manière d'acquit*, and that Seilern's maxim, that force of arms would prevail, would henceforth be followed. In this view Stepney was correct: on the same day on which the Conference was held the imperialists gained a victory over the insurgents at Tyrnau, with 11,000 men against 22,000 Hungarians. Rákóczy was present. When things went wrong for his army the cavalry fled, leaving the wretched foot, the Tolpatz, to be slaughtered. The commander of some French grenadiers was captured, brought to Vienna and displayed on New Year's Day, 1705, for about two hours in an open waggon as a spectacle for the people. Stepney took the opportunity of speaking to him.[17]

General Heister was unable to follow up his victory; but Landau had at last surrendered to the Allies (and Count Frise was made its Governor), so the year 1704 ended more cheerfully than it had begun. Stepney had leisure to attend to more personal matters.

XIX *The Quarrel with Wratislaw*
(1705)

<u>Stepney in Vienna to Stanhope</u>
<u>7 January (n.s.) 1705</u>

> Count Wratislaw does not find so many friends here as he expected
> at his return. He sticks close to Pr. E-[*sic*] and is generally call'd
> *Son Suisse*: It is not a little consolation to me to find most people
> here have the same opinion of him as I have.[1]

The antipathy which George Stepney felt towards Wratislaw dated
back to 1701, when the Count was establishing himself as imperial
Envoy to England (his first diplomatic post abroad), and Stepney
was at the start of his second mission in Vienna. In so many ways
Wratislaw was everything that Stepney was not. The Count, who
had had a legal education, was nephew to Ulrich Kinsky, the late
Chancellor of Bohemia. His brother-in-law was Count Schlick, one
of the leading imperial commanders. He was rich enough to
command couriers to take his dispatches express to Vienna, where
they were read and answered by Leopold I, sometimes without
consultation with any minister. The *London Post* reported
Wratislaw's arrival in the capital on 28 December (o.s.) 1700,
accompanied by a retinue. He mixed easily with the English
aristocracy, becoming friend and adviser to Marlborough himself.[2]

In 1701 Stepney had good cause for his jealousy. His Instructions
for Vienna included the command that he was to discover and report
on the Emperor's proposals and terms for joining the Grand
Alliance. When he arrived, on 1 May 1701, it was to find that a
courier from Wratislaw had just left on the return trip Vienna-
London, taking with him the imperial views on the matter. Later,
Sir Charles Hedges told Stepney explicitly that neither he nor the
King had asked Wratislaw to send his courier. Stepney, who had
his information from Kaunitz, therefore concluded that Wratislaw
had acted on his own initiative, to try to ensure that any negotiations
took place in London, and not in Vienna.[3]

Wratislaw's stay in England continued until the summer of 1703, when he returned to Vienna with the apparent intention of relinquishing his appointment. Stepney commented in August 1703 that this was merely a ploy on the Count's part, in order to obtain the reversion of a high office in Bohemia in exchange for his promise to return to London. And events took place as Stepney had anticipated: Wratislaw did indeed return, and is credited with first suggesting to Marlborough that the latter should march his army to the Danube, which eventually resulted in the victory at Blenheim in August 1704.[4]

When Stepney reached the Hague in November 1703 he found Wratislaw complaining to everyone that the English Fleet had retired from the Mediterranean without accomplishing anything. Stepney told him that his complaints were without significance because the imperial court had not been offended at Admiral Shovell's behaviour. Wratislaw claimed to have received the Emperor's objections under his own hand, thereby confirming Stepney's worst fears that a private line existed between the Emperor and his Envoy.[5]

Wratislaw's complaints against Stepney during the summer of 1704 have been described in Chapters XVII and XVIII. It is certain that Stepney's visit to Cron Weissembourg in September of that year was as distasteful to Wratislaw as it was to Prince Eugene. When the former wrote to the Emperor, first to voice his apprehensions of Stepney's visit and later, after George had left, to claim that Marlborough had secretly promised him (Wratislaw) to have Stepney removed from Vienna, it is unlikely that he knew of Stepney's own wish for a posting to the Hague, or that he had already discussed that possibility with Marlborough. As to the means of bringing the Hungarian uprising to an end, the views of Wratislaw and Stepney were diametrically opposed, the Count being fully in support of Prince Eugene's desire to see the military defeat of the rebels.

At the turn of the year 1704/5 (n.s.) Stepney became aware that Wratislaw had written disparagingly of him to Marlborough. On 27 December (n.s.) 1704 George sent to Cardonnel a copy of his report on the imperial Conference on Hungary, and told him that when it was over he had taken Kaunitz aside and told him:

> wt a Comfort it was to me to find him explain[ing] to me in so agreeable a maner the sense the Emp[r] had of me and my Service, since I found others were not so candid but had reported that ye Emp[r] was dissatisfyed with my Conduct and desired a change. He assured me he never heard any such thing.

Stepney reasoned that because Kaunitz was in a position equivalent to that of an English Secretary of State, any instructions given to Wratislaw should have passed through his hands. Since they had not, Wratislaw must independently and falsely have made use of the Emperor's name and authority in a letter to Marlborough, or he must have been acting on the advice of the Jesuits. Now, Stepney was skating on very thin ice. His Whitehall informant had been his cousin, Erasmus Lewis, who was at the time private secretary to Robert Harley, and thus in a position to see confidential correspondence. But the knowledge of Wratislaw's letter, in turn, could only have come from Marlborough's secretary and George's friend, Adam de Cardonnel.

Stepney was aware of the danger, and continued, in his letter of 27 December, that he would rather perish than put Cardonnel to any inconvenience; but he thought it would be a generous gesture on Marlborough's part if the Duke sent him Wratislaw's letter in the original, and allowed him to make use of it.[6]

Now occurred an event which, though not completely unexpected, could have been of little help to the English Envoy. On 11 January (n.s.) 1705, Dominic Andreas, Count Kaunitz, was found dead of apoplexy. Stepney had had official dealings with Kaunitz ever since his arrival in Vienna in 1701, and although he had once seriously clashed with him (cf. Chapter XVI above), he had grown used to the Vice-Chancellor and their dealings had been amicable. The imperial chancery was put into commission, pending the appointment of a successor to Kaunitz, and after some days Stepney was informed that the elder Count Harrach would be in charge of Hungarian affairs.

According to Stepney, Kaunitz before he died had advised him to write to Counts Harrach and Mansfeldt, as friends and advisers of the Emperor, to find out the truth behind Wratislaw's accusations, and whether he was under the Emperor's displeasure or not. George did so, on 14 January, addressing himself to both officials. On 28 January

> Harrach discover'd to me by word of mouth the Emperor's answer, in the terms following: '*Qu'il a ordre de me dire en reponse a Mon Billet Que Sa Ma*^{te} *Imp*^{ll} *n'avoit pas Sujet d'ecrire autrement que content de moy, Et si le Comte de Wratislaw avoit dit ou ecrit quelque chose contre moy, cela n'a été nullement par ordre.*' He was pleas'd to add That He would be very well satisfyed if I continued here at least till a generall Peace.

Yet Stepney was not satisfied. The same evening he sent a second letter to Harrach, this time demanding not only that Wratislaw be reprimanded, but that Harrach should put his reply in writing, and send copies to the new imperial Envoy in London, Count Gallas, his assistant, [Johann Philipp] Hoffmann, and to the imperial representative in the Hague, Count Goes.[7]

To Cardonnel, George confided that when he received Harrach's written statement he would send it to Harley to find out what further satisfaction he should demand; and apart from the addressees listed above, both Secretaries of State should be informed of the Emperor's good opinion of him.[8]

One must remember the length of time taken by correspondence between London and Vienna, sometimes as much as a month. On 2 January (o.s.) 1704/$\underline{5}$ Marlborough had written politely to Stepney, regretting Wratislaw's behaviour, to which Stepney had referred in his letter dated 16 December (n.s.) 1704. The Duke expressed pleasure that Stepney had decided to ignore the matter, and suggested (for the Envoy's private information only) that it was possible he might be sent to Turin and Richard Hill be posted to Venice. Marlborough asked for Stepney's views, to be sent to him personally. The Duke did not refer to a letter which he had written to Wratislaw, dated 27 December 1704 (o.s.):

> Je suis bien marri de voir qu'il n'y a pas une meilleure intelligence entre vous et M. Stepney. Je lui faire ecrire sur ce chapitre.

On 9 January (o.s.) 1704/$\underline{5}$, Marlborough wrote again to Wratislaw telling him that the Queen and the States General might send new mediators in the Hungarian dispute, and urging him meanwhile to remember Stepney's long service and to treat him with courtesy during the '*peu de temps*' which he had to remain in Vienna. A copy of this letter was sent to Stepney. On the same date Cardonnel sent George a warning:

> I have received your letters of the 27th past and 3d inst., to which I have time to write but two words in answer and to tell you my humble opinion is that it would not be best to break or clash actively with the Gent^m [i.e. Wratislaw] so that you may guess it would not be well he should know that you are appriz'd of what he says, tho he has continued since in the same strain.[9]

But the warning came too late. Stepney was in a high state of excitement at his apparent victory over his enemy. He sent back to Marlborough not only an account of the use he had made of Wratislaw's letters to the Duke, but he added a list of seven queries to be answered before he would set out for Italy, and a demand for money for equipage. Stepney's pride was enhanced by a letter which came in from his cousin Lewis, that Robert Harley, when discussing a possible replacement for him in Vienna, remarked 'Name me a man to succeed!.' In his euphoric state Stepney did not scruple to write the whole story to Count Auersperg (still in Italy), revelling in his triumph over Wratislaw. And he repeated his letter, not only to Tucker in Whitehall, but copied to all the Queen's representatives in Europe and beyond, Aglionby, Blathwayt, Raby, Poley, Whitworth, Robinson, Wich, Vernon [junior], Davenant, Shrewsbury, Blackwell, Broughton, Hill and Sutton.[10]

Retribution came, but did not reach Stepney until the beginning of March. Meanwhile he recorded the death of his *adorable Princesse*, Sophie-Charlotte, Queen of Prussia, from a cold caught during carnival. Stepney had been in correspondence with Sophia, Electress-dowager of Hanover [mother of Sophie-Charlotte] about a possible bride for her Catholic son, Duke Max, who was resident in Vienna. There is no record of any condolence sent by Stepney to Sophia, but he may have considered any such letter inappropriate, as coming from a commoner.

In mid-February, among other personal letters, Stepney reverted to a subject dear to his heart. The previous September, from Cron Weissembourg, he had found time to write to his publisher, Jacob Tonson, about the possibility of purchasing an ancient seat of his ancestors, the Manor of Aldenham, in Hertfordshire, from its present owner, the Duke of Newcastle. Stepney had evidently been to see the manor during his visit to England in 1703/4, but had found it in a ruinous condition. He had asked Tonson to enlist the help of 'Mr. van Brugg' to give an expert opinion on the condition of the building, and whether there was any garden, wood or wilderness round about, which would be included in the sale, to make an agreeable retreat for Stepney and his friends. Regrettably, the reply from [Sir John] Vanbrugh was not favourable; for Stepney now wrote to him [18 February 1705] to say that he had put Aldenham out of his mind, but that he would like something similar,

that I may jump in some Box ready cut and dry'ed, as soon as my days of wandring are at an end.

George went on to discuss theatrical scenery, designed by Father Pozzo in Vienna, for court performances, explaining that the particular scenes which Vanbrugh wanted had already been destroyed, owing to the Court's convention that the scenery for any play attended by the Emperor himself was immediately cast aside after one performance only. The canvas was re-used, painted over, for a new scene. Stepney would have liked to have saved some of Pozzo's designs, because of the excellence of the perspective; however the difficulty would have been the transport to England because, he remarked, no river flowed in that direction.[11]

Whilst these agreeable thoughts were in George's mind, elsewhere the clouds of disapproval were darkening. Stepney's second letter to Count Harrach had brought its desired result. On 20 February (n.s.), the Emperor wrote to Count Gallas in London in words which closely reflected Stepney's own phrasing in letters sent home. But the Emperor was no fool. In a postscript, specially marked to be sent in cypher, Leopold told Gallas that the official text had been written to calm Stepney who, although he had enthusiastically furthered the common cause against France, had lacked the discretion necessary in Hungarian affairs. Gallas therefore was to use his own discretion and be reserved in discussion with English ministers on the matter; and if the Queen had already decided to send another Envoy to Vienna, Gallas could delay his approach until any such new representative had actually left. Stepney of course was ignorant of the Emperor's postscript, and continued to believe that he enjoyed Leopold's good opinion.[12]

About 4 March (n.s.) 1705, an official rebuke reached Stepney from Marlborough. Wratislaw had sent the Duke a copy of Stepney's first letter to Count Harrach containing the mention that letters written by Wratislaw had been spread abroad in England. Marlborough told Stepney he could not understand his action, because the Envoy had so often been told that the Queen, to whom alone he was accountable, was satisfied with his behaviour. Marlborough demanded a fuller explanation. He did, however, send Stepney a copy of his reply to Wratislaw, in which he expressed umbrage that the Count evidently considered him capable of exposing extracts of their correspondence. Cardonnel, in composing the covering letter to this correspondence, wrote with anguish to George:

> We received yesterday the favour of yours of the 28th past, and at the same time my Lord Duke received one from you of the 31st and another of the like date from Count Wratislaw, I assure you nothing surprised me more for several years than the reading of these letters, for I am so farr from agreeing with you that you have gain'd a Victory, that I heartily wish it do not prove the contrary, your friends here are no ways satisfied with it, as you may perceive by my Lord Duke's letter, wherein his Grace desires you will explain that part of your letter to Comte Harrach that mentions the spreading here [of] Extracts of Count Wratislaw's letters, my Lord Duke vows never to have shewn them to any body and for my part I am confident no man alive had them from me, tho the whole reflexion lyes at my door, I shall be heartily glad to see that you put this part right . . . for Gods sake pursue

this matter no further, but put it up as well as you can, let us see your skill in bringing yourself off. I am confident you will wish it had not gone so farr.[13]

Stepney was unabashed: he took Cardonnel's rebuke in good part, but told him that he had pre-judged the case, and might have waited until he had read George's further defence of his action. Regarding the source of his information, Stepney claimed that he had had it from various friends in England and Holland, some of whom had listened to remarks 'let fall' by Hoffmann, [the imperial Resident in London]. Vigorously defending himself, Stepney mentioned that he hoped Marlborough would believe one of the Queen's ministers rather than 'a Forraigner.' To the Duke Stepney merely sent a formal reply, referring him to his longer letter to Cardonnel, and saying that it would be the greatest misfortune of his life if he should find Marlborough's protection withdrawn.

By the same mail (7 March (n.s.) 1705) Stepney wrote to Halifax asking for his support, and to Lewis on the tricky point of his knowledge of Wratislaw's letter:

You have reason and so has Adam for criticising *des Extraits* but your former letters about Hoffman lead me into that error, for from thence I understood as if Wrat [*sic*] had written to him to the same effect as to others; otherwise I might have worded the Phrase in another manner, but would never have stifled the information come wt will. . . . I have patch'd up a bad business as well as I could with good breeding and moderation enough, and if you can have disposed Lord H[alifax] to take any part of the blame upon himself *a la bonne heure*, I have left latitude enough to include him, otherwise *jacta est alea*, and let the world rubb.[14]

Then Stepney worked to improve his defence. He turned to his friend in the Hague, Alexander Stanhope, whom he wished to enlist the help of the Prussian and Danish envoys to the States General. The Dane had written to his counterpart in Vienna, hinting that reports of Stepney's imminent recall were current in the Hague. Stepney now hoped that Stanhope might persuade these men to admit openly that they had heard these reports and informed Stepney. Stanhope replied curtly:

Neither Schetteou [*sic* – read Schmettau] nor Stocken remember or will own anything material for yr service.

A few days later, on 14 April, Marlborough arrived in the Hague for the summer campaign. Then, Stanhope behaved as a true friend to George Stepney:

Before the Duke went out of my house I took the liberty to tell him yr story so farr as I was concerned therein and so farr as he would hear me with patience till at last he interrupted me by assuring me he is much yr friend, and bid me advise you to be quiet, and let things alone when they are well, that you are much mistaken in the opinion you seem to fancy he has of that Count, whom he said he knows as well as you do. I had touched the point a little before to Mr. Cardonnel, who appeared warmly your friend, telling me much the same the Duke did, afterwards desiring me to begg of you to be quiet, and stir no more in the matter, since it is already as well as you can desire. They tell me there is no more thoughts of sending my Lord Paget or anybody else for Vienna.[15]

This was good advice, and Stepney took it to heart. He considered he had vindicated his position and could now leave Vienna with reputation, and not in disgrace. The question of his replacement in Vienna took more than a year to resolve.

XX *The Hungarian Mediation (III)*
(January 1705-May 1706)

Stepney in Vienna to Harley, 16 May
(n.s.) 1705

> The Emperor [Joseph I] applyes very heartily to business and
> particularly shews an earnest desire of composing the Troubles in
> Hungary. He is concerned at the desolation of the Country and
> wishes to redress grievances, and observe the conditions of his
> Coronation Oath . . . [But] . . . if the Hungarians did not return to
> their allegiance he would pursue them with the utmost severity.
> His motto is *Amore et Timore*.[1]

Although the first attempt at mediation between the Emperor
Leopold and his rebellious subjects had failed in 1704, the two
maritime powers were still determined to continue their efforts to
achieve a peace. According to the *mores* of the age, it was firmly
believed – even in the Dutch Republic – that the more aristocratic
the delegation, the more likely it was to succeed. Before the end of
1704, the Dutch had proposed sending an Extraordinary Mission,
and in the new year nominated Adolf Hendrik, Baron d'Almelo
(1658-1731) to carry it out. The first English choice was the
experienced Lord Paget, but after some havering he declined the
honour.

Both Bruynincx and Stepney welcomed the new initiative,
although the latter doubted whether it would be successful. At the
beginning of February 1705, the Hungarians, in revenge for cruelties
inflicted by General Heister's troops upon them, carried out a raid
along the Danube as far as Schwechat [now the site of Vienna's
airport]. The Emperor was said to have watched the flames from
the windows of his palace.

The imperial court had not been completely inactive. New
proposals were sent to the Hungarians in mid-February, which
Stepney hoped might form the basis for a treaty. At this time the
elder Count Harrach was in charge of Hungarian affairs. He drew
the two Mediators into discussion, and even accepted some of their
suggested amendments.[2]

At the beginning of May 1705, Stepney heard from Marlborough that 'Mr. Mountague' would come to Vienna with d'Almelo. Stepney assumed that the Duke was referring to Christopher Montagu, the elder brother of Lord Halifax. Not so: the individual named was George Montagu, *nephew* to Halifax, a young man who not two years previously had passed through Vienna and stayed (with a tutor) with Stepney in order to enhance his education. To the twentieth century, this seems an extraordinary choice. Even Stepney was surprised that the substitute for Lord Paget should be a man 50 years his junior.

A few days later Vienna's court and society was plunged into mourning. At the age of 65, after a short illness, Leopold I died. Stepney wrote a full account of all the circumstances regarding the Emperor's death, for which he later received praise from Queen Anne. On the day itself, 5 May (n.s.), the Envoy was engaged in correspondence of a different nature:

> The inclosed Treaties abᵗ the Ear has been recommended to me some time ago by Dr. Garelli, Physitian to ye Empʳ, being the work of one Valsalva, a Professʳ in Bologna. It has layne by me near 2 months for want of a proper conveyance.

	I am, Sir
The Empʳ dyed	Yr most humble &
this evening	most faithfull Servᵗ
Dr. Sloane	G. STEPNEY

The recipient was the eminent Secretary of the Royal Society, of which Stepney had been a member since 1698.[3]

The reign of the Emperor Joseph I heralded a complete change of government. The old ministers – all friends of Leopold – were hurried into retirement. Karl Theodor, Prince of Salms (1648-1710), formerly tutor to the young monarch, was now First Minister. At his first interview, Stepney noted that Salms appeared to be no friend of Wratislaw who, he said, should be sent to his employment in Bohemia. On the other hand, Salms appeared to put great trust in Baron Seilern, who had always advocated that a strong hand should be used against the Hungarians. These latter had let it be known that they would not accept any mediation unless it were accompanied by a guarantee. Stepney claimed that he had always foreseen this difficulty, which was aggravated by Salms' statement to Bruynincx that a foreign 'Guaranty' was inconsistent with the new Emperor's dignity and reputation. By mid-June Stepney's worst fears about the imperial attitude towards Hungary began to be realised. As well as 6,000 Danish soldiers, the government had amassed 9,000 Austrian horse and 12,000 foot to take the field against the rebels.[4]

As if to belie these warlike preparations Joseph I appointed Marlborough's friend Count [Philip Ludwig] Sinzendorf to liaise with the English and Dutch Envoys. Sinzendorf at once asked their opinion on a large bundle of papers. Stepney had seen many of these before; nevertheless he had a list compiled for London and provided a *précis* of the most important passages. On 25 June, he and Bruynincx were summoned to a conference at which only Salms and Sinzendorf were present. Stepney, speaking for both the Mediators, remarked that the Hungarian demands could be reduced to two heads, '*Securitas Interna et Externa*'. By the latter, the Hungarians meant the guarantee, which they had for so long requested. This point was immediately rejected by Salms. Stepney then discussed '*Securitas Interna*', i.e. the establishment of rights. But this, he said, was a difficult subject because the enumeration of such rights had been postponed to a future Diet. The Archbishop of Colocza had suggested that the Emperor might declare that he was ready to renew and confirm laws enacted at the two last Hungarian Diets, held long since at Odenburg and Pressburg. If the inward security were settled, Stepney added, the Hungarians might not think so much of their external security. Salms agreed to this, as being at least an essay towards an accommodation. He indicated obliquely that the Court had accepted the Anglo-Dutch mediation. Stepney and Bruynincx were asked to convey as much to the Hungarians, together with an offer to employ their good offices towards an exchange of prisoners.[5]

On the last day of June 1705, Stepney heard from Lord Halifax that the idea of sending his nephew to Vienna had foundered, and that Marlborough's son-in-law, Charles Spencer, third Earl of Sunderland (1674-1722) had been appointed to make the compliment from the Queen to the new Emperor, and to try what could be done in the business of Hungary. The day following the arrival of this news George wrote to Sunderland, describing his own mission to Schemnitz the previous year, and providing copious information on the etiquette desirable in dealing with the Hungarians. Transcripts of all Stepney's dispatches had been sent to Marlborough, so that if the Earl travelled via the Duke's camp in Flanders he would find all there. To do Sunderland justice, as Envoy Extraordinary and Plenipotentiary he did stop over in Marlborough's camp and rose at 5.00 a.m. to read through Stepney's papers.

Sunderland was brilliant, hot-tempered and volatile. Since,

together with Halifax, he was a member of the Whig 'Junto' in England, it could be presumed he had had a nodding acquaintance with Stepney, at least during 1700. But there is no direct evidence on this point. George expressed pleasure at the appointment, and remarked that he 'loved and honoured' Sunderland. A little later he learned that he too had been promoted to Plenipotentiary, with the extra allowance of £3 a day, to date from 19 June (o.s.) 1705, which was the date of Sunderland's appointment. George also heard that he owed his promotion to Sunderland and Halifax, who had pushed it through at a time when Secretary of State Harley was out of town. Nevertheless Stepney was still anxious to be quit of Vienna and achieve the transfer to the Hague, because he considered that in Holland he would have every chance of the appointment of Third Ambassador when peace negotiations with France were eventually put in hand.[6]

Directly the news of Sunderland's appointment became known in Vienna Count Wratislaw wrote to Marlborough to voice his disquiet at the prospect. He feared Stepney's influence over Sunderland, and the latter's known republican tendencies. The Count referred to Stepney's 'malicious spirit.' But at no time did he raise the objection that Stepney was too lowly born to carry out his task. This judgement appears to have been made by nineteenth- and twentieth-century historians, following the lead given by Archdeacon Coxe in his *Memoires of John, Duke of Marlborough*, where he once described Stepney as 'obnoxious.' Wratislaw, on the other hand, told Marlborough a year later that he had never had anything against Stepney's person, and in his dealings with him he (Wratislaw) had only carried out the orders of his Court.[7]

The Dutch negotiator, Baron d'Almelo, arrived in Vienna on 14 August (n.s.) 1705, and was joined by Sunderland on 26 August. As befitted his status, the Earl did not travel alone. He was accompanied by at least seven Englishmen, including Messrs Hopkins, Onslow, Buckingham, Furnese, Porter and Molesworth, and by his physician, Dr Goodman. Sunderland lodged in Stepney's house, and Onslow wished to do so. The new Envoy set to work without delay. By 29 August, he had completed his formal calls on the Emperor and the imperial family, and with Stepney had had two meetings with Count Sinzendorf.

Sunderland had made his own *aide mémoire* on the advice which Marlborough had given him as he passed through the camp at Meldert, on his way to Vienna. In the main these instructions were not concerned with Hungary but with the Duke's difficulties with

Prince Louis, the Emperor's general in the west, and with the Dutch. For, during the campaign of 1705 both these allies seemed to have been more concerned with frustrating Marlborough's plans than with the resolute prosecution of the war. The Duke wished steps to be taken at the imperial court to enable Prince Eugene to serve during 1706 on the Rhine and for Prince Louis to be displaced. Sunderland was told to trust no-one at the Court except Count Wratislaw. And he was enjoined to do his best to cause both the Count and Stepney to forego their animosity towards each other. Stepney, of course, was not informed of this advice.[8]

Sunderland's mission to Vienna was not successful. Already on 9 September, Stepney wrote that after only two weeks' stay the Earl was suffering from the *Maladie des Suisses* [homesickness] and had written for leave to return in the event that he found little likelihood of success in the Hungarian negotiations. D'Almelo had sent a similar letter. By now Stepney was uneasy at the turn of affairs. He knew that his opinions were not in fashion, and that Wratislaw, now, had more influence at Court than the rest of the ministers put together. Stepney's only course was to remain passive.

The delay in advancing the mediation was by no means the fault of the Mediators. The imperial army was under way to Transylvania. The Hungarian chiefs were too far away to be easily reached. Hungarian Deputies who were charged with obtaining passports for the Mediators only returned on 20 September, with a message from Rákóczy, then at Szecsen [on the river Igol, about 60 miles east of Neuhäusel] that he would continue there with the Hungarian Assembly until the Mediators arrived. But his conditions were that the Imperial Court must consent to an armistice and keep their army 'on this' [i.e. the Vienna] side of the Danube. Taking into account the time necessary for messengers to pass back and forth between the parties, there was no likelihood of any quick decision on the matter, and Stepney speculated on the possibility that Transylvania might be entirely reduced by the Malcontents before the imperial army could arrive.[9]

The war in Italy was going badly. The Duke of Savoy was struggling to hold Turin, while Prince Eugene, in Lombardy, was desperate for reinforcements. Count Gallas, the imperial envoy in London, had presented a memorandum requesting a loan of 400,000 Crowns, from the Queen and the States General in the usual proportion of two-thirds from the English and one third from the Dutch. Should this be received, the Emperor would be prepared to march 20,000 men into Italy by October. In writing of this plan to

Sunderland, Harley remarked that he, the Earl, would of course know whether it was feasible [!]. The Secretary of State added that the Allies were disheartened to see the war in Italy and the gallant Duke of Savoy so much neglected by the Court of Vienna.

> and all their vigour applied to Hungary, which would have either submitted to reasonable terms or been reduced as soon as the French had been driven out of Italy.

It was Stepney who replied to Whitehall by courier:

> I may take the liberty to acquaint you that this Court seems a little concerned that Her Ma^{ty} instead of granting their request in their great necessity only reproaches them for their mismanagement in the affairs of Hungary, and I hear in their private reflections they attribute their present disappointment to some ill impressions which Mr. Bruyninx and I may have given of their affairs.

And George claimed that his 'relations' [i.e. dispatches] had always been candid, particularly about the loan, which he had recommended to Harley in earlier letters; and that he was not disturbed in the performance of his duty.[10]

On 7 October (n.s.) Cardonnel at Herontals wrote a distressed letter to Stepney:

> You will see by the enclos'd his Grace is determined to make you a visit, I have been dreading it this four or five months and tho' I would go a great way and take a great deal of pains to kiss your hands, I should almost as willingly have gone to the Gallys as undertake this Journey, and the visit by the ways, where I wish they don't poyson us.[11]

Indeed Marlborough had been organising his visit to Vienna ever since the summer of 1705, and Sunderland's notes included a paragraph on the project. The Earl was to persuade the Emperor and Wratislaw to write to Queen Anne and the States General to obtain permission for the visit. Sunderland carried out his task, and Cardonnel's worst fears were realised. But before the Duke could begin his journey east the situation in Hungary again changed. On 21 October Stepney reported that Rákóczy now seemed to be willing to keep up some sort of a treaty, and had appointed deputies to meet the Emperor's commissioners and the Mediators at Tyrnau [about 30 miles north-east of Pressburg]. Count Wratislaw had been named as the sole imperial commissioner because his colleague, the Bishop of Osnabrück (who was a Prince of Lorraine) had declined to attend this first meeting, arranged for 27 October. The Earl of Sunderland had by now received his letters of revocation. Nevertheless as a Mediator he accompanied Stepney to Tyrnau. Count Wratislaw, on the other hand, saw no advantage in proceeding further than Pressburg, and stopped there.[12]

On 30 October, Stepney at Tyrnau sent an official dispatch to his cousin Erasmus Lewis (Harley's secretary) and to the English envoys in the Hague, Berlin, Moscow, Turin, Venice and Frankfurt which was in essence a piece of propaganda for the Allied involvement in Hungary:

> The Plenipotentiaries of England and Holland, after having waited upon ye Emperour on the 20th inst. and received his last Orders, sett out ye next morning for Hungary, and lay that night at Pressburgh, on the 27th General Palffy ye Ban of Croatia at the head of part of ye Garrison accompanyed them half a mile out of Town, where they were rec'd by Colonell Götze at the head of 8 Standards or 800 Hungarian horse, who serv'd as Convoy on the Road. As they pass'd by St. George, the Burghers were drawn up at the Gates of ye City, and the Magistrates made a compliment at the Couch [sic] Side. They lay that night at Pösing, which was a rich and thriving town, but last winter was miserably drain'd by Gen[ll] Heister, and afterwards bombarded and taken by the Malcontents. On the 28th they arriv'd at this place [Tyrnau] which is a flourishing City being an Archiepiscopall Residence and the chief University of ye Kingdom. Count Berczeni having come hither two days before they were mett and complimented by some of his officers, and he sent his Coaches and led horses to bring them into Town, with very great pomp and ceremony, the Hungarian Nation being known to delight in such solemn appearances, and being willing particularly on this occasion to shew the highest Veneration for her Maj[ty] and the States General.

Privately to Lewis Stepney voiced less optimistic comments:

> Hitherto the Hungarians shew no disposition of admitting the project wch ye Court recommended to us, by drawing nearer to Pressburg, for wch reason we are now proposing to the Court that ye Imp[ll] Ministers may stay if they will at Pressburg and the Hungarian Deputies at this place while the Mediators have the disagreeable life of Couriers in plying between both: by next Post wee may know whether the Court will agree to this expedient. . . .

The Court did so; George continued (to Whitworth) on 2 November:

> in 2 days Ld Sunderland and I return to Vienna to meet ye D. of Marl[borough] (who intends to lodge under my roof) leaving our Allyes [i.e. D'Almelo and Bruynincx] to keep up the appearances of a Negotiation, till either wee come back again or send them word the Imp[ll] Court will make no other stepp. To make their being here [Tyrnau] more agreeable they have sent for their wives, clavsins and Base Viols, with wch god bless them.

And from Pressburg, on 4 November, Stepney wrote to Harley about the flattering life of the Mediators, to which he willingly submitted, if he could be so happy as 'to bring this perplext matter to any sort of Consistency.' He continued that word had come from Count Sinzendorf that he was moving from Pressburg to Vienna to receive new instructions as to the armistice, and that he wished some of the Mediators to accompany him. Thus it was arranged that Sunderland and Stepney should begin 'the dance,' leaving the two Dutchmen at Tyrnau to deal with the Malcontents.[13]

On 5 November, Sunderland and Stepney reached Vienna and the next day had audience separately with the Emperor about their mission. The same evening they received letters by courier from the Dutch Plenipotentiaries in Tyrnau, which they handed over to Salms. On 11 November Stepney reported that Sinzendorf had replied to Sunderland in a surprising manner: The Court was *not* willing to abate any of its territorial demands (contrary to the Mediators' declared opinion). Remonstrances were useless, because the Emperor had spoken. On 14 November, Sunderland and Stepney received fresh letters from Tyrnau. The Dutch Mediators wrote that the Court's conditions for an armistice would do more harm than good, and they desired Marlborough to intervene to get the terms moderated.

For on 12 November, the Duke had indeed arrived in Vienna, by river from Ratisbon. The same evening he had his audiences of the Emperor and the imperial family. He was received everywhere with marks of esteem:

> The Court offered to defray him, [wrote Stepney] and the Prince of Dietrichstein's Palace was prepared for his reception, but his Grace has been pleas'd to accept such Conveniences as I could make for him in my house.

What happened to the Earl of Sunderland and his entourage is not entirely clear. However Cardonnel's assistant, Harry Watkins (who had been left behind in Germany) wrote to Stepney in December 1705, that the 'whole family' [i.e. Marlborough's suite], were full of praise for George's generous treatment of them in Vienna. The Palais Lamberg was capacious and Stepney's steward, James Fury, had long experience of the ways of the imperial city.[14]

The Duke of Marlborough had not come to Vienna merely to discuss the Hungarian situation with the Emperor and the latter's advisers. The talks encompassed the entire war against France on all fronts – Germany and Flanders; Spain and Italy; as well as the pressing imperial need for money; and not least the Duke's claim to the principality which had been promised to him by the late Emperor Leopold. Although George Stepney was chiefly concerned with the Hungarian rebellion, he was nevertheless a highly experienced diplomat, and so it is surprising to find that he was excluded from a conference to which Marlborough was invited by the Emperor on 16 November, and which was attended by Salms, Sinzendorf and Wratislaw. There is no record in the Stepney papers as to what transpired. But the following evening the Duke had a long conversation at court with the Emperor and Empress, and according to the conventions of the day was not permitted to sit in their presence. The result – for Marlborough was then 55 years old – was the attack of gout which confined him to bed and delayed his departure from Vienna. He was able to see D'Almelo and Bruynincx, who had returned specially from Tyrnau to meet him (and had left their wives in Hungary as hostages against their return). Formally, the peace Congress had begun because the Mediators were collecting and exchanging the full powers on all sides. They had made the first proposals for an armistice in the terms suggested and dictated by the Court, Stepney reported, and had been assured of an answer from the Hungarians within four or five days. But, added Stepney, everyone was waiting to know the fate of the imperial army in Transylvania.

On 19 November Sunderland had his audience of *congé*. On the 22nd the Duke was visiting the Emperor's Chamber of Rarities, when Joseph appeared and gave him a ring. Marlborough took his formal leave the same evening and both he and Sunderland left on 23 November, heading for Berlin. Stepney accompanied them as far as Moravia, '8 German miles on their way to Breslau.' The Envoy who, as he remarked, had been left to 'jogg on after the old rate', could not resist an addition to his dispatch to the Secretary of State:

> N B: The Ring [presented to Marlborough] was worth m/14 florins; Mr. Cardonnel had one of 1400 fl. Lord Sunderland's picture [of the Emperor] was scarce of that value. The revenue of the Principality is computed at about m/16 fl. yearly.

On balance, George Stepney felt that the visits of Marlborough and Sunderland had been useful to him. He told Halifax he hoped he had contracted a lasting friendship with Sunderland, which he attributed to Halifax's patronage. Marlborough had been fair and open with him, and had left him with an Act of Substitution so that he (Stepney) could take possession of the principality of Mindelheim. George claimed he had never encouraged the Duke's pretension:

> but since the root of all evil is predominant I shall do my best to

serve him after his own way and thereby have an opportunity of acquiring the most essential merit.

Marlborough had asked Stepney if he still wanted to go to the Hague. George said that since he had cleared his name and had got the Court to agree that he had acted fairly as Mediator, he would rather go directly home and pass his life in quiet, having by his own fortune and by his employment at the Board of Trade enough to satisfy him. Marlborough then remarked that it might be for the Queen's service and his own satisfaction to have Stepney at the Hague, because he wished a minister there of experience, even if only for eight or ten months. Stepney said he would entirely submit himself to his Grace, and would be ready to move as required. So they parted; with Stepney in the hopes that his being at the Hague might be less precarious, and that Marlborough might treat him with more confidence and favour than otherwise. To Halifax he concluded that his first choice would be to be in England, now that there were fair prospects of happy days, by the [Whig] majority in Parliament and by the consequences to all who wished well to the Queen and the Succession.[15]

With the departure of the Duke and the Earl George Stepney's life resumed its routine. His first concern was to write to Lord Halifax about his unpaid Extraordinaries, which dated back to 28 February 1702. His account, set out in a somewhat complicated way, shewed that he was owed a total of £3,700 10s., and had received only £1,300. He now claimed that King William's promise had amounted to £1,000, and that the expense of life in Vienna would be attested by Marlborough and Sunderland. And during the month following, he found himself moving house, because the Palais Lamberg had been let to Count Schlick. George had found accommodation in the house of the Princesse de Longueval, situated in what is now Bankgasse 1-3, conveniently close to the Court. Before the upheaval of the move Stepney had a sad duty to perform towards Aubrey Porter, the father of one of the young men who had accompanied Sunderland:

> I'm heartily sorry the first letter I write to you must bring you the most disagreeable news I could send: but I hope you will have been prepared to receive it with temper and resignation. Your son sickened on the 21st November (two days before the Earl of Sunderland left this place); Dr. Goodman, who attended his Lordship, perceived it would be a violent feaver, and sought to prescribe proper remedies in time. But Mr. Porter would not be persuaded to use them, nor after that Doctor's departure from hence admitt of any other physician, till I brought one to him

allmost against his consent, who has attended him with great Care and Affection and I believe would have restor'd him if any man could; but the distemper encreased dayly, and yesterday about noon he expir'd after having performed all Christian Duties. I visited him frequently during his illness, and so did the Earl of Hartford and Mr. Maynhart, who were his chief acquaintance at Cambridge. They can bear witness no human means were neglected, and I may venture to assure you more could not have been done to save him if your self had been here present; for I have had really an esteem for him; and he was sensible of it to the last. The nature of his distemper and the methods us'd to cure it will be drawn up by his Physician, and sent you by next Post, to which I shall add the expences during his Illness and what is necessary towards a decent Buriall which will be performed too morrow. I must do justice to his Servant by acquainting you that He did his part very honestly and deserves to be recommended to you on that Account. I intend to find some opportunity of sending him towards England by the cheapest way, with the Cloathes etc which his Master left.

I heartily wish I might have had a better Subject for my first Correspondence with you; but on all occasions I desire you to be assur'd of my being very sincerely,

Two contrasting aspects of Stepney's character may be noted from this letter: on the one hand his (quite justified) promptitude in requesting the repayment of the funeral expenses; and on the other his care that the good behaviour of the young man's servant should not be forgotten.[16]

While the Envoy was watching over the illness of young Mr Porter he had to report to Whitehall the imperial victory at Cibo, in eastern Hungary, on 11 November 1705. Rákóczy and other leaders of the rebels were present with 10,000 Hussars, 5,000 foot and 1,200 Germans who had taken service with the Malcontents. The passage was disputed, and 1,000 imperialists died before it was forced, after which the rebels lost about 3,000 foot, including most of the German deserters. The Hussars, as usual, escaped into the mountains. Rákóczy was reported to have fled to Bistritz. But Berczenyi was still active, and Hungarian raids into Moravia and Austria were expected. Indeed, while regrouping, the tactic of the Hungarians was to spin out the peace negotiations as long as possible, and then try to pin the blame on the Court for any break. They objected to Stepney's commission, and demanded a new one. The Dutch Mediators, in accordance with the Malcontents' wishes, sent messages to Vienna trying to persuade the Emperor to soften the statement of his claim to the hereditary succession of the crown of Hungary.[17]

After leaving Vienna the Duke of Marlborough had travelled to Berlin in search of Prussian troops to help him carry on the war, and he had concluded a treaty with Frederick I, King of Prussia. But as usual he omitted to keep the English Envoy in Vienna informed of these developments. Stepney complained to Cardonnel that although he could get a copy of the treaty from Bartholdi, the Prussian Envoy,

> I was really ashamed to own to him or any body else that I had it not.

This letter crossed with one from Cardonnel, sending the treaty together with relevant documents. But it should be noted that Cardonnel sent the papers to Stepney on his own initiative, without informing Marlborough that he had done so.[18]

On 18 January (n.s.) 1706, General Count Leopold Schlick arrived in Vienna fresh from his military victory over the Hungarians. The following day the Court held a conference about Hungary, and Sinzendorf related the proceedings to Stepney. In turn George wrote to the Dutch Mediators in Tyrnau, sending them the text of the Emperor's Declaration to his Hungarian subjects, and a letter from the Mediators in general to the Hungarian Confederates then assembled at Miskolcz, this latter document having been approved by the Court with slight amendments. Sinzendorf told Stepney that the Emperor seemed to wish him to undertake the journey to Miskolcz himself. George civilly declined, pointing out that the Dutch ministers were already half way to Miskolcz and could undertake the task more easily. At this time Vienna was threatened, according to report, by 2,000 Hungarian raiders, who might well be in collusion with anti-Jewish riots which were taking place in the city.

Stepney had objected to the wording of the Emperor's Declaration, which he feared would do more harm than good if delivered as it stood to the Hungarians at Miskolcz. He sent the text back to Sinzendorf, asking that the offending passages be omitted. This was refused, and he was instructed to release the paper to the Dutch Mediators.

> The Express was scarce gott out of one Gate when Count Rechteren [Baron d'Almelo's new title] enter'd at another having been oblig'd to return by Anger on the Border of Moravia because of the Ice which stopp'd the passage over the Danube from Pressburgh.

Rechteren's intention was to support Stepney in requesting a more suitable Declaration from the Emperor than the one provided. He remonstrated with the Emperor at his audience, and, with Stepney, approached the Bishop of Osnabrück, the Emperor's First Commissioner. Once again this request was refused, as Salms and Sinzendorf made clear to the two Mediators at a meeting on 28 January. The only concession agreed by the Court was that the Mediators might present to the Assembly at Miskolcz a memorial, as coming from themselves, in which the offending points were omitted. Rechteren refused (as had Stepney) to travel to Miskolcz. But on 30 January he left Vienna to rejoin his colleague Bruynincz in Tyrnau, proposing to use Hungarian messengers to carry the unsatisfactory proposals onwards.[19]

George Stepney was not well: he excused himself to Cardonnel for using 'another hand' to write, owing to a defluxion in his eyes. It seemed he was suffering from the common cold. Work, however, was not interrupted, and he took time to approach 'Mr. Secry [sic] Harley about Toulon.'

> When the Duke of Marlborough was here I laid before him a plan of Toulon with a description how to attack that Poste and raise both the City and Fleet. It was given me by an Italian Ingener who some years ago was concerned in the works and Canal, and according to his representation the design seems feasible enough.

In fact, Stepney had discussed the matter with Marlborough in the coach as the latter was leaving Vienna *en route* for Count Sinzendorf's castle at Ernstbrunn. Now, the Envoy tactfully reminded Cardonnel of this episode by telling him that the plans had been forwarded to Harley. The incident is interesting because the idea for an attack on Toulon, which took place in 1707, has been described as Marlborough's brainchild. This may be so: but the concept appears to be attributable to an unnamed Italian civil engineer, passed on to the Duke by the English Envoy in Vienna.[20]

Nine days before Count Rechteren left Vienna for Hungary Prince Eugene reached the imperial capital from Italy. The military command in that country was always a thankless task, but Stepney had reported critically on the Prince in a letter to Cardonnel written on 9 January (n.s.) 1706; that Eugene would not wish to return to Italy for the campaign of 1706, and that if he were sent *nolens volens* he was unlikely to cooperate with the Duke of Savoy or with General Guido Starhemberg, but would certainly keep any allied troops under his own command.

Stepney was treading on dangerous ground. Eugene was immensely popular in England, and Lord Halifax had recently warned George that some of the Council thought he (Stepney) was too severe upon the Prince. On 28 December 1705, Cardonnel repeated the warning (in a private letter which Stepney subsequently burned). George wrote back that there had been rumours of an imperial intention to recall the Prince and end the war in Italy 'unless we took the whole burthen upon ourselves.' Therefore Marlborough had asked him to keep a close eye on events and report. He, George, was in no way prejudiced against Prince Eugene: nevertheless Cardonnel would hear no more on the subject. It took a personal letter from Marlborough to allay the fears of the Envoy: the Duke was anxious to have Stepney's frank reporting continued – only, he must not address himself to anyone else.[21]

In mid-February 1706, Stepney received Marlborough's command to attend to the reimbursement of the huge loan of £250,000 sterling which the Duke had grandly promised the Emperor during his visit to Vienna for carrying on the war in Italy. The money was to be raised by public subscription in England and was to be secured against revenue from the imperial States of Silesia. Stepney's old friend Franc Stratford, now based in London, was handling the complicated procedure for obtaining interest and repayments. Undoubtedly to Stepney's delight Stratford specified that any moneys obtained from Silesia should not pass through the hands of Wratislaw, lest the Count should be tempted to use them for purposes other than strict repayment.

As usual Stepney wasted no time, but requested a meeting with Salms, Wratislaw, the President of the Chamber and other officials the day following the arrival of Marlborough's and Stratford's instructions. Stepney decided he would subscribe £1,000 himself, and told his sisters to arrange this for him, provided they had received from the Lord Treasurer the £3,000 which was due to him as arrears.

The matter was complicated by the fact that Stepney was dealing not only with one loan, but with two. A smaller amount (christened by Stepney as 'The Little Loan') had been suggested by Count Gallas in London as far back as August 1705, to help to remount Prince Eugene's cavalry in Italy. 300,000 dollars were to be provided in the proportion of two thirds from Queen Anne and one third from the States General. Originally three instalments were envisaged, to be made in the months of October and November 1705, and in January 1706. But when these plans reached Stepney and Sunderland in October 1705, no-one knew whether the Dutch had agreed to their share. With some delay, payments of the Little

Loan were made directly from London to Venice through the bankers Thomas and Samuel Williams, with whom Stepney had to enter into correspondence; and besides this task he found himself instructing Prince Eugene in the niceties of banking and in the correct form of documents on which the Prince's signature was necessary.[22]

Negotiations with the Hungarians were dragging on. Bruynincx, in Tyrnau, was in bed with fever during February. Count Rechteren tried to jolt the Malcontents into cooperation by demanding peremptorily that they should either come to a treaty or give him a recredential so that he could return home. Stepney commented on the possibility that Rákóczy, who now appeared less moderate than hitherto, might be receiving support from the Turks – an eventuality always feared by the Court. However the Hungarians did request a suspension of arms, to which the Court reluctantly agreed, and Rechteren returned with the news to Tyrnau. About a week later (17 March, n.s.) the rebels were raiding between Vienna and Pressburg and on the frontiers of Moravia. But on 25 March, the Dutch ministers sent word to Stepney that a new suggestion had been made for a buffer zone, on the Vienna side of the Danube, from which the troops of either side should be withdrawn.

At the beginning of April Stepney's health was once more giving him trouble: he complained again of defluxion in the eyes and of rheumatism, for which cupping and bleeding were prescribed. He had no time to be ill, for on 13 April, Bruynincx arrived in Vienna, to confer with the Court about a truce, abruptly requested by the Malcontents, to begin at once on 15 April, and to last a fortnight. During this time it was hoped that a solemn armistice might be concluded, to extend to the further parts of Hungary. The rebels had provided passports, and Stepney and Wratislaw were due to travel within a few days to Pressburg, leaving Bruynincx to rest in Vienna. Stepney commented to Raby:

> I hope your Excy will think it a very edifying circumstance and a
> good omen to the peace of Hungary that C. Wrat and I are destined
> to go thither so lovingly in order to negotiate.

For the two adversaries had had to come to an accommodation; and in January 1706, George had explained the situation to his cousin Erasmus Lewis:

> C. Wrat and I (since my Lord Duke appear'd among us) have
> been oblig'd to have some sort of civill Commerce together more
> than we had otherwise, and in the transactions of Hungary we
> meet and discourse as if we had no grudge, for it would be
> impertinent in me to dispute the Emperour's making use of whom

he pleases, and I am satisfied the more Wrat sees of my behaviour in that Negotiation, the more sensible he is made of the wrong I suffer'd; which I know he has acknowledg'd on several occasions, both to the E. of Sunderland and others; I own I had rather have to doe with any body else and in any other business, but in our employment such accidents must be sometimes expected and bore with patience.[23]

On 21 April (n.s.) 1706, Wratislaw and Stepney left Vienna for Pressburg, where they expected to meet Count Rechteren. The latter, with Stepney, then continued to Tyrnau. On 27 April, Stepney informed Marlborough that he and Rechteren had been waiting for four days for an answer from the Malcontents to the Emperor's proposals. Rákóczy was staying a day's journey away from Tyrnau. Bercsenyi visited him on the morning of 27 April, to receive his instructions. Stepney decided to add two final paragraphs to his letter to Marlborough:

Now, my Lord, I am to return to your Grace my Dutyfull thanks for bearing me in your thoughts upon what may happen to Mr. Stanhope [who had fallen ill in the Hague]; I gladly accept that offer upon the hopes I have that while I am under your Grace's immediate influence and protection, I may have such opportunities of recommending myself by my Zeal for your service, as may entitle me to some peculiar degree of your favour and Confidence; without which consideration neither that Post nor any other would be acceptable to me, who having pass'd throughout almost all the stepps of foreign Service, proposed nothing more to myself but to end with the reputation and comfort of having faithfully discharg'd any trust your Grace shall be pleased to repose in me.

When and in what manner your Grace may be pleas'd to bring about my removal from this Court, is what I am no longer sollicitous of; yet I am humbly of opinion I ought to have some successor upon the place to receive from me the necessary informations as to the present state of our affairs here, otherwise Her Majesty's Service might suffer by my abrupt departure; if it were not for this only consideration I am ready at all time to obey Summons and to justify by my unalterable Devotion that I am . . . . [end of letter].

To Lord Halifax, on the same date, George explained himself more fully:

Mr. Cardonnel tells me he shew'd your Lp at Windsor a Postscript which his Grace was pleased to write to me with his own hand on the 29th past, desiring to know my opinion as to my removal to the Hague and promising to act accordingly.

And knowing that he owed this 'favourable motion' to Halifax's endeavours, George enclosed an extract of his letter to Marlborough so that Halifax could see that he proposed no condition save that of being in favour with the Duke. George continued:

> Otherwise my figure at the Hague would be more insignificant than some people endeavour to render it here; whereas I have served long enough to think myself above that usage and shall hardly submit to any employment on such mortifying terms. I know very well the uneasiness to which good Mr. Stanhope has been too frequently expos'd by that Starr of the first Magnitude, *Fulgore Suo qui depremit infra sepositos;* but he was forc'd to stifle his dissatisfaction for the benefit of his Family whereas my only aim is to be sustain'd and countenanc'd and then no man alive shall serve him with more application and integrity.

And George reminded his friend that he was now the eldest of all the Foreign Ministers and did not wish to be neglected at any peace treaty

> to which my Char[acter] of Plenipotentiary at the Congress will naturally intitle me.

And Stepney ended his letter with a request that it should be burned: so that it is with some surprise that one finds a copy carefully included in his letter-book.[24]

On 29 April, at noon Stepney wrote his dispatch to 'Right Honourable' [i.e. Harley] from Tyrnau, recounting the events of the last few days. He and Rechteren on 23 April, had delivered to the three Hungarian Deputies there present the Court's project containing the conditions for a truce. The Deputies said they must have time to consider these documents; and Wratislaw sent a message from Pressburg that he must return to consult the Court. Only five days remained of the original cease-fire period, and the Hungarians asked for this to be extended by 10 or 12 days. A similar extension had been suggested to Wratislaw by Rechteren and Stepney by way of a note sent to him the night before they left Pressburg for Tyrnau. Wratislaw made no reply, so from Tyrnau further application was made, as the Malcontents requested. The Courier returned on 26 April, late at night, with assurances from Bruynincx:

> Que Sa Majesté Imperiall [sic] avoit temoigné d'etre disposée à prolonger la suspension Provisionelle d'Hostilitez pour autant de jours qu'il seroir besoin, Et que le Comte de Wratislaw avoit ses ordres pour dela comme aussi pour faciliter la Negotiation de l'Armistice à un tel point, qu'au moins Elle étoit persuadée qu'on ne pourra aucunement imputer à Sa Majesté s'il ne vient à une heureuse conclusion.

But, continued Stepney, Count Wratislaw,

> instead of speaking distinctly to that article assumes the liberty

peculiar to himself by censuring us [i.e. the Mediators] for not giving him a detail of the Commissaries proceedings; and to this moment he has not informed us of the Emperor's pleasure in the most material point of the Prolongation, tho' we have sent another messenger after him to Pressburg to inquire what we are to depend on, there remaining but two days and half more before which the term is expired.

On 1 May, at Pressburg, Stepney continued his dispatch:

On the 29th afternoon Wratislaw answered the Mediators that the Emperor has consented to the Suspension of Arms being continued for four more days, viz. to 5 May inclusive, which days however are to be deducted from the two months' truce because H I M [His Imperial Majesty] has resolved not to extend that beyond the end of June unless there were very great appearances of a peace.

The Mediators decided to convey only the first part of this statement to the Hungarians, and they later received the Malcontents' answer to the imperial proposals. This paper was amended by the Mediators, and the morning of 30 April was spent in discussion of the revisions, and in making a fair copy. The final text was delivered to Rechteren and Stepney in Tyrnau in the evening of the same day. The two immediately set out for Pressburg and put the document into Wratislaw's hands the same night. There was no time to have any copies made.

But Stepney added one hopeful domestic circumstance to his dispatch: the Emperor had at last consented that Princess Rákóczy, who had been detained in Vienna with her two sons ever since the commencement of the troubles, should be allowed to visit her husband in Hungary. This concession had been requested two years previously, at Schemnitz, and refused. According to Stepney, it was one reason for the breakdown of the then negotiations. The present consent had been negotiated privately, over four months, between Wratislaw and the Princess. Stepney added that this move was designed as an instrument to dispose Rákóczy to come to reasonable terms; and also to sow discord among the Hungarian chiefs, who might suspect Rákóczy of making a private deal with the Court.

Wratislaw had sent a private messenger to Rákóczy, and had asked Stepney for an official passport for the man. The Courier returned with assurances from the Hungarian leader that the Princess would be returned to Vienna whenever the Emperor should decide. On 30 April, Wratislaw prepared a great feast for the lady, but she did not reach Pressburg until after midnight, so the celebrations had to be postponed by one day. Then she left with a great train to travel by way of Pösing and Schinta to meet her husband at Nyitra.[25]

As well as hosting the entertainment for Princess Rákóczy Count Wratislaw, as Imperial Commissioner, composed a Resolution which he put into the hands of Rechteren and Stepney before noon on 2 May, in Pressburg. The two Mediators at once left town with this document, and reached Tyrnau the same night. Messengers were sent to Rákóczy; but at Tyrnau, on 5 May in the morning, Stepney wrote:

> This moment C. Rechteren and I are desired to go over to P. Ragotzy at Neytra,'tis a long day's journey in very hot weather, but we must do what we can . . . . I am heartily weary of this hattering life but bear it the more patiently because I believe the business must end one way or other in three or four days.

Stepney hoped to finish the armistice by 8 May, so that he could go to Mindelheim on Marlborough's affairs and be back in time for the Congress of Peace, which was not scheduled to commence until 18 days after the armistice had been concluded. And the Mediators did indeed reach Nyitra on 5 May, at about five o'clock in the evening. To avoid disputes about ceremony they sent compliments only to the Princess, and had arranged with two Hungarian officials that the Prince would drop in to his wife's apartment 'as if by accident.' In that way they worked that night and all the day following with the Prince, Bercsenyi and other Hungarian Deputies.

> Our debates upon every article were very long and warm [wrote Stepney]; for C. Bercsenyi endeavoured, by all the subtilties he cou'd invent, to render our journey and attempts ineffectual; but the Prince by his own good sense rather than by the authority he uses over the Senators, prevail'd with them to come to an agreement with us.

On 7 May, in the morning, the Mediators were handed a paper of reasonable conditions which they sent forward to Wratislaw by two messengers who travelled all night. Rechteren and Stepney followed more slowly, arriving at Pressburg on the morning of 8 May. They had the satisfaction to find that Wratislaw was willing to sign the articles with very little alteration. Rechteren volunteered to return again to Tyrnau with the original document, to collect the signatures of the Hungarian Deputies. Stepney continued his dispatch in more optimistic vein than hitherto:

> C. Wratislaw and I go back toomorrow [9 May] for Vienna from whence I shall have the honour to write to you at large by next post. . . . The Truce is till ye end of June and after that time 12 days are allowed to give notice throughout Hungary and Transylvania if we are not so happy as during yt term to come to a conclusion of Peace: for which the Congress is to begin at

Pressburg on the 25th inst: by a specification of the Hungarian grievances and demands: whereby it will best appear whether they are in earnest or not: at last it is some satisfaction to me that we are got over the first difficulty wch till within these 24 hours I scarce thought wee shou'd have been able to surmount.[26]

But Stepney's hopes were dashed. On his return to Vienna he was to find that the Court had intercepted a letter from Rákóczy to Louis XIV, written about a month previously, from which it was clear that the Hungarian was expecting an increase in subsidy from France and a declaration from the King that he would support Rákóczy's claim to the Principality of Transylvania, by right of his having been freely and duly elected. And Stepney feared that if Louis XIV acceded to these demands the Mediators would find 'all our endeavours are only Amusements.'[27]

XXI *Interlude –*
The Principality of Mindelheim
(July 1704-May 1706)

> I was asked the other day if his Grace would accept the dignity of
> a Prince of the Empire. . . . I presumed that would be no great
> addition to his present state, and perhaps he neither could nor
> would receive any honours but from Her Majesty.

This letter from George Stepney to Secretary of State Harley, written
on 12 July 1704, is the first intimation of the Emperor Leopold's
desire to honour in distinctive fashion the Duke of Marlborough.
Stepney continued that he was asked what would be the best means
of managing the sense of obligation on the part of HIM [His Imperial
Majesty]. George admitted to some freedom in his reply: to give
reasonable terms to the Hungarians, and to find means of
prosecuting the war against France with more vigour than had been
done of late. Stepney sent a copy of this account to the Duke, adding
that the proposal had in fact been made by Count Sinzendorf,
probably on the order of his superiors.[1]

Stepney was later told that the Queen approved of his answer
to Sinzendorf. The matter did not come to his attention again until,
on 22 August (n.s.) 1704 – after the Battle of Blenheim – he read
in the copy of the *London Gazette* which had arrived that day that
the Duke had declined the Emperor's offer to make him a Prince.
Stepney was quick to assure Cardonnel that he had never mentioned
the subject to anyone except Harley, and that in a private letter of
which he had sent Marlborough a copy. The following day more
mail from Whitehall reached Vienna, and Stepney read Harley's
news that Hoffmann [the imperial Resident in London] had
delivered to the Queen a letter from the Emperor in his own hand,
urging her to allow Marlborough to accept a title. The Queen did
not wish to offend the Emperor; who duly wrote to Marlborough,
in Latin, according him the title of Prince. At least a copy passed
through Stepney's hands, who sent it on to Harley, requesting
instructions as to whether the Duke should become a Prince of the

Empire. But the honour had been duly gazetted; and now Stepney worried whether it would be correct to address the Duke as '*Altesse*' [Highness], because this was not usual except to those princes who enjoyed session and a vote at the imperial Diet. For reasons of etiquette, Stepney forbore to congratulate the Duke in writing. But as he was soon to visit Marlborough at Cron Weissembourg no doubt he made his compliment verbally.[2]

Imperial bureaucracy was slow and complex. On 19 November 1704, Stepney, then back in Vienna, reported to Cardonnel:

> A friend of mine has enquired underhand in the Chancery what has become of the Patent of Prince. It sticks there. . . and I believe will go no further.

George added that the Elector of Mainz [the Chancellor of the Empire] favoured Marlborough's having session and vote. The Patent might be presented when the Duke went down the Rhine; but as to the Principality itself, Stepney knew nothing.

Marlborough had entrusted Count Wratislaw with the formalities of his new honour. At the end of 1704, the Count had the support both of Prince Eugene and the King of the Romans for the lucrative appointment of Administrator of the newly conquered Bavaria. Stepney lost no opportunity to decry Wratislaw's efforts – or the lack of them – in Marlborough's private affair. On 10 December he wrote to the Duke:

> Count Wratislaw has neither interest enough here [i.e. in Vienna] to procure any such thing [the Principality], nor an heart to press it, now he has made his harvest, and that his Commission both with England and with your Grace is at an end. If it should prove otherwise, I shall be agreeably surprised. In the mean time I shall proceed with him as if I really believed he were in earnest; and it shall be my care to promote your just expectations to the best of my power.[3]

Marlborough was not the only individual with an interest in an imperial fief. Count Wartemberg, with the backing of his master, King Frederick I of Prussia, was looking for an imperial city which could be converted into a principality. Stepney was told that Nordhausen was a possibility. A few days later George was in conversation with an Italian agent who mentioned that a contact in the Circle of Suabia had suggested that some rich man in Genoa or Venice might like to purchase in the Empire a fief which, as a principality, would entitle the holder to session and vote at the Diet. The place proposed was Donauwehrt. Stepney shewed casual interest and extracted the relevant details. He offered himself to Marlborough as an intermediary in the matter, should Count

Wratislaw fail. And on 27 December, Stepney could crow to Cardonnel:

> He [Wratislaw] has never said one word to me yet of ye Principality, and I wish his Grace cou'd bring himself to think as little of it as the Count does.

Eventually, on New Year's Eve, Stepney asked Wratislaw about Marlborough's affair. The Count said he had reminded the Emperor about it, and a patent would be dispatched. But the fief was not Donauwehrt: a small town on the Danube was more likely, probably Munderkingen. Stepney at once wrote to Marlborough:

> I suppose it to be a very inconsiderable ruinous Town, which with much ado may be found in ye Map of Suabia, on this side of the Danube about 7 German miles above Ulm.

To Cardonnel, in his covering letter, Stepney was more frank:

> In my letter to My Lord Duke I have given some information what sort of Principality is designed for him; may I perish if I would accept it, so inconsiderable as I am; but I dare give no opinion and shall keep faithfully to the instructions I receive.[4]

Later, in January 1705, Stepney took trouble to establish the exact income to be expected from Munderkingen, which was not enough to defray the tax to which Princes of the Empire were subject. Stepney was delighted to pass on this information, because Wratislaw had told Marlborough that everything had been arranged for him. And George even added a remark that Marlborough was of course free to consult anyone in England who knew more about the affairs and methods of the Empire than he (Stepney) did. In this letter, as in others which he wrote at the beginning of the year 1705, George Stepney revealed that side of his character which was the most irritating to his superiors.[5]

Nevertheless Marlborough accepted Stepney's judgement about Munderkingen, and told Stepney politely to refuse the offer. In February, George reported that Count Sinzendorf was looking for an estate for Marlborough in Holland, near Ruremonde. But this project too came to nothing.

After the death of the Emperor Leopold the subject of the Principality seemed to lapse: Joseph I had to find his feet as successor to his father, and Marlborough was conducting the campaign in Flanders. But when the Duke visited Vienna, and possibly on his last evening when he was surprised by the Emperor in the Chamber of Rarities, the location of the Principality was revealed as Mindelheim, [about 50 km south-west of Augsburg.] Stepney reported the matter to Harley two days after the Duke had left Vienna for Berlin. And (as noted in Chapter XX above) George

The Einlasstor, Mindelheim, Bavaria.

was to act for Marlborough when it came to taking over the Principality.[6]

One of the officials with whom Marlborough was already in contact was Baron Staffhorst, *Grand Maître* to the Duke Regent of Württemberg. Stepney wrote to Staffhorst, hoping that the latter would be present when the inaugural ceremony of its new ruler took place in the Principality. And Stepney now took over the organisation of the imperial patent, sending to Cardonnel a packet of documents, including a new Instrument of Authorisation, for Marlborough to sign and seal:

youle [*sic* – you'll] find a corner marqued for your name.

When Cardonnel returned this paper he remarked that money

matters [i.e. the fees to various officials] were to be at Stepney's discretion. By a courier returning to the Hague on 30 December 1705, Stepney sent to Stanhope a box wrapped in seercloth in which were contained the three original patents for the Principality. George listed all his disbursements: to the *Référendaire* of Austria; to his friend [Caspar Florentin] Consbruck (who refused the 100 dollars proffered – and Stepney remarked that his usual fee was three times as much, so Marlborough should make a 'handsome compliment'); and to several other functionaries, so that the total came to 570 dollars. Stepney was awaiting from the *Référendaire* details of the investiture and the fief. All these formalities had to be completed before Marlborough could draw any profits. And the Chamber of Innsbruck must first deliver the possession. Stepney promised to press for this as much as possible.

Marlborough had the grace to acknowledge Stepney's efforts. He wrote from St James' on 11 January (o.s.) 1705/6, to say that the patents had reached the Hague two days before he embarked for England. He did not dispute any of the fees: and Stepney should make his compliment to Consbruck.[7]

Stepney's next move was to send on to Cardonnel a recommendation from Prince Eugene in favour of Baron Imhoff to be continued as Administrator of Mindelheim. There were two competitors for this appointment, the other being the Baron's younger brother. Prince Eugene's word was enough, and the elder brother, Johann Josef, got the job. Stepney also sent forward to Cardonnel his own view that, as all the inhabitants of Mindelheim were Catholic, things should be left alone in the Principality and that those of other professions should not be employed. Already on 6 March 1706, George expected to visit Mindelheim during the summer.

> The Compliment which his Grace is pleas'd to make of leaving me the disposall of Offices there is by no means what I can receive.[8]

The visit took place during May. Stepney was at Pressburg on 8 May and in Vienna on the 12th. It seems that he left the next day for Mindelheim, whence he wrote to Erasmus Lewis on the 21st:

> Pray acquaint my Sister that I got hither yesterday after a very agreeable journey thro' Munich and Augsburg. . . . It is a very pleasant country and more profitable than I thought it was. I have a covey of English Nuns next door to me and over against me a knott of Jesuits who will be damned if they are not honest and good subjects.

Stepney continued to recount the behaviour of some of Marlborough's most recent recruits for the war

> The Palatin troops march like snails and devour like locusts. . . . I
> wish they may fight like dragons. In six days they have exacted near
> a thousand florins of our people of Mindelheim; but I have ferreted
> them out and at least they promised to move on the 24th inst.[9]

His stay lasted only a week. On 27 May, Stepney was writing to
Cardonnel 'Within a Post from Ratisbonne' [where he would take
to the river for his journey back to Vienna]. Now he estimated the
contributions exacted by the Palatine troops to have been 2,828
florins; but it was lucky for the people of Mindelheim that he had
arrived when he did, because after receiving Stepney's
remonstrance, Brigadier Offeren forbore exacting any more
supplies. Stepney also tried to divert other regiments from
descending on the town, and sent Cardonnel the details.

As for the ceremony of Inauguration, Stepney hoped no
circumstance had been omitted which might have been for his
Grace's Glory and Interest. He was preparing a full account, which
would be sent to Cardonnel, together with a list of expenses, as
soon as possible.

At Ratisbon Stepney was able to report that the Emperor's
Requisitional Letter for admitting Marlborough into the Diet was
presented by the Emperor's representative, Cardinal Lamberg, to
the Elector of Mainz on 20 May. Stepney said he would thank the
Cardinal and thought matters would now take their natural course
without opposition. He had made contact with the Hanoverian
representative at the Diet, [Christoph, Freiherr von] Schrader, who
did indeed pilot the Duke's application through the labyrinth of the
imperial administration.[10]

The next day [28 May] Stepney, catching up on correspondence,
told Stanhope he was

> in a kind of Noah's Ark being on ye Danube in my way to Vienna
> and so down again to Pressburgh.

He was pleased with his reception at Mindelheim, and continued:

> the people were kind and hearty and seem'd so well satisfyed
> with my way of treating them, that at parting (contrary to my
> expectation and desire) they obliged me to accept one of the finest
> Bason & Ewers that I have seen, worth about 60[ll] [£60] Sterl.

George repeated these remarks to Lord Halifax, and could not resist
the additional comment that had he not plied with great application
and skill in the affair of Mindelheim, it might have been protracted
for a year or two longer.

On 31 May (n.s.) 1706, Stepney was back in Vienna, where he
was greeted with the good news, first of the fall of Barcelona to the
Allies, and second of Marlborough's great victory at Ramillies,

which returned the Spanish Netherlands to imperial control.

Stepney had little more to do with Mindelheim. But in July 1706, from Tyrnau in Hungary, he addressed himself

A la reverende Dame

La Dame Kundienne à la Maison des Religieuses Angloise
à Mindelheim,

to tell her, in reply to her letter, that Marlborough would continue the pension to the English Cloyster, and that he (Stepney) had written to Baron Imhoff accordingly. George sent his good wishes, and particularly asked that his humble service might be presented to 'Mrs. Skelton and ye rest of our Nation.'[11] The nuns in Mindelheim belonged to the *Gesellschaft der englischen Fräulein* or, the Institute of the Blessed Virgin mary, established in the sixteenth century by Mary Ward. It seems likely that 'Mrs Skelton' was a relative – perhaps a daughter – of Sir Bevil Skelton, who had preceded Sir Peter Wyche as Resident in the City of Hamburg during good King Charles's golden days. Stepney maybe, was reminded of his first days abroad under his Catholic friend and master.

XXII *The End of the Hungarian Mediation and the Transfer to the Netherlands*

(June-October 1706)

George Stepney to his friends,
June 1706

You must own, this is a very hattering life. . . . This piece of service has been the most painful & vexatious of any I have mett with thro'out the Course of my life. . . . The Horse you design me will be acceptable at all times as coming from a person whom I honour sincerely, but I am very sensible such a present is more than I have deserv'd and I have had so much troublesome business of late that I have had no leisure for any exercise, and scarce believe that I am likely to have any.[1]

On the fourth evening after his return from Mindelheim George Stepney had audience not only of the Emperor, but of both Empresses – that is Eleanor, the Empress-Dowager (the widow of Leopold I) and the reigning lady, Amalia Wilhemine (1673-1742). In the flush of the victory of Ramillies the Envoy from England was well received. But he was commanded by the Emperor to leave for Hungary the very next day (5 June (n.s.) 1706); and so, following his audience, Stepney sat down to write to Cardonnel, apologising that he had no time again to write to Marlborough, to whom he had already sent congratulations on 2 June. Early on 5 June, he was on his way, taking no-one except [John] Laws (his new secretary), Heyman and a footman with him.[2]

The Court, not having heard from Count Rechteren since 24 May, was impatient to learn the Malcontents' demands. Stepney found Rechteren at Tyrnau and the two set out for Neuhäusel, taking with them Baron Onstein, who had been sent to Vienna with the news of the battle of Ramillies. They arrived at Rákóczy's fortress on 7 June, where they met the Prince in his wife's apartments. Onstein's task was to inform the Hungarians of the victory in

Brabant and thus counter the rumours being spread by emissaries from the Elector of Bavaria (who had appeared, according to Stepney, in 'religious habit'). But the Mediators found Rákóczy more determined than ever not to relinquish his disputed title of Prince of Transylvania; and he insisted that Deputies from that country should participate in the peace congress.

More sinister was the fact that Stepney encountered at Neuhäusel his old acquaintance from Berlin days, the French diplomat Des-Alleurs. The latter happened to 'drop in' to the Princess's suite when the Mediators were there. Finding Rákóczy so immovable as regarded Transylvania Stepney concluded that the Frenchman had indeed given the Prince the assurances from Louis XIV requested in the intercepted letter of the previous month (cf. Chapter XX). Both Rákóczy and the Princess hinted to the Mediators that hopes had been given them by a certain minister in credit with the Emperor [presumably Wratislaw] that the Court might give way on this material point. The Mediators disclaimed all knowledge; but they did send Onstein back to Vienna with letters for the Bishop of Osnabrück and Count Wratislaw on this aspect. During the visit Stepney had an hour's talk with DesAlleurs

in public, not to fall under the penalty of the last Act of Parliament,
for holding correspondence with Her Ma[tys] Enemies.

On 9 June, Stepney and Rechteren returned to Tyrnau. There they were joined by Hungarian Deputies, and the formalities of the Congress began, with the examination of the full powers which had been accorded to the Emperor's Commissioners. It must be remembered that the two sides had still not agreed to meet face to face, and the Mediators left Tyrnau for Pressburg to meet the imperial side *before* any Deputies from Transylvania could reach Tyrnau and obstruct the proceedings. To their surprise, at Pressburg, they found not one Imperial Commissioner. Stepney sent another courier to Vienna to the Bishop of Osnabrück to say that the Mediators had brought the Hungarians' demands, and wished to know whether Imperial Commissioners could be expected at Pressburg, or whether the Mediators should travel to Vienna.

On 14 June, Bruynincx arrived from Vienna, followed next day by the Bishop, attended by his own guard. The Archbishop of Colocza came from Tyrnau, and two Imperial Commissioners also appeared, but not Wratislaw, who was said to be indisposed. After matters of precedence had been settled, the Bishop of Osnabrück agreed to receive the 23 Hungarian articles. Stepney commented on these:

You will find them of three Classes: 1st, what the Emperor is obliged to grant in conscience as founded on Reason, Justice and Law; 2dly, what he may further allow out of fatherly affection as well as for his own convenience and that of his Allies without doing any violence or Injury to his Regall Authority; and 3rdly, what he cannot but reject as insolent and impertinent; especially their Proposalls that half the yearly Revenue arising from his Gold and Silver Mines should be assigned for making good the Copper money, which is now the only coin to be seen throughout the country; and that His Imperial Majesty should think of some methods of rewarding the two Chiefs for their Virtue, Fatigue and Injuries, which cannot but be received at Vienna with the highest Indignation: but that cannot be imputed to any fault of the Mediators since we are oblig'd by our office to hand all Proposalls good or bad from one Party to the other.

At Pressburg, too, the Mediators heard from Wratislaw of the Court's reaction to the appearance of Transylvanian Deputies at the Congress. This was so unsatisfactory that all three Mediators decided to return to Vienna to see if they could not persuade the Court to adopt a softer attitude. And Stepney sadly concluded his dispatch with the observation that the language of the Court had changed since the great victories in Spain and in the Netherlands:

And it were to be wished that these successes may not defeat our endeavours at present, as those at Hochstädt [Blenheim] and Landau rendered ineffectual our Negotiations at Schemnitz.[3]

On 16 June the Envoy, back in Vienna, was writing to his cousin:

I am returned hither this evening, very weary.

He enclosed his dispatch to Harley, although doubting that the Secretary of State would have time to read it:

I wish however that somebody of Patience, Judgment and Integrity would take the points a little under consideration, and give some opinion how far the Queen ought to appear or not appear in favour of the Hungarians, for perhaps never so little attention was given to a matter which was certainly of consequence, otherwise Parliament would not have recommended it, or Her Maty thought fitt to employ people in it. The Laws of Hungary with Tripartitum to which the points refer may be borrowed to [sic] Lord Sunderland, Mr. Unguy or Dr. Goodman.[4]

The Court, of course, held conferences on the Hungarian demands. A paper was to be prepared for presentation to the Emperor, to set out his Final Resolution, which the imperial commissioners would deliver to the Mediators 'in form' at Pressburg. These activities took time, so Stepney was able to enjoy a break of 12 days in Vienna, during which time he dealt with his routine correspondence. He noted however that Wratislaw had gone to Pressburg, in advance of his colleagues, on 19 June.

On 28 June Stepney took up the story to Cardonnel:

> Ime [*sic*] going again to Hungary tho I am in a very ill state of health, for I think it my Duty to await ye criticall minute of that Negotiation.

The ministers of the Court had not kept their promise to shew the Mediators the Court's answer to the Hungarian propositions before handing the text over officially. George continued:

> Many of them are very insolent in their discourses since your late victory [i.e. Ramillies], and one of the greatest benefits they proposed from it, is, persuading ye Queen and ye States to assist ye Emperor either by men or money towards subduing ye Hungarians by force of arms if this Court should think fitt *de rompre avec Eclat*, wch is Wr's ordinary expression . . . .

And, weary as he was of his task, Stepney told his friend he was not reporting these remarks officially. But he hoped Marlborough's conquests

> whereby he has so gloriously secured our Religion and the liberties of Europe may never prove a means of enslaving a free people and of destroying the Reformed Churches in Hungary, where five parts of six are of our profession.[5]

On 28 June, the three Mediators returned to Pressburg and the same evening were invited to a conference by the Bishop of Osnabrück, who told them that the imperial answer to the Hungarians was ready, and he thought the impartial world would recognise that the Emperor had gone as far as possible towards reclaiming the Malcontents. Stepney made a suitable reply. When the imperial paper was read the Mediators demurred at one clause, but were told that it was too late for any alteration to be made. In fact, according to Stepney, the Court's attitude towards the Malcontents was as unyielding as ever. The Mediators had expected a prolongation of the cease-fire, which was immediately refused by Wratislaw. The three therefore requested the Bishop to send a courier to Vienna to request the prolongation once again.

At midnight the Mediators and Wratislaw left Pressburg for Tyrnau, where they arrived early in the morning of 29 June. Wratislaw wished to visit Rákóczy, to try to get him to accept an equivalent for Transylvania. and he continued his journey to Neuhäusel the same evening.

The Mediators, in Tyrnau, intended to present the Court's reply to the Hungarian Deputies, but the latter refused to accept it because no-one from Transylvania was present; and in turn the Mediators would not accept any document from the Hungarians owing to the title which they accorded to Rákóczy. The Hungarian delegation withdrew.

Next day (30 June) a courier arrived from the Bishop of Osnabrück with the welcome news that the truce was extended for another 12 days [i.e. until 24 July]. The Mediators informed Wratislaw by an Express Courier, and agreed with Count Bercsenyi a complicated formula which might accommodate a delegation from Transylvania. On 2 July, Wratislaw returned to Tyrnau, and set out immediately for Vienna. Over the next four days couriers passed between Tyrnau and Vienna in both directions, until at length Stepney and Bruynincx decided to travel themselves to Court, leaving Tyrnau early in the morning of 7 July. Their objectives were to try to get the Court to treat the Transylvanians more favourably, and to obtain yet more time for carrying on the negotiations. As Stepney remarked:

> Unless we obtain these two points, all we would do is but lost labour.[6]

Back in Vienna the Mediators found that although they had not yet been able officially to deliver the Court's reply to the Hungarians, copies of it in Latin and German were being circulated in Vienna, 'which is no very regular proceeding,' said Stepney. Again the Court, after another conference, reiterated its decision not to allow any status to confederates from Transylvania, nor to allow any further prolongation of the truce. Reluctantly, Stepney and Bruynincx prepared to return once more to Hungary, and Stepney wrote to Harley:

> By some letters I have seen from Prince Rakoczy he seems extreamly dissatisfyed with the conversation he lately had with Count Wratislaw, who instead of encouraging him by gracious assurances of the Emperor's Protection and by some favourable Expedient in the point of Transylvania, flattly declar'd to his face that in case HIM should find himself oblig'd to leave the Transylvanians to a free choice, He might depend upon it that HIM would admit the meanest subject of Hungary and Transylvania to that Dignity rather than allow of him. After which disobliging expression the Court ought not to be much surpriz'd if the Prince is chang'd of a sudden from the good dispositions he discover'd of late by promoting everything that might be judg'd proper towards facilitating the Treaty, and seems for the future very indifferent whether the negotiation be continued in its ordinary course, or interrupted by new Hostilities.[7]

On 13 July, at 4.00 p.m., Stepney and Bruynincx left again for

Tyrnau, crossing at Pressburg the path of Count Rechteren, who was travelling in the opposite direction. The Count's news was that the Hungarian Deputies were about to break up the Congress of Tyrnau because no answer had come from the Court on the two essential points, and they were aware that the imperial army was preparing to surprise and attack them. Rechteren still hoped to convince the Court of the necessity for a prolongation of the armistice, and of the sincere inclinations of the Hungarians. But he achieved no more success than had Stepney and Bruynincx, and returned to Tyrnau on 16 July, in the morning, bearing the flat refusal given him by the Prince of Salms and Count Wratislaw. Stepney recommended that the negotiations should be broken off at once, but Rechteren insisted that the Bishop of Osnabrück would make a last direct approach to the Emperor, and that he (Rechteren) had left his secretary behind in Vienna to bring good news, if any. And a messenger did arrive – yet another conference would be held at Court, on 16 July; the result would be sent immediately to the Mediators, and if the Hungarians made a swift and satisfactory answer, nothing would be omitted by the Court to facilitate peace. Stepney wrote:

> our negotiation here has been like a Stagg *aux abois*; it is impossible it should recover, yet neither Party will venture to give the Death's wound.

Meanwhile strange events had taken place at Rákóczy's stronghold of Neuhäusel. His wife had left him to take the waters at Carlsbad. This was perhaps not surprising, since Charlotte-Amélie had not seen her German relatives for at least five years. According to Stepney's dispatch to Harley, the Princess's place was taken by Rákóczy's elder sister, Countess [Juliana] d'Aspremont, whom 'the Emperor was pleas'd to employ.' This lady had arrived at Neuhäusel on 16 July, and Stepney claimed to be ignorant of how she got there. He merely remarked that she had been successful in persuading her brother to move to Schinta [on the river Waag] which was only two hours' journey from Tyrnau and thus within easier reach of both the Mediators and the Hungarian Deputies.

What Stepney did not reveal to his Secretary of State was that on 1 July he had replied to a letter from Juliana's husband, Count d'Aspremont, who appears to have been travelling in the Low Countries. Stepney referred to Wratislaw's activities in going to Neuhäusel, which he did not think would be successful; and promised that if d'Aspremont wished to visit his estates in the Pas de Calais, '*mon P^{ce} de Mindelheim*' would help him take possession of the lands. The only reference to the Countess reads, just before the final salutation:

J'espere que l'addresse [sic] *de Mad* remettra un peu ses affaires Domestiques dont vous aurey des d'Elle meme.*

A little later, after he had returned to Vienna, Stepney wrote to one of his acquaintances, a merchant of Cracow named Alexander Rosse, recommending to him the estates of 'Princesse Aspremont' which were at Patak in Hungary, and from which the steward had remitted no money:

I entreat you to be assistant to ye Lady (for whom I have a most particular esteem) by buying up her wines preferably to any other . . . . I have given her my word that she may relye on yr zeal and integrity.

The wording of this paragraph would appear to bear out Alexander Stanhope's opinion of the year 1704 that George had formed an attachment to Juliana. And indeed Stepney himself had never denied their acquaintance. It seems incredible, therefore, that he should have been ignorant of her journey to visit her brother. But it was no doubt to bolster his claim to impartiality in the mediation that he made no earlier mention of it in any document.[8]

Rákóczy sent a message to the Mediators that he would be pleased to see all three at Schinta. They went there on 18 July and talked to him without ceremony in his sister's apartment, as they had formerly done in his Lady's. The discussion was about the methods of carrying on the Treaty, which he maintained was impossible unless the truce was prolonged. The Prince also assured the Mediators that the Hungarians were preparing their reply to the Emperor's last missive, which would be ready before the present armistice expired, provided the Court before 20 July, consented to a reasonable term for treating. Otherwise he and Bercsenyi (who was present) would not deliver anything in writing but would print their manifesto (as the imperialists had done) so that the impartial world would have a chance to sympathise with them.

The Mediators returned to Tyrnau the same evening. Nothing had come from the Court, and so yet another messenger was dispatched to the Bishop of Osnabrück, requesting the extra time. On 19 July, a courier arrived from the Bishop and from Wratislaw, in answer to the Mediators' earlier plea of 16 July,

whereby you see [wrote Stepney] violent Councells have prevail'd so farr that whatever the Mediators can or would do, is not sufficient to preserve our negotiation from an unnaturall end.

And he added that the imperialists' main argument – that the army in Transylvania was in distress – was notoriously false: it had never been so well supplied, and the commander, General Rabutin, in a recent letter had made no mention of any shortage.

On 20 July, the Mediators again visited Rákóczy at Schinta, in the evening. They told him they saw little hope of the truce being prolonged, and that the Emperor persisted in his intention of governing Transylvania as had been agreed at the Peace of Carlowitz – that is, by a Governor and 12 Counsellors, all appointed by imperial authority. Rákóczy was surprised at this double negative, having been assured by his sister that the Court would be reasonable. The Mediators agreed not to deliver this answer to the Hungarian Deputies until the following day, still hoping against hope that a courier would arrive from Vienna. But no news came to Tyrnau, and so the Mediators delivered their final Declaration on 21 July, before noon, to two Deputies who, with tears in their eyes, expressed their very sensible concern for the pains the Mediators had taken to no purpose, and over the calamities to which their country was likely to be exposed.

They also gave the Mediators a Protestation, justifying their proceedings and laying the blame for the rupture at the door of the imperial Court. Stepney read the paper, saw that it was violent, and begged the Deputies to withdraw certain expressions. This they would not do without Rákóczy's consent, and so they went to see him, followed in the evening by the Mediators, to take leave. The Prince refused to moderate the paper, and told the Mediators to expect his manifesto.

> In this visit the Prince seem'd more bitter than in any of our former conversations; however he promis'd us not to enter into desperate measures with the Turk or any other Potentate; but to wait at least until Wee had made our Report, and try'd if it were yet possible to bring the Court to a more moderate sense.

The Mediators returned the same evening [21 July] to Tyrnau and visited the only Hungarian Deputy left there. The next day they broke up the Congress and transported all goods and domestics to Pressburg and thence to Vienna, where they arrived on 23 July. Next morning Stepney saw the Bishop of Osnabrück and the Prince of Salms and related all that had happened. The Emperor warned his subjects of the resumption of hostilities, referring to the Hungarians as rebels who did not deserve the terms of the armistice. James Fury, who had remained in Vienna throughout Stepney's absences, wrote that the talk of the city was solely of extirpating the Hungarians with fire and sword, and that he (Fury) expected greater cruelties than ever.

On 1 August, the Mediators had audience of the Emperor. It fell to Stepney 'to deliver the Harangue' in which the recent turn of events was described, and the breakdown attributed to the councils of the hawks of the imperial court [to use a modern expression], with much reasonableness being credited to the Hungarian side. The speech was printed in London on 28 August (o.s.) 1706, and was reprinted into German, Swiss and Italian gazettes in translation.[9]

George Stepney was by now a sick man. He wrote to Cardonnel on 31 July, in reply to a letter from Adam dated 17 July:

> I thank you for the kind Sense you express in relation to my health: My too frequent journeys to Hungary have indeed much impair'd it; and I am often troubled with faint sweats and Feavours, which convince me I have no longer that Iron constiution I had formerly. But I hope a little ease and regular living may sett me up again or I must endeavour to change air, on which subject I intended to write to you by this post, but I have neither leisure nor force at present.

And indeed George had been almost continuously on the move since his return to Vienna from Mindelheim [see Appendix VII]. In 48 days he had covered about 950 km, often at night in a bumping, swaying coach – although during the summer it was cooler to travel by night rather than by day. Food and drink would have been provided locally. George enjoyed the Tokay wine, and made no comment as to provisions, but in a war-torn land these could not have been plentiful. He was still complaining of his fever a week after his letter to Cardonnel.[10]

Stepney's spirits were raised at the thought of his impending transfer. In mid-September he received a private letter from Mr Secretary Harley, tactfully expressed as ever:

> Whitehall – 6/17 August 1706
>
> The Queen thinks this a proper time to express her approbation of the good service you have rendered Her Ma^{ty} in so many distant places, by removing you nearer home; and to a place more agreeable to yourself: I mean the Hague.

Stepney was to prepare his departure, but await official revocation because an answer from Lord Raby was still awaited, whether he would accept the post. In fact, the Queen had suggested Stepney's transfer much earlier, in May 1706, as soon as she learned of Alexander Stanhope's illness. The change was of course postponed owing to the critical negotiation taking place in Hungary. It is pleasant to read that Godolphin headed off a bid from Richard Hill for the post in the Hague because he remembered Marlborough's promise to Stepney and his wish to have him there. In the course of their exchange of letters the Duke described George to Godolphin as 'capable and honest.'[11]

Cardonnel claimed the credit for the transfer, writing to Stepney from Helchin on 14 August (n.s.):

> Since you seem to be so willing to leave Vienna pray prepare for a sudden call, I have vanity enough to think I have contributed a little towards it by my preaching to my Lord Duke and Lord Halifax for a proper person to go to Brussels. His Grace was pleas'd to do the other & this morning ask'd my opinion about yr coming thither, you may believe my friendship for you as well as my concern for the Public readily suggested to me what was proper on this occasion, since in this case you are to be join'd with his Grace as Plenipotentiary for the Government of this Country, you will be ridd of Mr. Wratislaw and instead of him may meet three here, but you'le have more authority and be supported . . . I assure you, you are the only person I ever thought qualified for this business since our being here.

Adam was referring to the task of governing the Spanish Netherlands. After the victory of Ramillies the country had been claimed for King Charles III of Spain by Count Goes, who was the King's as well as the Emperor's Envoy at the Hague. Already in July Stepney knew from court gossip that Marlborough had been offered the governorship of the country by the imperial court, and by the end of that month he knew that this offer had been declined. On 24 August Bruynincx presented to the Emperor a long letter from the States General [which he seems to have communicated to his friend Stepney] demanding that the Dutch 'Barriers' in the Netherlands should be settled according to the 9th Article of the Grand Alliance, before Marlborough or any other person should be appointed as Governor of the Spanish Netherlands either by the Emperor or by the King of Spain.

George answered Cardonnel on 28 August (before he had received Harley's letter quoted above):

> You are a bold friend to mention me as a Person fully qualified for a business which I'm afraid exceeds my reach; but I am Clay in the hands of a Potter and can only promise you that your recommendation shall never be discredited as far as Application and Integrity can make it good.

And George wished to be informed as to his successor, because of his having to dispose of equipage and movables, in order to return as light as possible. He recommended his cousin, Charles Whitworth 'the poor Muscovite' as the successor, but this suggestion was not followed.[12]

Before leaving there was much to be done. Stepney was already in correspondence with Godolphin about details of the 'little loan' to the Emperor from the maritime powers. It had been destined for Prince Eugene in Italy, but direct transmission of the funds had caused the President of the Chamber [the imperial finance minister] to take umbrage that the transaction had not passed through his hands. Now, there was a dispute as to the banking costs involved, and which government should bear them. Stepney wished the Lord Treasurer's advice.

Rákóczy had written to the Queen as well as to the States General. Stepney recommended that Her Majesty should reply in the same vein as had her allies: – that is with compassion. He did not believe rumours of peace negotiations between France and the Emperor: the French could not offer any terms with which the imperial court could be contented. Commenting on the European situation, Stepney averred that the English were in a good way of obtaining their trade, through dominance in Spain; the Dutch were likely to get their Barrier; but the Austrians were far from obtaining their desire, which was sovereignty of Naples and Sicily.

The King of Sweden [Charles XII] invaded Saxony, via Silesia, which caused the Vienna Court to speculate that this move was made in concert with France, and to the advantage of Hungarians. All this was worrying for a man hopeful of leaving his post. At last, on 18 September, the longed-for Letter of Revocation arrived. George had already told Cardonnel he would be 'wing'd with Joy and Impatience till I reach you.' On 21 September, he had his audience of *congé* from the Emperor, and was pleased at the cordiality of the interview. Next day he bade farewell to the imperial family, and on 25 September, he was under way.

On 26 September, Stepney passed through Amstetten [130 km west of Vienna] and wrote to his steward, James Fury, who replied to him at length. Stepney had been worried about his wine, so Fury went into great detail about its packing and transportation. The house had been re-let to Count Fuchs, who was taking over some of the wine and other objects. Fury had more than one complaint against Heyman, who had not been helpful over the move. He had not told Fury who was to take care of the two horses, or how much grooms in charge of them should be paid (Stepney noted in the margin, 17d. per day [in modern money, about 7p]). And the iron hearth to the chimney in the room where Cardonnel had lodged was missing: only Heyman could tell Stepney what had become of it, because he had had the keys to that chamber from beginning to end. Fury continued:

> I told ye Countess of Aspremont that I have orders to pay her
> some money, but she said she wanted none yet. Yr hon^r will receive
> a letter from hereabout what Mr. Walstorff [Stepney's banker in
> Vienna] has in Comission, he arrived an hour after yr hon^{rs}
> departure.

Regrettably, there is no explanation of either of Fury's statements.[13]

On 1 October, Stepney was in Munich, writing to Count
Löwenstein [the Governor] to say he had had information from
Wratislaw that the Emperor had decided to make Marlborough a
present of three or four pictures, apart from any which his brother
King Charles might have given, and could not the Count give orders
for the immediate dispatch of two by Rubens and one other, without
waiting for any new orders from Vienna because he (Stepney) had
the means of transporting the pictures with his own baggage. If this
was not possible, Stepney suggested that Löwenstein should write
to Wratislaw for confirmation, and send the pieces to Frankfurt
addressed to M. Behagel, banker. This man had in the past been
used by Stepney on various occasions for forwarding mail and
goods. George ended his letter by remarking that his eye had been
caught by *Mars and Venus*, and by *Lot with his two daughters*,
both of which were by Rubens. The outcome of this request is not
known.

Something of a mystery surrounds George Stepney's subsequent
movements. In the mid-eighteenth century the Swiss historian
Guillaume de Lamberty published his *Mémoires pour servir à
l'histoire du XVIII siècle*. This volume has been much used by
subsequent historians in the nineteenth and twentieth centuries.
Lamberty prints a letter, in French, which he claims was written by
Stepney, although no date or recipient is quoted. The text describes
a visit which Stepney is said to have made to Saxony, without
permission, to observe the three kings there assembled – Augustus
the Strong of Saxony, Charles XII of Sweden and the latter's puppet,
Stanislas Leszczynski of Poland. The vivid description of Charles
XII has often been reproduced and could well have been written
by Stepney. The remarks about Augustus are meagre; but prefacing
the description of Stanislas is the statement that George was
travelling incognito, with a (male) friend and a valet as his only
companions. Nevertheless Stanislas at a reception singled him out,
with his friend, because both were strangers.

Not one word of this visit survives in any of the Stepney papers.
It is possible that he might have visited Dresden and Leipzig (where

he is said to have met Stanislas) between 1 October, when he was in Munich and 10 October, when he reached Frankfurt am Main. He could not have accompanied Marlborough when the Duke made his famous visit to the three kings the following spring.

Despite being 'winged with Joy' Stepney did not hurry to travel across Europe. There was one other possible diversion on the way: the Countess of Aspremont was in Frankfurt a week after Stepney left that city; the length of her stay is not known. But a man called 'Talon' wrote to Stepney from Cologne in late October, having heard from George, and sending to him an enclosure from the Countess, who was then awaiting the arrival of her husband.

Once again, there is no explanation of the inclusion of this letter among the Stepney papers. But if Stepney did go through Carlsbad he may well have encountered there Princess Rákóczy, who was reported by her sister-in-law to be under arrest for entertaining some Swedish officers in her apartments. If they were handsome young fellows it was thought to be unlikely that they were involved in any 'public design.' George, following his usual practice about his private life, kept mum.[15]

XXIII *George Stepney's Poetry*

<u>Translation of a verse from Lucan</u>
(Undated)

Victrix causa Diis placuit, sed victa
Catoni

The gods and Cato did in this divide,
They choose the conqu'ring, he the conquer'd side.

This epigram of George Stepney's was included in Dr Samuel Johnson's *The Works of the most Eminent English Poets, with Prefaces, Biographical and Critical* (London, 1779-81), Volume 12, together with all Stepney's output hitherto published. But the Doctor accompanied this collection with a judgement so damning that the poet's reputation has never since recovered. To quote Johnson:

> It is reported that the juvenile compositions of Stepney *made grey authors blush.* I know not whether his poems will appear such wonders to the present age.
>
> He apparently professed himself a poet . . . but he is a very licentious translator, and does not recompense his neglect of the author [Juvenal] by beauties of his own.
>
> In his original poems, now and then, a happy line may perhaps be found, and . . . a short composition may give pleasure; but there is, in the whole, little either of the grace of wit, or the vigour of nature.[1]

Literary men of the earlier eighteenth century took a different view. Giles Jacob, who brought out his *Poetical Register* in 1720 (13 years after Stepney's death) remarked:

> He [Stepney] was very happy and successful in all his Negotiations, which occasioned a constant Employment in the most weighty Affairs. At his leisure hours he wrote some Pieces of Poetry, which are very much admir'd for the Politeness and Elegancy of his Style, as well as his great Wit.

And Samuel Wesley, who published *An Epistle to a Friend concerning Poetry* in 1700, included the lines:

> Who can th'ingenious S[tepney]'s Praise refuse,
> Who serves a grateful Prince, and grateful muse?

Later critics have followed Johnson's lead: John Sergeaunt, who published his *Annals of Westminster School* in 1898, once referred to George Stepney's 'wretched verses.' The poet was not included in *The Penguin Book of Restoration Verse* (Harold Love, ed. 1968). James Sutherland, in his *English Literature of the late Seventeenth Century* (Oxford, 1969) remarked that Stepney was 'a Platonic pattern of the minor occasional poet' and that 'the chief authority on the career and moribund reputation of Stepney is Johnson.'

No-one could claim that Stepney was among the great men of English literature, but he was at least no worse a poet than many of his contemporaries. An attempt has been made here to place his poems as far as possible within his career, and to draw attention to some of them in a more kindly fashion than did Johnson.

The two lines from Lucan set at the head of this chapter are undated, but in imagination they might be ascribed to the years which George spent at Westminster School; and one hopes he was duly rewarded with a tit-bit from the headmaster's table [cf. Chapter II].

The poems which Stepney wrote at Cambridge have been indicated in Chapter II. A curious feature of the poem *On the University of Cambridge's burning the Duke of Monmouth's picture* is that, while it begins in the regular iambic measure with the usual line of ten syllables, half way through and without warning Stepney wrote dodecasyllabic lines in the anapaestic rhythmic pattern, for example:

Then in comes mayor Eagle, and does gravely alledge
He'll subscribe, if he can, for a bundle of sedge:
But the man of Clarehall that Proffer refuses,
'Snigs, he be beholden to none but the muses:

and this rhythm continues to the end of the poem. There seems to be no explanation for this change, other than carelessness.

No verses of Stepney's can be traced to the years which he spent in Hamburg as secretary to Sir Peter Wyche, except one poem, dated surely in 1688, entitled *The Audience*, which was attributed to Stepney in 1749. This is a satirical piece, mocking those Jacobites who, in imagination, came to seek audience of the baby Prince of Wales. The phraseology is vulgar. The main reason, however, for doubting Stepney's authorship is the fact that during the whole of 1688 he was at his post in Hamburg, and would hardly have had the opportunity of acquainting himself with the various characters named in the poem, other than from news-sheets which might have reached him.

The start of 1691, saw Stepney in the Hague, composing his

long laudatory poem to the King, the *Epistle to Charles Montague, Esq.* on which comments have been made in Chapter IV. It would not have been proper for a mere secretary to have addressed the King directly.

At about this time Stepney composed his *Letter to Mr. Prior upon his grave Epistle to Mr. Montagu,* beginning:

How'ere tis well – and nding [*sic*]
& Phyllis but a perjured Whore.

[The poem is given in full at Appendix VIII.]

Prior's poem (to be found in *The Penguin Book of Restoration Verse*, p.84) was first published in 1692. Stepney stayed with Prior in the Hague during the winter of 1690/91, when the two friends were competing for the approbation of Charles Montagu, their prominent contemporary. The first verse of Prior's offering runs:

Howe'r, 'tis well, that whilst Mankind
Thro' Fate's Fantastick Mazes errs,
He can imagin'd Pleasure find,
To combat against real Cares

and he continues to anticipate the well-known maxim, later expressed by R. L. Stevenson, that to travel hopefully is better than to arrive. Prior ends disconsolately:

We wearied should lie down in Death
This Cheat of Life would take no more;
If you thought Fame but Stinking Breath,
& Phillis but a perjur'd Whore.

Stepney's response is practical in outlook. The pleasures of the moment are to be enjoyed, with no questions asked; and ignorance is bliss. The philosophy agrees well with George's optimism at the start of his career.

During his posting to Dresden in 1693, Stepney produced three Latin pieces. The first was the epitaph for his predecessor Sir William Colt [see Chapter VI]. The second was an epigram which he sent to Blathwayt on 7/17 October 1693, in the context of the lifting of the siege of Belgrade by the Duke of Croy, which had not helped the Emperor's war against the Turks:

In Ducem Croia
Perdere Croie potes Belgradum, reddere nescis;
Infoelix bellum, te Duce, Caesar agit
Aut tantis transisse Savum nec oportuit ausis,
Aut non tam trepido mox remeasse metu.

An subitae te est haec causa, fuga; quod sis memor olim
Quam tibi vix licuit, Caute, referre pedem?
Laudo Consilium quod nil temerarius audes

Sed tibi perpetus [*sic – perpetuo*] *haec laus erit opprobrio.*
This has been translated:

Against the Duke of Croy

You may lose Belgrade, Croy, but you can't return it;
It's a miserable war the Emperor wages, with you as Commander,
Either you ought not to have crossed the Sava with such daring,
Or not immediately turned back with such anxious fear.

Or was flight a sudden thought? And will you one day remember
How you were scarcely allowed, Cautious, to retreat?
I praise the Counsel which tells you to dare nothing rash,
But such praise is to your eternal disgrace.

As usual, Stepney circulated his epigram to his friends. Sir Paul Rycaut, in Hamburg, wrote that it was 'very severe.' It was a propaganda piece, designed to castigate any commander of the Grand Alliance who preferred retreat to attack.[2]

The third Latin poem which Stepney wrote at the turn of the year 1693/94 (on the French King's offer of the Netherlands to the Elector of Bavaria), has been noted in Chapter VII and has been reproduced, together with Stepney's English version, at Appendix III.

During 1693, Stepney was engaged on the translation of the Eighth Satire of Juvenal, a project into which he was drawn by John Dryden. The manuscript of the translation is now in America, and the work has been subjected to detailed scrutiny by American authorities on Dryden and his circle. Stepney is given little credit for his contribution, which was revised by Dryden.[3]

The spring of 1695 was the date of Stepney's longest and most successful composition, *A Poem Dedicated to the Blessed Memory of Her Late Gracious Majesty Queen Mary.* To quote one short stanza:

Thus to the Noon of her high Glory run
From her bright Orb, diffusive like the Sun,
She did her healing Influence display
And cherish'd all our nether World that lay
Within the Circle of her radiant Day:

and the acclaim which it received was justified, for the Queen was well loved. James Vernon (senior) wrote to Stepney:

You will see by the Gazette you are gott into Print & I'le assure you 'tis to the Encrease of your Reputation. . . . Congreve was thought to have done well onely for Hanging the Roomes & painting a dismall Scene, but tis Mr Stepney onely shews the Queen.

As well as sending the poem to Vernon, Stepney also posted it direct to his publisher, Jacob Tonson, under a covering letter which not only contained many suggested amendments, but pointing out that the poem ends with a recommendation to the King to return to the war in Flanders. These sentiments Stepney wished removed, should Parliament decide to the contrary. However the ending remained intact.[4]

Stepney's next work to which a certain date can be given is the song written to celebrate the victory at Namur at the end of 1695. Mention has already been made of this piece in Chapter IX.

Events soon imposed on a good Whig the necessity for another political composition. The 19 lines entitled *On the late horrid Conspiracy* were circulated in late 1696, and published by Francis Saunders in 1697. The author cites Alexander the Great and Julius Caesar, both of whom took revenge on their enemies' betrayers, and concludes his poem:

> So WILLIAM Acts – And if his Rivals dare
> Dispute his Reign by Arms, He'll meet 'em there
> Where Jove, as once on Ida, holds the Scale,
> And lets the Good, the Just, and Brave, prevail.

Is this so much worse than *Rule Britannia*, included in the *Golden Treasury of Songs and Lyrics*?

Stepney's next known epigram was composed in Brandenburg for the Electress's new palace [see Chapter XII]. It ran as follows:

> *Auspicÿs fundata tuis Domus, amula* [sic – ?*amicula*]
> *gestit*
> *ut natalities Domino persolvat honores:*
> *Sis Bonus, et gratis succede Penatibus; hospes*
> *Sponsa rogat tenerique secundant Omen Amores.*

He sent Blathwayt four translations in French (composed by members of the court) and one in German. All were in verse. A prose version might run:

> Palace, founded on your own auspices, my sweetheart passionately
> longs to give the birthday honours to her Lord: be good, and
> prosper with favourable *Penates* [household gods]; the bride
> invites her guests, and the tender Loves give us a favourable omen.[5]

Before 1701, Stepney wrote his best poem, *The Nature of Dreans,* which appears in *A New Miscellany of Original Poems on Several Occasions*, printed for Peter Buck and George Scraben in that year.

> At dead of night imperial reason sleeps
> And fancy with her train loose revels keeps,
> Then airy phantoms a mixt scene display,
> Of what we heard, or saw, or wish'd by day;
> For memory those images retains,
> Which passion form'd, and still the strongest reigns.
> Huntsmen renew the chace they lately run,

And gen'rals fight again their battels won.
Spectres and furies haunt the murd'rers dreams,
Grants or disgraces are the courtier's themes.
The miser spys a thief, or a new hoard,
The cit's a knight, the sycophant a lord.
Thus fancy's in the wild distraction lost,
With what we most abhor, or covet most.
But of all passions, that our dreams controul,
Love prints the deepest image in the soul;
For vigorous fancy, and warm blood dispense
Pleasures so lively that they rival sense.
Such are the transports of a willing maid,
Not yet by time, and place to act betray'd
Whom spies, or some faint virtue force to fly
That scene of joy, which yet she dares to try.
Till fancy bawds, and by mysterious charms,
Brings the dear object to her longing arms;
Unguarded then she melts, acts fierce delight,
And curses the return of envious light.
In such blest dreams Biblys enjoys a flame,
Which waking she detests, and dares not name.
Ixion gives a loose to his wild love
And in his airy visions cuckolds Jove.
Honours and state before this phantom fall;
For sleep, like death, its image, equals all.

Yet another Latin epigram appeared in 1701, this time addressed to the Pope, Clement XI, who was pro-French, and who had issued a decree forbidding discussion of the affairs of Italy, Stepney wrote:

Quid Germanus agat, quid Gallus junctus Ibero
Roma loqui. Gallo sic cupiente vetat
Nitimur in vehhem [sic]; linguas vis scire ligandi
Artem! Germanis disce ligare manus.

These lines have been translated:

Rome says what Germany does to France, in conjunction
with Spain, but forbids France's desire for the same.
We fall back on invective; if you want to know how to
hold tongues, you must teach the Germans to hold their
hands.[6]

Also in 1701, Stepney probably composed the Latin poem *Ad Regem Sueciae* [To the King of Sweden] which was published by W. Mears in London twenty years later. The author's name was given as 'Georgio Stepney, Arm[iger]' and a translation was provided by one 'Mr. B—', who remains unidentified. The content of the ten Latin lines is to urge matrimony on the King of Sweden [Charles XII]. The reason for attributing this poem to 1701 is that

Stepney during that autumn was sending to Whitehall copies of various documents relating to Charles XII's victory over Augustus the Strong of Saxony, so the Swedish monarch would have been on his mind. Equally, the poem could have been written in 1703, when Stepney was expecting to be sent to the King of Sweden in order to mediate in the latter's quarrel with Saxony, [cf. Chapter XVI].

It seems reasonable to date Stepney's poem *The Austrian Eagle* in 1703, since the six (English) lines could be taken as a compliment to the young Archduke Charles as he was about to set off on his journey to Spain. However the surviving correspondence does not supply definite confirmation.

Two poems written at the end of Stepney's life deserve comment. The first is the charming and self-deprecatory *Verses imitated from the French of Monsieur Maynard to Cardinal Richelieu:*

I

When money and my blood ran high
My muse was reckon'd wond'rous pretty
The sports and smiles did round her fly,
Enamour'd with her smart concetti

II

Now, who'd have thought it once with pain
She strings her harp, whilst freezing Age
But feebly runs thro' ev'ry vein
And chills my brisk poetic rage.

III

I properly have ceas'd to live
To wine and women, dead in law:
And soon from fate I shall receive
A summons to the shades to go

IV

The warriour ghosts will round me come
To hear of fam'd Ramillia's fight
Whilst the vex'd Bourbons thro' the gloom
Retire to th'utmost realms of night

V

Then I, my Lord, will tell how you
With pensions every muse inspire
Who Marlb'rough's conquests did pursue
And to his trumpets tun'd the lyre.

VI

But should some drolling sprite demand
Well sir, what place had you, I pray?

How like a coxcomb should I stand!
What would your lordship have me say?

The last English-language poem of Stepney's life was that written to Mr Edmund Smith (1672-1710), playwright, following the failure of Smith's tragedy *Phaedra and Hippolitus* in April 1707. No correspondence between Stepney and Smith has survived, so it is not easy to understand what prompted Stepney, in Holland, to write his poem in praise of the dramatist. The two men must have been well known to each other, because in addressing Smith Stepney uses a diminutive of Smith's Christian name – 'Mun.'

The dedicatee of Smith's play was Charles Montagu, Lord Halifax, who was probably the 'My Lord' of Stepney's poem written after the Battle of Ramillies, which is quoted above.

No collection of Stepney's poetical works was ever made. The complete list of his poems in English as well as in Latin, is shewn in Appendix IX.

XXIV *The Netherlands*
(October 1706 – September 1707)

> I beg leave to congratulate you upon your removal to a province
> that requires all those great abilities for which you are so
> deservedly celebrated . . . . I have often had an opportunity of
> mentioning my obligations to you, and the great respect I shall
> always have for so extraordinary a character as well in other
> countrys as in England.[1]

As he travelled through Europe George Stepney would have been
encouraged by Joseph Addison's laudatory remarks, quoted above.
The latter was by now employed in the Secretary of State's office
(Southern Department) and his correspondence would be useful to
an Envoy who was about to take up a new appointment.

From Frankfurt Stepney continued to Cologne and then followed
advice from Cardonnel to travel via St Tron, Tirelemont, Louvain
and Vilwoorde to Marlborough's camp at Cambron, where he
arrived on 19 October (n.s.) 1706. Since 9 September, the Duke
had been insistent that Stepney should first come to meet him at
the camp before they went on to Brussels together. Already two
Dutch Deputies, Johan van den Bergh and Johan Hop, were with
Marlborough. These men were charged with supervision of the
government of the Spanish Netherlands on behalf of the States
General. But relations between the Allies were not good: the Dutch
envisaged a much stricter rule over the captured territories than
did the English. Marlborough, who was expecting to return to
England having completed the summer campaign, wished to brief
Stepney thoroughly as to his views. He had, after all, been
designated by the Emperor as Governor of the Spanish Netherlands
but, on the advice of Heinsius, had refused the appointment, not
without regret. When Stepney joined the Duke a new Council of
State for the Spanish Netherlands had been set up, composed of
representatives of the conquered nobility, few of whom were
competent. Later, in January 1707, the supervisory 'Conference'
was established, which consisted of Marlborough and two Deputies
from the States General. The Duke appointed as his own deputy
George Stepney.

Complicating the situation in the Spanish Netherlands was the fact that the former Governor – the defeated Max Emmanuel – still controlled some of the southern provinces, and held court at Lille. In mid-October 1706 he wrote to Marlborough and to the Dutch suggesting peace negotiations. The Duke was unwilling to commit himself until he had seen the terms in detail. In any case, he did not wish personally to be involved in any preliminary negotiations; 'Mr. Stepney will be very proper,' he told Godolphin. And he proposed to take Stepney to Brussels on 27 October.[2]

The new Envoy was now in correspondence with both Secretaries of State in London – with Hedges (Southern Department) over what concerned the Spanish Netherlands, and with Harley, as he had been previously, in matters concerning the Dutch. He wrote to both men from Brussels on 4 November. During the one week which he had spent in that city he assembled facts and figures about the trade between the conquered provinces and the Queen's dominions, a subject which was of passionate interest to Brabant and Flanders. He sent home a history of the trade from 1669, two printed tariffs dated 1680 and 1700 (which were too bulky to be enclosed with his letter), and emphasised that what the local magistrates most desired was the removal of the English prohibition on the import of lace.

But the Queen's Instructions for her Envoy Extraordinary at Brussels did not reach him until he had joined Marlborough at Rotterdam on 8 November:

> Whereas since the victory obtain^d at Rammeliess by the Blessing of God upon our Arms and those of the States General, the Cities of Louvain, Brussells, Antwerp, Ghent, Bruges and Ostende, with the greatest part of Brabant and Flanders, have own'd King Charles the 3d [sic] for their lawfull Souveraign, and it will now be necessary to have settled regular Gouvernement in those Countries, which by reason of the great difficulties the King of Spain is [in] at present, He cannot give directions therein so soon as the necessity of Affairs may require; For preventing therefore the Inconvenience which may happen, It is Our Pleasure and you are hereby empowered, as Our Envoy Extraordinary, to conferr with the States General or such of them or their Ministers as you shall judge most conducing to the Service, And to agree with them (until the King of Spain's pleasure can be known) for settling such Governors and Method of Government in Flanders, Brabant and the respective Cities Towns and Places which shall submitt to King Charles as you shall judge will induce them to continue in their Allegiance to this King, and be most for the Security and Advantage of the Common Cause. A.R.[3]

In fact, Stepney was left with much less latitude than is implied in this document. Arrived at the Hague on 9 November, he reported again to both Secretaries of State. He had received his Instructions and Credentials as Envoy Extraordinary and Plenipotentiary to the States General of the United Provinces, with full powers in general to treat with the ministers of all Princes and States. But in regard to the government of the Spanish Netherlands he understood that Marlborough was to regulate the matter with the States General, depending on the report of their Deputies who were returning to the Hague from Brussels and from the army. Stepney was merely to see executed whatever the Duke and the States General should decide.

As usual George was concerned about his allowances. He instructed Richard Powis to get his new Privy Seal passed. He hoped for an equipage allowance of £800, to suit his daily allowance as Plenipotentiary of £8 a day. He claimed that as he was accredited both to the Hague and to Brussels he would be entitled to an equipage for each station. Powis was to see that there was no hiatus between the expiry of the former Privy Seal relevant to Vienna and the commencement of the new one. Arrears of 'extrys' were still outstanding. To these George added a new claim, which included £180 for his journey westwards from Vienna. He swore that in fact it had cost him more, for he had had to pay for an escort from Cologne to the army.[4]

Together with Marlborough Stepney attended a conference of all ministers concerned in the Grand Alliance, at which the peace proposals put forward by Max Emmanuel were rejected. Then, on 26 November the Duke left Holland, Stepney attending him as far as the Brill. He had been warned to be ready to go again to Brussels, and hence recommended to Harley that the efficient English secretary at the Hague, Jacques Dayrolle, should be continued in employment and given an allowance. Dayrolle duly received, in January 1707, an increase in his allowance to 40s. per day.

In northern Europe Charles XII of Sweden had made peace (on conditions) with Stepney's friend Augustus of Saxony. The news reached Stepney via John Wyche in Hamburg, and was quickly transmitted to London. The speedy transit time of mail between the Hague and Whitehall may have been agreeable to one used to the month's delay in replies to letters from Vienna. Stepney's dispatch to Harley dated 23 November (n.s.) 1706 was answered three days later, and Stepney in turn acknowledged the reply on 3 December. To Marlborough, again at St. James', Stepney wrote about the Dutch hopes and fears about their Barrier, and in

December recommended to the Duke that he should yield to the Dutch desire for possession of the towns of Ostende and Dendermonde. But he reported that he had warned Heinsius (as had the Duke) that the Dutch should be moderate in their attitude towards the Spanish province, so that the people should not consider themselves treated as a conquered country.

At the end of the year Stepney's plan to revisit Brussels had to be postponed: no Dutch Deputies could be found to undertake this joint mission because the allowance of 27 Guilders a day was too little. And, of more significance, was news which had reached the States General that the Landgrave of Hesse might withdraw his troops from Italy. Since the Allies had decided to continue the war, the winter negotiations for the next season's troops were of the utmost importance. The Landgrave had been under contract for some years to supply troops. But their condition in Italy was lamentable; the Dutch were in arrears with subsidy; and no move had been made to hand over to Charles of Hesse the fortress of Rheinfels, which he dearly wished to possess. George Stepney was well known to this prince – and who was better qualified to conclude a satisfactory treaty? At the turn of the year a letter from Cardonnel in Whitehall foreshadowed the last winter journey which George Stepney was destined to make.[5]

Rather naturally, Stepney was not enthusiastic about going to Cassel. But the task was managed above his head, in correspondence between Marlborough and Heinsius, because he was to act for the States General as well as for the Queen. At one point Stepney had hopes of avoiding the unpleasant travel because two emissaries from the Landgrave arrived in the Hague and there seemed to be no reason why negotiations could not be carried out in that comfortable city. But the Hessians denied having brought with them any instructions to treat, and so, reluctantly, on 30 January (n.s.) 1707, Stepney began his journey, on the first evening travelling as far as Utrecht.[6]

On 5 February he reached Cassel and was greeted by the Marshal of the Court, Baron [Frederick] Kettler, who offered him the same courtesy – an apartment in the Palace – as he had done nine years previously when Stepney made his first visit. George desired to be excused, but he was immediately conducted to the Landgrave, presented his letters of credence, and stayed with His Highness until late in the evening. The two men discussed the situation of the Hessian troops in Italy, Stepney advancing the arguments for their retention in that country. The Landgrave wished to see an attack made into Burgundy via Hunningen. [This proposal was consequent on the recent death of Prince Louis of Baden, hitherto the imperial commander on the Rhine.] It was not difficult for George to counter the suggestion by saying that any military operations must be concerted with Prince Louis' successor, who had not yet been named. Kettler and another official were nominated by the Landgrave to arrange with Stepney the practical details of any new agreement for troops. They called on him on 7 February, but had nothing substantial to offer. Stepney asked them to submit their proposals in writing.

Couriers passed from the Hague to Cassel and back. Stepney understood that the Dutch had vetoed the idea of a march through Hunningen. And the Landgrave continued daily to receive complaints from his generals and officers in Italy. Prospects for a treaty appeared very bleak.[7]

To Dayrolle, but to no-one else, Stepney admitted he was ill. The Secretary in the Hague received on 10 February, Stepney's packet of mail written on the 7th. He forwarded the official report to Heinsius, and was busy making copies of items for Cardonnel. Dayrolle had social news to impart to his chief. The society ladies in the Hague were upset that Stepney [still a bachelor] had absented himself from a ball which had been given the previous Tuesday by the Prussian Envoy, Monsieur Schmettau, and which had continued until dawn. The assembly would meet once a week in various houses, and would undoubtedly reach Stepney's residence before long, particularly because the ladies would not forgive him for being absent on the anniversary of the Queen's birthday [6/13 February].

Dayrolle had still more domestic news. It appears that Stepney shared a house in the Hague with the Russian Ambassador – a man named Artemonitz – who was also accredited to Queen Anne. During George's absence in Cassel Madame Artemonitz introduced to Dayrolle a certain Mrs Northwick, who had a house to let and wanted Stepney to take it at Fl. 3,000. Dayrolle objected that this price was too high, but he discovered that the Hanoverian Envoy, Bothmar, was also interested in leasing the house. Dayrolle, however, did not think that Bothmar would offer as much as Stepney. The secretary kindly sent on to George his private mail, so that he could amuse himself on the return journey by reading his sisters' letters and the prints; he would have less to deal with on his return. He reported some defects in the Stepney household: beds and the roasting-jack [*tournebroche*] were missing, unless they had arrived with items sent from England.[8]

Stepney was unsuccessful in his mission, despite the last-minute arrival of instructions from Harley, that he could negotiate for Hessian troops for a six-month period only, until November 1707, if that would make the Landgrave's compliance easier. Stepney reported that agreement had been reached for that period, for a force of five battalions, a regiment of horse and one of dragoons who were to stay in Italy. But he had not been able to get a man more, and His Highness stuck to his resolution to command his remaining forces to begin their march out of Italy on 10 March. Any further negotiations were to take place in the Hague with the Hessian ministers there. George wrote his report on 14 February from a castle at Neuhaus, near Paderborn, which belonged to the Bishop. The Bishop had offered hospitality at other places in his territory, which was on the direct road from the Hague to Cassel. On Stepney's outward journey the Bishop had been at his devotions three miles away, but now

> he has lay'd hold of me and I am oblig'd to stay Supper with him after wch I intend to proceed on my journey, that the imperial ministers (whom I shall likewise call on at Münster) may not censure me for too great partiality.[9]

Ill or no, Stepney reached the Hague on 20 February and had an interview with Heinsius the following day. The States General were not satisfied with the Landgrave's declaration, and a few days later despatched to him Stepney's former colleague, Count Rechteren, who had abandoned the mediation in Hungary about the same time that Stepney was recalled. Stepney emphasised to the Dutch the necessity of regulating their payments to the Landgrave and to his officers, before any positive decisions were likely to be taken in Cassel.

Then, on 1 March, Stepney heard that the Dutch Deputies appointed to the 'Conference' to supervise the Spanish Netherlands were due to leave within 10 or 12 days, and so he prepared to accompany them. Meanwhile Marlborough, still in England, wrote to him that in conjunction with the States General he (Stepney) was to treat with the Saxon minister in the Hague for foot-soldiers, for which the Queen had allocated £50,000. The negotiation was to be hastened, and was left entirely to Stepney's prudent management.[10]

On 15 March he had a meeting with some Deputies of the States General and with the minister from the Landgrave of Hesse, to examine the convention which Rechteren had signed in Cassel for the Hessian troops which were to remain in Italy. The Landgrave's minister demanded money, including the payment of debts incurred during the previous war. A long discussion ensued; but Stepney was convinced that the Dutch could be relied on to make the hardest possible bargain with the Hessians, and therefore he was prepared to sign any convention, if the Duke of Marlborough himself did not arrive in Holland in time to do so. As soon as the conference was over, another started with the Saxon Envoy and an emissary from King Augustus, who had arrived in the Hague with a letter offering the Queen and the States General a body of 6,000 Saxon troops. There was no time for a copy to be made, so Stepney begged Harley to pass the document on to Marlborough. The same afternoon he left for Brussels via Rotterdam, where a yacht had been put at his disposal by the States General. His secretary, John Laws, described the journey in a letter to Erasmus Lewis:

> On the 16th [March] in the evening Mr. Stepney and Baron de Renswoude [one of the Dutch Commissioners] sail'd from Rotterdam, and on the 18th in the morning the former arrived at Antwerp; where the day following, being the Anniversary of Her Majesty's happy Accession to the Crown He celebrated the same (as well as he cou'd, on board) and when the Canon [*sic*] were fir'd from the Yacht they were answered by those on the Castle, Town and Cittadell, and by 3 Salvoes of the Garrison, the Governor Marquis de Tarracena and the Magistrates being very desirous on that occasion to distinguish their Zeal for Her Majesty's Person and Government. In the evening He continued his Voyage and arriv'd here [Brussels] yesterday [20 March] in the afternoon where he was received with more ceremony than was expected, Count Tilly the Governor having order'd the Canons round the town to be thrice discharg'd upon the approach of the Yacht, and in the evening He receiv'd the visits and compliments from the chief Nobility in Town.[11]

From Antwerp Stepney took time to write to his friend Lord Lexington:

> My dear Lord,
>
> I rec^d the hon^r of a letter from yr Lp some few days before I left Vienna, & since my removall to these parts I have been tumbled & toss'd from Pillar to Post as if I were still Her Mat$^{y's}$ Itinerant Minister, being no sooner return'd from Cassell, than I am commanded to Brussells, where a Creature of the opera must make me amends for all fatigues; This I mention to retort upon yr Lp wt you tell me of yr having so much money, a good Cook & excellent Wine, for in these Countries wee have no reason to complain; & I fancy if you cou'd find means to defrawd the Customs, a little Champagne & Burgundy wou'd not come amisse to yr Lp, If I can serve yr Lp either yt way or any other, either in ye Dutch or

Spanish Netherlands (for I am divided between two stations) you will be pleas'd to command me.

One successful Campagne more will I believe be attended by an happy hon^{ble} & lasting Peace – when I hope to sett up my Rest upon some pleasing seat upon ye Thames, & being sometime so happy as to receive yr Lp there, wch is ye ultimate end of ye felicity I propose to myself.[12]

The Envoy's hattering life was not over: he had not been in Brussels more than two-and-a-half weeks when a letter arrived from Cardonnel telling him to return to the Hague at once to greet Marlborough. During this brief spring visit to the capital of Brabant Stepney made no report on the Spanish Netherlands, but signed the treaty with the Landgrave, wrote to Sunderland to congratulate him for his part in the Anglo-Scottish Union, to Harley about the affairs of northern Europe and to Addison about Lord Halifax's intention of forming an assembly of '*beaux esprits*': remarking that

the difficulty will be to regulate ye Company, for every man will fancy he has a right to appear there.

On 9 April, in the evening, he was back in the Hague. Marlborough had not arrived, having been delayed by contrary winds. Stepney wrote that he had kept quiet:

being willing to expect my Lord Duke's superior direction.

One suspects that the brief interlude of inactivity may have been more than welcome to a sick man.[13]

Marlborough arrived in Holland on Sunday 17 April (n.s.), and stayed overnight at the Brill, reaching the Hague during the afternoon of the 18th. He saw Stepney, and expressed satisfaction at the latter's handling of affairs; but he was hastening on to Saxony, by way of Hanover, to make sure that the promised troops would materialize, and to do his best to avert a Northern war. Charles XII of Sweden, his puppet King of Poland, Stanislaus, together with the ex-King of Poland – Stepney's friend Augustus – were all together at Leipzig. Augustus was of course still Elector of Saxony, and as such was still powerful in Eastern Europe. Stepney accompanied the Duke as far as Utrecht and then returned to the Hague, to sign the treaty agreed with the Saxon Envoy about that troop contingent. By 10 May Marlborough had returned to the Hague, in time to learn of the defeat inflicted on the allied forces at Alamanza in Spain, which presaged the eclipse of the Habsburg power in that country. Stepney was busy chivvying the Dutch authorities to provide their marine quota – the number of ships which would support the allied war effort during the summer – when Marlborough commanded his presence forthwith on another journey to Brabant.[14]

The Duke and the Envoy both reached Brussels on 13 May. Stepney had had time at Antwerp to confirm to Sunderland the French reports of their victory. Gloomily he commented that the only footing which the Allies could hope to keep in Spain would be at Barcelona and Gibraltar. Another mail had arrived from England, causing Stepney to reply to Harley:

> I should gladly have serv'd Sir Philip Meadows at the Hague if he had found me there and given him the best information I could of the Court of Vienna tho' in nine months that I have left that Court their Maxims seem to be much chang'd from what they were. Nor can I distinguish at this distance who are cheifly concern'd in the Direction. But by appearances one may be allowed to suspect their Influence is not very propitious for 'tis pretty plain their menagement makes the warr move heavily in all parts.

Stepney's successor at Vienna [Sir Philip Meadows the younger – d. 1757] had arrived in the Hague about 24 May (n.s.), to find he had missed both Duke and Envoy. He wrote to the latter, but complained of having received no reply. This he tactfully ascribed to the activity of 'impudent parties' between Antwerp and Brussels, and proposed in future to use the reliable M. Clignet of Leyden to forward the mail.[15]

The Envoy was following the Duke to war. On 26 May he wrote:

> While I was at the Camp a fire broke out at Lembeck [22 km south of Brussels] where the Duke of Marlborough had his quarters. In an hour and half it had destroyed about 50 houses and a Church. My Lord Duke's house (belonging to the Princesse of Steinhouse [sic]) was sav'd and all the Horses, but some of Our Friends have suffer'd in several parts of their Equipage.[16]

In mid-June Stepney, back in Brussels, announced that he had no news for Harley or Sunderland because his time was taken up with the government of the Spanish Netherlands.

During the previous winter English attempts to ameliorate the harsh Dutch attitude to the conquered provinces had been partially successful. On 6 October 1706, the Council of State, acting on the instructions of the Allies, had issued a decree regulating the amount of subsidy to be contributed by the province of Flanders, and accusing the local authorities of misappropriation of funds and maladministration. The Estates of Flanders reacted vigorously. They sent a delegation to the Hague which claimed that the misery of the people was entirely the result of the war and of the exclusion of any Fleming on the Council of State. The States General, prompted no doubt by Marlborough and by Stepney, realised their unwisdom in creating disaffection in the heavily populated Flanders. On 31 January 1707 they wrote to the Council of State that the decree about the subsidy should be suspended and the complaints of the province investigated. Stepney, they added, was in agreement. In fact, the decree was never reactivated, and a Flemish nobleman was appointed to the Council of State.

Now, in the summer of 1707, the Conference instructed the Council to publish a decree forbidding the negotiation of bills of exchange drawn on France. The Council made difficulties, which caused the States General to explode in wrath, and to inform the Council that it had no power to put obstacles in the way of resolutions taken by the Allies. The Council obeyed, and drew up a decree in the name of King Charles III, dated 3 August 1707.[17]

Similarly, Stepney during his last weeks in Brussels wrote to his friend Harry Watkins, who was then temporarily acting as Marlborough's secretary:

Sir,   Bruxelles, 14 June 1707
                                            at noon -

I'me sorry to find by yr letter to Mr. Lawes that our friend Mr. Cardonnell is gone off indisposed to Malines; yr letter to Mr. Seule is sent after him; & in a day I'le visit Mr. Cardonnell.

During his absence you'le allow me to direct to you wt I have to represent to his grace; . . . .

I see by Mr. Geldermalsen's letters to Mr. van den Berg that his grace had promis'd I shoud joyn with my colleagues here in solliciting that all provisions design'd for ye Army may pass free & without paying any duties: Perhaps that was his grace's intention, but it has not yet been signifyed to me: However from wt I have seen of Mr. Geldermalsen's letter, I shall act in conformity with ye Deputies; tho' ye Council of State much oppose that franchise, since thereby ye King's Revenue will suffer great diminution.

I am ever,
Sir,
yr most humble
& faithfull sert

G. STEPNEY[18]

Adverse comments on George Stepney are to be found in the memoirs of Field Marshal the Count of Mérode-Westerloo (1674-1732) which were published in 1840 by his great-great-grandson. Westerloo came of an ancient family, was a soldier of fortune and in the course of a respectable military career changed his allegiance regularly to whichever monarch provided the best opportunities to a man convinced of his own excellence and high station in life. At Blenheim he fought against the Allies, but by Ramillies he was on their side. The Duke of Marlborough thought him worth cultivating, and would have liked to see him a member of the Council of State, but Westerloo refused the appointment because it was not sanctioned by his then superior, King Charles III of Spain. He was unsparing in his criticism of the Allied appointments to the Council of State and of the arrangements for the government of his country:

> Stepney, grand Tory,[!] revenant de sa mission de Vienne, étoit le premier ministre de la part d'Angleterre, et placé par le duc de Marlborough dans ce qu'ils appelèrent la Conférence. Il voulut en faire grand bruit, mais je le fis taire; il alla bientôt mourir en Angleterre, et laissa à sa place son valet de chambre, garcon d'esprit, que le duc de Marlborough y maintint longtemps; à la fin cet homme partit riche, et d'autres vinrent s'engraisser à nos depens.[19]

Obviously, the Count's knowledge of English politics was deficient. But his second sentence, that the Envoy wished to make an impression but that he, Westerloo, had silenced him, may well be true, and is discussed below. Stepney did not, of course, leave his valet to succeed him: John Laws was his competent secretary; but whether he or his successors – among them Cadogan – enriched themselves by their appointments is a matter beyond the scope of this volume.

Stepney's own comments on Westerloo have not survived. But from Marlborough's letters, both to the Count himself and to Stepney, it appears that the two men did not get on well with each other. Indeed, Westerloo may have assumed, in Stepney's eyes, the rôle of another Wratislaw.

The trouble started in March 1707 when Marlborough (then in London) assured the Count that Stepney and the Deputies of State had been instructed to assist him in obtaining from the Council of State the money necessary to put his regiment of cavalry and one of dragoons into a state of service. As soon as Marlborough was settled at his camp at Meldert [23 km west of Brussels] he wrote to Westerloo again on 7 June:

> je suis marri en même temps de ce que vous vous en prenez si fort à M. Stepney, qui n'y a eu presque autre part que de vous remettre ma lettre. . . . Aussi j'ose vous assurer que quand vous connaîtrez mieux M. Stepney, vous trouverez qu'il n'est pas homme à vouloir jamais troubler les cartes, mais tout le contraire.

Nevertheless Westerloo, obviously furious, sent a trumpeter to the Duke, who wrote to him again four days later in similar vein. But

Westerloo would not be placated, and so on 18 June the Duke wrote to the Envoy:

> Sir,
> I have this morning received another letter from the Marquis de Westerloo, which I send you here enclosed, as I shall continue to do all that I receive from him. I have returned him a civil answer, and doubt not but your prudence will incline you to consider he is a person to be treated with management in the present conjuncture.

This letter crossed with one to the Duke from Stepney, for on 19 June, Marlborough wrote again, assuring the Envoy he would always be welcome to visit the camp, but that he himself was the best judge whenever the service at Brussels would allow of his absence. If Stepney did not take up the invitation, the Count of Westerloo did, for on 22 June, the Duke told Stepney that Westerloo had been with him that afternoon, and that he had agreed to be more tractable and complaisant in future. Stepney was to help him as far as possible in his dealings with the Council. There the matter rested, until a month later Marlborough wrote to Westerloo, that members of the Council of State had complained about an affront, and added sharply that Westerloo was to put a stop to the affair, which was prejudicial to the interests of the King [of Spain]. The Count obeyed this good advice.[20]

During July Stepney spent two days at Marlborough's camp (returning to Brussels on 17 July). He remarked that there was no sign of any action. And he wanted to dissuade the Queen from writing again to the Emperor about the troubles in Hungary. The Austrian generals would not listen, and life would be made difficult for Meadows. The Dutch had urged the matter merely because they did not wish any action near their frontiers.

The States General had forbidden the transport of coin into France, and wished similar placarts displayed in the Spanish Netherlands. Stepney and the Dutch Deputy got the Council of State to agree. He was also able to inform Sunderland that, as the Secretary of State had directed, a 'little fleet' would shortly be equipped at Ostend, to guard the pacquet-boats:

> I have worked at it underhand, and believe I shall bring it to bear.

But time was running out, although Stepney could conclude a letter to Joseph Addison by acknowledging one received from Lord Halifax by the last post:

> and hope to answer it in 2 or 3 days, having found myself better this morning than I have been these six weeks.[21]

On 1 August (n.s.) 1707 Marlborough, then at the camp at Meldert, instructed Stepney to urge the Council of State to publish placarts forbidding the use of French *billets de monnaie* in the Spanish Netherlands. The Duke emphasised that this proclamation should be made on the same day that a similar prohibition was published in the United Provinces. If Stepney could not achieve this aim, he was to come over to the camp for further consultation with the Dutch colleagues.[22]

It is not known whether Stepney obeyed the Duke's order. In any case Marlborough moved his camp to Soignes, whence on 18 August Cadogan wrote to Lord Raby commenting on the abominable weather, wet and cold, and that most roads were impracticable.

On 19/30 August Dayrolle in the Hague reported to Harley: Since my last to you I have received the honour of your two letters of Aug 12/23 and 15/26 in answer to which I will tell you that as to Mr. Stepney's condition of health, he has been very ill for some time, his distemper being, as he supposed, an Ulcer between the Colon and intestinum rectum but is much better since by our advices and sollicitations, he has made use of the Vulneral herbs of Switzerland, having an instance here of Mons. d'Elbourg the Duke of Savoy's minister, who has formerly been cured of the same distemper with the s^d Vulnerals when no other remedy would do. By Mr. Stepney's last letters, he was able to go for England, and having received, I suppose by your means, Her Maties leave, was preparing for that voyage, staying only for the news of the arrival of the Henrietta yacht at Ostende, whither she is to come from Calais wth a ffrench pass procur'd off Mons. de Vendome.[23]

Dayrolle's information was correct. Marlborough had made a direct approach to the enemy commander for a pass for the yacht, which was duly granted. But the weather intervened, and no move could be made from Brussels by the sick man. On 30 August Stepney made his will, and a week later wrote a dignified and moving farewell to the Duke, the letter being in the hand of his secretary, John Laws, and only the signature being his own:

Brussels, 7th Septem^r
My Lord,
I am with the deepest Sense of Gratitude to return to Your Grace my most dutyfull Thanks for the Severall degrees of your Protection, wherewith you have been pleas'd to honour me; But most particularly for the generous Compassion which Your Grace has shewn me during my Indisposition, and having procur'd for me a quick and easy Passage to England, which is the only hopes I have of my Recovery for I am reduc'd to as low a State as is possible.

If I have the good fortune to be restor'd the remains of my

life shall be most zealously consecrated to Your Grace's Service, and shall chiefly owe it to your Goodness and I'le make the best diligence I can to return to my Station. In all events my most zealous wishes shall be employed till the last moment, That Your Grace may long enjoy the fruits of your many signal Victories, and have yet one glorious day, whereby the misfortunes of this Campaign in other parts of the world may be redress'd and forgotten.

I send this letter to Your Grace by Mr. Laws, my Secretary, whom I have employ'd with me here in Brussells ever since the opening of our Campaign, and chose to leave him here while I was absent at the Hague that he might have a perfect Insight of what was Transacting by my Colleagues: He has been very exact in the business, and has kept the Journal and Papers very well together; I therefore judge it for Her Majesty's Service , That he may be continued here during my absence, and allowed to frequent the Conferences to which Mr. Vanden Bergh has consented, and I now recommend him to Your Grace's Favour and Protection.

If Your Grace has any particular instructions for me in England, or any thing that Your Grace would have carefully convey'd thither, Your Grace may be pleas'd to lett me know it by the return of my Secretary to Ghend, where I shall be on Friday night, and wait Your Grace's commands.

Once more I begg God's Providence may protect your Lordship, and that you will be pleas'd to accept the most Sincere Assurances of my being with the greatest Duty and Veneration
My Lord
Your Grace's
Most humble and most
obedient Servant
G. STEPNEY[24]

The day following, Marlborough (at Helchin) acknowledged George's letter and apologised that he could not himself travel to Ghent to see him. But he sent Cardonnel, who returned with optimistic news from the physicians. Stepney was delayed again at Ostende by contrary winds, but finally left for England on 11 September (n.s.) 1707.[25]

XXV *England*
(September 1707)

From George Stepney's Will,
30 August 1707

Having observed in myself of late a very visible decay and having
reason to doubt that my Constitution may not be strong enough to
gett the better of my present indisposition . . . I recommend my
Spirit with the deepest Resignation to the mercy of its Creator
. . . . I choose to be interr'd in Westminster Abbey being the place
of my Educaton. . . .

I can reflect on certaine passages of my life with a sort of
Consolation and Assurance of my having serv'd my Souveraine
and Countrey with Reputation for which reason I think it my Duty
to the publick that some Enumeration may be made of my Services
which some of my Contemporaries at Westminster will be intreated
to doe with plainness and truth.[1]

Little is known of the last fortnight of George Stepney's life. To
revert to the English (i.e. old style) of dating, he left Ostend on 31
August 1707. Perhaps his yacht brought him up the Thames as far
as Westminster. The Latin inscription beneath the bust in
Westminster Abbey records that he died in Chelsea. This location
is narrowed by Thomas Faulkner, author of *An Historical &
Topographical Description of Chelsea and its Environs*, published
in 1829, who states that George resided for some time in Paradise
Row, and died there on 15 September 1707. The maximum duration
of his residence was only two weeks. There is no sign of George or
his sisters having taken a house in Chelsea: and certainly they did
not buy one. However, various acquaintances might have offered
hospitality to a sick man, whose overwhelming desire was for fresh
air. A Mr Jermyn Wyche was a rate-payer in Paradise Row, and a
little further away from the river were Madame Aglionby and Mrs
Powis. Mr Lowndes was at the Gate House; Lord Carbery (from
Wales) at the imposing Gough House. This last building was three
storeys high and commanded beautiful gardens leading towards
the river. One may imagine George enjoying the sweet Thames

running softly during his last days.[2]

His will had already been prepared. To his two sisters, Frances and Dorothy, he left his whole estate, apart from specific bequests to his friends. Lord Halifax was to choose from George's books 'a hundred Tomes if there be any which may deserve to have place in his Library.' And Charles was left, as well, a golden goblet which had been a present from the Landgrave of Hesse. Adam de Cardonnel acquired the 'gilt Bason and Ewer' which had been George's trophy for receiving the Principality of Mindelheim on Marlborough's behalf. A monteith and five decanters went to Harry Watkins, and George had no doubt but that this friend would make good use of them. Matt Prior was not required to repay the 50 guineas he had borrowed; Uncle Bernard was forgiven, similarly, £100. Erasmus Lewis 'my deare Cozen' was left £100 (and a recommendation was made to the sisters that they should remember this nearest Stepney relative when they should come to consider their own wills).

The God-daughter, Mrs. Ann Baker, was left £100. 'My honoured Uncle Captain James Partridge' received £50. George felt that he had already furthered Charles Whitworth's career, but as a pledge of friendship he left him the small diamond ring which he ordinarily wore.

Finally:

I have been removed soe suddenly from one forrayne Commission to another that I have not had Leisure to digest my Letters and Transactions into any tolerable order or Consistency for which reason I desire my Writings of all sorts may be consigned into the hands of Mr. Lewis and that none of them may be made publick who is desired to dispose of any particular Letters he shall find relating to any of my owne private or Domestick Affaires since the constant distraction I have beene [in] has not allowed me to take that precaution myself.

Regrettably, to the twentieth-century mind, Erasmus Lewis carried out his task only too well.

In accordance with his wishes, the body of George Stepney was laid to rest in Westminster Abbey in the night of Monday-Tuesday, 22-23 September 1707, in great state. It is recorded that the pall was carried by two Dukes, two Earls and two Barons. No names are mentioned. The Dukes perhaps were Montagu and Buckingham; the Earls (one hopes) Halifax and (probably) Westmorland. It is not possible to hazard a guess at the Barons.[3]

Officially, his passing was regretted. Marlborough, at Helchin, heartily condoled with Harley on the loss of poor Mr Stepney.

Heinsius, at the Hague (before Stepney died) was '*bien faché que Mr. Stepney n'y pourra pas travailler.*' Addison remarked to Christian Cole:

> I need not tell you how much he [Stepney] is lamented here.

And the same sentiments were expressed by Isaac d'Alais, the Embassy secretary in Hanover, writing to Lewis. Missing are any more personal expressions of grief – a fact which would have caused no disquiet to George's spirit; for he had remarked, apropos of the death of young Porter in 1706, that

> everybody has his time allotted, and there is no need of any more melancholy Reflexions on that subject.[4]

At the beginning of November 1707 a detailed inventory (in French) was made of the belongings which Stepney had left in the Hague. The list indicates the size of the house, which probably had been taken over from Alexander Stanhope, because nine armchairs belonging to that diplomat were still in place. The ground-floor consisted of two reception rooms, to the left and right of the front door; an antichamber, a cabinet and two small rooms at the back. There were about six rooms on the first floor, including one which was occupied by Heyman, and one in which Watkins had left various possessions. Stepney's furnishings were carefully enumerated, and in the margin it was noted that 'the rest' belonged to the Ambassador of Moscow.

Stepney's own possessions were very modest, as the first entry illustrates:

> *Dans la chambre gauche en entrant*
> *Il y a une Tapisserie d'un espece de Satin rayé*
> *4 tables, 1 grille avec un petit Ecran,*
> *un tapit de table de cuire*
> *12 chaises de paille et ii Cuissans,*
> *et 14 jalousies de Gaze devant les fenestres.*

The tapestries are of interest, because Lamberty alleged that Marlborough had placed in Stepney's house valuable hangings of gilded leather, each containing in its centre a painting attributed to Titian. The Duke is said to have taken them to England after Stepney's death. There is no reference to these pieces in the inventory. Indeed, the remark set down after the remnants of satin tapestry found on the first floor states merely that it was worn. [*qui a servi*].

Among the various items were found a case containing two flutes – it is not known when Stepney last practised on these instruments – and a box containing a cup, spoon, knife and fork all of silver-gilt [*vermeil doré*]. This, remarked the inventor, was believed to belong to Mr. Heyman. Knowing the bad reputation of that gentleman in the mind of Stepney's former steward, James Fury, one might suspect that Heyman had taken possession quickly of an attractive travelling-set belonging to his deceased chief. For nearly everything else was marked as old, used or worn out.

Not so in the stables: here were six carriage horses, one Arab horse and one servant's horse; together with eight harnesses including bridles and three saddles. Also a bed for the coachman and '*Un Carosse coupé très propre*'.

The Arab horse was presumably the one presented to Stepney by Sir Robert Sutton. On 2 October (o.s.) 1707, Erasmus Lewis wrote to Harley:

> I acquaint Lord Treasurer by this post that Mrs. Stepney desires him to accept of a beautiful Arabian horse their [*sic*] brother left at the Hague.

Lord Godolphin was a founder-breeder of English bloodstock. It is to be hoped that Stepney's horse contributed to his stud.[5]

Jacques Dayrolle took possession, for safe-keeping, of the silver-chest, and of the wine, of which the cellar contained a considerable amount.

When Stepney died he was owed by the Treasury some £7,000. His sisters, who were joint executrices of the will, found that to extract money from the Treasury was not easy. In February 1708 money warrants were issued to the executors of George Stepney for £779 10s. in respect of 'extrys' dating back to 1706-7; together with £477 7s. 11 $\frac{1}{4}$d. which was outstanding on his salary of £1,000 *per annum* as Commissioner of Trade.

In August 1708 a warrant was ordered under Royal Sign Manual for £1,890 4s. 2d.

> to the executors of George Stepney, late Envoy Extraordinary & Plenipotentiary to the Emperor of Germany, for so much expended by him in that service pursuant to Her Majesty's commands more than has yet been paid or allowed him in any bills of extraordinaries: the Queen being well satisfied upon perusal of the particulars that the same was laid out & disbursed by her directions & having also a due regard to the merit & faithful services of the said Stepney in his several negotiations during the said employ.

But despite the laudatory remarks above, two weeks later one J. Taylour, in the absence of William Lowndes [Secretary to the Treasury] wrote to the Auditor of Receipt that the money warrant quoted above was to be satisfied out of loans to be made by Stepney's executors on the sale of tin; and that the repayment money orders for which loans were to be drawn without interest and to remain in the Auditor's office until they came up 'in course' for repayment. All of which manipulation would not have surprised George Stepney, had he still been alive, in the least.

The Stepney ladies were by no means helpless in dealing with money matters, as a letter from Frances to Marlborough illustrates:
Feb 14th [annotated in pencil as 1711]

My Lord,
The person who was my Brothers Steward being ordered to bring over hither most of the furniture, and other things, that were found in his House, acquainted me that He had by your Grace's express command carried back from the ship, and delivered into your Grace's celler [sic] at the Hague, an hundred and eight bottles of Tokch [i.e. Tokay] wine which He told me your Grace was pleased to say you would pay for. Haveing heard nothing from your Grace since that hapned tho it is now above three years agoe, I beg leave to remind your Grace it was valued at a Guinea a bottle besides the carriage to the ship, and back again, which I desire your Grace to consider of and remit the Mony
To your Grace's
Most humble servant
FRANCES STEPNEY[6]

Frances died in 1718, aged 61. Her sister Dorothy at some time moved away from Whitehall and settled in Lisle Street, Soho. At the time of her death, in 1724, her household included a maid-servant, cook, footman and coachman. She left numerous bequests to cousins, including Erasmus Lewis, who had borrowed heavily both from her and from his younger brothers and sister. Dorothy left strict instructions that his promissary-note to repay the debt should not be returned to him until he had settled in full with his siblings. And she left a small legacy to a cleaning-woman who was to look after the grave of her brother in Westminster Abbey.

But the most notable feature of Dorothy's will is the fact that her residuary legatee – in the amount of £8,000 – was a Mrs. Charlotte Whetstone, who at the time of Dorothy's death was living with her. Nothing is known about Charlotte, and since the appellation 'Mrs' was given in the eighteenth century both to married and to unmarried women it cannot be established whether she was born a Whetstone or married into that family.

The Whetstones of Woodstock, Essex (where grandfather Sir Thomas Stepney had found his bride) disappeared from county records during the seventeenth century. A Rear-Admiral [William] Whetston in April 1704 commanded the convoy which protected the Duke of Marlborough when he travelled from Harwich to Holland, but there is no evidence which connects the Admiral with Charlotte. Nevertheless Dorothy Stepney returned to a Whetstone a small fortune, the result of the industry and labour of the grandchildren of a Stepney younger son.[7]

On 6 November 1724, Sir Erasmus Philipps [5th Baronet, d. 1743] noted in his diary:

Was a Bearer at the Funeral of Cosin Dorothy Stepney, sister to the famous George Stepney Esq. . . . Mr. Francis Whitworth (brother to Lord W) was Chief Mourner and She was buried from her House in Lisle Street in West^r Abbey & laid in the same Grave with her Sister & Brother. This was a very handsome Funeral.[8]

XXVI *Epilogue*

Vir
Ob Ingenii acumen,
Literarum Scientiam,
Morum Suavitatem,
Rerum Usum
Virorum Amplissimorum Consuetudinem
Linguae, Styli, ac Vitae Elegantiam,
Praeclara Officia cum Britanniae tum
Europae praestita,
Sua aetate multum celebratus
Apud posteros semper celebrandus;
Plurimus Legationes obiit
Ea fide, Diligentia ac Felicitate,
Ut Augustissimorum Principum
Gulielmi et Annae
Spem in illo repositam
Nunquam fefellerit,
Haud raro superaverit.
Post longum honorum Cursum
Brevi Temporis Spatio confectum
Cum Naturae parum, Famae satis vixerat
Animam ad altiora aspirantem placido efflavit.

A man who, for the sharpness of his intellect, knowledge, scholarship, sweetness of character and experience of affairs was intimate with men of the highest position, noted for the refinement of his language, style and life, who in his time was greatly celebrated for having performed remarkable service in Britain as in Europe, and who by posterity will always be honoured.

Eighteenth-century tombs were usually provided with effusive epitaphs. It is not known who composed George Stepney's, though according to Samuel Johnson, it was 'transcribed by Jacob.' How true do these phrases ring, after the passage of 300 years?

Sharpness of intellect, scholarship, knowledge of men and affairs were characteristics certainly evinced by Stepney during his career. To these may well be added a high sense of duty and punctuality in carrying out his orders. He was useful to his employers both for the very detailed dispatches which he provided as well as for his ability to reduce complicated documents to manageable length and to extract from them the nub of the matter, [cf. Chapter VI].

And Stepney was a squirrel, throwing no document or letter away. For example, he kept full details of his negotiations with the Saxon court 1693-1695, and included a treaty paper dated 1557. Other documents reveal the receipts and disbursements made by the court during the years 1686-1688, each member of the court being listed, including the Italian musicians. Similarly, a volume of his papers is devoted exclusively to the relations between Poland and Saxony between May 1701 and October 1702. The first paper sets out the starting-point, the 'Peace of Oliva', in Latin and French, dated 3 May 1660. No wonder that he was able to brief not only his own monarch but also foreign officials, as required, with facts and precedents.[1]

Sweetness of character was not always one of Stepney's attributes. He could be querulous. He was never averse to putting other people right, often with asperity. He bore grudges over long periods. His correspondence reflects a growing cynicism as his hopes of early promotion faded, and as his patron, Charles Montagu, fell from favour. However, his greatest professional defect was his extreme sensitivity about his personal popularity – or lack of it – at any court in which he served. Set against this failing must be placed the tenacity with which he held his own among contemporaries who were, for the most part, men of greater social standing and wealth than himself.

The epitaph mentions his intimacy with men of the highest position. This was true. Stepney possessed an unerring eye for the people who could help him in his diplomacy. He had, after all, begun as a schoolboy to cultivate the friendship of Charles Montagu. He enjoyed the esteem of his first chief, Sir Peter Wyche, and within two years of the start of his independent career in 1692 he had won the confidence of Eberhard Danckelmann in Berlin, of Borgomañero the Spanish Ambassador to Vienna, and also in that city of Count Kinsky. He had already found the favour of Sophia, Electress of Hanover, and her daughter the Electress of Brandenburg. His good standing with the former lady caused him to become the channel of communication with her on behalf of the Whigs, in the year 1700, to persuade her to accept her succession to the English crown.

Stepney's part in this delicate affair may well be claimed as a 'remarkable service' in Britain. It was not Stepney's only achievement. His rôle in negotiating for Hessian troops in November 1694 has already been described. Later in his life he was to find that the Duke of Marlborough – as had King William – was ready to toss over to him any thankless task which the great man found convenient to pass on. In 1704, it was to make excuses to the Emperor for liberties which the Duke had taken in concluding his treaty with the King of Prussia, in 1706, to take over the Principality of Mindelheim and in the winter of 1706/7, to seek once again from Hesse-Cassel the replenishment of troops.

Refinement of language, style and life: the truth of these words of the epitaph are borne out by the number of young Englishmen who were sent to Stepney to complete their education and to whom he accorded care and attention.

Stepney's poetry has been discussed in Chapter XXIII. His prose style deserves greater praise, for its lucidity and strength:

The Fact, my Lord, is evident: the injury notorious & ye consequences might be dangerous . . . .

These phrases from Stepney's letter to Trenchard of 9 March (n.s.) 1694, have already been quoted in Chapter VII. Here, the rhythm of the words may be noted. No doubt but that Trenchard, as Stepney intended, was jerked into consideration of the whole text.

In the main, Stepney did fulfil his many missions to the satisfaction both of King William and Queen Anne, and did not betray the trust placed in him. He failed in his efforts to achieve at least an armistice between the Hungarian Malcontents and the imperial army, and has been adjudged by most writers always to have been prejudiced in favour of the rebels. It is true that his part was warmly noted by Hengelmüller, the Hungarian historian, and that three volumes of Stepney's letters, translated into Hungarian, are to be found in the *Nationalbibliothek* in Vienna. His defence against the charge of prejudice is set out in this book. Sadly, the difficulties of mediation between intransigent adversaries in the Balkans have been made only too obvious to the twentieth-century reader.

Honoured by posterity . . . ? If Stepney has slipped from view during the twentieth century there are good reasons for a revival of interest in him. In some ways he was ahead of his time. He was critical of the social conditions which he found in central Europe, where excessive taxation was loaded on to those least able to bear it. His skepticism with regard to witchcraft is apparent from a letter to John Robinson in September 1694, that the Saxon court regarded him as little better than an atheist, 'for not entring into their Credulity

S. Cole Sculp.

of Witches.' This was written in the context of the trial of Frau
Neidschütz for witchcraft [cf. Chapter VIII].[2]

One other aspect of Stepney's philosophy may be viewed with
sympathy: although he lived and died a Protestant, he was never a
religious fanatic. He was critical of certain Patholic practices, in
particular the expensive and ostentatious rites observed by the
Imperial Court [cf. Chapter VI]. But he honoured true devotion
where he found it, as is evident from his comment on a Capucin
monk who was said to work miracles. Stepney said he was not
competent to judge such matters, but

> they say he is an honest good man, and in this world that is
> sufficient.[3]

The epitaph reflects on the short space of time accorded to Stepney
in this world. His spirit passed peacefully away. In the Latin, of
which he was such a master:

> Requiescat in pace.

Appendix I

(Verso)
Pet[n] of George Stepney
for a fellowship from Trinity Coll.

(Recto)
To the King's most Excellent Ma[tie]
The humble Peticon of George Stepney
Sheweth

That yo[r] Pet[r] hath been Student in Trinity College near Six Yeares, being Elected thither from Westm[r] : and is at present imployed by Sir Peter Wych at Hamburgh in Yo[r] Ma[ts] Service by the Colledges Consent : And that according to the Custome of the said Colledge Yo[r] : Pet[r] : hath a Right by his standing and a Certaine expectation of being elected.

  Therefore and in Consideracon that Yo[r] Pet[rs] : ffather and Grandffather S[r] Thomas Stepney and George Stepney were Servants to Yo[r] : Maj[ts] Royall Grandfather, ffather and Brother of blessed memory, and allwayes Loyall and dutifull, Yo[r] : Pet[r]: doth humbly pray that Yo[r]: Maj:[tie] will be graciously pleased to grant Yo[r]: Pet[r]:, Yo[r]: Maj:[ties] Letters to the said Colledge to elect him into the next ffelowship, according to his Standing and Seniority tho' he be absent, or into a ffelowship in Jesus Colledge now Vacant, by the death of Mr. Wakefield.

And Yo[r]: Pet[r]: shall ever pray, etc.

[BL: Add.MS.41804 (Middleton Papers) f.318]

Note: The above is the last paper in the volume. It is unsigned. There is no indication of what happened to it, nor how it came to be included in the Middleton Collection, except that Lord Middleton was Secretary of State in 1687. There is a faint pencilled note: 'In Hamburg papers.'

Appendix II

James II's Mandate to Trinity College, Cambridge, to admit George Stepney as a Fellow:

> George Stepney to be
> Fellow of Trinity Colledge
> Cambridge

> Trusty & well beloved etc.
> Whereas George Stepney hath by his petition informed Us that he hath been Student in yt your Colledge near six years, whither he was chosen from Our Royall Schoole of Westminster, and is thereby Scholar of the foundation of your House, and soe aptly qualified to be Fellow, besides his parts and endowments of Learning, which have rendered him moreso; as Wee have had very good information; And whereas the said George Stepney is now, as he hath been some time employed in fforeigne partes for Our service, Wee cannot thinke it reasonable, that his absence from yt our Colledge upon such an occasion should be any way prejuciall to him; Wee have therefore thought fitt to signify Our pleasure unto you in his favour hereby requiring you that upon receipt of these Our Royal Letters Mandatory you meete together, and Elect him ye said George Stepney a Fellow of yt Our Colledge, to be admitted when present, and to Enjoy all proffits, priviledges, benefits and advantages, belonging to such Fellowship next aftersuch as have already obtained Our former Letters to the like purpose;any Statute, Custome or usage of our said Colledge to the contrary notwithstanding with wch Wee are graciously pleased to dispence in this behalfe; For ye doeing whereof this shall be your Warrant,
> Given at Our Court at Windsor the 17th day of July 1687.

> Our Trusty and
> welbeloved Master and
> Senior Fellowes
> Trinity Colledge in Our University
> of Cambridge.

[PRO: SP105/82 - Original Letters to George Stepney - f.7]

Appendix III

Epigramme sur la Cess[at]ion que le Roy de France
veut faire des Pays bas [à] S A E de Baviere
[*by George Stepney*]

Subdolus excelsi Satanas de vertice montis
Ostendens Christo, quas habet orbis, opes,
'Inflexo, dixit, tangas modo poplite terram
'Atq[ue] haec obseqüy praemia, Cultor, habe.
Haud minus insano Ludovicus percitus oestro,
Nunc jactat Bavaro talia verba Duci,

'Jus atq[ue] Imperium, genibus minor, Accipe Nostrum
'Et quocunq[ue] patet Flandria, tota Tun [sic – ?Tuum] est.

Quam bene conveniunt? hic sanguine gaudet et irâ,
Immitiq[ue] Suos sub Ditione premit:
Humani generis Satanas est perfidus osor
Ut pote cui placeant flamma, flagella, rota.

Luciferum mala praecipitem detrusit abttato [sic – ?attracto]
Ambitio, Hac eadem te quoque, Galle, rapit.
Nec tanto fracta est inferna superbia lapsu;
Neve animum imminuit prona ruina Tuum:

Ambos persequitur dominandi caeca Libido:
Offertis quod non Ipse, nec alter, habes,
Artifices estis, similes; Hoc discrepat unum
Insidias struxit cautiùs ille suas
Obtulit Imperium cui (dum Deserta peragret)
Torpebant longâ languida membra fame:
Tu contra, Terras, (licet Ipse famelicus) offers,
Dum satiat Belgas luxuriosa Ceres.

Credatur merito sua nunc Audacia Gallis;
Fronte Ipsum superant Doemona [sic – ?Daemonia] Vasconicâ.

[PRO: SP81/87 (German States 1693-97) f.59. Undated, but placed at January (n.s.) 1694. The English rendering is at f.58, also undated.] George Stepney's English version of the preceding Latin epigram:

Upon ye French king's off'ring to give up
ye Spanish Netherlands in favour of ye Elr
of Bavaria

Upon the Desert Mountains airy head
Where tempting Satan the Messiah led
'Thy knee (said he) with Reverence incline
'And all this spacious Empire shall be thine

By this example, & an heart as vain
The Gallick king wou'd now Bavaria gain
And Courts him in a like Romantick strain

'The Universall Monarchy be mine
'And I the Spanish Netherlands resign.

By these two parallels wee plainly see
How well both Tempters, & their Bribes agree:
Rapine and Blood this Tyrants soul possess,
And thoughts his slavish people to oppress:
Man to torment, is Satan's sole desire
He revells in ye midst of Groans & Fire.

Drag'd by ambition the Curst Angell fell
Down to ye Regions of ye lowest Hell.
Such, Louis, is thy sin; & such ye Fate
Wch threatens Thee, & thy declining State.
Nor Satans Pride is lessned by his end;
Nor thine, by pregnant judgments wch impen'd.
Both, your old hearts, in Misery retain
And in your lowest Ebb affect to Reign.
Dispose of Provinces, present a Throne,
& Bribe with large Possessions, not your own.

Both the same ends by the like means pursue;
Yet Satans were ye Wiser of the Two:
In a sad Desert his Intrigues he layd,
For one, whose heart (he thought) by Want decayd:
Lewis (himself by sickening Dearth opprest)
Dares tempt a Prince with Joy & Plenty blest.

Thus, tho ye Fiends in Craft the French excell
A Gascon is more Impudent than Hell.

[The last two lines are corrected in Stepney's own hand:]

In craft the Fiends may farre the French excell
But Gascons are more Impudent than Hell.

Appendix IV

Johann Graf von Clary und Aldringen to the Emperor Leopold I (undated, but annotated as 1694, March):

Aller durchleuchster Kaÿser Erb König Undt Herr Allergnädigster Herr Herr:
Euer Königsterliche Maÿst gerühen nicht Ungnädig zu vermercken da? eine unterstehe deroselben hiebeyliegenden imediate ad Augustissimas Manus in allertiefester submission zu übersenden, welches mir mit meiner Postberichten zuhanden komen, Und ich untherstehend in mainung, da? solches an mich seye, eröthert, Undt in dessen beÿlag sich etwan etwas zu dero wissenschaft dienliches finden möchte, alstrer zu mich die gegen E K M [Euer Kaiserliche Majestät] allerunterthänigste Devotion, Undt treugehorsambster Furster mich betrogen hat, Undt weile es eine etwas Anlossliche Schrift ist, als habe solches durch meinen ältisten Sohn abcopieren lassen, nicht wissendt, ob da? darinnen Unterstrichene recht Seÿe; anbey zu beherrliche Kaÿserliche Clementz mich allerunterthänigst empfehle Undt verbleibe ersterbe
E K M treygehorsammester Unterthäner
Johan Graf von Clary Undt Aldringen

(Enclosure to the above:)

a D[resde] ce 12/22 de Mars 94
Monsieur
Je vous suis fort sensible au billet que vous avez eu la bontè de m'écrire du 13/3 du courant, que Monsieur de Stepney me fit insinuer dans le moment de sa reception, mais Mr. de Holz-bringt etoit dejà parti, quatre jours passès, de sorte que suivant vos ordres ie [sic – je] vous renvoye sa lettre, quoique Mr. le Baron, et Chambellan de Rechenberg, où il etoit descendu à son arrivée dans cette ville – me l'ayt fait demander, pour la luy faire tenir. Je n'ay point receu le petit paquet avec le plan du Trou ou roo de Pescabare, et sa description, dont Mr. de Holzbringt s'est voulu Charger pour moy: et quoyque je n'aye pas l'honneur de le conaitre, et que ie je trouve allette depuis un mois, je n'en aurois pas manquè de trouver un amy, qui l'auroit été voir de ma part, le remercier come il faut de sa peine: s'il l'avoit donnè â un laquay,

où page dans la maison du Baron de Rechenberg, gendre de Mr.
le Feldt Marêchal, car ils me conoissent tous. Ce mr. de Holzbringt
donc m'en a pas trop bien usé avec vous, en se Chargeant du dit
paquet, et ne ne faisant pas delivrer: et pour cela ie vous supplie
Monsieur, de le luy faire redemander – pour me le faire tenir par
une voye plus secure; Car si il me l'avoit fait insinuer, il auroit
pu vous apporter le paquet des livres, que j'ay retirè enfin avec
tant de peine des grifes de ceux qui l'avoient voulu confisquer
avec quelques bibles luteriennes, dans le quel ballot un libraire
d'icy avoit mis ce paquet-là. Pour ce qu'est de la fème de Mr. le
Hofrath Willius, ie n'ay point entendu de ceux qui me viennent
voir, que S A Ele [sic – Son Altesse l'Electeur] luy ait donè la
permission de venir voir son mari dans sa detention; au Contraire
l'on dit, que ce Monsieur pourroit bien à la representation de
Messieurs du Conseil, obtenir sa libertè. L'on attend icy avec
impatience, quelle resolution le lieut. Zedlitz apportera de la Cour
Imperiale, au sujet de l'enlargissement de Mr. le General de
Schöning, Car Mgr l'Electeur semble prendre toutes les mesuresla
dessùs pour la Campagne prochaine. Les Notables des E^tats,
apres avoir accordè à S A Ele presque tout ce qu'on leur avoit
demander, de sorte que on n'en a pas usé avec eux, comme le Roy
votre Maitre dernierement avec ses Etats assembles à Stockholm.
Je vous fait un recit bien ample de le maison de Mr. Lemel dans
la lettre que j'ay jointe au paquet des livres, que ie vous feray
tenir par le premier Courier, qui Se rendra Chez vous; en attendant
je vous baise tres humblement les mains, étant avec beaucoup de
zele, et de verite
Monsieur
Votre tres obeissant et
tres acquis serviteur

(No signature.)

[HHStA Vienna: Reichshofkanzlei - Berichte aus Dresden l693-94
Fazikel 4b Bündel 3 (5l8/95) ff.1 and 2.

Note: These two letters have been copied word for word from the
originals. No attempt has been made to correct grammar or accents.

Appendix V

<u>The Treaty I made with Baron Goerz [Goertz] at the Hague</u>:

Comme Son Altesse le Landgrave de Hesse Cassell s'engage par la presente a entretenir contre l'ennemi commun tout le tems que cette guerre durera, comme Il a fait par le passe, un Corps de Trouppes au de La de celles qu'il est oblige de fournir de son Contingent a l'Empire, Sa Majeste le Roy de la Grande Bretagne, en consideration des services que sa dite Altesse rend au public par ce secours extraordinaire, et pour subvenir en partie aux frais que sa dite Altesse doit faire pour la Subsistance des dites Trouppes, promet aussi de son cote de payer ou faire toucher a sa dite Altesse par maniere de subsides, outre les payments qui ont ete deja faits, la somme de dix mille ecus ou vingt cinq mille florins par mois, a compter douze mois dans l'annee, qui commencera a premier jour de Janvier prochain, En foy de quoy nous, les Ministres de sa dite Majeste et de sa dite Altesse, etants suffisamment autorise et commis a cela de part et d'autre, avons signe cette convention, et fait apposer les sceaux de nos Armes.

Fait a la Haye le 4/14 Novembre l'an 1694

LS G. STEPNEY B. GOERTZ LS

<u>Note</u>: The text of this agreement appears twice in the Stepney papers:
(a) PRO: SP105/55 (Stepney's Letter Book 1694-5) f.54
(b) BL: Add.MS.46535 (Lexington Papers, Vol. XV) f.4
The wording of (a) above is a little fuller than that found in (b): hence (a) is the text used here. The seventeenth-century disregard for French accents is common to both versions.

Appendix VI

<u>George Stepney's travel, 23 February-27 May (n.s.) 1697</u>
(written in his own hand)

I left the Hague the 13/23 febr. 1697
and arrived at Dusseldorf   16.26 [Feb]
      at   Cologne   1 Mars   ns
           Newwitt [*sic*]   3 Mars
           Coblentz   4 "
           Wiesbaden   7 "
           Francfurt   <u>8 March</u>

26 Febr

I went to Mentz [Mainz]   7.17 March
returned to Francfurt   9.19 March
I went to Steinheim where ye
Elr of Mentz was a-hunting   22 March/1 April
returned to Francfurt   2 April ns
I went to meet ye Landgrave
at Swallbach   24 Aprill/4 may
Returned to Francfurt   26 April

I went from Francfurt to Marpurg   16/26 May
to Cassell the   17.27 "

from ye   Travelling charges
Decr 4   for my servants &
       goods from Hague to
       Dusseldorf   548 gd
12/22   From Dusseldorf to
febr   Francfurt   201 Rx [Reichsthaler]

My journey to Mentz-
back again   100 gulders
gave to Elrs Servants   100 gulders
My journey to Steinheim
& gave to Servants   20 gulders

[PRO: SP105/57 (Stepney's Letter Book 1697) ff.44-45 (undated).]

Appendix VII

June

		km
5	Vienna-Pressburg (early morning)	65
	Pressburg-Tyrnau	50
7	Tyrnau-Neuhäusel (afternoon)	70
9	Neuhäusel-Tyrnau	70
13	Tyrnau-Pressburg (arrival at midnight)	50
16	Pressburg-Vienna (arriving 'very weary')	65
28	Vienna-Pressburg	65
	Pressburg-Tyrnau (midnight departure)	50

July

7	Tyrnau-Pressburg-Vienna	115
13	Vienna-Pressburg-Tyrnau (departure 4.00 p.m.)	115
18	Tyrnau-Schinta (20 km) - Tyrnau	40
20	Tyrnau-Schinta-Tyrnau	40
21	Tyrnau-Schinta-Tyrnau	40
22	Tyrnau-Pressburg-Vienna (arriving 23 July)	115

950 km

Note: This itinerary has been compiled from Stepney's letters and dispatches – see the various notes to Chapter XXII.

Appendix VIII

National Library of Wales MS.5303 E (Herbert Papers) ff.23-24
(in George Stepney's handwriting):

'A letter to Mr. Prior, upon his grave Epistle
to Mr. Montagu, beginning

How'ere tis well – and nding [*sic*]
& Phyllis but a perjured Whore

'While in a melancholy strain
you raile & preach The World is vain,
I only sigh to think you've grown
so wise, so wondrous wise, so soon:
Ime sure as yet nor Age nor Care
have plowd yr face or chang^d yr hair;
No starving Bratts, nor scolding Wife
have made thee weary of thy Life;
No Pox has ript thy blooming youth
& taught thee such a dismall truth;
Thy fortune's neither large, nor scant,
The temp'rate zone twixt wealth & want.
Why then shou'd Wee in Prior find
a Cato's brow, or Timon's mind?

'Suppose ye World an errand [*sic*] Cheat
Where none but Rooks & rascalls gett;
Learn to be cautious how you play,
& you may thrive as well as they.

'Ile own all pleasures when possesst
are only Conterfeit at best;
yet while our [?hearts] are deceiv'd
those joys are reall if believed.

'Jaion [?Jason] when he hug^d the Air
& thought the Queen of ffrance was there;
had all ye transport of ye charms
wch Jove ere found in Juno's arms:
Such is ye Vigor of Conceit,
Fancy can, like a God, create:
Whereas to pry, is but to know

wt being known procures our woe.
Had limping Vulcan ne'er been led
to trap his wife with Mars in bed,
He'd still been ignorant & blest
& she not only fair but chast:
'Twas nothing but this curious Itch
made him a jest, & her a Bitch.

'In Smithfield faire Ive seen a clown
(who took y^t time to Walk to Town)
transported with ye Witty Strife
'Twixt Punchinello & his Wife,
before he had ye Sense to know
The puppet squeek'd not, but D'Avaux;
At last he peep'd behind ye Scenes,
nicely discovered ye Machines,
then Swore (like you) you're Rogues & Cheats
Scarce cou^d his 2 pence quell his threats;
The Mob had sure embroyld ye Faire
But for ye prudence of ye Mayor.
'Such mischief comes, when wee will know

if wt wee like be true or no;
'As men, who may with pleasure eat
Examine first, then loathe the meat,
When age & impotence draw nigh   )
'tis time with Solomon to cry   )
after enjoym^t, Vanity   )

'Before you shou'd pronounce this doom
You've Whole Seraglio yet to come;
& ought not to conspire with those
who on our Infancy impose
& make us at ye Font defy
That world wch wee want sense to try

'Then let but Phyllis ease thy pain   )
& through thy Codpiece cool thy brain   )*
You'le find ye World not half so vain   )

'Wt matters it if she's untrue
So there be room enough for you:
After her conduct to enquire
is nicely to forestall desire:
Be to ye Sexes frailty blind
If for ye minute she be kind
& prove no fould contagious whore
In justice you shou'd ask no more'
(Undated)
*Note: Stepney scored through the middle line of this triplet.

Appendix IX

George Stepney's published poems.

Date composed	Title	First published
?1676-82	Translation of a verse from Lucan (two lines)	F. Cogan, *Works of the Minor Poets*, Vol. 3 (1750)
1682	*Subprofessor Graecae Linguae*, Cantabr.	(as above)
1683	*In Nuptias P. Georgii et D. Annae*	*Hymenaeus Cantabrigiensis* (1683)
1684	Ovid's *Elegies*, Book III, No. 9, Upon the Death of Tibullus	Dryden, ed., *Miscellany Poems*, (1st ed. 1684)
1684	Odes of Horace: The Ninth Ode of of the Fourth Book	(as above)
?1684	Horace: The Seventh Ode of the Third Book	Cogan, Vol. 2 (1794)
?1684	To the Evening Star (English'd from a Greek Idyllium)	(as above)
1684	To the Earl of Carlisle, upon the Death of his Son	Dryden, ed., *Miscellany Poems*, (3rd ed. 1706)
1685	*In Obitum Caroli Secundi*	Cogan, Vol. 3 (1750)
1685	A Poem to King James the Second upon his Accession to the Throne	Cogan, Vol. 2 (1749)
1686	On the University of Cambridge's burning the Duke of Monmouth's Picture, 1685	(as above)

1688	The Audience (?by Stepney)	Cogan, Vol. 3 (1750)
1691	An Epistle to Charles Montagu on His Majesty's Voyage to Holland	F. Saunders* (1691)
1693	Translation of the Eighth Satyr of Juvenal (edited by Dryden)	J. Tonson (1693)
1695	A Poem Dedicated to the Blessed Memory of Her Late Gracious Majesty Queen Mary	J. Tonson (1695)
1696	On the late horrid Conspiracy	F. Saunders* (1697)
pre-1701	The Nature of Dreams	Buck & Scraben, *A New Miscelany of Poems* (1701)
?1703	The Austrian Eagle	Cogan, Vol. 2 (1749)
?1703	*Ad Regem Sueciae*	W. Mears, *The Grove . . .* (1721)
1706	Verses imitated from the French of M. Maynard to Cardinal Richelieu	Cogan, Vol. 2 (1749)
1707	To Mr. Edmund Smith	Cogan, Vol. 3 (1750)

No date has been allotted to the following poem:

	The Spell	Cogan, Vol. 3 (1750)

Notes: * Broadsheets, in BL: *Poetry, 1670-1729*
         # Broadsheets, in BL: *Poems, 1680-1729*

The bulk of Stepney's published poems are most easily available in the following collections:

Samuel Johnson, LL.D (ed.): *The Works of the most Eminent English Poets* (London, 1779-81), Vols. 12, 17.
Robert Anderson (ed.): *A Complete Edition of the Poets of Great Britain* (London & Edinburgh, 1793), Vol. 6.
Alexander Chalmers (ed.): *Works of the English Poets* (London, 1810), Vol. 8.

Unpublished poems and epigrams by George Stepney

Date	Title	Reference
1691-2	A Letter to Mr.Prior, upon his grave Epistle to Mr.Montagu, beginning . . .	cf. App. VIII
1693	Epitaph on Sir William Colt (Latin)	PRO: SP80/17, f.359
1693	Epigram on the Duke of Croy (Latin)	PRO: SP105/60, f.15
1693-4	Epigram *Upon ye French King's Off'ring to give up ye Spanish Netherlands* . . . (Latin and English)	cf. App. III
1695	*Song to ye King at Loo after the taking of Namur*	BL: Add.MS. 28897. f.319
1699	Epigram inscribed on the Electress of Brandenburg's house (Latin)	PRO: 105/53 4/14 July 1699
1701	Epigram on the Pope's Decree . . .	PRO: SP105/63 p.427

Note: 1. This song was printed by H. T. Swedenberg Jr. in his article *George Stepney, My Lord Dorset's Boy*, Huntingdon Library Quarterly, No. 1 (November 1946).

Notes and References

I *Antecedents*

1. PRO: SP105/60, f.29v (Stepney's Letter Book), Stepney in Dresden to Charles Montagu, 24 Oct/3 Nov 1693. Stepney was stating his claim to be appointed a Gentleman of the Privy Chamber. However, his statement that he was three years old at the time of his father's death was incorrect; he was six.
2. *The Dictionary of Welsh Biography down to 1940* (London, 1959), p.924.
3. CSPD 1629-31, p.462. (The entry is undated.)
4. *Transactions of the Carmarthenshire Antiquarian Society and Field Club*, Vol. XI, pp.71, 79, 80. I am grateful to Mr Alwyn J. Roberts of the Department of Manuscripts and Records, The National Library of Wales, for providing this reference.
5. Guildhall Library: Court Minute Books of the Grocers' Company: MS.11588/4 *Orders of the Court of Assistants*, 22 April 1640 to 15 June 1669 pp.384, 421, 461, 468, 568, 643, 649, 668. MS.11593/1 *List of Apprentices, 1629-1666*, p.310.
6. The christenings of all the Stepney children are found in the microfiche records of the IGI for London. A third daughter, Mary, was born in 1661, but died as a three-year-old and was buried in the church of St. Martin-in-the Fields in 1664. Details of Wilmot House are taken from *The Survey of London*, Vol. XVI, part I (1935), pp.222-3, in the British Library.
7. For George Stepney senior's appointment and relinquishment of his post as Groom of the Privy Chamber (supernumerary) see CSPD 1664-5, p.138 and CSPD 1668-9, pp.216-7. Details of Stepney's debts are contained in PRO: C.5/551/72 *Chancery Proceedings Series II (Bridges Division)*; June-September 1684.
8. Information about the Moseley family is based on the IGI Microfiche for Lancashire; PRO: *The Calendar for the Committee for the Advancement of Money*, p.1484; *V C H Lancashire*, Vols. IV, VI and VII; PRO: PROB 11/109/30 *The Will of Anthony Mosley of Manchester* (proved 10 April 1607).
9. PRO: *The Calendar for the Committee for the Advancement of Money*, pp.714-5; SP19/108 (Committee for the Advancement of Money) ff.13-18 and ff.48-55 (1647-1652).
10. PRO: C.5/551/72 *Chancery Proceedings Series II (Bridges Division)* June-Sept. 1684; George Stepney's will (1707) is at PRO: PROB 11/498, f.246; For James Partridge the stationer, see BL: *The Survey of London*, Vol. XVI, p.97.
11. Jane Stepney's will is at PRO: PROB 11/426, f.122; For Stepney's letter to his sisters, see PRO: SP105/54, f.99 (Letter Book), 22 June/2 July 1695. Correspondence about 'the door' is in the same volume at f.98 (same date).

II *Education*

1. PRO: SP81/87, f.136 (German States, 1693-6), Stepney in the Hague to James Vernon (the elder) 19/29 April 1695.
2. John McMaster, *St Martin-in-the-Fields* (privately printed, 1916).
3. The description of Westminster School is based on John Sargeaunt, *Annals of Westminster School* (London 1878).
4. PRO: SP105/54, f.188 (Stepney's Letter Book), Stepney in the Hague to Heneage Montagu, 22 Oct/1 Nov 1695.

5. G. F. Russell Barker and Alan H. Stenning, *The Record of Old Westminsters* (London, 1928).
6. PRO: SP105/60, f.13v (Stepney's Letter Book), Stepney in Dresden to Dr [Lionel] Gatford 29 Sept/9 Oct 1693.
7. Stepney's poems here referred to are to be found in Alexander Chalmer's *Works of the English Poets* (London, 1810), Vol. VIII.

III *Apprenticeship*

1. PRO: SP105/54, f.36 (Stepney's Letter Book), Stepney in Dresden to Blathwayt 10/20 July 1694.
2. PRO: SP105/50, f.111v (Stepney's Letter Book), Stepney at Mechlin to Vernon 15/25 July 1692. *Note*: In 1685 Dr Owen Wynne was Under-Secretary of State.
3. PRO: SP105/54, f.109, Stepney in Frankfurt to Trumbull, 7/17 July 1695. *Note*: Stepney's 'nine years ago' would seem to refer to 1686. Trumbull went to Paris in November 1685, so Stepney's memory was inaccurate by one year.
4. For Jane Stepney's advice to her son, see PRO: SP105/60, f.31 (Stepney's Letter Book), Stepney in Dresden to his mother, 24 Oct/3 Nov 1693. 'My first patron. . .', SP105/60, f.320, Stepney in Dresden to Prior, 5/15 June 1694. For Falkland's appointment and death, see HMC Reports, Vol.II, *Buccleuch Papers*, pp.65, 70.
5. Rous & Venn: *Admissions to Trinity College Cambridge*, Vol. II (Cambridge, 1913). BL: *Calendar to Downshire Mss*, Vol. I, Part I, Wyche to Trumbull, 22 Jan/1 Feb 1686.
6. For information about Wyche, see DNB and BL: Add.MS.41824 (Wyche's letters from Hamburg), particularly f.233 of 22 May 1685.
7. I owe the information about the English Company to Dr Sielemann of the *Staatsarchiv*, Hamburg, who most kindly sent me an extract from Heinrich Hitzigrath's *Die Kompagnie der Merchant Adventurers und die englische Kirchengemeinde in Hamburg 1611-1835*, (Hamburg, 1904). The recommendation of Wyche is at PRO: SP82/16, f.269 (Hamburg), Allestree to Sir Leoline Jenkins, 30 Dec 1681.
8. BL: Add.MS.41825, f.152 (Wyche's letters from Hamburg), Wyche to Middleton 7 May, 1686. *Note*: The excerpts from Stepney's first letter has been set out as he wrote it, with the small letters in 'yᵉ' and 'yᵗ' written as superscript. However, for ease both of the reader and the making of the transcription subsequent quotations shew all letters set on the base line.
9. For Frytag's visit, see BL: Add.MS.41825 (Wyche's letters from Hamburg) f.156 Wyche to Middleton, 18 May (n.s.) 1686. *Note*: The original mediator between Hamburg and Zell was an Aulic Counsellor named Ackenhausen. Baron Frytag carried more weight. For Stepney's mission, see Add.MS.41825, f.162, 21 May 1686.
10. BL: Add.MS.41825, f.194, 6 July 1686.
11. The account of the siege of Hamburg is largely taken from Stepney's *Relation* which he sent to the Vice-Master of Trinity College (Dr Babington) via Charles Montagu. This paper is now in the Bodleian Library at RAWL MS.A.326. It is undated, but was acknowledged by Montagu on 6/16 Nov 1686, who told Stepney he had received it by pacquet dated 18 October: see PRO: SP105/82, f.5 (Original Letters to George Stepney). Further details are based on Wyche's dispatches, in BL: Add.MS.41825, ff.207-283, 20 July-12 October 1686. Stepney's own later reminiscences are at PRO: SP105/59, ff.37v, 152 (Stepney's Letter Book), 1 July and 9 Sept 1693.

12. PRO: SP105/82, f.4, Wynne to Stepney, 5 Nov (o.s.) 1686.
13. PRO: *ibid.*, f.5, Montagu at Trinity College to Stepney 6/16 Nov 1686.
14. For details of the emoluments attached to Stepney's Fellowship, I am indebted to Mr Alan Kucia, Archivist of Trinity College Library (May 1987).
15. BL: Add.MS.7077, f.1 (Stepney Papers, Vol.XX), Egert in Stockholm to Stepney, 17 Aug 1687. For Storer, see Stepney's letter to him at PRO: SP105/60, f.33v (Stepney's Letter Book), 17/27 Nov 1693.
16. For Prince George's visit, see BL: Add.MS.41826, f.135 (Wyche's dispatches), Wyche to Middleton, 24 June 1687. For Millison, see PRO: SP105/60, f.13v (Stepney's Letter Book), 29 Sept (o.s.) 1693. Wyche's mourning is at BL: Add.MS.41826, ff.157, 159 (Wyche's dispatches), Wyche to Middleton, 2 and 12 Aug 1687.
17. BL: *ibid.* ff.254, 256, 24 and 27 Jan 1688.
18. PRO: SP105/82, ff.11, 14 (Original Letters to Stepney), Charles Montagu to Stepney, Feb 1688, Anne Montagu to Stepney, 10/20 Feb 1688; BL: Add.MS.41827, f.1 (Wyche's dispatches), Wyche to Middleton, 13 March 1688.
19. BL: *ibid.* f.35, Wyche to Middleton, 5 June 1688.
20. BL: *ibid.* f.36, Wyche to Middleton, 19 June 1688, PRO: SP81/87, f.124 (German states), Stepney to James Vernon, 12/22 March 1695.
21. BL: Add.MS.41827, f.72, Wyche to Middleton, 17 Aug 1688.
22. BL: *ibid.* ff.63, 76 Wyche to Middleton, 7 & 24 Aug 1688 and Add.MS.41823 (Middleton Papers, Vol.XXI) Middleton to Wyche, 4 Sept 1688.
23. BL: Add.MS.41827 (Wyche's dispatches), Final folio, undated.
24. BL: Add.MS.45731, f.88 (Letters to E. Poley, 1688-89), Wyche to Poley, 21 Dec 1688.
25. BL: *ibid.* f.103, Wyche to Poley, 1 Feb 1689.
26. Heinrich Hitzigrath, *Die Kompagnie der Merchant Adventurers*, p.32, note 2 (Hamburg, 1904).
27. PRO: SP105/82, f.9 (Original Letters to Stepney), Rycaut in London to Stepney, 12/24 May 1689 [*sic*]. *Note*: Probably the date of this letter was 14/24 May. The difference between old and new styles in 1689 was 10 days. I am indebted to Miss Sonia Anderson of the HMC for pointing out the subscript to Rycaut's letter.
28. PRO: SP105/82, f.10 (Original letters to Stepney). *Note*: The late Dr Albert Hollaender (PRO) commented that it is not known how this letter came to be among the Stepney papers, possibly it was never dispatched.
29. The departure of Wyche from Hamburg and the arrival of Rycaut are recorded in a list of resident diplomats and consuls in the City up to the year 1870, compiled by Johann Martin Lappenberg and Christian Mahlstedt. A copy of the relevant page was most kindly sent to me by Dr Sielemann of the *Staatsarchiv*, Hamburg.

IV *Tutelage*

1. Alexander Cunningham, *History of Great Britain, 1688-1714*, (London, 1787), p.106.
2. Jane Stepney's will is at PRO: Prob/11/426. Montagu's letter is at PRO: SP105/82, f.13 (Original letters to George Stepney). John Laughlin was Chaplain and Librarian at Trinity College.
3. J. Macky, *Memoirs of Secret Service* (London, 1733). Macky's 'Characters' are sometimes attributed to Burnet, and are in any case suspect. However the sketch of Johnston is in part borne out by Stepney, and so is included here.
4. Cal.Tr.B. 1689-92, pp.349, 762 and 1011.
5. Dr. Alfred Pribram, *Oesterreich und Brandenburg 1688-1700*, p.57 (Vienna, 1885).

6. For Johnston's movements, see: PRO: SP84/221, ff.92 & 111 (Holland, July 1689 - Dec 1690). Aglionby at the Hague to Warre, 4/14 Apr and 25 Apr/5 May 1690. For Leibniz, see Eduard Bodemann, *Der Briefwechsel Gottfried Wilhelm Leibniz* (Hanover 1889).

7. By 1690, owing to the German custom of partible inheritance, Brunswick had been split between Lüneburg and Wolfenbüttel, and Lüneburg in turn between Calemberg (or Hanover) and Zell. The Wolfenbüttel branch leaned towards the French 'interest.' For a clear description of the situation, see J.M. Kemble, *State Papers & Correspondence – from the Revolution to the accession of the House of Hanover* (London, 1857) – Introduction. Colt's letters to Johnston survive in PRO: SP105/84 (Original letters to George Stepney, 1690-93) i.e. those letters which Stepney himself saved.

8. Stepney's letter to Colt is at PRO: SP105/50, f.133 (Stepney's Letter Book), 7/17 Sept 1692.

9. J.M. Kemble, *State Papers & Correspondence...*, p.45 (London, 1857). BL: Add.MS.34095, f.71 (Sir W. Colt's correspondence), Johnston at Grez to Colt, 21/31 July 1690.

10. BL: Add.MS.34095, f.90 (Sir W. Colt's correspondence), Stepney to Colt, 7/17 Aug 1690.

11. BL: *ibid.*, ff.98, 106 Johnston at Halle to Colt, 14/24 and 18/28 Aug 1690.

12. PRO: SP105/82, ff.19, 21 (Original Letters to Stepney), Montagu in London to Stepney 1/10 Sept & 6/16 Oct 1690. BL: Add.MS.34095, f.170 (Sir W. Colt's correspondence), Dursley in the Hague to Colt, 16 Nov 1690.

13. Cal.Tr.B. (1689-92), p.1164.

14. PRO: SP84/221, f.286 (Holland, July-Dec 1690), Prior in the Hague to Richard Warre, 29 Dec (n.s.) 1690.

15. For Johnston's movements, see BL: Add.MS.34095, f.216 (Sir W. Colt's correspondence), Johnston in the Hague to Colt, 2/12 Jan 1691. For William III's journey, see Stephen B. Baxter, *William III* (London, 1966).

16. For James Montagu's letter about Stepney's poem, see: PRO: SP105/82, f.15 (Original letters to Stepney), 24 Feb (o.s.) 1690/91.The Chaplain in Hamburg on Sir Paul Rycaut's arrival was J. Walls; see: PRO: SP105/82, f.16 Walls in Hanover to Stepney 28 Feb (o.s.) 1690-91. For Johnston's movements, see PRO: SP105/84, f.21(Original letters to Stepney) Colt at Hanover to Johnston 27 March (o.s.) 1691; and BL: Add.MS.34095, ff.303,316,328 (Sir W. Colt's correspondence), Johnston to Colt, 31 Mar/10 Apr, 6/16 Apr, 20/30 Apr 1691.

17. Johnston wrote from Carlsbad to Colt, see BL: Add.MS.34095, f.363 (Sir W. Colt's correspondence), 21/31 May 1691; and from Berlin, see BL: Add.MS.36662, f.58 (Correspondence of Sir W.D. Colt), 7/17 July 1691. Stepney's news-letters are in the last sheets of PRO: SP105/50 (Stepney's Letter Book 1692), beginning at 14 July 1691. Montagu's letter is at PRO: SP105/82, f.26 (Original Letters to Stepney), 15 Sept (o.s.) 1691.

18. PRO: SP105/60, f.64 (Stepney's Letter Book), Stepney in Dresden to l'Enfant 23 Nov/3 Dec 1693.

19. PRO: *ibid.*, f.100v, Stepney to Polier, 29 Dec (o.s.) 1693.

20. Johnston's last letter to Colt in 1691 is at BL: Add.MS.36662, f.241 (Colt's correspondence), Johnston in Berlin to Colt, 26 Dec 1691.

V *Independence*

1. PRO: SP105/60, f.320 (Stepney's Letter Book), Stepney in Dresden to Prior, 5/15 June 1694

2. PRO: SP105/50, f.20 (Stepney's Letter Book), Stepney in Berlin to Prior.

3. PRO: *ibid.* f.10, Stepney in Berlin to Charles Montagu 1 March (n.s.) 1692.

4. For Stepney's account of Cresset, see PRO: SP105/50, f.49, Stepney in Berlin to John Robinson in Stockholm, 6 April (n.s.) 1692. It is possible that Johnston employed Cresset in Berlin, but this is not an established fact. Stepney's queries on his allowances are at PRO: SP105/50, f.1v, Stepney to Warre, 9/19 Feb 1692. *Ibid.* f.10v, Stepney to 'Mr. Poulteney' 1 March (n.s.) 1692. Stepney's congratulations to Montagu: PRO: SP105/50, f.17, Stepney in Berlin to Montagu 15 March (n.s.) 1692.

5. PRO: SP105/50, f.10v, Stepney to 'Mr. Poulteney', 1 March (n.s.) 1692.

6. PRO: SP105/50, f.22, Stepney in Berlin to the Earl of Nottingham, 19 March (n.s.) 1692.

7. PRO: SP105/84, f.30 (Original Letters to George Stepney, 1690-1693), Schweinfurt in Hanover to Stepney, 7/17 Feb 1692.

8. PRO: SP105/50, f.29, Stepney in Berlin to Blathwayt, 22 March (n.s.) 1692.

9. *Ibid.* f.58v, Vernon at Loo to Stepney, 14/24 April 1692.

10. *Ibid.* f.58vm Stepney at Torgau to Vernon, 27 April (n.s.) 1692. *Ibid.* f.37v, Stepney in Berlin to Prior, 29 March (n.s.) 1692.

11. *Ibid.* f.55, Stepney in Berlin to Danckelmann 11 April (n.s.) 1692.

12. Stepney's description of the Saxony/Brandenburg wedding is contained in several letters, all to be found in his Letter-Book SP105/50, viz: PRO: SP105/50, f.57v, Stepney in Torgau to Rycaut, 22 April (n.s.) 1692; f.60, Stepney in Leipzig to Lord Nottingham and to Blathwayt, 18/28 April 1692 PRO: SP105/50, f.61 Stepney in Torgau to Nottingham and to Blathwayt, 23 April (n.s.) 1692. *Ibid.* f.62, Stepney in Torgau to Blathwayt, 29 April (n.s.) 1692.

13. PRO: SP105/82, f.45 (Orig. Letters to G. Stepney), Blathwayt at Loo to Stepney, 29 April (o.s.) 1692.

14. PRO: SP105/50, f.74v (Stepney's Letter Book), Stepney in Berlin to Vernon, 14 May (n.s.) 1692.

15. Cal.Tr.B. 1689-92, pp.1845-6.

16. PRO: SP105/50, f.82, Stepney in Berlin to Blathwayt, 21 May (n.s.) 1692.

17. PRO: *ibid.* f.88, Stepney in Cleves to Johnston, 6/16 June 1692.

18. PRO: *ibid.* f.97v, Stepney in Cleves to Blathwayt, 10/20 June 1692

19. The Stepney/Molesworth quarrel is contained in PRO: SP105/84, ff.54-66 (Orig. Letters to G. Stepney,1690-93), Colt or his secretary (Schweinfurt) to Stepney, 8 July (o.s.) to 5/15 August 1692 and SP105/82, ff.55-60 (Orig. Letters to Stepney, 1686-95), Vernon and Blathwayt at Lembecq to Stepney, between 27 July/6 Aug and 8/18 August 1692.

20. PRO: SP105/60, f.98 (Stepney's Letter Book), Stepney in Dresden to Stratford, 29 Dec (o.s.) 1693.

21. PRO: *ibid.* f.97, Stepney in Cleves to Montagu, 8/18 June 1692. *Ibid.* f.114, Stepney in Liège to Montagu, 24 July/3 Aug 1692. The journey timetable is at SP105/50, f.109 (undated). Cleves [Kleve] is about 17 km east of Nijmegen; Grave is 15 km to Nijmegen's south-west; this sector involved the crossing of the Maas. Bois-le-Duc ['s Hertogenbosch] is 26 km west of Grave; Bois-le-Duc to Hoogstraten, along the old road, probably involved passing through Breda, in which case the stretch is about 80 km. On to Antwerp (35 km); and to Brussels by the old road, c. 50 km. Genappe is 12 km south of Waterloo, or 30 km from Brussels. 'Wechtern' is Werchter, on the Djile, north of Louvain and about half-way between Brussels and Diest. According to the timetable, Stepney's caleche travelled at about 6 km per hour. The dates recorded by Stepney, on this occasion, are all old-style.

22. BL: Add.MS.37991, f.117 (Blathwayt's Letter Book), Blathwayt (?at Genappe) to Lord Nottingham, 18/28 July 1692. PRO: SP105/82, f.54 (Orig. Letters to Stepney 1686-95), Vernon at Lambecq to Stepney, 22 July (o.s.) 1692. PRO: SP105/50, f.128 (Stepney's Letter Book), Stepney at Cleves to Dr. Wynne, 24 Aug/3 Sept 1692.

23. PRO: *ibid.* f.110v, Stepney at Mechlen to Blathwayt, 15/25 July 1692. *Ibid,* f.115, Stepney at Cleves to Blathwayt, 29 July/8 Aug 1692. *Ibid,* f.122, Blathwayt at Ninove to Stepney, 21 Aug (n.s.) 1692. *Ibid,* f.123, Stepney at Cleves to Blathwayt, 16/26 Aug 1692.

24. PRO: SP105/50, f.117, Stepney at Cleves to Blathwayt, 2/12 Aug 1692 and *ibid.* f.124v, Blathwayt at Ninove to Stepney, 23 Aug (n.s.) 1692. The name of the Danish secretary is not given: he could have been Bartholomew Meuschen, later Danish secretary at Dresden, and an 'old friend' of Stepney's.

25. PRO: SP105/50, f.138, Blathwayt in Gramen to Stepney, 5/15 Sept 1692 and *ibid.* f.146, Stepney in Magdeburg to Blathwayt, 15/25 Aug 1692.

26. PRO: SP105/50, f.104, Stepney in Cleves to Blathwayt, 1/11 July 1692. *Ibid,* f.131v, Stepney in Cleves to Rycaut, 3/13 Sept 1692. *Ibid,* f.132v, Stepney in Cleves to Blathwayt, 6/16 Sept 1692.

27. PRO: SP105/50, f.133, Stepney in Cleves to Colt, 7/17 Sept 1692. SP105/84, f.87, Schweinfurt in Zell to Stepney, 19 Nov (o.s.) 1692.

28. PRO: SP105/82 (Orig. Letters to Stepney, 1686-95), f.69, Vernon at the Hague to Stepney, 7 Oct (n.s.) 1692.

29. PRO: SP105/50 (Stepney's Letter Book), f.145, Stepney at Cell [Zell] to Blathwayt, 4 Oct (o.s.) 1692. *Ibid.* f.146, Stepney in Berlin to Blathwayt, 8/18 Oct 1692. *Ibid.* f.146, Stepney in Magdeburg to Blathwayt, 15/25 Oct 1692. *Ibid.* f.152, Stepney in Berlin to Blathwayt, 1/11 Nov 1692.

30. PRO: SP105/50, f.167, Stepney in Berlin to Blathwayt, 6 Dec (n.s.) 1692.

31. The exchange of letters between Stepney and Leibniz is to be found in J. M. Kemble *State Papers & Correspondence,* p.103ff. (London, 1887). The letters are given in Kemble's English translation of French originals. The date of Stepney's letter is erroneously given as 6 November: it should be 6 December 1692. Stepney did not record the exchange in his letter book. The text of his poem to the Duchess of Hanover seems to have been lost.

32. Stepney told Leibniz about his posting to Vienna in his letter of 6 December 1692, referred to above. His letter to Prior is at PRO: SP105/50, f.169 (Stepney's Letter Book). Stepney in Berlin to Prior. 11/21 Dec 1692.

VI *The Imperial Court*

1. PRO: SP105/58, f.4v (Stepney's Letter Book), Stepney in Vienna to Lord Nottingham, 28 Dec 1692/7 Jan 1693.

2. PRO: SP105/58, f.9, Stepney to Nottingham, 10 Jan (n.s.) 1693. *Note:* The Duke of Hanover had been pressing for admission to the College of Electors [of the Holy Roman Emperor] in exchange for his military support for Leopold I. The latter was willing enough to grant the Duke's request, but the move was opposed by other rulers on political or religious grounds. A full account of the Ninth Electorate is to be found in Aloys Schulte, *Markgraf Ludwig Wilhelm von Baden und der Reichskrieg gegen Frankreich 1693-97* (Karlsruhe, 1892).

3. PRO: SP105/58, f.10v Stepney in Vienna to Lord Portland, 14 Jan (n.s.) 1693. SP105/82, f.80 (Original letters to Stepney 1686-95) Portland at Kensington to Stepney, 27 Jan/6 Feb 1693.

4. PRO: *Ibid.* f.78, Blathwayt to Stepney ,13/23 Jan 1693; f.82 Balthwayt to

Stepney, 27 Jan (o.s.) 1693. A copy of Stepney's Privy Seal for £3 a day is at SP105/82, f.93, 16 March 1693.

5. Stepney's dispatch is at PRO: SP105/58, f.10v, 23 Jan (n.s.) 1693.

6. *Note*: The imperial State-Secretary [*Staatssekretär*] should not be confused with the similar English title. Consbruck did not enjoy ministerial rank, but was responsible for serving the Chancery in a secretarial (small 's') capacity. Stepney's circle of friends in Vienna are disclosed in several letters which he later wrote from Dresden, e.g. PRO: SP105/60, f.11, Stepney to Bruynincx, 29 Sept/9 Oct 1693; f.116v, to Blumenthal, 2/12 Nov 1693; f.67v, to Bothmar 1/11 Dec 1693; f.155c, to Ehrenburg 16/26 Oct 1693, SP105/58 f.93, to Colt, 30 March 1693.

7. PRO: SP105/58, Stepney in Vienna to Leibniz, 4 Feb (n.s.) 1693.

8. PRO: SP105/58, f.69 (Stepney's Letter Book), Stepney in Vienna to Nottingham, 7 March (n.s.) 1693; f.74v, 1/11 March 1693.

9. PRO: *Ibid.* f.59, Stepney in Vienna to Nottingham, 22 Feb/4 March 1693 PRO: SP105/82, f.103 (Original Letters to Stepney), Blathwayt at Loo to Stepney, 11/21 April 1693. *Note*: In his correspondence Stepney referred freely to Crowns (one-quarter of £1 sterling) and/or *Reichsthaler* (or Dollars). The value of the two was approximately equal. The Florin was about 1/10th of £1 (cf. John J. McCusker, *Money and Exchange in Europe and America, 1660-1775*, (London, 1978)).

10. PRO: SP105/58, f.85, Stepney in Vienna to Blathwayt, 11/21 March 1693.

11. *Ibid.* f.133, 19/29 April 1693. Stepney's *Harangue* is at f.136.

12. PRO: SP80/17, f.317 (Germany, Imperial Court, 1689-1700), Stepney in Vienna to Vernon, 14/24 June 1693.

13. PRO: SP105/59, f.40 (Stepney's Letter Book), Stepney in Vienna to Blathwayt 4 July (n.s.) 1693; f.59v, Stepney to Paget, 28 June/8 July 1693. *Note*: Stepney had met Paget briefly at Mechlen in July 1692 when Paget was travelling to England for leave. See SP105/50, f.111v, Stepney to Vernon, 15/25 July 1692.

14. PRO: SP105/58, f.180, Stepney in Vienna to Blathwayt, 17/27 May 1693; SP105/59, f.12v, 3 June (n.s.) 1693.

15. PRO: *Ibid.* f.14, Stepney in Vienna to Blathwayt, 10 June (n.s.) 1693; SP80/17, f.318 (Germany, Imperial Court, 1689-1700), Stepney in Vienna to Vernon, 14/24 June 1693; SP105/59, f.37v, Stepney in Vienna to Blathwayt, 1 July (n.s.) 1693; f.79, 12/22 July 1693; SP105/60, f.5v (Stepney's Letter Book), Stepney in Vienna to Vernon, 22 July (n.s.) 1693.

16. PRO: SP105/59, f.92v (Stepney's Letter Book), Stepney in Vienna to Paget 19/29 July 1693;. f.97v, Stepney in Vienna to Blathwayt, 1 Aug/22 July 1693; PRO: SP80/17, f.316 (Germany, Imperial Court, 1689-1700), Stepney in Vienna to Vernon, 20 June (n.s.) 1693. The *Corpus Christi* incident was the subject of an essay by the late Dr. A. E. Hollaender, *Mr. Resident George Stepney and the Pietatis Austriaca* (London, 1976) in which he emphasized Stepney's anti-Catholic bias. However Stepney's letter to Vernon cited above is merely a factual account of the incident. Stepney recognised true piety in Catholics as well as in Protestants.

17. PRO: SP105/59, f.105v Blathwayt at Nether Hespen to Stepney, 17/27 July 1693; f.106, Stepney in Vienna to Blathwayt, 2/12 August 1693; f.109, Stepney to Paget (same date).

18. PRO: SP105/82, f.132 (Original letters to Stepney), Blathwayt at Lembecq to Stepney, 11/21 Aug 1693; SP105/59, f.113v, Stepney in Vienna to Blathwayt, 9/19 Aug 1693. The text of Stepney's epigram on the Duke of Croy is at PRO: SP105/60, f.15, Stepney at Leipzig to Blathwayt, 7/17 Oct 1693; cf. also BL:

Add.MS.7060, f.110 (Sir Paul Rycaut's correspondence) Rycaut in Hamburg to Stepney, 25 Oct 1693. For the description of the pilgrimage to Mariazell, see PRO: SP105/59, f.167, Stepney in Vienna to Blathwayt, 9/19 Sept 1693.

19. PRO: *ibid.* f.123, Stepney in Vienna to Trenchard, 19/29 Aug 1693, enclosing ff.126-133. Documents relevant to the peace proposals, f.16v, Stepney to Paget (about the compliment), 3/13 June 1693; PRO: SP105/58, f.38v, Stepney in Vienna to Nottingham (about Schöning), 11 Feb 1693; BL: Add.MS.46533, f.118 (Lexington Papers), Stepney at the Hague to Lexington, 28 Oct/7 Nov 1695.

20. PRO: SP105/59, f.65v, Stepney in Vienna to Blathwayt, 8 July (n.s.) 1693, f.68v, 1/11 July 1693. *Note*: The confusion in the high command was noted by Christoph Dietrich von Bosen ('young Bose'), who reported that during the summer of 1693 there were 36 commanding generals in the Rhine Army, including three sovereign commanders [Prince Louis, the Elector of Saxony and the Landgrave of Hesse-Cassel], plus four Field-Marshals [cf. Richard Fester, *Die armirten Stände u. die Reichskriegsverfassung, 1681-1697* (Frankfurt/Main, 1886), p.130].

21. PRO: SP105/84, f.173 (Original Letters to Stepney), Colt at Zell to Stepney, 1 June (o.s.) 1693; f.177, Colt at Frankfurt to Stepney, 27 June (o.s.) 1693.

22. The account of the campaign, and of the death of Sir William Colt are to be found in PRO: SP105/84, f.187, Colt at Neudenau to Stepney, 14 July (o.s.) 1693; f.195, Colt at Sontheim to Stepney, 3 Aug (o.s.) 1693; f.197, 6/16 Aug 1693; f.200, 3/13 Aug 1693; f.204, Schweinfurt at Aschaffenburg to Stepney, 25 Aug (o.s.) 1693; f.211, Schweinfurt at Frankfurt to Stepney, 5/15 Sept 1693. *Note*: Schweinfurt had been locally employed by Colt for at least two years. The anglicised version of his name was Swinfurt. He always signed himself with his surname only, so his first name is unknown. After Colt's death he seems to have found employment in the Secretary of State's office in London, because Stepney mentions him as being competent to translate German into English, as required.

23. PRO: SP105/82, f.142 (Original Letters to Stepney), Blathwayt at Linnick to Stepney, 4/14 Sept 1693 [a copy of this letter is also to be found in SP105/59 – Stepney's Letter Book – at f.173].

24. PRO: SP105/82, f.145 (Original Letters to Stepney), Vernon in Whitehall to Stepney 12 Sept (o.s.) 1693; f.148, Charles Montagu to Stepney (same date).

25. PRO: SP105/59, f.178 (Stepney's Letter Book), Stepney in Vienna to Blathwayt, 30 Sept (n.s.) 1693.

VII *Romance, Death and Subsidies*

1. PRO: SP105/60, f.11v (Stepney's Letter Book), Stepney in Dresden to Storer, 29 Sept/9 Oct 1693.

2. PRO: *ibid.* f.104v, Stepney to Blathwayt, 29 Sept/9 Oct 1693. *Note*: The folio sheets in Stepney's letter-books (particularly in SP105/60) are *not* always arranged in chronological order. Thus it is possible that two letters written on the same date, as above, are 93 folios apart.

3. Information about Blauenstein and Jane (née Stepney) is derived from Burke's *Extinct & Dormant Baronetcies,* (2nd edition, 1844); and PRO: SP105/54, f.74 (Stepney's Letter Book 1694-5), Stepney in Dresden to Couneau, 15 Aug 1694. SP105/84, f.169 (Orig. Letters to G. Stepney), Colt in Dresden to Stepney, 14 May (o.s.) 1693; SP105/60, f.99 (Stepney's Letter Book), Stepney in Dresden to his mother, 29 Dec (o.s.) 1693. Blauenstein's first names were Frideric Mörsz, according to Eduard Bodemann, *Der Briefwechsel des Gottfried Wilhelm*

Leibniz in der Königlichen offentlichen Bibliothek zu Hannover, (Hanover, 1889), p.17. Blauenstein wrote four letters to Leibniz between 1685-1687, about the delivery of heavy guns and other weapons, and about chemistry. The tenancy agreement between Stepney and Frau Schröder is at SP 105/86, ff.355, 357, 29 Sept/9 Oct 1693. The first reference to Mme. Pflug is at SP105/60, f.20 Stepney in Dresden to Stratford, 20 Oct (o.s.) 1693. It has not been possible to discover her first name. In a list which he compiled of the Saxon Court in 1692 (BL: Add.MS.37165, f.7), Stepney says she was born a Bruchdorf of Holstein, and was possibly a daughter of the Electress Dowager of the Palatine. She seems to have been much younger than her husband, for Stepney at first mistook her for Pflug's daughter. He later referred to her as 'the tall Saxon'.

4. PRO: SP105/60, f.147, Stepney in Leipzig to Blathwayt, 4 Oct (o.s.) 1693.

5 PRO: *SP81/87, f.8 (German States, 1693-96), Blathwayt at Loo to Stepney, 2 Oct (n.s.) 1693

6 PRO: SP105/60, f.144v, Stepney in Leipzig to Stratford, 4 Oct (o.s.) 1693. *SP105/82, f.156 (Orig. Letters to G. Stepney), Blathwayt at Loo to Stepney, 2 Oct (n.s.) 1693. *Notes:* (i) The two references marked (*) above are to the same letter. Stepney made a copy of an extract which he sent to Vernon. (ii) Stepney's method of expressing numerical thousands was often to use the abbreviation m/—. To the non-mathematical reader this is easy on the eye, and I have followed Stepney's practice. (iii) It was the general philosophy of most seventeenth-century diplomats that the minds of rulers could be swayed by judicious presents to their mistresses.

7. PRO: SP105/60, f.15 (Stepney's Letter Book), Stepney in Leipzig to Blathwayt 7/17 Oct 1693.

8. PRO: *ibid.* ff.142v, 143 Stepney in Dresden to Mrs Holmes, and to Prior 29 Sept/6 Oct 1693. *Note:* 'betty' was Prior's mistress in the Hague. It has not been possible to identify the other people mentioned.

9. PRO: SP105/60, f.12v, Stepney in Dresden to Lady Bellomont, 9 Oct (n.s.) 1693; f.156, to Bruynincx, 14/24 Nov 1693; f.107, to Mr Walter, 23 Oct/2 Nov 1693.

10. PRO: *ibid.* f.31, Stepney in Dresden to his mother, 24 Oct/3 Nov 1693.

11. *Ibid.* f.157, Stepney in Dresden to (probably) Vernon, 10/20 Oct 1693.

12. *Ibid.* f.41v, Stepney in Dresden to Blathwayt, 7/17 Nov 1693.

13. *Ibid.* f.11 and f.42v Stepney in Dresden to Bruynincx, 29 Sept/9 Oct and 6 Nov (o.s.) 1693.

14. PRO: SP105/60, f.33, 'PS to Mr. Blathwayt', dated 10/20 Nov 1693, and probably enclosed with the letter at f.41v above, dated 7/17 Nov. Stepney sent Colt a 'character' of Ham (SP105/58, f.77v – Letter Book, 1/11 March 1693), from which this account is derived. The King's approbation of Ham is contained in BL: Add.MS.34504, f.3, of 16/26 April 1689. PRO: SP105/82, f.168 (Orig. Letters to Stepney), Charles Montagu to Stepney, 30 Nov (o.s.) 1693; SP105/60, f.95, Stepney to the Earl of Dorset 26 Dec (o.s.) 1693, f.95v to Charles Montagu – same date. Stepney's letter to Lord Dorset (above) is the only one to survive. It is quoted in full in Brice Harris, *Charles Sackville, Sixth Earl of Dorset,* (Univ. of Illinois Press, 1940), p.190. However, the reason there given for Stepney's writing of the letter is incorrect: Dorset had nothing to do with Stepney's posting to Dresden, and the letter of thanks was written to acknowledge Dorset's part in getting his protégé appointed a Gentleman of the Bedchamber.

15. PRO: SP105/82, f.152 (Orig. Letters to Stepney), Vernon in Whitehall to Stepney, 26 Sept (o.s.) 1693; SP105/60, f.106 (Stepney's Letter Book), Stepney in Dresden to Vernon, 17 Oct (o.s.) 1693; *ibid.* f.59v, 17/27 Nov 1693; *ibid.*

f.95v, Stepney in Dresden to Charles Montagu, 29 Dec (o.s.) 1693.

16. PRO: *ibid.* f.44, Stepney in Dresden to Stratford, 31 Oct/10 Nov 1693. *ibid.* f.63, Stepney in Dresden to Prior, 24 Nov/4 Dec 1693.

17. PRO: SP105/60, f.85v (Stepney's Letter Book), Stepney in Dresden to Trenchard, 19/29 Dec 1693; SP81/87, f.48 (German States, 1693-96), N. v. Danckelmann in Vienna to Stepney, 9 Jan (n.s.) 1694; SP105/60, f.164, Stepney in Dresden to N. v. Danckelmann, 5/15 Jan 1694.

18. PRO: *ibid.* f.93v, Stepney in Dresden to Vernon and Blathwayt, 22 Dec 1693/ 1 Jan 1694; *ibid.* f.101v, 2/12 Jan 1694.

19. PRO: *ibid.* f.76v, Stepney in Dresden to Blathwayt and Vernon, 12/22 Dec 1693; *ibid.* f.190, 9/19 Jan 1694; *ibid.* f.191v, 12/22 Jan 1694; *ibid.* f.193, Stepney in Dresden to Trenchard, 16/26 Jan 1694

20. *Ibid.* f.197v, 19/29 Jan 1694; *ibid.* f.200, Stepney in Dresden to Trenchard, Blathwayt and Vernon, 23 Jan/2 Feb 1694.

21. The poem (Latin version) is at PRO: SP81/87, f.59 (German States, 1693-97) – no date and in English; f.58 ditto; PRO: SP105/60, f.177 (Stepney's Letter Book), Stepney in Dresden to 'young Stratford', 22 Jan/1 Feb 1694; BL: Add.MS.7060 (Sir P. Rycaut's correspondence), f.128, Rycaut in Hamburg to Stepney, 3/13 Feb 1694,

22. PRO: SP105/60, f.203, Stepney in Dresden to ?Vernon, 30 Jan (o.s.) 1694; *ibid.* f.204v, 2 Feb (o.s.) 1694; *ibid.* f/204v, Stepney in Dresden to Trenchard, 3/13 Feb 1694.

23. PRO: *ibid.* f.213, 16/26 Feb 1694.

24. PRO: *ibid.* f.214, 20 Feb/2 March 1694. *Note*: Willius was later released by the Elector Frederick Augustus.

25. PRO: SP105/60, f.216, Stepney in Dresden to Trenchard, 23 Feb/5 March 1694; f.220 to Vernon (same date).

26. PRO: SP105/60, f.223, Stepney in Dresden to Trenchard, 27 Feb (o.s.) 1693. *Note*: Stepney's account of this affair is corroborated by letters which Benebourg wrote to Kinsky, and which are preserved in the *HHStA* in Vienna. In particular Benebourg wrote on 15 Feb (n.s.) 1694 to Kinsky informing the latter of Carlowitz's mission and recommending Kinsky to receive and listen to him. Cf *HHStA: Staatskanzlei Sachsen, Korrespondenz 1694-1738, 2A Fasc. 1.2. ff28-29,* Benebourg to Kinsky, 15 Feb (n.s.) 1694.

27. PRO: SP105/60, f.230v (Stepney's Letter Book), Stepney in Dresden to Blathwayt, 2 March (o.s.) 1694; SP105/82, f.180 (Orig. Letters to Stepney), Shrewsbury in Whitehall to Stepney, 16 March (o.s.) 1694; SP105/60, f.232, Receipt signed by Christoph Thierry Bose, 2 March (n.s.) 1694; *ibid.* f.177, Shrewsbury in Whitehall to Stepney, 9 March (o.s.) 1694; *ibid.* f.234v, Stepney in Dresden to Trenchard, 10 March (o.s.) 1694. *Note*: Three members of the Goertz family occur in Stepney's correspondence. The family seat was at Schlitz, near Frankfurt/Main. Johann, in 1694, was sent for a second time to Vienna by William III. (The first time had been during 1688, to persuade the Emperor to acquiesce in the projected invasion of England, when for William to have sent a Dutch envoy would have been too dangerous.) Johann's brother, Friedrich Wilhelm, was in the service of the Duke of Brunswick-Lüneburg (the later Elector of Hanover). Stepney wrote a note on both these Goertz brothers at PRO: SP105/56, f.64 at 1 Oct 1696. The third Goertz was a nephew of Johann and Friedrich Wilhelm. He was in Holstein service in 1701, and then transferred to the Emperor in 1704. His first name is unknown. Cf PRO: SP105/72, f.191, 23 June 1704, and SP105/75, 17 June 1705.

28. *HHStA: Reichshofkanzlei, Berichte aus Dresden, Fasz 4b, 3rd Paket, ff 1 and*

2: Clary to the Emperor, undated, but annotated as March 1694, plus enclosure. PRO: SP105/60, f.11v (Stepney's Letter Book), Stepney to an unknown correspondent, undated but placed at 29 Sept/9 Oct 1693. *Note*: Ehrenburg's name is found spelled in a variety of ways, e.g. Ehrembourg, or Ehrenberg. He is *not* identical with Konrad Ehrenschildt, who was Danish, although Stepney in June 1693 once (wrongly) referred to 'Ehrenschild' as Swedish Ambassador in Vienna. The correspondence between Colt and Stepney about Monceau is at PRO: SP105/84, f.91 (Original Letters to Stepney), Colt at Zell to Stepney, 23 Nov (o.s.) 1693; SP105/58 (Stepney's Letter Book), 25 Jan (n.s.) 1693.

29. PRO: SP105/60, f.238, Stepney in Dresden to Shrewsbury, 21 March (o.s.) 1694; f.240, 24 March (o.s.) 1694.
30. PRO: *ibid.* f.248v, No addressee. Stepney may have written this as an *aide memoire,* on 27 March (o.s.) 1694; *ibid.* f.249v, Stepney in Dresden to Blathwayt, 30 March (o.s.) 1694.
31. PRO: *ibid.* f.253, Stepney in Dresden to Vernon, 30 March (o.s.) 1694.
32. PRO: *ibid.* f.285, Stepney in Dresden to Shrewsbury, 6 April (o.s.) 1694; *ibid.* f.287, Stepney in Dresden to Blathwayt, 10 April (o.s.) 1694; PRO: SP105/82, f.191 (Orig. Letters to Stepney), Blathwayt in Whitehall to Stepney, 20 April (o.s.) 1694.
33. PRO: SP105/60, f.289 (Stepney's Letter Book), [Johann] Goertz in Vienna to Ham, 4/14 April 1694 (French); PRO: SP105/60, f.266 (Stepney's Letter Book), Stepney in Dresden to Shrewsbury, 17 April (o.s.) 1694; *ibid.* f.273, Stepney in Dresden to Goertz, 30 April (o.s.) 1694 (French). *Note*: To explain the arithmetic of the subsidy: The amount in question was the 'missing' m/50 Rx of the 1694 subsidy. The Emperor promised one-third, i.e. Rx 16,666. Subtracted from Rx 50,000 this left Rx 33,333 (or Rx 33,334) to be paid by the States General of the Netherlands and by the King of England. It had become accepted practice that any such sum should be divided in the proportion of one third from the States General and two thirds from the King.
34. PRO: SP105/60, f.270 (Stepney's Letter Book), Stepney in Dresden to Shrewsbury, 20/30 April 1694. *Note*: In this assessment, Stepney was wrong: Frederick Augustus was more forceful politically than Stepney thought.
35. PRO: SP105/60, f.275, Stepney in Dresden to ?Blathwayt, 28 April (o.s.) 1694; *ibid.* f.283v, Stepney in Dresden to Shrewsbury, 4/14 May 1694.
36. PRO: *ibid.* f.293, Stepney in Dresden to Blathwayt, 8/18 May 1694; f.297, 15/25 May 1694.
37. King William's dislike of Charles Montagu is described in Stephen B. Baxter *William III*, p.316 (London, 1966). Blathwayt's optimistic forecast of Stepney's future is referred to in the latter's letter to Vernon, at PRO: SP105/60, f.301,18/28 May 1694.
38. PRO: SP105/54, f.59 (Stepney's Letter Book 1694-5), Stepney in Dresden to Shrewsbury, 8/18 June 1694.
39. PRO: SP105/60, f.311v (Stepney's Letter Book), Stepney in Dresden to Vernon, 29 May/8 June 1694. Note: Compliments of condolence or congratulation were sought after by all diplomats, because personal presents from the recipient ruler were usually involved. Blathwayt's letters to Stepney are quoted by the latter to Vernon, at PRO: SP105/54, f.20 (Stepney's Letter Book 1694-5), Stepney in Dresden to Vernon, 12/22 June 1694.
40. PRO: SP105/60, f.312 (Stepney's Letter Book), Stepney in Dresden to Blathwayt, 29 May/8 June 1694; PRO: SP105/54, f.20v (Stepney's Letter Book 1694-5), Stepney in Dresden to Prior, 12/22 June 1694.

VIII *Hope Deferred*

1. PRO: SP105/82, f.201 (Original letters to Stepney), Shrewsbury in Whitehall to Stepney, 26 June (o.s.) 1694. This letter is in the hand of James Vernon (senior) who may also have composed it.

2. PRO: SP105/54, f.59 (Stepney's Letter Book), Stepney in Dresden to Vernon, 7/17 Aug 1694.

3. PRO: *ibid.* f.29v, Stepney in Dresden to Blathwayt, 22 June/2 July 1694. *Note*: Stepney was partly correct: *La Générale* was tortured, but in 1696 and then not with full rigour. She behaved with great courage, admitted nothing, and was eventually banished to her estates, being released in 1699. Cf: *Archiv für d. sächsische Geschichte*, Vol. VIII, pp.213-8 (1870) under '*Miscellan*'. No author is quoted.

4. PRO: SP105/54, f.40v, Stepney in Dresden to Blathwayt, 10/20 July 1694.

5. PRO: *ibid.* f.47, Stepney in Dresden to Portland ,20/30 July 1694; f.47v, to Blathwayt, same date.

6. PRO: *ibid.* f.43v, Stepney in Dresden to Charles Montagu, 10/20 July 1694; *ibid.* f.57, to Blathwayt, 3/13 August 1694; *ibid.* f.44, to Dr Montagu, 17/27 July 1694; PRO: SP105/82, f.224 (Orig. letters to Stepney), Dr Montagu to Stepney, 21 August (o.s.) 1694.

7. PRO: SP105/54, f.65 (Stepney's Letter Book 1694-5), Stepney in Dresden to Shrewsbury, 10 August (o.s.) 1694; f.67, Stepney to Frise (French), same date; PRO: SP105/55, f.48 (Stepney's Letter Book), Stepney in the Hague to Shrewsbury, 23 Oct/2 Nov 1694.

8. PRO: SP105/82, f.231 (Orig. letters to Stepney), Blathwayt at Sombreff to Stepney, 9/19 Aug 1694; PRO: SP105/54, f.77v (Stepney's Letter Book 1694-5), Stepney in Dresden to Blathwayt, 31 August (o.s.) 1694; BL: Add.MS 34354, ff.1-3 (Letters to W. Blathwayt), Stepney in Dresden to Blathwayt, 7/17 Sept 1694. Cf also: Heinrich, Freiherr v. Friesen, *Julius Heinrich, Graf von Friesen*, p.52 (Leipzig, 1870), quoting Stepney's letter of 11/21 Sept 1694 to Friesen (Frise). *Note*: Aloys Schulte, in his biography of *Markgraf Ludwig Wilhelm von Baden* [Prince Louis] (Karlsruhe, 1892), comments (p.225) that from the material available to him, including Stepney's letter to Frise of 11/21 September 1694, he was unable to decide whether Schöning was indeed guilty of having engineered the withdrawal of the Saxon troops from the Rhine.

9. PRO: SP105/82, f.241 (Orig. Letters to Stepney), Blathwayt at Wontgern near Deinse to Stepney, 5 Sept (n.s.) 1694; f.243, 7 Sept (n.s.) 1694.

10. BL: Add.MS.7060, f.158 (Sir P.Rycaut's correspondence), Rycaut in Hamburg to Stepney, 29 Aug (n.s.) 1694; BL: Add.MS.28897, f.45 (Ellis Papers, Vol.2), Cresset at Zell to Ellis, 7 Sept (n.s.) 1694. PRO: SP105/55, f.19 (Stepney's Letter Book), Stepney at Brunswick to Blathwayt, 20 Sept (n.s.) 1694.

11. PRO: *ibid.* f.21, Stepney at Zell to Blathwayt, 21 Sept (n.s.) 1694; *ibid.* Stepney at Ebstorff to Blathwayt, 25 Sept (n.s.) 1694; f.22, Stepney at Ebstorff to Mme. Pflug, 24 Sept (n.s.) 1694.

12. PRO: *ibid.* f.33, Stepney at Zell to Blathwayt, 2 Oct (n.s.) 1694.

13. For Count Frise's remark on Stepney's presence in the Hague see Heinrich, Freiherr v. Friesen, *Julius Heinrich, Graf v. Friesen* (Leipzig, 1870), p.270. Frise mentioned Stepney in a letter from the Hague to the Elector of Saxony dated 16 Oct (n.s.) 1694. Stepney's letters to Shrewsbury and Montagu asking for promotion are in PRO: SP105/55, f.48 (Stepney's Letter Book), Stepney in the Hague to Shrewsbury, 23 Oct/2 Nov 1694; f.40 to Montagu on the same date.

14. Stepney's letter to his sister is at PRO: SP105/55, f.26, 26 Oct/15 Nov 1694.

Note: The Librarian of the English Folk Dance and Song Society has very kindly informed me that the Book of Country Dances which Stepney wanted would almost certainly have been John Playford's *English Dancing Master*, first published in 1651, but which went into 18 editions and 3 volumes before 1728.

15. PRO: SP105/55, f.51 (Stepney's Letter Book), Stepney in the Hague to Vernon, 26 Oct/5 Nov 1694.
16. PRO: *ibid.* f.54. Text of the Stepney/Goertz agreement.
17. PRO: *ibid.* ff.50, 50v, Stepney in the Hague to Charles Montagu, 30 Oct/9 Nov 1694.
18. PRO: *ibid.* f.59, Stepney in the Hague to Shrewsbury, 30 Oct/9 Nov 1694; SP105/82, ff.247 & 248 (Original letters to Stepney), Vernon in London to Stepney, 30 Oct (o.s.) and 2 Nov (o.s.) 1694.

IX *Diplomat, Soldier and Country Gentleman*

1. BL: Add.MS. 46535, f.9 (Lexington Papers, Vol.XV), Stepney at Wesel to Lexington, 23/13 Feb 1695.
2. BL: *ibid.* f.5, Stepney in London to Lexington, 21 Nov (o.s.) 1694; PRO: SP105/55, f.67 (Stepney's Letter Book), Stepney in Whitehall to Madam the Electrice of Saxony, 28 Dec (o.s.) 1695; PRO: SP105/82, f.249 (Original Letters to Stepney, (1686-95), Sophia, Electress of Hanover (own hand) to Stepney (French), 10/20 de Janvier 1695.
3. BL: Add.MS.28897, f.64 (Ellis Papers), Stepney to Ellis, 15 Dec (o.s.) 1694. Stepney's request for instructions is at PRO: SP105/55, f.69, Stepney in Whitehall to Blathwayt, 9 Jan (o.s.) 1695; the reply is at PRO: SP105/55, f.73,'Instructions for our trusty and well beloved George Stepney, Esq.' January, 1695. For Stepney's leave-taking in London, see PRO: SP81/87, f.112 (German States), Stepney in Dresden to Vernon, probably dated 22 Feb/4 March 1695
4. BL: Add.MS.46535, f.9, Stepney at Wesel to Lexington, 23/13 Feb 1695.
5. PRO: SP105/55, f.76 Stepney in Leipzig to Blathwayt 19 Feb/1 March 1695. SP81/87, f.111 Stepney in Leipzig, probably to Vernon, 19 Feb/1 March 1695.
6. PRO: SP105/55, f.112 Stepney in Dresden to Vernon The date is given as 2 Feb; but it was more probably 22 Feb/4 Mar 1695. *ibid.* f.114 Stepney in Dresden to Shrewsbury 26 Feb/8 March 1695. *ibid.* f.119 Stepney in Dresden to Vernon 1/11 March 1695.
7. PRO: SP105/55, f.122v (Stepney's Letter Book), Stepney in Dresden to [Richard] Hill in Antwerp, 19/29 March 1695. Note: Stepney gives details in this letter of the Cossart brothers, merchants and bankers. Isaac was based in Amsterdam and assisted Stepney frequently in money transactions, and forwarding letters. Isaac's brother Jean was based in Rotterdam. PRO: SP81/87, f.127 (German States), Stepney in Dresden to Vernon, 19/29 March 1695.
8. BL: Add.MS. 46535, f.39 (Lexington Papers, Vol. XV) Stepney in Dresden to Lexington, 22 March/1 April 1695.
9. BL: *ibid.* f.49, 3 April (n.s.) 1695.
10. BL: *ibid.* f.97, Stepney in Leipzig to Lexington, 16/26 June 1695 (sending extracts of his correspondence with Blathwayt); PRO: SP105/55, f.188, Lexington in Vienna to Stepney, 4 May (n.s.) 1695 (Copy of letter).
11. PRO: *ibid.* f.188, Stepney in Dresden to Blathwayt, 30 April/ 10 May 1695. BL: Add.MS.46535, f.76, Stepney in Dresden to Lexington, 3/13 May 1695.
12. *ibid.* f.69, Stepney in Dresden to Lexington, 15/25 April 1695; PRO: SP105/

55, f.199, Stepney in Dresden to Count Frise, 7/17 May 1695 (French); *ibid.* f.192, Stepney in Dresden to Charles Montagu, 30 Apr/10 May 1695; BL: Add.MS.46535, f.88, Stepney in Dresden to Lexington, 20/30 May 1695.

13. PRO: SP105/55, f.203v, Stepney in Dresden to Mr.Beintema, 10/20 May 1695. It has not been possible to identify the recipient of this letter. He seems to have been a medical doctor, and a member of the Stepney/Bruynincx/ Ehrenburg circle in Vienna. Cresset's letters are at BL: Add.MS. 28897, (Ellis Papers. Vol. II), f.240, Cresset at Zell to Ellis, 13 Aug (probably n.s.) 1695. Cresset mis-spelled Monceau's name as 'Mongeau', but the identification seems firm. BL: Add.MS 28897,f.228, Cresset at Zell to Ellis about Stratford, 9 Aug (n.s.) 1695.

14. PRO: SP105/55, f.225 (Stepney's Letter Book), Stepney in Dresden to Trumbull, 24 May 3 June 1695; PRO: *ibid.* f.233, Stepney at Carlsbad to Blathwayt, 4/14 June 1695.

15. PRO: *ibid.* f.207, Stepney in Dresden to Stratford, 14/24 May 1695 (with enclosures).

16. PRO: *ibid.* f.186, Stepney in Dresden to Cardonnel, 26 Apr/6 May 1695.

17. PRO: *ibid.* f.220, Stepney in Dresden to Cardonnel, 21/31 May 1695 (two letters). *Note:* John Falconbridge's name recurs throughout the Stepney correspondence, spelled in a variety of ways, e.g. Fauconbridge. Together with his brother James, John Shurley and Morgan Price, he is listed as servant to Stepney in January 1695, and seems to have accompanied him to England. He does not seem to have served Stepney after 1699, but became a rolling stone; applied to join the army (in 1705) and a year later took service with Henry Davenant in Frankfurt. There the latter complained bitterly of Falconbridge's behaviour; that he was over-bearing, caused trouble among the other servants, and favoured a particular footman, who went everywhere with him. This last allegation gives rise to the suspicion that Stepney's long employment of Falconbridge (1693-1699), together with his desire to keep his 'little Dutch boy' in his service, might indicate a homosexual household. It is fair to note that when I raised this possibility with the late Dr Albert Hollaender (who until his death in 1989 was carrying out the most scholarly calendar of the Stepney papers in the PRO), he told me he had seen no evidence of homosexuality on Stepney's part.

18. PRO: SP105/55, f.96v (Stepney's Letter Book), Stepney in Dresden to Bruynincx, 4/14 March 1695.

19. BL: Add.MS 28897, f.93 (Ellis Papers, Vol. 2), Stepney in Dresden to Ellis, 21/31 May 1695; Add.MS 46535, f.89 (Lexington Papers Vol XV), Stepney in Dresden to Lexington, 24 May/3 June 1695; PRO: SP105/55, f.230, Stepney in Carlsbad to Count and Countess Reuss, 2/12 June 1695 (French); PRO: SP105/55, f.231 (Stepney's Letter Book), Stepney in Carlsbad to Madame Schellendorf (Count Frise's sister), 2/12 June 1695; SP105/54, f.79 (Stepney's Letter Book), Stepney in Leipzig to Blathwayt, 14/24 June 1695.

20. PRO: SP105/55, f.237, Stepney to Mme. Pflug (copied into the Letter Book in Stepney's own hand), 8/18 June 1695.

21. PRO: *ibid.* f.213, Stepney in Dresden to Blathwayt, 17/27 May 1695; SP105/ 54, f.79, Stepney in Leipzig to Blathwayt, 14/24 June 1695.

22. BL: Add.MS. 28897, f.154 (Ellis Papers, Vol. II) Stepney in Frankfurt to Ellis, 2/12 July 1695.

23. BL: Add.MS. 46535, ff.101, 103 (Lexington Papers, Vol. XV), Stepney in Frankfurt to Lexington, 2/12 and 6/16 July 1695.

24. PRO: SP105/54, f.134 (Stepney's Letter Book), Stepney in Frankfurt to Cresset,

20/30 July 1695.

25. PRO: SP105/54, f.137, Stepney in Mainz to Trumbull, 25 July/4 August 1695; *ibid.* f.138v, Stepney to Blathwayt (same date); *ibid.* f.145, Stepney in Frankfurt to Blathwayt, '6 in the morning', 30 July/9 August 1695.

26. PRO: SP105/54, f.145v, Stepney in Frankfurt to Powis, '3 in ye morning', 30 July/ 9 August 1695.

27. PRO: *ibid.* f.147, Stepney in Cologne to Trumbull, 2/12 August 1695; f.146v Stepney in Cologne to Blathwayt, 2/12 August 1695.

28. PRO: *ibid.* f.153, Stepney at Aix to Prior, 8/18 August 1695.

29. PRO: *ibid.* f.150, Stepney at Aix to Heneage Montagu (same date).

30. BL: Add.MS. 46535, f.111, (Lexington Papers, Vol.XV), Stepney at Namur to Lexington, 16/26 August 1695.

31. BL: Add.MS. 28897, ff. 278, 282 (Ellis Papers, Vol. II) Stepney to Ellis, 22 Aug/1 Sept and 26 Aug/5 Sept 1695. *Note*: Stepney's account of the fall of Namur is contained in BL: Add.MS. 46535, f.113, dated 20/30 August 1695, and is also in the printed edition of the Lexington Papers (The Hon. H. Manners-Sutton, ed. – London, 1851).

32. BL:Add.MS. 28897, f.292 (Ellis Papers, Vol.II) Stepney at the Hague to Ellis 10/20 Sept 1695.

33. BL: *ibid.* f.296 12/22 Sept 1695. *ibid.* f.302 16/26 Sept 1695.

34. Stepney's verses in full are at BL: Add.MS. 28897, f.319 (Ellis Papers, Vol.II) Stepney at the Hague to Ellis, 1/11 October 1695.

35. BL: Add.MS. 46535, f.117 (Lexington Papers, Vol.XV), Stepney at the Hague to Lexington, 10/20 Oct 1695.

36. PRO: SP105/54, f.179 (Stepney's Letter Book), Stepney at the Hague to Ham (no date, but copied into the Letter Book immediately following a letter to Bruynincx dated 15/25 Oct 1695).

37. PRO: SP105/54, f.188, 22 Oct/1 Nov 1695 (no addressee: but the late Dr Albert Hollaender considered Heneage Montagu to be the most likely recipient.).

38. BL: Add.MS 46535, f.115 (Lexington Papers, Vol. XV), Stepney at the Hague to Lexington, 28 Oct/7 Nov 1695.

39. BL: Add.MS. 28897, f.384 (Ellis Papers, Vol.II), Stepney at the Hague to Ellis, 15/25 Nov 1695; f.386, Cresset at Zell to Ellis, 26 Nov (o.s.?) 1695; f.390, Abstract of Stepney's letter toTrumbull, 29 Nov/9 Dec 1695. This letter, in full, is at PRO: SP84-223, f.83 (Holland, 1692-7).

X *The Envoy to the Princes of the Rhine*

Note: No Letter Book exists for the period January-June 1696. Stepney's progress is recorded in the PRO volume, SP81/87 (German States, 1693-96) and in Volume XV of the Lexington Papers, BL, Add.MS. 46535. The principal references are shewn below.

1. BL: Add.MS.46535, f.124, Stepney in the Hague to Lexington, 17/27 Dec 1695; Add.MS.28897, f.422 (Ellis Papers, Vol. II), 'Copy of letter to Mr Secretary' [Trumbull] – the date is incorrectly given, but should read 13/23 Dec 1695; Add.MS.34354, ff.6, 8 (G. Stepney Letters to W. Blathwayt). Two letters from Blathwayt to Stepney written at the end of 1695. The dates on both are obscure.

2. William III's letters to Heinsius are in BL: Add.MS.34504, f.190, 22 Oct/1 Nov 1695; f.205, 7/17 Jan 1696. Montroyal was close to Trarbach, on the Moselle.

3. Stepney's Instructions are attached to his letter to Lexington, dated 17/27/Dec

1695 (see above).

4. BL: Add.MS.46535, f.129 Stepney in Düsseldorf to Lexington, 2/12 Jan 1696. 'The Circles' are those of Franconia and Suabia, whose merchant citizens were frequently asked to contribute cash to German princes for defence. During the Nine Years' War both Circles relied heavily on the skill of Prince Louis, as the local commander, to defend them.

5. PRO: SP81/87, f.145 'Extract of a letter from Mr.Stepney', 6 Jan (n.s.) 1696.

6. Stepney's letters reporting to Trumbull on his stay in Düsseldorf are at PRO: SP81/87, ff.149-161, 3/13 Jan to 17/27 Jan 1696 (five letters).

7. Stepney's long dispatch from 'The Castle at Ehrenbreitstein, over against Coblentz' is at PRO: SP81/87, f.164, 5 Feb (n.s.) 1696.

8. PRO: *ibid.* f.173, 2/12 Feb 1696.

9. PRO: SP81/87, f.178, Stepney in Frankfurt to Trumbull, 16/26 Feb 1696.

10. *Ibid.* f.183, Stepney in Cassel to Trumbull, 2/12 March 1696.

11. BL: Add.MS 46535, f.132, Stepney in Cassel to Lexington, 29 Feb/10 March 1696.

12. Stepney's further letters from Cassel in March/April 1696, and Whitehall's comments on them are at PRO: SP81/87, ff.186-190. *Note:* The word 'rolle' should be 'roule' and signified that the Post of Honour should be allocated to the commanders on alternate days.

13. Stepney's letters on his return to Frankfurt are at PRO: SP81/87, ff.194/5-211; and in BL: Add.MS.46535, f.147 (11/21 Apr 1696) to f.168 (16/26 May 1696), all these addressed to Lexington.

14. BL: *ibid.* f.168, Stepney in Frankfurt to Lexington, 12/22 May 1696.

15. Stepney's report to Blathwayt on his visit to Prince Louis is at PRO: SP81/87, f.219, 'Copy of My letter to Mr. Blathwayt, 30 May/9 June 1696. (This was written at Schwalbach). Stepney's letter (in French) to Prince Louis is quoted in full in Aloys Schulte's *Markgraf Ludwig Wilhelm von Baden und der Reichskrieg gegen Frankreich, 1693-97* (Karlsruhe, 1892), p.207.

16. BL: Add.MS.46535, f.169, Stepney in Frankfurt to Lexington, 2/12 June 1696.

17. BL: Add.MS.34504, f.223, William III *Au Camp de Waveren* to Heinsius, 15 June (n.s.) 1696.

18. BL: Add.MS.46535, f.171, Stepney in Cologne to Lexington, 17/27 June 1696.

19. The Tilly episode begins in Stepney's Letter Book (which he resumed again at 1 July 1696), PRO: SP105/56, f.2, copy of Blathwayt's 'Instructions about Tilly', 23 June (n.s.) 1696 and continue to f.31, Stepney at Gembloux to Trumbull, 6/16 July 1696.

20. PRO: SP105/56, f.9, Stepney in Düsseldorf to his sisters, 21/31 (*sic*) June 1696. Daniel Steingens was Counsellor and Secretary of State to the Elector Palatine. He fell under displeasure, then was reinstated. He kept in friendly touch with Stepney until 1707. His wife did not figure in later correspondence, and nothing is known of her after her visit to London in 1696. In 1707 Steingens became Resident of the Palatinate in London, and was married to an English wife, so perhaps the first Mme. Steingens died young. Cf Stepney's letter to Steingens at SP105/77 of 10 Feb 1706.

21. PRO: SP105/56, f.34, Stepney at Gembloux to Rycaut, 13/23 July 1696.

22. *Ibid.* f.34v, Stepney to Trumbull (same date).

23. Carmarthen Record Office: F.65 (George Stepney's letters to Mr. Hill) from Nivelle, 16/26 July, 1696.

24. The King's visit to Cleves is described in PRO: SP105/56, f.59, Stepney at Loo to Trumbull, 8/18 Sept 1696.

25. PRO; SP105/57 (Stepney's Letter Book 1697 – no folio numbers) Stepney to Lord Villiers, 24 March/3 April 1697.

26. PRO: SP105/56, f.67, Stepney in the Hague to Trumbull, 2/12 Oct 1696; *ibid.* f.85, 23 Oct/2 Nov 1696; BL: Add.MS.46535, f.183, Stepney in the Hague to Lexington, 4/14 Dec 1696; PRO: SP105/56, f.92, Stepney in the Hague to 'Lancil' Stepney, 3/13 Nov 1696. Stepney's list of his debts is at SP105/56, f.116, 11/21 Dec 1696.

27. Stepney's comment on the Emperor Leopold I is to be found at BL: Add.MS.46535, f.179, 5/15 Nov 1696. It was included in the printed version of the Lexington Papers and used by Aloys Schulte in his biography of *Markgraf Ludwig Wilhelm v. Baden.* . . , p.325. Prior's letter to Lexington was dated 17/27 Nov 1696, and is in the Lexington Papers at p.230.

28. PRO: SP105/56, f.97, Stepney in the Hague to Blathwayt, 10/20 Nov 1696. *ibid.* f.102v, 17/27 Nov 1696; PRO: SP105/56, f.104, Stepney to Heinsius, 29 Nov (n.s.) 1696; *ibid.* f.108v, Stepney in the Hague to Blathwayt, 1/11 Dec 1696.

29. PRO: SP105/56, f.108v, Stepney in the Hague to Blathwayt, 1/11 Dec 1696. *ibid.* f.115, 8/18 Dec 1696. William III's letter to Heinsius is at BL: Add.MS.34505, f.15v, 15/25 Dec 1696; PRO: SP105/56, f.117, Stepney in the Hague to Ellis, 15/25 Dec 1696; *ibid.* f.118, Stepney in the Hague to Watkins, 18/28 Dec 1696. *Note*: According to Chambers' Twentieth Century Dictionary (Revised edition, 1964) 'Lamb's-wool' was a wholesome old English beverage composed of ale and the pulp of roasted apples, with sugar and spices. BL: Add.MS.46535, f.174, Stepney at Dieren to Lexington, 21/31 August 1696.

XI *The End of the Nine Years' War*

1. Aloys Schulte: *Markgraf Ludwig Wilhelm v. Baden.* . . (Karlsruhe, 1892), p.360.

2. PRO: SP105/56, f.110 (Stepney's Letter Book), Stepney in the Hague to Blathwayt, 18/28 Dec 1696; f.117v, Stepney in the Hague to Heinsius, 25 Dec (n.s.) 1696.

3. *Ibid.* f.125, Stepney in the Hague to Blathwayt, 1 Jan (n.s.) 1697. The '3 Stoicks' to whom Stepney refers were the Plenipotentiaries appointed by the King to negotiate peace with the French. They were Thomas Herbert, Eighth Earl of Pembroke (1656-1733); Edward, Viscount Villiers (1656-1711), who at the time was the King's Envoy in the Hague (he was soon to be created Earl of Jersey); and Sir Joseph Williamson (1633-1701), former Secretary of State and diplomat. Pembroke was very learned, especially in mathematics. (Cf entries for all three in the DNB).

4. PRO: SP105/56, f.131, Stepney in the Hague to Blathwayt, 5/15 Jan 1697; f.116, 11/21 Dec 1696.

5. *ibid.* f.137, Stepney in the Hague to Charles Montagu, 12/22 Jan 1697.

6. *ibid.* f.138, Goertz in Frankfurt to Stepney (French), 10/20 janvier 1697.

7. BL: Add.MS.46535, f.189 (Lexington Papers, Vol.XV), Stepney in the Hague to Lexington, 5 Feb (n.s.) 1697. Stepney was referring to Joost van Keppel, Earl of Albemarle, Henri de Massue de Ruvigny, Earl of Galway, and Count Frise.

8. PRO: SP105/56, f.152v, Stepney in the Hague to Blathwayt, 5 Feb (n.s.) 1697; f.153v, Stepney to Ellis (same date), f.160v, Stepney in the Hague to Romswinckel (French), 6/16 février 1697.

9. PRO: SP105/57, f.46 (Stepney's Letter Book), *Protocolle de ce que c'est passé dans la Conférence chez Mr. Le Pensionnaire à la quelle Mr. le Comte de Frise et moy assistames le 6/16 de février 1697. Note*: This volume of Stepney's Letter Book was wrongly bound. The first 42 leaves contain Stepney's correspondence between June and August 1697. The earlier letters begin at f.44. But the folio numbering stops abruptly at f.95 (23 March/2 April 1697).

10. PRO: SP105/57, f.52, Stepney in Cologne to Heinsius, 1 March (n.s.) 1697 (French).

11. *ibid.* f.64, Stepney in Coblenz to Heinsius (Fr), 5 March (n.s.) 1697.

12. BL: Add.MS.46535, f.193 (Lexington Papers, Vol XV), Stepney at 'Wisbaden' to Lexington, 25 Feb/7 March 1697. *Note*: This letter was *not* included in the nineteenth-century selection of Lexington's correspondence, published in 1851. Stepney was by 1697 on 'old boy' terms with Lexington. At some time during the year he gave introductions to both Lexington and Count Frise to 'Crown Court' in London – presumably a brothel, for both men visited a lady. See the Calendar of the Bath MSS, Vol. III, p.199, which prints Richard Powis' letter to Matthew Prior, and note that the date of this letter, given as 3/13 March 1697, should read 1698 by the modern calendar.

13. PRO: SP105/57, f.82v Stepney in Frankfurt to Trumbull, 11/21 March 1697; f.85, Stepney in Frankfurt to Goertz of Hanover, 13/23 March 1697 (French).

14. *Ibid.* – Stepney in Frankfurt to Heinsius (French); 27 Apr/7 May 1697, Stepney to Blathwayt, 29 Apr/9 May.

15. *Ibid.* – Stepney in Frankfurt to Mr. le Comte d'Autel, 2/12 May 1697. *Note*: Schulte gives the German version of d'Autel's name as Feldzugsmeister (FZM) Graf Johann Friedrich von Eltern. (*op. cit.*, p.104).

16. PRO: SP105/57, Stepney in Frankfurt to Blathwayt (private letter), 6/16 May 1697; *ibid.* Blathwayt at Breda to Stepney, 12/22 May 1697.

17. *Ibid.* Stepney at 'Fridberg' to Blathwayt, 16/26 May 1697; *Ibid.* Stepney at Cassel to Blathwayt, 20/30 May 1697.

18. *Ibid.* Stepney in Cassel to Mr. Chanc^{llr} of the Exchequer, 20/30 May 1697.

19. *Ibid.* Stepney in Frankfurt to Blathwayt, 30 May/9 June 1697.

20. *Ibid.* Stepney 'on ye Rhine', and at Bonn to Blathwayt, 4/14 and 5/15 June 1697.

21. Stepney's letter to the King is at PRO: SP105/57, 12/22 June 1697, and to Ellis at f.13v, 2/12 July 1697 (note that the folio numbers start again at the date 14/24 June 1697).

22. PRO: SP105/57, f.8, Stepney at Cocklenberg to Count Frise (French), 5 juillet (n.s.) 1697; f.21, Stepney at Cocklenberg to Trumbull, 12/22 July. *Note*: This date is given as '12/22 of Juin' – but this is an error made by Stepney's clerk.

23. PRO: SP105/57, f.25, Stepney at Cocklenberg to Mr Dorville (French), 16/26 Juillet 1697; *ibid.* f.30, Stepney in the Hague to Blathwayt, 10 Aug (n.s.) 1697. Lord Westmorland was Thomas Fane, (1679-1736) the Sixth Earl, whose diary is in the British Library at Add.MS.34223. He makes no mention of this journey. Stepney's visit to Amsterdam is at PRO: SP105/57, f.38, Stepney in the Hague to Trumbull, 3 Sept (n.s.) 1697.

24. Narcissus Luttrell: *A Brief Historical Relation of State Affairs from September 1678 to April 1714*, Vol. IV, p.272 (Oxford, 1857).

XII *Brandenburg and Poland*

1. PRO: SP105/51, p.4, No.1, Stepney's Letter Book 1698. *Note*: This volume of the Letter Books bears no folio numbers. On the first few leaves Stepney himself wrote in page-numbers.

2. BL: Add.MS.34505, f.56v (Mackintosh Collections, Vol.XIX), William III at Kensington to Heinsius, 24 Dec/3 Jan 1697/8.

3. PRO: SP105/51, p.4, No. 2. Stepney's Instructions are given in a slightly abbreviated form: however it should be possible to judge how well he carried them out.

4. PRO: SP105/51, p.5, Stepney in Whitehall to Vernon, 28 Jan (o.s.) 1697/8.

Note: Eventually, Stepney was not involved in 'the affair of Neufchatel'. But he briefed himself on the subject, which concerned conflicting claims to the territory. One of the claimants was King William, from whom the Elector of Brandenburg expected to inherit (cf. Stepney's letter to Vernon, written from the Hague on 4/14 Feb 1698, in SP105/51). Neuchâtel (modern spelling) now lies within Switzerland, on the lake which bears its name, about 50 km west of Berne.

5. BL: Add.MS.28900 (Ellis Papers, Vol. V), Stepney at Rotterdam to Ellis. (This letter is wrongly dated 1/11 Jan 1698: it should be 1/11 *February* 1698, when Stepney wrote a similar account of his travels to Vernon.)

6. PRO: SP105/51. Stepney in Hamburg to Sophia, 27 Feb (o.s.) 1697/8; and Sophia at Herrenhausen to Stepney, 3/13 Mar 1697/8.

7. Stepney's account of his journey is contained in SP105/51 between the dates 11/21 February and 5/15 March 1697/8.

8. PRO: SP105/51. 'Relation of the Ceremonial at my Audience', 6/16 Mar 1697/8.

9. The letters about the Danckelmann affair are in SP105/51, between 8/18 March and 29 March/8 April 1697/8.

10. PRO: SP105/51. Stepney in Berlin to Vernon, 27 Mar/6 Apr 1697/8.

11. PRO: SP105/51. Stepney in Berlin to Ellis, 22 Mar/1 Apr 1697/8.

12. *Ibid.* Stepney in Berlin to Charles Montagu, 22 Mar/1 Apr 1697/8.

13. PRO: SP105/51, Blathwayt in Whitehall to Stepney, 29 Mar (o.s.) 1697/8, Stepney in Berlin to Blathwayt, 16/26 Apr 1698.

14. The account of Stepney's travel to Danzig and Warsaw is in SP105/51 between the dates 27 April/7 May and 21/31 May 1698.

15. PRO: SP105/51, Stepney in Königsberg to Vernon, 31 May/10 Jun and 3/13 Jun 1698.

16. Correspondence about Stepney's visit to Königsberg is in SP105/51 between 31 May/10 June and 1/11 July 1698; Stepney's comments to Raby are in SP105/63, p.259 of 14 August 1701.

17. Stepney's long dispatch is at SP105/51, dated 2/12 Aug 1698. His comments about Ham, and about his own success are dated 6/16 Aug 1698.

18. PRO: SP105/51, Stepney in Berlin to Blathwayt (private letter) 9/19 Aug 1698.

19. PRO: SP105/51, Blathwayt at Loo to Stepney, 9 Aug 1698 (marked 'rec'd at Berlin 6.15 Aug); Stepney in Berlin to Blathwayt, 20/30 Aug 1698.

20. Stepney's Letter-Book for the period September-December 1698 is missing. The account of his visit to Goer is found in BL: Add.MS.28901, f.423 (Ellis Papers, Vol. VI), 13/23 Sept 1698; f.426, 25 Sept/5 Oct 1698; and in Add.MS.28902, f.35-f.63 (Ellis Papers, Vol.VII), 4/14-11/21 Oct 1698. In some of these papers the dates are confusingly given in old style (o.s.): in the text these have been transcribed into new style (n.s.).

21. The party is recorded in Stepney's letters to Ellis and Blathwayt at BL: Add.MS.28902 (Ellis Papers, Vol. VII) at f.106 of 1/11 Nov 1698 ff.116 and 121 of 5/15 Nov 1698. Readers are reminded of the accuracy of Shakespeare's description of a state banquet in northern Europe, given in *Hamlet* Act I, Sc.IV: 'The king doth wake tonight and take his rouse.'

22. BL: *Calendar of the Bath MSS.* Vol. III, p.298, Blathwayt in the Hague to Prior, 5 Dec 1698.

23. BL: Add.MS.28902, Stepney in Berlin to Ellis, f.211, 27 Dec/6 Jan 1698/9.

24. PRO: SP105/52 (Stepney's Letter Book – no folio numbers), Stepney in Magdeburg to Vernon, 15 Jan (o.s.?) 1698/9.

25. *Ibid.* Stepney in Berlin to Robinson 8 Feb (probably o.s.) 1698/9. Stepney's account of the Elbing situation is contained in his letter to Paget, 11/21 Feb 1698/9.

26. PRO: SP105/74, f.133v (Letter Book), Stepney in Vienna to Mlle Pelnitz, 26 Nov (n.s.) 1704. The French Envoy's full name was Pierre Puchot, marquis

DesAlleurs. He came from Normandy. Stepney liked him. The first name of the Danish Envoy, Mr. Ahlfeldt, is not known.

27. PRO: SP105/52, Stepney in Berlin to Ellis, 14/24 Mar 1698/9.

28. *Ibid.* Stepney in Berlin to Sir Peter Wyche and to Charles Montagu, 8/18 Mar 1698/9.

29. Correspondence about the Protestant refugees begins with Stepney's letter to Ellis dated 18 April (o.s.) 1699 in SP105/52, and continues through this and the following Letter Book, SP105/53. At times long lists of the names of the refugees are included.

30. PRO: SP105/52, Stepney in Berlin to Ireton, 24 Jun 1699. *Note*: In the late seventeenth-century, 'jockey' signified a dealer in horses, rather than a rider.

31. PRO: SP105/52 Stepney in Berlin to Blathwayt, 4/14 Jul 1699. The Latin epigram is given in Chapter XXIII.

32. PRO: SP105/53 (Stepney's Letter Book – no folio numbers) Stepney in Berlin to Blathwayt, 1/11 Aug 1699. The musician was John Abel [I], (1650-1724), for whose career see Grove's *Dictionary of Music*.

33. PRO: SP105/53, Stepney in Berlin to Blathwayt (private letter), 12/22 Aug 1699.

34. *Ibid.* Stepney to Blathwayt, 19/29 Aug 1699. It should be noted that the King agreed with Stepney's judgement as to the unsuitability of the masquerade. See SP105/53, Blathwayt to Stepney on 2/12 Sept 1699.

35. Bodleian Library: RAWL.MS C.936, f.94, 'To Mr.Blathwayt', 17 Oct 1699. *Note*: This volume comprises Stepney's Letter Book for the period October-November 1699. It is not known how this section became detached from the series of Letter Books in the Public Record Office, and was deposited in Oxford.

36. BL: Add.MS.34505 (Mackintoch Collections, Vol. XIX), William III at Kensington to Heinsius, 10/20 Nov 1699.

37. PRO: CO 389/16, pp.402-3 (Board of Trade papers – no title), 7 Dec (o.s.) 1699.

XIII *The Commissioner of Trade*

1. Carmarthen Record Office F.65 (G. Stepney's Letters to Mr Hill) Stepney at Königsberg to Hill, 17/27 June 1698.

2. Information on the Board of Trade and its members is based on J. P. Greene *Great Britain and the American Colonies (1606-1763)* (New York, 1970), p.127, *et seq.*, and on the *Dictionary of National Biography*. The Secretary to the Board was William Popple, assisted by his son (also William). *Note*: that the Earl of Bridgewater is always spelled thus in the Board of Trade Journal. His son, Scroop Egerton (the first Duke of Bridgwater) omitted the first 'e' in the name. In the Journal, the Board collectively is often referred to as 'their Lordships', this courtesy apparently dating back to the first Lords Commissioners for Trade established by King Charles II. It must have pleased Stepney.

3. The business of the Board of Trade on 6 and 7 September (o.s.) 1697 is related in PRO: CO391/10, ff121 & 121v (Board of Trade Journal), Stepney's intervention on behalf of Orford is at PRO: CO192/10, f.164v, 28 Oct (o.s.) 1697. The Order in Council was read on 8 November (f.169v).

4. PRO: CO391/10, f.138, 23 Sept (o.s.) 1697; f.139v, 27 Sept; f.141v, 30 Sept; f.163v, 26 Oct; f.174v, 17 Nov.

5. Blathwayt's letter is at PRO: CO 391/10, f.141v; 30 Sept (o.s.) 1697. Orth's letters are at PRO: CO 388/6 (Trade Foreign); 5 and 15 Oct 1697. The papers about the wool manufacture at Sada begin at PRO: CO388/6, 4 Oct 1687. The wool trade (or smuggling) between Scotland and Holland is revealed in PRO: CO 388/5, ff.217-226v (Trade Domestick), 8 Oct-11 Nov (o.s.) 1697.

6. The General Report on Trade is in PRO: CO 389/15, pp.265-282 (Board of Trade

Entry Book), 23 Dec (o.s.) 1697. Blathwayt's comment is in PRO: SP105/51 (Stepney's Letter Book), Blathwayt in Whitehall to Stepney, 18 Feb (o.s.) 1697/8.

7. PRO: SP105/51 (Stepney's Letter Book), Stepney in Berlin to Robinson, 12/22 March 1697/8.

8. PRO: *ibid.* Stepney in Berlin to Ellis, 21 March/1 April 1697/8.

9. PRO: *ibid.* Vernon in Whitehall to Stepney, 8 April (o.s.) 1698; *ibid.* Stepney in Berlin to Vernon, 16/26 Aug 1698.

10. PRO: *ibid.* Stepney in Königsberg to Blathwayt, 14/24 June 1698.

11. PRO: *ibid.* Stepney in Königsberg to Popple, 20/30 June 1698.

12. PRO: SP105/53 (Stepney's Letter Book), Stepney in Berlin to Blathwayt, 19/29 Aug 1699 and 12/22 Sept 1699.

XIV *The Turn of the Century*

1. PRO: CO391/12, f.152v (Board of Trade Journal), 22 Dec (o.s.) 1699.

2. PRO: *ibid.* f.154v, 3 Jan (o.s.) 1699/1700; f.184v, 9 Feb (o.s.).

3. PRO: CO391/13, f. 35 (Board of Trade Journal), 12 June (o.s.) 1700.

4. PRO: *ibid.* f. 47v, 28 June (o.s.) 1700; f.57v, 17 July (o.s.) 1700.

5. Stepney's days of absence from the Board of Trade are taken from the Journal in the CO391 series. The clerk listed (in order of seniority) each member who attended day by day. Stepney wrote on 10/20 May 1698 to Charles Montagu about rooms at Hampton Court (see Letter Book, SP105/51). Montagu eventually confirmed the arrangement in 1699; cf BL: Add.MS.28903, f.398 (Ellis Papers Vol. VIII), Stepney in Berlin to Ellis, 22 July/1 Aug 1699.

6. BL: Add.MS.28855, f.154 (Ellis Papers, Vol. XI) Stepney at Newmarket to Ellis 13 Apr (o.s.) 1700. The King's decision not to go to Newmarket is shewn in the contemporary Newsletter *The Post Boy,* microfilm in BL: Burney Collection of Newspapers, Reel 122, Nos. 773, 776 and 779.

7. The text (in French, as he wrote it) of Stepney's first letter to Sophia is in Onno Klopp (ed.), *Correspondenz von Leibniz mit der Prinzessin Sophie,* (reprinted at Hildesheim, 1973), Vol. II, p.208 *et seq.* Sophia's reply is in BL: Hardwick State Papers, Vol. II, printed as *Miscellaneous State Papers 1501-1726,* p.442, headed 'Princess Sophia to Mr. Stepney, (transcribed from the original in Lord Somers' hand). The announcement of the King's dining with Lord Macclesfield at 'Bushe Park' is also in *The Post Boy,* No. 812 [see Note 6 above]. Stepney's second letter to Sophia is in PRO: SP105/89, f.24 (Stepney's Miscellaneous Papers – unbound).

8. PRO: SP105/68, p.423v (Stepney's Letter Book), Stepney in Vienna to Buckingham, 23 June (n.s.) 1703. SP105/77 (Stepney's Letter Book) Stepney in Vienna to young Vernon, 17 March (n.s.) 1706. Stepney's distrust of Vernon senior is shewn in a letter which he wrote to his cousin Erasmus Lewis from Vienna at PRO: SP105/63, p.411 (Stepney's Letter Book), 20 Sept (n.s.) 1701; 'I have had my reasons why I have not corresponded with Secretary Vernon since I left England.'

9. Stepney's *Essay upon the Present Interest of England* is now to be found in the Somers Collection of Tracts, Third Collection, Vol. IV, according to which it was printed in 1701. From the text, it was written after the death of the Duke of Gloucester (28 July (o.s.) 1700) and before that of King James II (September 1701).

XV *The Grand Alliance*

1. BL: Add.MS.34505, f.190v (Mackintosh Collections, Vol. XIX) William III to Heinsius, 1 Apr (o.s.) 1701.

2. Stepney's Instructions are contained in BL: Add.MS.34354, f.? (Letters to W. Blathwayt), 2 Mar (o.s.) 1700/1; PRO: SP105/62, f.1 (Stepney's Letter Book).

3. PRO: *ibid.* f.6, Stepney at Sheerness to Hedges, 19 March (o.s.) 1700/01.

4. PRO: *ibid.* f.10, Stepney in the Hague to Hedges, 25 March/3 April 1701.

5. *Ibid.* f.12, Stepney to Hedges (private letter) – same date.

6. Details of Wratislaw's arrival in London and of his dispatch to the Emperor regarding Stepney are taken from E. Jarnat-Derbolav *Die Oesterreichische Gesandtschaft in London, 1701-11*, (Bonn, 1972). The King's irritation with Wratislaw can be seen in his letter to Heinsius from Hampton Court dated 25 March 1701 (BL: Add.MS.34505, f.189).

7. PRO: SP105/62, ff.18, 19 Stepney at Bonn to (respectively) Stanhope and Hedges, 7/18 April 1701. Hedges' reply is at f.68, dated 18 April (o.s.) 1701.

8. Stepney's journey is recounted in his Letter Book, SP105/62, ff.31-44, between the dates 9/20 April and 23 Apr/4 May 1701. He reported on the situation in Germany as he progressed.

9. PRO: SP105/62, f.51, Stepney in Vienna to Hedges, 23 April/4 May 1701. Stepney's suspicions about Wratislaw's 'hidden channels' are at f.107 (31 May/11 June) and f.118 (4/15 June 1701). Stepney was suspicious of Vernon's behaviour ever since the latter had 'shopped' him to the King a few months earlier.

10. Stepney's dispatches to Hedges describing his first days in Vienna are in the Letter-Book, SP105/62, ff.57 to 72 (26 Apr/7 May – 7/18 May 1701). Details of the Palais Lamberg are taken from the typescript of Paul Harrer Lucienfeld, *Wien, seine Häuser, Menschen u. Kultur,* Vol. VII, Part 1 (Vienna, 1948) in the *Bibliothek der Stadt Wien.* The rent paid by Stepney for the house is given in his Letter Book SP105/66, writing to Tucker from Vienna on 11 October (n.s.) 1702. (No folio numbers in this volume).

11. Stepney's expenses and reports are all contained in his Letter-Book, SP105/62 from f.122 (7/18 June 1701) onwards.

12. PRO: SP105/63 (Stepney's Letter Book – page numbers only) p.31 Stepney in Vienna to Prior, 9 July (n.s.) 1701. *Note:* In early July 1701 Stepney was instructed by the Earl of Albemarle to correspond with a Colonel Montmollin, who had been sent by the King to Munich to try to persuade the Elector of Bavaria to join the Grand Alliance. Stepney carried on the correspondence throughout the summer, but since the Colonel's efforts came to nothing and Stepney was not directly involved with Max Emmanuel, the exchange of letters is ignored here.

13. PRO: SP105/63, p.44, Stepney in Vienna to Hedges, 13 July (n.s.) 1701; *ibid.* p.98, 27 July (n.s.) 1701.

14. *Ibid.* p.130, 6 Aug (n.s.) 1701.

15. Stepney's description of the dinner is at PRO: SP105/63, p.318, Stepney in Vienna to Blathwayt, 7 Sept (n.s.) 1701.

16. The letter to Godolphin about Boscawen is at PRO: SP105/63, p.210, 17 Aug 1701. Hedges' suggestion about Addison is at BL: Add.MS 7074, f.21 (Stepney Papers Vol. XVII). Ellis in Whitehall to Stepney, 20 May (o.s.) 1701, and f.43?, July 1701. Addison arrived in Vienna in December 1702.

17. PRO: SP105/63, p.400, Stepney in Vienna to Blathwayt, 17 Sept (n.s.) 1701. The Governor of Brunn was probably Count Philipp Christoph Breuner (d.1709), *Oberster Erb Cammerer in Nieder-Oesterreich* (Zedler). The Sinzendorf family was long resident at Ernstbrunn. In 1989 there was alas no trace of the artificial lake which Stepney describes.

18. PRO: SP105/63, p.460, Blathwayt at Loo to Stepney, 13 Sept (n.s.) 1701.

19. The account of Stepney's exclusion from the knowledge of the Grand Alliance negotiations is at PRO: SP105/63, p.238, Stepney in Vienna to Blathwayt (private letter), 20 Aug (n.s.) 1701; p.404, Marlborough at the Hague to Stepney, 23 Aug (n.s.) 1701; p.460, Blathwayt at Loo to Stepney, 13 Sep (n.s.) 1701; p.462, Stepney in Vienna to Blathwayt, 24 Sep (n.s.) 1701; SP105/64 (Stepney's Letter Book), f. 27, Stepney in Vienna to Blathwayt, 28 Sep (n.s.) 1701; f. 69 Stepney in Vienna to Hedges, 5 Oct (n.s.) 1701.

20. PRO: SP/105/64, f.101, Stepney in Vienna to Obdam, 13 Oct (n.s.) 1701. The account of Stepney's new clothes, and of the ball, is taken from his letter to Tucker in PRO: SP105/66 (Stepney's Letter Book), 11 Oct 1702.

21. Stepney's letter to Frise (undated) is printed in Heinrich Freiherr v. Friesen, *Julius Heinrich, Graf von Friesen* (Leipzig, 1870), p.154. Curiously, Stepney's Letter Book for the months of January and February 1701/2 is missing. The next volume, SP105/65, begins with copies of Vernon's letters of 3, 6 and 8 March (o.s.) 1701/2, describing the King's illness and death. The last of these letters reached Vienna on 30 March (n.s.) 1702 via the Hague. During the first two months of the year letters exist from both Vernon and Ellis to Stepney, from which it is evident that he corresponded with them as usual. However the content of the Whitehall letters is routine, and has been omitted here.

XVI *The New Reign*

1. PRO: SP105/65 (Stepney's Letter Book – no folio or page numbers), Stepney in Vienna to Vernon, 1 Apr (n.s.) 1702 – PS to letter.

2. Stepney's claim on the King is set out in his letter to Lord Treasurer Godolphin in SP105/65 of 10 May 1702. Vernon's reference to the expense account is in *The Letters of James Vernon*, G. P. R. James (ed.) (London, 1841, p.174), Vernon in Whitehall to Stepney, 10 Feb 1701/2.

3. PRO: SP105/65, Stepney in Vienna to Blathwayt, 10 Apr (n.s.) 1702.

4. *Ibid.* Stepney in Vienna to Vernon,13 and 17 May 1702.

5. *Ibid.* Stepney in Vienna to Hedges, 19 July 1702.

6. PRO: SP105/66, Stepney in Vienna to Prince Eugene, 11 Oct 1702. *Note*: This volume of Stepney's Letter Books was given folio numbers for the first 167 sheets. Then the numbering ceases abruptly. The letter to Prince Eugene above is the first *without* a folio number. The Prince's reply is in the same letter-book.

7. PRO: SP105/66, Powis in Whitehall to Stepney, 10 November 1702.

8. Stepney's account of his quarrel with Kaunitz is contained in his two letters to Hedges in SP105/66 at 19 Nov 1702. For the other view of the affair, see Guillaume de Lamberty, *Mémoires pour servir à l'Histoire du XVIII Siècle* (Amsterdam, 1735), Vol. II, pp.286-7. Stepney's letter to Lord Nottingham is in SP105/66 at 11 Nov 1702.

9. The Vigo celebrations are in SP105/66 at 29 Nov and 2 Dec 1702.

10. The end-of-the-year conference and relevant letters are in SP105/66 at 23 and 26 Dec 1702. The full name of the Amirante of Castile was *Don Juan Tomes de Cabrera, Conde de Melgar, Duque de Rioseco*. On 22 Aug 1705 Stepney reported his death.

11. All the events and rumours of January 1703 (n.s.) are contained in the next volume of Stepney's Letter-Books, SP105/67, to which he allotted page numbers. The original of Stanhope's letter is in BL: Add.MS 7069 (Stepney Papers, Vol. XII), f.1, 2 Jan (n.s.) 1703.

12. Godolphin's letter to Stepney is at PRO: SP105/67, p.241 and the reply is at p.243, dated 17 Feb (n.s.) 1703, with the follow-up letter to Hedges at p.250.

21 Feb (n.s.) 1703.

13. Stepney's intervention in the Portuguese negotiations is at PRO: SP105/67, p.301, Stepney in Vienna to Hedges, 28 Feb (n.s.) 1703 and at pp.322 and 326, both of 1 March 1703. Hedges' approbation is in the next volume of the Letter-Books, SP105/68, p.52, 19 March (o.s.) 1702/3.

14. The Bavarian battle is at PRO: SP105/67, p.420, Stepney in Vienna to Hedges, 17 March (n.s.) 1703 and at p.466, undated, but inserted under 24 March. Prince Louis' pleas, and Prince Eugene's threat to resign are in PRO: SP105/68, p.1 4 April (n.s.) 1703. The news of the Oppenheimer bankruptcy is at PRO: SP105/68, p.139, Stepney in Vienna to Hedges, 2 May 1703 and p.294 2 June (n.s.) 1703.

15. PRO: SP105/68, p.88v, Stepney in Vienna to Cardonnel, 19 April (n.s.) 1703. Cardonnel's reply is recorded in Rebecca Warner, *Epistolary Curiosities,* (London, 1813), Part II, p.71.

16. PRO: SP105/69 (Letter Book – no folio or page numbers), Stepney in Vienna to Hedges, 4 July (n.s.) 1703.

17. *Ibid.* Stepney in Vienna to Marlborough, 20 July 1703.

18. The tentative Venetian negotiations are at PRO: SP105/69. Stepney notes in his own hand, *Private letter to Mr. Secretary ab¹ the negotiations with Venice,*8 Aug (n.s.) 1703, and in Stepney's letter to Tucker of 26 Sept 1703.

19. PRO: SP105/69, Stepney in Vienna to Hedges 4, 8 and 16 Aug 1703. Stepney's letter to Hill, dated 15 August 1703, is printed in *The Diplomatic Correspondence of Richard Hill,* W. Blackley (ed.) (London, 1845) Vol. I, pp.12-14; and is also in SP105/69, the text being attached to Stepney's letter to Hedges dated 22 Sept (n.s.) 1703.

20. Stepney's Instructions are contained in Lord Nottingham's letter of 31 August (o.s.) 1703 (SP105/69); and his self-congratulation is in his letter to Hedges of 29 Sept (n.s.) 1703. His report on the French action in Savoy is in the next volume of the Letter-Books, SP105/70 (no folio, but page numbers provided), at p.53 Stepney in Vienna to Hedges, 10 Oct (n.s.) 1703. Stepney had his information about Hill from Count Auersperg (who was then in Zürich with William Aglionby, the English Secretary),; cf PRO: SP105/70; p.58v, Extract of a letter from Aglionby, 10 Oct (n.s.) 1703; p.62, Stepney in Vienna to Auersperg (in French), 13 Oct 1703.

21. PRO: SP105/70, p.98, Stepney in Vienna to Hedges, 'A Private and familiar letter' 20 Oct (n.s.) 1703.

22. *Ibid.* pp.166, 168, 202, as above, dated 4, 7 and 10 Nov 1703 respectively.

23. BL: Add.MS.7063 (Stepney Papers, Vol. VI), f.38, Cardonnel in Whitehall to Stepney, 19 Nov (o.s.) 1703.

24. PRO: SP105/70, p.254, Stepney in the Hague to Tucker, 'Ab¹ Mr. Hill', 30 Nov (n.s.) 1703.

25. Heinsius' recommendation to Stepney is at PRO: SP105/70, p.361, Stepney in the Hague to Hedges, 25 Dec (n.s.) 1703. The Bill of Extraordinaries is in the same volume at p.455.

XVII *The Hungarian Mediation*

1. Gustav Ratzenhofer, ed. *Feldzüge des Prinzen Eugen* (Vienna, 1879), Vol. VI, Part I, p.726.

2. PRO: CO391/16, ff.165v-177, Board of Trade Journal. The new members of the Board were Thomas Thynne, first Viscount Weymouth (1640-1714), William Legge, first Earl of Dartmouth (1672-1750) and 'Mr. Cecil', probably Robert

Cecil, brother of James, fourth Earl of Salisbury. All these were Tory.

3. PRO: SP105/71, f.168 (Stepney's Letter Book), Stepney to Tucker, 8 Feb (n.s.) 1704.

4. Snyder, Vol. I , Letter No. 269, Marlborough at the Hague to Godolphin, 1/12 Feb (n.s.) 1704. 'You will see by my letter to Mr. Secretary Hedges the measures Mr. Stepney and I have taken with the Pensioner as to the negociations with [the Elector of] Bavaria.'

5. The background to the Hungarian situation is based on R. W. Harris, *Absolutism and Enlightenment* (Revised edition, London, 1967); Hengelmüller; and Hugo Hantsch, *Die Geschichte Oesterreichs*, (Graz, 1968). Stepney's letter to Lexington is in BL: Add.MS 46535 (Lexington Papers, Vol. XV), f.245, 7 Sept 1701. The Emperor's letter to Prince Louis is printed in Röder: Vol. I, Part II, p.231. Whitworth's dispatches are contained in PRO: SP105/71 (Stepney's Letter Book).

6. PRO: SP105/68, p.294 (Stepney's Letter Book), Stepney in Vienna to Hedges, 2 June 1703; SP105/71, f.160 Stepney in the Hague to Hedges, 5 Feb (n.s.) 1704.

7. Stepney's account of his journey is in PRO: SP105/7, ff.191-216, 1/12 – 15/26 Feb 1704. Raby's letter to Cadogan is in BL: Add.MS.22196, f.13 (Strafford Papers), 4 Mar (n.s.) 1704.

8. Stepney's Memorandum is undated, but filed in SP105/71 under 13 March (n.s.) 1704. The incident concerning Lady Colt's jewel is at PRO: SP105/54, f.108v, 5/15 July 1695.

9. PRO: SP105/71, f.386, Stepney in Vienna 'to Mr. Secretary', 19 Mar (n.s.) 1704.

10. Stepney's interception of Rákóczy's letter is at PRO: SP105/72, f.31 (Letter Book), Stepney in Vienna to Hedges (private letter), 12 Apr (n.s.) 1704; f.41(as above), 18 Apr (n.s.) 1704. Stanhope's letters are in PRO: SP 105/72, f.80 (Stepney's Letter Book), 'Extract of a letter from the Hague', 18 Apr (n.s.) 1704; and BL: Add.MS.7069, f.142, Stepney Papers, Vol. XII. Stanhope in the Hague to Stepney, 13 May (n.s.) 1704. A copy of an extract of Baron Obdam's letter to Bruynincx is in PRO: SP84/574, f.139 (Holland, Misc. 1700-1708), 8 Avril 1704. Stepney's rebuttal of the accusations is in PRO: SP105/72, ff.80/135, Stepney in Vienna to Stanhope, 30 Apr and 24 May (n.s.) 1704 .

11. Bruynincx' encounter with Prince Eugene is at PRO: SP105/72, f.117, Stepney in Vienna to Hedges (private letter – the underscoring is Stepney's own), 17 May (n.s.) 1704. The conversation about the fleet is in the same volume, f.82v, 3 May (n.s.) 1704.

12. Marlborough's letters to Stepney and to Sinzendorf, dated 10 and 11 May 1704, respectively, are printed in Murray, Vol. I, pp.258 and 259.

13. Stepney's letter (in French) to Kaunitz is at PRO: SP105/72, f.124, 20 May (n.s.) 1704, and to Marlborough, in the same volume, f.128, 21 May 1704. Marlborough's reply, dated 30 May, is in Murray,Vol. I, p.288 Cardonnel's letter is in BL: Add.MS.7063 (Stepney Papers, Vol. VI), f.50, 24 May 1704.

14. PRO: SP105/72, f.148, Stepney in Vienna to Halifax, 4 June (n.s.) 1704.

15. The attack on the menagerie is described at PRO: SP105/72, f.158, Stepney in Vienna to Marlborough, 10 June (n.s.) 1704. Stepney's remarks about the Protestants: PRO: SP105/72, f. 169, Stepney in Vienna to Hedges, 11 June (n.s.) 1704.

16. PRO: SP105/72, ff.178/9, Stepney in Vienna to Harley, 18 June (n.s.) 1704.

17. Stepney's opinion of the imperial terms for the Malcontents is at PRO: SP105/72, f.185, Stepney in Vienna to Harley, 21 June (n.s.) 1704. The Elector Palatine's reaction to the Mediators' suggestion is at PRO: SP105/72, f.196 (Stepney's Letter Book), Stepney in Vienna to Harley, 25 June (n.s.) 1704. Marlborough's letter to

Hedges, dated 29 June 1704, is in Murray, Vol. I, p.329.

18. PRO: SP105/73 (Stepney's Letter Book, no folio but page numbers), p.18, Stepney in Vienna to Harley, 9 Jul (n.s.) 1704, p.27 (as above), 12 July 1704.

19. Stepney sent the *Nuremberg Gazette* dated 21 July 1704 to Cardonnel (SP 105/73, p.67). The intercepted letters are referred to in PRO: SP105/73, p.63, Stepney in Vienna to Marlborough, 25 July (n.s.) 1704. Stepney wrote to Cardonnel on 5 August 1704 (same volume, p.68v). The arrival of the news of the battle of Blenheim in Vienna was best described by Stepney when he wrote 10 days later to his colleagues in Italy and Switzerland. (SP105/73, p.137, 26 August (n.s.) 1704). His letter of congratulation to Marlborough is in the same volume, p.108v.

XVIII *The Hungarian Mediation (II)*

1. Murray, Vol. I, p.436.

2. PRO: SP105/73, p.92 (Stepney's Letter Book), Stepney in Vienna to Cardonnel, 9 Aug (n.s.) 1704.

3. *ibid.* pp 141, 153, Stepney in Vienna to Harley, 27 Aug and 3 Sept (n.s.) 1704 and p.165, 6 Sept (n.s.) 1704.

4. BL: Add.MS.7077, ff.30, 32, 34 (Stepney Papers, Vol .XX – Misc. Letters and Papers), Fury in Vienna to Stepney 13, 17 and 20 Sept (n.s.) 1704. *Note*: James Fury joined Stepney's household in 1701 or 1702. He was 'German bred' and had served James Vernon senior when the latter was briefly in Vienna in 1692. Fury had also served Blathwayt in Flanders for several years. John Ellis provided these personal details to Sir Paul Rycaut when recommending Fury as a secretary. Ellis added that the appropriate salary would be 200 Crowns, or £40 per annum, living in, plus any travel costs (cf. BL: Add.MS.28901, f.133, 17 May 1698). Fury stayed with Stepney throughout the latter's service in Vienna, and stayed on in the city after Stepney's departure in 1706. He had a brother (unnamed) who lived in Vienna. It is possible that Fury overlapped with Stepney's previous major-domo, John Falconbridge. After 1701 there is only one reference to the latter, in 1703, when Stepney received a letter from Henry Davenant (Frankfurt) and marked it, 'I desired Falkonbridge to thank ym.' However it is possible that Stepney carelessly wrote in the name of the old steward rather than that of the new! Davenant's letter is in BL: Add.MS.7066, f.1, 21 May 1703.

5. Gustav Ratzenhofer, ed., *Feldzüge des Prinzen Eugen,* Vol. VI, pp.184-5 and 200-1, Prince Eugene to Hofkriegsrath Johann von Thiell, 22 Sept and 6 Oct (n.s.) 1704.

6. Stepney's description of his visit to Landau with Marlborough is taken from his letter to Whitworth, PRO: SP 105/73, p.193, 25 Sept (n.s.) 1704 and *ibid.* p.200, Stepney to Erasmus Lewis, 26 Sept 1704.

7. Wratislaw's dispatch to the Emperor was dated 21 7^{bris} [September] 1704 '*Im Lager bei Cron Weissenburg. . .*' and is to be found in HHStA England 38 (Berichte). The original of the Emperor's reply is in HHStA: England 38 (Weisungen), Konvolut *Weisungen an Wratislaw 1704 X-XI.* I have used the translation given in Hengelmüller, p.175, slightly amended by myself.

8. PRO: SP105/74, pp.236-243 (Stepney's Letter Book, Oct-Dec 1704). The report for Marlborough is dated 5 Oct (n.s.) 1704 but is filed at the back of the volume.

9. Wratislaw's dispatch to the Emperor dated 18 October (n.s.) 1704 is in HHStA: Bavarica 89 (alt 67a). Whitworth's letters are in SP105/74, pp.1-20, between the dates 1 and 18 Oct (n.s.) 1704. Stepney's journey and his preliminary reports

to Harley are in the same volume, pp.45-48v, 22-23 Oct 1704.

10. PRO: SP105/74, p.77, 'Short narrative to Mr. Secretary Harley', 3 Nov (n.s.) 1704 and *ibid.* p.82, Stepney in Vienna to Harley, 12 Nov (n.s.) 1704.

11. PRO: *ibid.* p.95, Stepney in Vienna to Harley, 15 Nov (n.s.) 1704; *ibid.* p.106, 19 Nov (n.s.) 1704.

12. Stepney's account of his audience is at PRO: SP105/74, p.119, Stepney in Vienna to Harley, 22 Nov (n.s.) 1704. The Emperor's comments are in HHStA: England 32 (Weisungen), Konvolut *Weisungen an Wratislaw 1704 X-XI.*

13. Stepney's varied duties are recounted in his letters in PRO: SP105/74, pp.126-149, 22 Nov-6 Dec (n.s.) 1704.

14. PRO: *ibid.* p.165, Stepney in Vienna to Cadogan, 10 Dec 1704.

15. The booklet containing Stepney's Inscription bears the British Library reference 7711.c.28. In April 1993, the Curator of the *Heimat Museum der Stadt Höchstädt a.d. Donau* (Herr Georg Strobel) told me he had no knowledge of any monument contemporary with the Battle of Blenheim having been built. A nineteenth-century memorial had been destroyed during the Second World War. Two modern monuments exist: one of carved stone just outside Höchstädt; the other a plaque in the churchyard wall at Blindheim (the German village name corrupted to 'Blenheim').

16. Marlborough's letter to Stepney about the provisioning of the troops was written from Hanover on 3 Dec 1704 (see Murray, Vol. I, p.550).

17. Stepney's report on the Conference is at PRO: SP105/74, p.201, Stepney in Vienna to Harley, 27 Dec 1704, and on Heister's victory, at PRO: SP105/75 (Stepney's Letter Book, Jan-June 1705 – no folio or page numbers), 3 Jan 1705 .

XIX *The Quarrel with Wratislaw*

1. PRO: SP105/75 (Stepney's Letter Book – no folio or page numbers).

2. Wratislaw's career is set out in the ADB. The entry in the *London Post* is in BL: Burney Collection of Newspapers (Microfilm Reel 123a).

3. PRO: SP105/62, f.93v, Hedges in Whitehall to Stepney, 9 May (o.s.) 1701 (see also Chapter XV, in this context).

4. PRO: SP105/69, Stepney in Vienna to Hedges, 23 Aug (n.s.) 1703 (see also Chapter XVI, for Marlborough's favourable report on Wratislaw to the imperial court).

5. PRO: SP105/70, p.315, Stepney in the Hague to Hedges (private letter), 11 Dec (n.s.) 1703.

6. PRO: SP105/74, p.208v, Stepney in Vienna to Cardonnel, 27 Dec (n.s.) 1704; SP105/75, Stepney in Vienna to Lewis, 17 Jan (n.s.) 1705.

7. Stepney reported the death of Kaunitz in his letter to Harley, at PRO: SP105/75, 14 Jan (n.s.) 1705. His letter to Harrach (and its follow-up) are preserved in Vienna in the *Allgemeines Verwaltungsarchiv* (Harrach Archiv Fasc. 101, Stepney G, 1705. Stepney kept his own copies in SP105/75 at 14 and 28 January (n.s.) 1705.

8. PRO: SP105/75, Stepney in Vienna to Cardonnel, 28 Jan (n.s.) 1705.

9. Marlborough's letter to Stepney dated 2 Jan (o.s.) 1704/5 is to be found in SP105/75 under the date 28 Jan (n.s.) 1705, when it was received, thus conveying the time needed for transit, London-Vienna (15 days). The Duke's letter to Wratislaw of 27 Dec (o.s.) 1704 is printed in Murray, Vol. I, p.564. Cardonnel's letter to Stepney of 9 Jan 1704/5̲ is in BL: Add.MS.7063 (Stepney Papers, Vol. VI). f.40. Cardonnel wrote the year as 1704, which was correct under the Old Style; but resulted in the letter's being placed at the start of the modern calendar year 1704, rather than at January 1705, where it belongs. The correct dating is clear from the remainder of the text, which deals with the

negotiations for Marlborough's Principality.

10. PRO: SP105/75, Stepney in Vienna to Marlborough, 31 Jan (n.s.) 1705; *ibid.* Lewis in Whitehall to Stepney 29 Dec (o.s.) 1704; *ibid.* Stepney in Vienna to Auersperg, 1 Feb (n.s.) 1705; *ibid.* Stepney in Vienna to Tucker, 14 Feb (n.s.) 1705.

11. PRO: SP105/73, p.199v, Stepney at the Camp at Weissembourg to Jacob Tonson, 26 Sept (n.s.) 1704; SP105/75, Stepney in Vienna to Mr.Vanbrugh, 18 Feb (n.s.) 1705. *Note:* Father Andreas Pozzo (1642-1709) was a renowned baroque artist, expert on perspective and on *tromp l'oeil*, who had been brought to Vienna by the Emperor Leopold (see Michaud).

12. The Emperor's letter is in HHStA England Kart.32 – Weisungen, *Konvolut Leopold I u. Joseph I an Gf Gallas, 1703-5.*

13. Both Marlborough's and Cardonnel's letters are in SP105/75 at 7 and 6 February (o.s.) 1705 respectively. Marlborough's letter to Wratislaw (in French) was composed by Cardonnel, but to comply with the courtesy of the day the Duke was expected to write it out himself. Cardonnel explained that his Grace was very busy, so that the original, to Wratislaw, missed the post. However Marlborough told Cardonnel to let Stepney have a copy, none the less.

14. PRO: SP105/75, Stepney in Vienna to Lewis, 7 March (n.s.) 1705.

15. Stepney's letter to Stanhope is in PRO: SP105/75, 11 March (n.s.) 1705. Stanhope's two letters are in BL: Add.MS.7069 (Stepney Papers Vol. XII), f.204, PS to a letter of 10 Apr (n.s.)1705; f.208, 16 Apr (n.s.) 1705.

XX *The Hungarian Mediation (III)*

1. PRO: SP105/75 (Stepney's Letter Book, Jan-June 1705).

2. *Ibid.* Stepney's dispatches are at 21, 25 and 28 February 1705. General Siegbert Heister commanded the imperial troops in Hungary from late 1703 to mid-1705. He was succeeded by Count Leopold Schlick.

3. Marlborough's letter announcing the arrival of 'Mr. Mountague' is at PRO: SP105/75, Marlborough in the Hague to Stepney, 21 Apr 1705. Stepney's letter to Sir Hans Sloane is in BL: Add.MS.SL4040, *Letters to Sir Hans Sloane,* Vol.V, f.28, 5 May 1705.

4. Stepney's dispatches about the changes in the imperial administration and on the Court's attitude to Hungary are in PRO: SP105/75, Stepney in Vienna to Harley on 23 and 27 May; 6 and 13 June (all n.s.).

5. *Ibid.* 27 June (n.s.) 1705. *Note:* Paul Szechenyi, Archbishop of Colocza, was deeply involved in Hungarian politics and had already tried, without success, to mediate between the rebels and the imperial government.

6. PRO: SP105/76 (Stepney's Letter Book, July-Dec 1705 – no folio or page numbers), Stepney in Vienna to Lord Sunderland, 1 July (n.s.) 1705. Sunderland's early rising is remarked in BL: Add.MS.7063, f.112 (Stepney Papers, Vol.VI), Cardonnel at Meldert to Stepney, 6 Aug (n.s.) 1705. Stepney's view of Sunderland and of his own prospects are in PRO: SP105/76, Stepney in Vienna to Harley, 18 July (n.s.) 1705; to Erasmus Lewis on 22 July; and to George Montagu on 29 July (n.s.) 1705.

7. Wratislaw's letters to Marlborough, dated 19 and 30 July 1705 are printed in Coxe, Vol. II, pp.222-224. Coxe's damaging remark about Stepney is to be found in the 1885 edition of his *Memoires of the Duke of Marlborough,* p.269. Wratislaw's later comment to Marlborough was made in 1706, when he and Stepney had to cooperate in negotiations with the Hungarians. Marlborough had the extract of the Count's letter copied out and sent it to Stepney from

Tongres on 14 May 1706. Stepney included it in his Letter Book, SP105/77, under the date 2 June 1706, when he replied to Marlborough.

8. The names of Sunderland's entourage are given in BL Add.MS.7067, f.171 (Stepney Papers, Vol. X), James Dayrolle in the Hague to Stepney, 31 July (n.s.) 1705. It has not been possible to identify them all. Molesworth was probably a son of Robert, the first Viscount (see Chapter V), and '*le jeune Onslow*' is likely to have been Thomas, son and heir of Richard, first Baron Onslow (1654-1717), who was described by Burnet as 'worthy' – i.e. he was a Whig (DNB). The fact that Sunderland stayed in Stepney's house is apparent from PRO: SP105/76, Stepney in Vienna to Plantamou,r 7 Sept (n.s.) 1705. Sunderland's *aide mémoire* is printed in Snyder, Vol. I, p.464.

9. Sunderland's homesickness is described in PRO: SP105/76, Stepney in Vienna to Raby, 9 Sept (n.s.) 1705. Stepney's forebodings are in the same volume, writing to Lewis on 12 Sept (n.s.) 1705; his dispatch on the state of affairs in Hungary, addressed to 'Right Honourable' (i.e. Harley), same volume at date 23 Sept (n.s.) 1705.

10. PRO: SP105/76, Harley in Whitehall to Sunderland, 28 Aug/8 Sept 1705; Stepney in Vienna to Harley, 28 Sept (n.s.) 1705.

11. BL: Add.MS.7063, f.146 (Stepney Papers Vol. VI), Cardonnel at Herontals to Stepney 7 Oct (n.s.) 1705.

12. The Bishop of Osnabrück was Carl Joseph Ignatius (d.1715) brother of the Duke of Lorraine. He later became Archbishop and Elector of Trier (Trèves). On 9 September 1705 Stepney reported the Emperor's invitation to the Bishop to mediate in the Hungarian dispute, and on 21 October the prelate's arrival in Vienna.

13. PRO: SP105/76, Stepney at Tyrnau to Lewis, Raby, Stanhope, Whitworth, Hill, Broughton, Davenant, 30 Sept (n.s.) 1705; and privately to Lewis on the same date. Stepney's letters to Whitworth and to Harley are in the same volume. Stepney also wrote to Raby on 4 November 1705; 'Accordingly ye L. of Sunderland and I have begun the dance by removing from Tyrnau hither [i.e. to Pressburg].'

14. Stepney's reports on the continuing Hungarian negotiations and on Marlborough's arrival in Vienna are in PRO: SP105/76, Stepney in Vienna to Harley, 7, 11 and 14 Nov (n.s.) 1705; Watkins' praise of Stepney's hospitality is in BL: Add.MS.7063, f.160 (Stepney Papers, Vol. VI) Watkins in the Hague to Stepney, 15 Dec (n.s.) 1705. Stepney was about to move house (see p.) but it seems that Cardonnel was already given a room in the new accommodation: see BL: Add.MS.7077 (Stepney Papers Vol. XX – Misc. Papers & Letters), Fury in Vienna to Stepney, 29 Sept (n.s.) 1706.

15. PRO: SP105/76, Stepney in Vienna to Harley, 18 and 25 Nov (n.s.) 1705; and to Halifax on 25 Nov. Stepney's remark about his being left to 'jogg on' is in his letter to the Duke of Shrewsbury, same volume, 14 Nov 1705.

16. Stepney's letters to Halifax and to Aubrey Porter are both in PRO: SP105/76 at 25 Nov and 16 Dec (n.s.) 1705 respectively. Details of the house at Bankgasse 1-3 are taken from Paul Harrer-Lucienfeld, *Wien, seine Häuser, Menschen u. Kultur* (Vienna, 1952), Vol. VII, p.114, in the *Bibliothek der Stadt Wien*.

17. For the imperial victory at Cibo, and the rebels' subsequent tactics, see PRO: SP105/76 Stepney in Vienna to Harley 9 and 29 Dec (n.s.) 1705.

18. Correspondence about the Berlin Treaty (which includes its text), is at PRO: SP105/77 (Stepney's Letter Book, Jan-June 1706 – no folio or page numbers), Stepney in Vienna to Cardonnel, 9 Jan (n.s.) 1706; and Cardonnel in the Hague to Stepney, 31 Dec (n.s.) 1705. Stepney's own comments on the treaty are to be found in his letter to Cardonnel, same volume, at date 11 Jan (n.s.) 1706.

19. The details of Rechteren's negotiations, as described by Stepney, have been omitted. Stepney's dispatches, from the time of Schlick's arrival in Vienna, are in PRO: SP105/77 between 20 and 30 Jan (n.s.) 1706.
20. PRO: SP105/77, Stepney in Vienna to Harley, 27 Jan (n.s.) 1706; and to Cardonnel on the same date. For 'Marlborough's brainchild' see Nicholas Henderson, *Prince Eugen of Savoy*, p.138 (London, 1964).
21. PRO: SP105/77, Stepney in Vienna to Cardonnel, 9 Jan (n.s.) 1706 (two letters); and 20 Feb (n.s.) 1706; *ibid.* Marlborough at St James to Stepney, 26 Feb (o.s.) 1706.
22. For Marlborough's loan, see PRO: SP105/77, Marlborough in Whitehall to Stepney, 15 Jan (o.s.) 1706; and Stratford's letter of the same date; also Stepney's reply to Cardonnel, 17 Feb (n.s.) 1706; Stepney in Vienna to Marlborough, 27 Feb (n.s.) 1706. Correspondence about the Little Loan begins with PRO: SP105/76, Harley in Whitehall to Stepney, 14/25 Sept 1705 and Stepney's reply dated 10 Oct (n.s.) 1705. Stepney's correspondence with the Williams brothers and with Prince Eugene continue in SP105/77 at 10 April and 4 June (n.s.) 1706.
23. Stepney's health is the subject of his letter to Emmanuel Howe at PRO: SP105/77, 7 April (n.s.) 1706. The report of Bruynincx' return, and Stepney's letter to Raby are in the same volume, at 14 April (n.s.) 1706. Stepney wrote to Lewis about Wratislaw at PRO: SP105/77, 16 Jan (n.s.) 1706; the last four words of this letter are written out in Stepney's own hand, in the Letter Book.
24. PRO: SP105/77, Stepney at Tyrnau to Marlborough, 27 April (n.s.) 1706; and to Halifax on the same date.
25. PRO: SP105/77, Stepney at Tyrnau to Harley, 29 April (n.s.) 1706, continued from Pressburg on 1 May. *Note*: Princess Rákóczy was Charlotte-Amelie of Hesse-Rheinfels. According to Stepney she was of a 'resolute and intriguing spirit', and had helped her husband to escape from captivity in Wiener Neustadt in 1701.
26. Stepney's comments on the prospect of his journey to Nyitra are taken from his letter to Raby: PRO: SP105/77 at 5 May (n.s.) 1706; and to Harley on the same date. Stepney's dispatch of 8 May (from Pressburg) is in the same volume.
27. PRO: SP105/77, Stepney in Vienna to Harley (private letter), 12 May (n.s.) 1706.

XXI *Interlude – The Principality of Mindelheim*

Note: The negotiations about the principality of Mindelheim have been minutely described in Coxe, Vol. I, particularly the ceremony of Inauguration, to be found on pp.383-9. An excellent modern account is in Peter Barber's *Marlborough as Imperial Prince* (*British Library Journal* Vol. VIII, 1982). This chapter is included to illustrate more fully Stepney's part in the affair, based on his correspondence.

1. PRO: SP105/73, p.27 (Stepney's Letter Book, July-Sept 1704), Stepney in Vienna to Harley, 12 July (n.s.) 1704.
2. PRO: SP105/73, p.128, Stepney in Vienna to Cardonnel, 22 Aug (n.s.) 1704, p.128v, Harley in Whitehall to Stepney, 25 July/5 Aug 1704. Stepney forwarded the Emperor's letter in PRO: SP105/73, p.170 Stepney in Vienna to Harley (private letter) 6 Sept (n.s.) 1704. Stepney's worries over etiquette are voiced in PRO: SP105/73, p.173v, Stepney in Vienna to Cardonnel, 8 Sept (n.s.) 1704.
3. PRO: SP105/74, p.163, Stepney in Vienna to Marlborough, 10 Dec (n.s.) 1704. Wratislaw was not in fact given the Bavarian appointment, but later became

Chancellor of Bohemia.

4. PRO: SP105/74, p.182, Stepney in Vienna to Marlborough, 17 Dec (n.s.) 1704. *ibid.* p.208v Stepney in Vienna to Cardonnel 27 Dec (n.s.) 1704. *ibid.* pp.210 Stepney in Vienna to Marlborough and 215v and to Cardonnel 31 Dec (n.s.) 1704. Stepney did not name the Italian agent. The modern spelling of Donauwehrt is Donauwörth.

5. PRO: SP105/75 (Stepney's Letter Book, Jan-June 1705), Stepney in Vienna to Marlborough, 21 Jan (n.s.) 1705.

6. PRO: SP105/76 (Stepney's Letter Book, July-Dec 1705), Stepney in Vienna to Harley, 25 Nov (n.s.) 1705.

7. PRO: SP105/80 (Documents relating to Mindelheim – no folio numbers), Cardonnel at Breslau to Stepney ,26 Nov (n.s.) 1705. Stepney in Vienna to Staffhorst, 16 Dec (n.s.) 1705. The Baron did not comply with Stepney's request: cf. SP105/77, Stepney at Straubing to Cardonnel, 28 May 1706. PRO: SP105/76, Stepney in Vienna to Cardonnel, 9 Dec (n.s.) 1705 BL: Add.MS.7063, (Stepney Papers, Vol.VI), ff.163, 165 Cardonnel in the Hague to Stepney,18 and 22 Dec (n.s.) 1705. PRO: SP105/76, Stepney in Vienna to Cardonnel, 30 Dec (n.s.) 1705. SP105/77 Marlborough at St James' to Stepney, 11 Jan (o.s.) 1705/6.

8. PRO: SP105/77, Stepney in Vienna to Cardonnel, 13 Feb (n.s.) 1706; SP105/80, Stepney in Vienna to Cardonnel, 6 March (n.s.) 1706.

9. PRO: SP105/77, Stepney in Mindelheim to Lewis, 21 May (n.s.) 1706.

10. *Ibid.* Stepney 'within a post from Ratisbonne' to Cardonnel 27 and 28 May (n.s.) 1706. I owe the identification of Schrader to Mr Peter Barber's essay referred to above.

11. PRO: SP105/77, Stepney at Straubing to Stanhope, 28 May (n.s.) 1706; and to Halifax on the same date; *ibid.* Stepney in Vienna to Harley, 2 June (n.s.) 1706; SP105/80, Stepney at Tyrnau to *La Dame Kundienne*, 18 July (n.s.) 1706.

XXII *The End of the Hungarian Mediation and the Transfer to the Netherlands*

Note: The last existing volume of Stepney's Letter Books – SP105/77 – ends abruptly on 28 June 1706. Thereafter some of his original letters are traceable in the Public Record Office and British Library in various collections. It has not been possible to discover what happened to the Letter Books for the last year of Stepney's life. They surely existed, for he had no reason to break his 20-year-old habit of keeping copies of his outgoing official letters and of many which he received.

1. Stepney's remarks are taken from his letters written at Neuhäusel and Tyrnau to Richard Warre, Sir James Montagu and Sir Robert Sutton on 8, 10 and 12 June (n.s.) 1706 respectively (all are in PRO: SP105/77). The horse was a somewhat surprising gift from Sutton: but he was indebted to Stepney and his staff for news reaching him from England.

2. PRO: SP107/77 (Stepney's Letter Book, Jan-June 1706), Stepney in Vienna to Cardonnel, 4 June (n.s.) 1706. SP80/28, f.249 (Germany: Mr. Stepney 1706, No.10), Fury in Vienna to – no addressee, but probably to Lewis, since this paper follows a letter from Stepney addressed to his cousin, dated 5 June 1706. Fury included the month, but not the exact date. *Note*: Amalia Wilhelmine was a princess of Brunswick-Lüneburg: i.e. she was closely related to the house of Hanover. John Laws or Lawes became Stepney's secretary during 1705. Stepney

wrote to Edmund Poley on 18 Feb 1705 that he was expecting him to arrive with a 'budget' of pamphlets and scandal. Cardonnel complained of the fees which Laws was charging during Marlborough's visit to Vienna in 1705. Nothing is known of Heyman (or Hayman) except that he had a room in Stepney's house in Brussels in September 1707. He may have been a senior steward. James Fury disliked him.

3. Stepney described the visit to Neuhäusel and his meeting DesAlleurs in his dispatch to Harley and a letter to Raby from Pressburg. Both in PRO: SP105/77, 15 June (n.s.) 1706.

4. PRO: SP105/77, Stepney in Vienna to Lewis, 16 June (n.s.) 1706. It has not been possible to identify 'Mr. Unguy'.

5. PRO: SP105/77 Stepney in Vienna to Cardonnel 28 June (n.s.) 1706.

6. PRO: SP80/28, f.305, f.323 Stepney at Tyrnau to Harley, 2 and 6 July (n.s.) 1706.

7. PRO: SP80/28, f.331, Stepney in Vienna to Harley, 10 July (n.s.) 1706; f.347, 13 July (n.s.) 1706. *Note*: Hengelmüller described the interview between Rákóczy and Wratislaw rather differently: neither man would yield, though without rancour. Wratislaw is said to have told Rákóczy that if he trusted France he would join those princes who had come to grief owing to that country's broken promises. Stepney's assertion that the breach in the negotiations was caused by Wratislaw's 'impertinence' to Rákóczy was contradicted in the Prince's own memoirs. These, however, were not published until many years after the event.

8. Stepney's dispatches from Tyrnau are in PRO: SP80/28, f.353, Stepney to Harley, 16 July (n.s.) 1706; f.355, Stepney to Harley, 20 July (n.s.) 1706. His letters to Count Aspremont and to Rosse are in BL: Add.MS 7075, f.23 (Stepney Papers Vol.XVIII – Misc. Letters), 1 Juillet 1706; f.35, 9 August (n.s.) 1706 respectively.

9. PRO: SP80/28, f.355, Stepney in Tyrnau to Harley, 20 July (n.s.) 1706; f.371, Stepney in Vienna to Harley, 24 July (n.s.) 1706; f.381, Fury in Vienna to Lewis, 21 July (n.s.) 1706; ff.393, 395, *et seq.*, Stepney in Vienna to Harley, 4 Aug (n.s.) 1706. This includes his speech to the Emperor (French). A marginal note indicates that the speech was received in London on 11 August (o.s.) 1706.

10. BL: Add.MS.7063 (Stepney Papers Vol.VI), f.228 (scored through): copy of Stepney's letter to Cardonnel from Vienna dated 31 July (n.s.) 1706. Cardonnel's letter of 17 July is not in this volume. BL: Add.MS.7064 (Stepney Papers, Vol.VII – Misc. Letters), f.6, Stepney in Vienna to Henry Davenant, 7 Aug (n.s.) 1706.

11. BL: Add.MS.7059 (Stepney Papers, Vol. II), f.107v, Harley in Whitehall to Stepney, 6/17 Aug 1706; Snyder, Vol. I Godolphin to Marlborough, p.534, 3 May (o.s.) 1706; p.543,Marlborough to Godolphin, 9/20 May 1706; p.547, Godolphin to Marlborough,14 May (o.s.) 1706.

12. Cardonnel's letter is at BL: Add.MS.7063, f.230 (Stepney Papers, Vol. VI), Cardonnel at Helchin to Stepney, 14 Aug (n.s.) 1706. Stepney's knowledge of the offer to Marlborough of the governorship of the Spanish Netherlands is at BL: Add.MS.7064, f.2 (Stepney Papers Vol.VII – Misc. letters), Stepney in Vienna to Cardonnel, 10 July (n.s.) 1706; f.3, Stepney to Stanhope (same date, and on f.5v), 28 July (n.s.) 1706. The letter to the Emperor from the States General is reported in BL: Add.MS.7059, f.170 (Stepney Papers Vol.II), Stepney in Vienna to Harley, 25 Aug (n.s.) 1706; Stepney's reply to Cardonnel is at BL: Add.MS.7064, f.14, 28 Aug (n.s.) 1706.

13. The letter about the 'Little Loan' is at BL: Add.MS.7059, f.162, Stepney in Vienna to Godolphin, 18 Aug (n.s.) 1706. Stepney's other recommendations

and comments are in the same volume, at f.176. Stepney in Vienna to Harley, f.183, 4 and 8 Sep (n.s.) 1706. He acknowledged his revocation in letters to Harley at f.191, f.195, 18 and 22 Sep (n.s.) 1706. Fury's letter is in BL: Add.MS.7077, f.36 (Stepney Papers Vol. XX – Misc. Letters and Papers), Fury in Vienna to Stepney, 29 Sept (n.s.) 1706.

14. BL: Add.MS.7075, f.53 (Stepney Papers Vol. XVIII – Misc. Letters), Stepney in Munich to Löwenstein, 1 Oct (n.s.) 1706.

15. Information about Countess Aspremont is in BL: Add.MS.7066, f.168 (Stepney Papers Vol. VIII). Henry Davenant in Frankfurt to Stepney, 24 Oct (n.s.) 1706; BL: Add.MS.7077, f.62 (Stepney Papers Vol. XX) 'Talon' at Koeln to Stepney, 28 Oct (n.s.) 1706. Talon was possibly Countess Aspremont's steward.

XXIII *George Stepney's Poetry*

1. Samuel Johnson, *Lives of the English Poets* (Everyman edition, London 1954), Vol. I, p.272.
2. Rycaut's comment on the epigram is in BL: Add.MS.7060, f.110 (Sir P. Rycaut's correspondence), Rycaut in Hamburg to Stepney, 25 Oct (n.s.) 1693.
3. The American criticism of Stepney is in H. T. Swedenberg Jr, *The Works of John Dryden* (General ed.), Vol.I V, (Berkeley, Calif., 1974).
4. Vernon's comment on the poem is in PRO: SP105/82, f.241 (Original Letters to Stepney), Vernon in Whitehall to Stepney, 12 March (o.s.) 1694/5. Stepney's letter to Tonson is printed in *The Gentleman's Magazine*, Vol. VIII (1837) pp.362-4. Stepney wrote it from Lippstadt on 14/24 Feb 1695.
5. PRO: SP105/53 (Stepney's Letter Book), Stepney in Berlin to Blathwayt, 4/14 July 1699.
6. PRO: SP105/63 (Stepney's Letter Book), p.427, Stepney in Vienna to Hedges and Blathwayt, 21 Sept (n.s.) 1701.

Note: I am indebted to Miss Audrey Fellowes of Norwich for the translations of the Latin epigrams which are printed in this chapter.

XXIV *The Netherlands*

1. Joseph Addison in Whitehall to George Stepney, 3 Sept 1706 (printed in Rebecca Warner, *Epistolary Curiosities,* London, 1813).
2. Cardonnel's suggestions for Stepney's travel are in BL: Add.MS.7063, f.250 (Stepney Papers, Vol. VI – Cardonnel's Letters), Cardonnel at Grainds to Stepney, 11 Oct (n.s.) 1706. Marlborough's plans for Stepney are contained in his letters to Godolphin of 9 Sept and 24 Oct (n.s.) 1706; (printed in Coxe, Vol. III, pp.11 and 76-8 respectively). Information about the situation in the Spanish Netherlands after the battle of Ramillies is based on Henri Pirenne, *Histoire de Belgique*, Vol. V, (Brussels, 1926), and L. P. Gachard, *Recueil des anciennes ordonnances de la Belgique, III Série, Tome 2*, (Brussels, 1867) – from the preface.
3. Stepney's report on Trade is at PRO: SP84/230, f.5 (Holland, 1706) Stepney in Brussels to Hedges, 4 Nov (n.s.) 1706. His Instructions are in BL: Add.MS.7058, f.1 (Stepney Papers, Vol. I), 'Additional Instructions for George Stepney', 15 Oct (o.s.) 1706.
4. BL: Add.MS.7075, f.54 (Stepney Papers Vol. XVIII), Stepney in the Hague to Powis, 12 Nov (n.s.) 1706.
5. Stepney's correspondence from the Hague during November and December 1706 is contained in PRO: SP84/230, ff.46-116, 16 Nov-31 Dec (n.s.) 1706;

BL: Add.MS.7064, ff.21-36 (Stepney Papers, Vol. VII – Misc. Letters), 30 Nov-21 Dec (n.s.) 1706; Add.MS.7059, f.230 (Stepney Papers, Vol. II), Stepney in the Hague to Cardonnel, 28 Dec (n.s.) 1706. Cardonnel's letter is in BL: Add.MS.7063, f.261, Cardonnel in Whitehall to Stepney, 27 Dec (o.s.) 1706.

6. For Stepney's reluctance to travel, see PRO: SP84/230, f.180, Stepney in the Hague to Addison, 28 Jan (n.s.) 1707. Marlborough's correspondence with Heinsius is in t'Hoff, p.289, Marlborough at St James' to Heinsius, 7 Jan (o.s.) 1707; p.291, Heinsius to Marlborough, 16 Jan (n.s.) 1707. Stepney wrote from Utrecht to Harley, PRO: SP84/230, f.182, 30 Jan (n.s.) 1707.

7. Stepney's reports on his negotiations are in PRO: SP84/230, f.184, 190, Stepney in Cassel to Harley, 7 and 11 Feb (n.s.) 1707.

8. BL: Add.MS.7067, ff.243, 254 (Stepney Papers, Vol. X – Letters from Dayrolle), Dayrolle in the Hague to Stepney, 11 and 18 Feb (n.s.) 1707. House rents were calculated *per annum*. Fl. 3,000 was approximately £300 in contemporary currency. cf. J. McCusker *Money and Exchange in Europe and America, 1660-1775*, p.9.

9. PRO: SP84/230, f.197, Stepney at Neuhaus to Harley, 14 Feb (n.s.) 1707. The Bishop of Paderborn was Prince Metternich, and was the candidate favoured by the States General to be appointed Bishop of Münster, which see had fallen vacant in May 1706. His rival was the Bishop of Osnabrück, brother to the Duke of Lorraine (formerly the Emperor's First Commissioner for treating with the Hungarians), who, on Stepney's recommendation, had been promised the diplomatic support of the English government. Hence, in 1707, Stepney's tactful courtesy to both clerics.

10. PRO: SP84/230, ff.211-247, Stepney in the Hague to Harley, 22 and 25 Feb, 1, 8 and 11 Mar (n.s.) 1707. Marlborough's instructions to Stepney are in Murray, Vol. III, p.318 Marlborough at St James' to Stepney, 16 Feb (o.s.) 1707.

11. Stepney's account of his last day in the Hague is in PRO: SP84/230, f.275, Stepney at Rotterdam to Harley, 16 Mar (n.s.) 1707. Laws' letter is in PRO: SP77/57 (Flanders, Misc. 1696-1707), Laws in Brussels to Lewis, 21 Mar (n.s.) 1707.

12. BL: Add.MS.46535 (Lexington Papers, Vol. XV) Stepney in Antwerp to Lexington, 18 March (n.s.) 1707 (this is the last paper in the volume).

13. The account of Stepney's short stay in Brussels is based on various letters in PRO: SP84/230, ff.294-312 (Holland, 1706-7), 24 Mar-12 Apr (n.s.) 1707.

14. Ff.318-360, 19 Apr-12 May (n.s.) 1707.

15. Stepney's comment in Meadows is at PRO: SP84/230, f.362, Stepney in Brussels to Harley, 16 May (n.s.) 1707. Meadows' remarks are in PRO: SP80/29 (Germany, 1707-9 – no folio numbers), Meadows at the Hague to Harley, 13/24 May 1707.

16. PRO: SP84/230, f.378, Stepney in Brussels to Harley ,26 May (n.s.) 1707.

17. Gachard, p.68 *et seq.*

18. Carmarthen Record Office, Stepney Papers, F.65.

19. *Mémoires du Feld-Maréchal Comte de Mérode-Westerloo, publiés par M. le Comte de Mérode-Westerloo son arrière-petit-fils*, (Brussels, 1840), Vol. II, pp.203-207.

20. Marlborough's letters to Westerloo and to Stepney are contained in Murray, Vol. III, pp.334 - 485.

21. PRO: SP84/230, f.409, Stepney in Brussels to Harley, 18 July (n.s.) 1707, f.423, to Sunderland, 25 July, f.329 to Addison, 27 July.

22. Murray, Vol. III, p.496.

23. PRO: SP84/229, f.388 (Dayrolle in Holland, 1700-1707), Dayrolle to Harley,

19/30 Aug 1707.
24. BL: Add.MS. 61144, f.170 (Blenheim Papers), Stepney in Brussels to Marlborough, 7 Sep (n.s.) 1707.
25. Murray, Vol. III, p.551, Marlborough at Helchin to Stepney, 8 Sep (n.s.) 1707. Cardonnel's report is contained in pp.553-4, Marlborough to Harley, 12 Sep (n.s.) 1707. The date of Stepney's departure is given by Dayrolle in PRO: SP84/229, f.400, Dayrolle in the Hague to Harley, 5/16 Sep 1707.

XXV *England*

1. PRO:Prob.11-498, f.346.
2. Chelsea Record Office: Orders of Vestry and Poor Rates 1662-1718, Poor Rates, 1695-1707, and 1707-16. Addison recorded Stepney's death in a letter to Christian Cole dated 16/27 Sept 1707. This is printed in *The Letters of Joseph Addison*, W. Graham (ed.), (Oxford, 1941). See also Luttrell, Vol. VI, p.213. Madame Aglionby is likely to have been the widow of Stepney's colleague, Dr. William Aglionby (d. 1706), who had been Envoy in Switzerland 1702-5, and with whom Stepney occasionally corresponded. Richard Powis was of course Stepney's agent at the Treasury.
3. Luttrell, Vol. VI, p.215.
4. Marlborough's letter is in Murray, Vol. IV, p.6, Marlborough at Helchin to Harley, 3 Oct (n.s.) 1707. Heinsius' remarks are in t'Hoff, p.342, Heinsius in the Hague to Marlborough, 10 Sept (n.s.) 1707. For Addison's letter, see Note 2 above. D'Alais letter to Lewis, dated 7 Oct (n.s.) 1707 is in BL: HMC Calendar to the Portland MSS, Vol. IV, p.455. Stepney's sentiments on the subject of death are at PRO: SP105/77, Stepney in Vienna to Richard Whitworth (the father of his cousin Charles), 24 Mar (n.s.) 1706.
5. The inventory is in BL: Add.MS.61144, f.172 (Blenheim Papers), 6 Nov (n.s.) 1707. For Lamberty's remarks on the wall hangings, see Sir Winston Churchill, *Marlborough, His Life & Times* (London 1933) Vol. II, p.257, Lewis' letter about the horse is in BL: HMC Calendar to the Portland MSS, Vol. IV, p.454.
6. The Treasury's debt to Stepney was noted by Addison – see his letters (W. Graham, ed.), as in Note 2 above, p.77. The government's repayment of part of the debt is in Cal.Tr.B.:1708, pp.136-7, 150, 377, 389. Frances Stepney's letter to Marlborough is in BL: Add.MS.61144, f.176.
7. Dorothy Stepney's will is at PRO: Prob.11-600, f.256. Whetston's command is referred to in BL: Add.MS.7063, f.47 (Stepney Papers, Vol.VI), Cardonnel in the Hague to Stepney, 22 April (n.s.) 1704.
8. Notes & Queries, 2nd Series, Vol. XI, Jan-June 1861, p.225 *et seq*.

XXVI *Epilogue*

1. Stepney's collection of Polish documents are in PRO: SP105/61; and the Saxon ones may be found in SP105/83 and /86.
2. PRO: SP105/55, f.26v, Stepney in Ebsdorf to Robinson, 27 Sept (n.s.) 1694.
3. PRO: SP105/76, Stepney in Vienna to the Electress of Hanover, 18 Aug (n.s.) 1705.

Bibliography

The bibliography for Stepney's diplomatic career is shewn below. For his poetry, see the notes and references to Chapter XXIII, together with Appendices VIII and IX.

Manuscripts and Local Sources

United Kingdom

BRITISH LIBRARY

Add.MS. 7058 through 7079, The Stepney Papers, Vols. I-XXII
SL4040	Letters to Sir H. Sloane, Vol. V
Add.MS. 5881	W. Cole, Alphabetical collection for an Athenae Cantab. . .
19514	Sir P. Rycaut's Letter Book, Oct 1689 – Apr 1690
21551	G. Stepney, Correspondence
22196	Strafford Papers (Correspondence Raby-Cadogen, 1703-10)
28876	Ellis Papers, Vol. II
28885	Ellis Papers, Vol. IX
28896-28898	Ellis Papers (Foreign) Vols. I-III
288900-288905	Ellis Papers Vols. V-X
33273	Letters to H. Watkins, 1702-14
34095	Sir W. D. Colt's correspondence 1690-91
34223	Diary of Thomas Fane, 6th Earl of Westmorland
34354	Letters to William Blathwayt
34504 and 34505	Mackintosh Collection, Vols XVIII and XIX, (William III's letters to Heinsius)
36662	Sir W.D.Colt's correspondence
37155 and 37156	Diplomatic correspondence of G. Stepney
37348	Whitworth Papers, Vol. I
37407	Letters to G.Stepney, 1691-1706
37663	Sir P. Rycaut's Letter Book,1692
37991	Blathwayt's Letter Book
41804	Middleton Papers, Vol. II
41823-41827	Middleton Papers, Vols. XXI-XXV (Sir P. Wyche's correspondence)
Add.MS 45731	Letters to E. Poley, 1688-89
46533	Lexington Papers, Vol. XIII
46535	Lexington Papers Vol. XV
61144	Blenheim Papers

Stowe MS 222 Hanover State Papers, Vol. I, (1692-1706)
Burney Collection of Newspapers, (Microfilm, Reels 122, 123a)
Calendars to the Bath MSS., Vol. III
                       Downside MSS., Vol. I, Part I
                       Portland MSS., Vol. IV

The Gentleman's Magazine, Vol. VIII
Hardwick State Papers, Vol. II Misc. State Papers, 1501-1726
HMC Report, The Buccleuch Papers, Vol. II
Notes &.Queries, Second series, Vol. IX
Somers Collection of Tracts, Third Collection, Vol. IV
The Survey of London, Vol. XXI, Part 1

BODLEIAN LIBRARY
RAWL MS A.326, G. Stepney, Letters from Dresden and Berlin
C.936, Stepney's Letter Book, October-November 1699

CARMARTHENSHIRE RECORD OFFICE
MS F.65, George Stepney's Letters to Mr. Hill
Robert Harrison, *Some Notes on the Stepney Family*, (London, 1870 – privately printed)

CHELSEA RECORD OFFICE
Orders of Vestry and Poor Rates 1662-1718

DORSET RECORD OFFICE
D.60, X23 and X38 Bloxworth Estate: Letter from Sir J. Trenchard to Stepney, and the latter's reply, Dec 1693 and Jan 1694 (n.s.)

GUILDHALL LIBRARY
Court Minute Books of the Grocers' Company
MS 11588/4, Orders of the Court of Assistants, 22 Apr 1640 - 15 June 1688
MS 11593/1, List of Apprentices, 1629-1666

INTERNATIONAL GENEALOGICAL INDEX
Microfiche records of all counties of England

NATIONAL LIBRARY OF WALES
Transactions of the Carmarthenshire Antiquarian Society and Field Club, Vol. XI
Dictionary of Welsh Biography down to 1940 (London, 1959)
Herbert Papers MS.5303 E.

NOTTINGHAM UNIVERSITY Portland Papers
PwV64	J. J. H-Bruynincx, Letters, 1694-6
PwV65, PwV66	Count Frise, Diplomatic Correspondence, 1695-96
Pw2Hy 1371	Sir R.Sutton's letter to Stepney from Turkey, 7 Jan 1704/5
Pw2Hy 1372	Count Sinzendorf's letter to Stepney, 22 Aug 1705, and Stepney's reply.
PwA 2721	Mme. Schellendorf's letter to Stepney (undated)
PwV67	W. Blathwayt's correspondence, 1693
PwA 166-7	Blathwayt's letters to the Earl of Portland, July 1693

PEMBROKESHIRE RECORD OFFICE
Francis Green's Genealogical Notes, Vols. 8, 15, 16, 20
Transactions of the Historical Society of West Wales, Vol. VII, (1917-18) Francis Green, *The Stepneys of Prendergast*

PUBLIC RECORD OFFICE
SP105/50 through SP105/89, The Stepney Papers
Board of Trade Papers

CO388/5	Trade Domestick, 1697
CO388/6	Trade Foreign, 1697
CO389/15	BoT Entry Book, 1697
CO389/16	BoT Papers, 1699
CO391/10	BoT Journal, 1697
CO391/12	BoT Journal 1699-1700
CO391/13	BoT Journal 1700
CO391/16	BoT Journal 1703-4
CO391/19	BoT Journal 1707

Calendars
Committee for the Advancement of Money (1647-1652)
State Papers (Domestic) – all volumes, 1660-1702
Treasury Books, 1660-69, 1674-9, 1689-93, 1702, 1708
Treasury Papers, 1556-1696

Legal Papers
C.5/551/72, Chancery Proceedings, Series II (Bridges Division), June-Sept 1684

State Papers

SP19/108	Committee for the Advancement of Money, 1647-1652
SP32/12	State Papers (Domestic) 1700
SP77/57	Flanders, (Misc.), 1696-1707
SP80/17	Germany, Imperial Court, 1689-1700
SP80/28	Germany (Mr. Stepney), 1706
SP80/29	Germany, 1707-9
SP81/87	German States, 1693-6
SP82/16	Hamburg, 1676-86
SP84/221	Holland, July 1689-Dec 1690
SP84/223	Holland, 1692-97
SP84/229	Holland (Dayrolle's letters) 1700-1707
SP84/230	Holland, 1706
SP84/574	Holland (Misc.), 1700-1708

Wills

Prob 11/109	Anthony Moseley of Manchester (1607)
Prob 11/118	Alban Stepney (1611)
Prob 11/178	Sir Edward Moseley (1638)
Prob 11/426	Jane Stepney (1684)
Prob 11/498	George Stepney (1707)
Prob 11/600	Dorothy Stepney (1722)

VICTORIA COUNTY HISTORIES
Hertfordshire, Vol.II, Lancashire, Vols. II, VI, VII, Middlesex, Vols. II, III

WESTMINSTER City Record Office and Library
560370 (Microfilm) St. Martin in the Fields Register of Baptisms, 1660-1672

F.390, 391, 403
F. 404, 407, 1106
F. 1116, 1123, 1127
F. 3666, 3671, 3679
F. 3685, 4534
} St. Martin in the Fields, Parish Rate Books for the years 1662, 1664, 1666, 1670-77, 1679, 1683, 1686, 1687

Austria

LOWER AUSTRIA

Exhibition Catalogue: *Prinz Eugen und das Barocke Österreich* (1986)

VIENNA Allgemeines Verwaltungsarchiv

MSS, *Fasc.101, Harracharchiv*

Bibliothek der Stadt Wien

Paul Harrer-Lucienfeld, *Wien, seine Häuser, Menschen u. Kultur, 7 Band, I.Teil* (Vienna, 1948)

Haus- Hof- u. Staatsarchiv

MSS *England, II, Korrespondenz (Berichte u. Weisungen)* 1691-3
Reichshofkanzlei, Berichte aus Dresden, 1690-93 u. 1694-5
England 32 (Weisungen)
England 38 (Berichte)
England 38 (Weisungen)
Bavarica 89
Staatskanzlei Reich,   Berichte 1671-1711
*   Saxonica, 1693-94*
*   England Varie, 1687-1700*
Staatskanzlei Sachsen, Korrespondenz, 1694-1738
W.540 Handschriften: Graf Heinrich Stratmann – Correspondence
No. W6768, Brodbeck,Christian, Philipp Wilhelm, Reichsgraf zu Boineburg (1656-1717), Kurmainzischer Statthalter zu Erfurt, (1927)
Mitteilungen des Oesterreichischen Staatsarchiv, Band 32 (1979)
Müller, Klaus, *Habsburgischer Adel um 1700, Die Familie Lamberg*

Österreichische Nationalbibliothek

Arneth, Alfred, Ritter v. (ed.), *Die Relationem der Botschafte Venedigs im 18 Jahrhundert-Relation des Daniel Dolfin, 1708* (Vienna, 1863)
Mach, Elizabeth, *Johann Wenzel, Graf von Gallas, K.u.K. u spanischer Botschafter am Hof der Kgn, Anna von England* (Dissertation der Universität Wien, 1966)
Mezgolith, Elfriede, *Graf Johann Wenzel Wratislav v. Mitrowitz – sein Wirken während des spanischen Erbfolgekrieges* (Dissertation der Universität Wien, 1967)

Belgium

BRUSSELS Archives générales du Royaume

Conseil de la Régence: Pièces concernant l'établissement du Conseil d'Etat en 1706 et ses démélés avec la Conférence Anglo-Batave, Nos. 19, 20

France

WISSEMBOURG Archives municipales

Vol.13, *Ratsprotokolle, 1704*

Germany

DRESDEN Staatsarchiv (1988)
Band 8, Archiv für d. sächsische Geschichte (1870)

FRANKFURT/MAIN Stadtarchiv
Schoffenratsprotokolle, 1696

HANOVER Niedersächsisches Hauptstaatsarchiv
Georg Schnath, *Geschichte Hannovers im Zeit-alter der neunten Kur und der englischen Sukzession, 1674-1714, Band 4,* (Hildesheim, 1938-82)

WÜRZBURG Staatsarchiv
MSS No.153, *Gräflich Schönbornisches Archiv Korrespondenz, Lothar Franz, Kurfürst v. Mainz und Philipp Wilhelm, Graf Boineburg, 1693*
No.155   *ibid. 1695*
No.156   *ibid. 1696*
No.157   *ibid. 1697*

Printed Works

ARNETH, Alfred, Ritter v. *Prinz Eugen von Savoyen* (Vienna, 1864)

BARBER, Peter *Marlborough as Imperial Prince* (British Library Journal, Vol. VIII, 1982)

BAXTER, Stephen B. *The Development of the Treasury, 1660-1702* (London, 1957); *William III* (London, 1966)

BITTNER, L. *Repertorium der diplomatischen Vertreter aller Länder* (Graz, 1965)

BLACKLEY, W. (ed.) *The Diplomatic Correspondence of Richard Hill, Vol. I* (London, 1845)

BODEMANN, Eduard *Der Briefwechsel des G.W. Leibniz in der Königlichen offentlichen Bibliothek zu Hannover* (Hanover, 1889)

BOYER, Abel *Annals of Queen Anne* (London, 1710)

BRAUBACH, M. *Der Aufstieg Brandenburg-Preussens 1640-1815* (Freiburg, 1933)

BRESSLAU, H. *Aktenstücke zur Geschichte Joseph August du Cros* (Berlin, 1875)

BROOKS, E. St John *Sir Hans Sloane, the Great Collector, and his Circle* (London, 1954)

BURKE, *Extinct and Dormant Baronetcies* (London, 1844)

BURNET, Gilbert *A History of My Own Time* (Martin Routh, ed., Oxford, 1833)

CAULFIELD, James *Memoirs of the Kit-Cat Club* (London, 1821)

CHANDLER, David *Marlborough as Military Commander* (London, 1973)

CHURCHILL, Sir Winston *Marlborough, his Life and Times* (London, 1933)

COKE, Roger *A Detection of the Court and State of England, Vol. III* (London, 1719)

COXE, William *Memoirs of the Duke of Marlborough* (London, 1820)

CUNNINGHAM, Alexander *History of Great Britain, 1688-1714* (London, 1787)

FABER, Johann H. *Topographische, politische u. historische Beschreibung der Reichs-Wahl-u. Handelsstadt Frankfurt am Main,* (Frankfurt/Main 1788)

FESTER, Richard *Die armirten Stände u. die Reichskriegsverfassung, 1681-97* (Frankfurt/Main, 1886); *Kurfürstin Sophie v. Hannover, (Wissenschaftliche Vorträge, Neuefolge 8)* (Hamburg, 1894)

FINSTER, Reinhard and HEUVEL, Gerd van den *Gottfried Wilhelm Leibniz,*

(Reinbek bei Hamburg, 1990)

FRESCHOT, Casimir *Mémoires de la Cour de Vienne*, (Cologne, 1706)

FRIESEN, Heinrich, Freiherr v. *Julius Heinrich, Graf v. Friesen*, (Leipzig, 1870)

FRICKE, Waltraut *Leibniz u. die englische Sukzession des Hauses Hannover,* (Hildesheim 1957)

GACHARD, L.P. *Receuil des anciennes ordonnances de la Belgique, 1706-1715, III Sérié, Tome 2* (Brussels, 1867) *Histoire de la Belgique au commencement du XVIIIe siècle* (Brussels, 1880)

GAEDEKE, Arnold *Die Politik Oesterreichs in der spanischen Erbfolgefrage* (Leipzig, 1877)

GRAHAM, W. (ed.) *The Letters of Joseph Addison* (Oxford, 1941)

GREENE, J. P. *Great Britain and the American Colonies, 1606-1763* (New York, 1970)

GRIMBLOT, Paul (ed.) *The Letters of William III and Louis XIV, 1697-1700* (London, 1848)

HAAKE, Paul *Hans-Adam v. Schöning,* (Vienna,1910)

HANTSCH, Hugo *Die Geschichte Österreichs (Zweiter Band)* (Graz, 1968)

HARLEIAN SOCIETY Vol. X, *Westminster Abbey Registers,* (1869); Vol. XIII, *Visitations of Essex,* (1878); Vol. XXIV, *Marriage Licences issued by the Archbishop of Canterbury, 1543-1869*, (1886); Vol. XXVI, *Marriage Licences issued by the Bishop of London 1611-1828,* (1887)

HARRIS, Brice *Charles Sackville, Sixth Earl of Dorset* (Univ. of Illinois Press, 1940)

HARRIS, R.W. *Absolutism and Enlightenment* (London, 1967)

HATTON, R., and BROMLEY, J. S. (eds) *Essays, 1680-1720, by and for Mark A. Thomson* (Liverpool University Press, 1968)

HAVELKA, Hans *Das Dorf, wo einst der Eber hausste* (Vienna, 1971)

HENDERSON, Sir Nicholas *Prince Eugen of Savoy* (London, 1964)

HENGELMÜLLER, Baron Ladislas *Hungary's Fight for National Existence* (London, 1913)

HITZIGRATH, Heinrich *Die Kompagnie der Merchant Adventurers u. die englische Kirchengemeinde in Hamburg, 1611-1835* (Hamburg, 1904)

t'HOFF, B. van *The Correspondence, 1701-11, of John Churchill, First Duke of Marlborough, and Anthonie Heinsius, Grand Pensionary of Holland* (The Hague, 1951)

HOLBORN, Hajo *A History of Modern Germany* (1964)

HOLLAENDER, Dr A. E. *Mr. Resident George Stepney and the Pietatis Austriae,1693*, in Emmison & Stephens (eds), *Tribute to an Antiquary - Essays presented to Marc Fitch* (London, 1976)

HORN, D. B. *British Diplomatic Representation, 1689-1789* (Camden Series, Vol. XLVI, 1932)

JACOBSEN, G. A. *William Blathwayt* (Yale and Oxford University Presses, 1932)

JAMES, G. P. R. (ed.) *The Letters of James Vernon* (London, 1841)

JARNAT-DERBOLAV, E. *Die Oesterreichische Gesandtschaft in London, 1701-11* (Bonn, 1972)

JOHNSON, Samuel J. *Lives of the English Poets, Vol. I,* (Everyman Edition, London, 1954)

KEMBLE, J. M. *State Papers & Correspondence, from the Revolution to the Accession of the House of Hanover* (London, 1857)

KLINGENSTEIN, Grete, *Der Aufstieg des Hauses Kaunitz* (Göttingen, 1975)

KLOPP, Onno (ed.) *Korrespondenz von Leibniz mit der Prinzessin Sophie, Vol. II* (reprinted Hildesheim, 1973); *Der Fall des Hauses Stuart* (1875-88)

KOCH, H. W. *A History of Prussia* (London 1978)

KRALICK, Richard and SCHLITTER, Hans *Wien, Geschichte der Kaiserstadt und ihrer Kultur* (Vienna, 1912)

KÜHN-STEINHAUSEN, Hermine *Johann Wilhelm, Kurfürst von der Pfalz (1658-1715)* (Düsseldorf, 1958)

LAMBERTY, Guillaume de *Mémoires pour servir à l'histoire du XVIII Siècle* (Amsterdam, 1735)

LANCASTER-BROWN, Peter *Halley and his Comet* (Blandford, 1985)

LANE, Miss M. *The Diplomatic Service under William III, in Transactions of the Royal Historical Society, Series IV, Vol. X (1927)*

LODGE, Richard *The Political History of England, Vol. VIII (1660-1702)*, (1910)

LUTTRELL, Narcissus *A Brief Historical Relation of State Affairs from September 1678 to April 1714* (Oxford,1857)

MANNERS-SUTTON, H. (ed.) *The Lexington Papers* (London,1851)

MACKY, J. *Memoirs of Secret Service* (London, 1733)

McCUSKER, John J. *Money and Exchange in Europe and America, 1660-1773* (London, 1978)

McMASTER, John *St. Martin in the Fields* (privately printed, 1916)

MERODE-WESTERLOO *Mémoires du Feld-Maréchal Comte de Mérode-Westerloo, publiés par M. le Comte de Mérode-Westerloo, son arrière-petit-fils* (Brussels, 1840)

MICHAUD, J. Fr. (ed.) *Biographie Universelle ancienne et moderne* (Paris, 1854)

MÜLLER, Klaus *Der kaiserliche Gesandtschafts-wesen im Jahrhundert nach den westfälischen Frieden, 1648-1740* (Bonn, 1976)

MUNCK, Thomas *Seventeenth-Century Europe* (London, 1990)

MURRAY, Sir George *Letters & Dispatches of John Churchill, Duke of Marlborough* (London, 1845)

PIRENNE, Henri *Histoire de Belgique, Vol. V* (Brussels, 1926)

PRIBRAM, Dr. Alfred *Oesterreich und Brandenburg, 1688-1700* (Vienna, 1885)

RATZENHOFER, Gustav (ed.) *Feldzüge des Prinzen Eugen, Vol. VI* (Vienna, 1879)

REDLICH, Oswald *Weltmacht des Barock-- Oesterreich in der Zeit Kaiser Leopold I* (Vienna 1921, reprinted 1961)

ROBB, Nesca A. *William of Orange – a personal portrait, Vol. II* (1961)

RÖDER, Philipp, (ed.) *Kriegs- u. Staatsschriften des Markgrafen Ludwig Wilhelm v. Baden über den spanischen Erbfolgekrieg* (Karlsruhe, 1850)

ROUS and VENN, *Admissions to Trinity College, Cambridge, Vol. II* (Cambridge, 1913)

RUSSELL-BARKER, G. F. and STENNING, A. H. *Record of Old Westminsters* (London, 1928)

SARGEAUNT, John *Annals of Westminster School* (London, 1878)

SCHULTE, Aloys *Markgraf Ludwig Wilhelm v. Baden u. der Reichskrieg gegen Frankreich, 1693-1697* (Karlsruhe, 1892)

SEIFER, Herbert *Die Oper am Wiener Kaiserhof im 17 Jahrhundert* (Tutzing, 1985)

SMITHERS, Peter *The Life of Joseph Addison* (Oxford, 1954)

SNYDER, Henry L. *The British Diplomatic Service during the Godolphin Ministry,* in R. Hatton and M. S. Anderson (eds), *Studies in Diplomatic History* (London, 1970) *The Marlborough-Godolphin Correspondence* (Oxford, 1975)

SRBIK, Heinrich, Ritter v. *Wien und Versailles, 1692-7* (Munich, 1944)

SUTHERLAND, James *English Literature in the late Seventeenth Century* (Oxford, 1969)

SWEDENBERG, H.T., Jr. *George Stepney, My Lord Dorset's Boy,* in *The Huntingdon Library Quarterly*, No. 1, Nov. 1946; *The Works of John*

Dryden, Vol. IV (Berkeley, Calif.,1974)

THOMAS, Daniel H., and CASE, Lynn M. (eds) *The New Guide to the Diplomatic Archives of Western Europe (2d. ed.)* (Univ. of Pennsylvania Press, 1975)

THOMSON, Mark A. *Louis XIV and William III, 1689-97,* in *English History Review,* 1961

TOLAND, John *Relation des Cours de Prusse et de Hanovre . . .* (translated from the English in Holland, 1706)

TREVOR, Arthur *The Life and Times of William III* (London, 1835)

WARNER, Rebecca *Epistolary Curiosities* (London, 1813)ı

ICKHAM-LEGG, L.G. *Matthew Prior, A Study of his Public Correspondence* (ambridge, 1921)ıW

KES, David *Preface to Dryden* (London, 1977)

ZEDLER, Johann Heinrich (ed.) *Universal Lexicon* (Leipzig and Halle, 1740)

ZEE, Henri & Barbara, van der *William and Mary* (London, 1973)

Nominal Index

Subject and Place Index

9, 73, 84, 163, 199, 221, 225, 226, 242, 268, 288, 296
Tyrnau (Hungary), 242, 245, 261, 262, 265-6, 268-72, 280, 281, 282, 284-8
Tyrol (Austria), 221, 237, 260

Ulm, City of, 209, 215, 276
United Provinces of the Dutch Republic, 2, 18, 22, 34, 45, 62, 63, 69, 116, 130, 131, 151, 203
Upper Rhine, Circle of, 21, 24, 62, 63, 69, 116, 130, 131, 151, 203
Upper Saxony, Circle of, 69, 98
Utrecht, 33, 38, 39, 63, 127, 193, 227, 303, 309

Velau, Treaty of (1657), 171
Venice, 220, 249, 260, 268, 275
Venetian Republic, 219, 243
Vienna, 1, 2, 5, 19, 20, 22, 42, 48, 60-4, 44-70, 73-80, 82-5, 87, 88, 90-101, 103-7, 109, 112-7, 119-22, 127, 134, 137, 143-5, 148, 149, 157, 162, 165-7, 170, 175, 188-93, 195-200, 201-10, 211-8, 220-6, 228-38, 240-3, 245-55, 256-66, 267-9, 271-6, 278, 279, 281-92, 304, 308, 310, 312
Vigo, 213
Virginia, 184

Wallachia, 162
Warsaw, 5, 162, 163, 174, 184
Wechtern, (or Werchter) (Brabant), 54-6
Weissenfels, 121
Wesel (Duchy of Cleves), 36, 111, 112, 194
West Indies, 202, 209
Westminster Abbey, 14, 316, 317, 320, 321
Westminster, City of, 7, 8, 9, 13, 14, 316
Westminster School, 10, 12-16, 18, 174, 295
Westphalia (Circle of), 69, 158
Whitehall, 10, 21, 22, 24, 26, 38, 43, 44, 47, 63, 64, 73, 75, 89, 94, 104, 105, 110, 111, 118, 127, 129, 131-4, 154, 157, 162, 165, 168, 177, 179, 181, 184-8, 195, 197, 207, 211, 213, 219, 245, 248, 250, 259, 264, 274, 289, 300, 304, 305
Wiener Neustadt, 226
Wiesbaden, 137, 148
Wilmot House (Westminster), 8
Wissembourg, 237, 238, 240, 244, 247, 250, 275
Wolfenbuttel, Duchy of, 108

Zeeland (Netherlands), 154
Zell, Duchy of, 19, 20, 34, 35, 80, 135
Zell (Celle), City of, 39, 53, 59, 106-9, 128, 166, 168, 179